PRINCIPLES OF

COST ACCOUNTING

8TH EDITION

Test
1 = 81
2 = 55
3 = 60
4 = 42
5 = 92
6 = 74

ROBERT E. SCHMIEDICKE, MA, CPA
Vice President for Administration and Finance
Davenport College of Business
Grand Rapids, Michigan

CHARLES F. NAGY, PhD, CPA
Professor of Accounting
Cleveland State University
Cleveland, Ohio

EDWARD J. VANDERBECK, MS, CPA
Chairman, Department of Finance and Accounting
Xavier University
Cincinnati, Ohio

Published by

A68 **SOUTH-WESTERN PUBLISHING CO.**

CINCINNATI   WEST CHICAGO, IL   CARROLLTON, TX   LIVERMORE, CA

Copyright © 1988
by South-Western Publishing Co.
Cincinnati, Ohio

ISBN: 0-538-01680-9

Library of Congress Catalog Card Number: 87-63207

3 4 5 K 1 0

Printed in the United States of America

COVER PHOTO: © Carl Flatow

PREFACE

The eighth edition of PRINCIPLES OF COST ACCOUNTING is dedicated to providing the student with a thorough understanding of cost concepts, cost behavior, and cost accounting techniques as they are applied to manufacturing cost systems. The text, designed for a one-term course, presents the principles and procedures of job order costing, process costing, and standard costs in a logical, concise, and clear manner. Analysis of cost data and the uses of cost information for management decision making are integrated with discussions of cost accounting systems and procedures. In addition, the last chapter in the text is devoted to the special-purpose reports and analytical techniques of managerial accounting.

FEATURES OF THE EIGHTH EDITION

The fundamental approach of PRINCIPLES OF COST ACCOUNTING has been retained in the eighth edition. However, several new features have been added with the objective of facilitating the learning process for the student and enhancing the teachability of the text for the instructor. Following is a summary of the new features and the significant features retained from previous editions of the text.

Learning objectives have been added at the beginning of each chapter. The objectives are intended to guide students in their study of the chapter and to provide them with a basis for evaluating their understanding of the material presented in the chapter.

Key terms are highlighted as they are introduced and are listed, along with page references, at the end of each chapter. A comprehensive **glossary** has been added at the end of the book which provides definitions for all of the key terms.

Questions, exercises, and problems at the end of each chapter have been revised, and a brief description of each exercise and problem has been added at the beginning of the exercise or problem.

Illustrations and examples are used extensively throughout the text to explain and reinforce the principles and procedures introduced.

SUPPLEMENTARY MATERIALS

An improved and expanded package of supplementary materials is available with the eighth edition of PRINCIPLES OF COST ACCOUNTING to assist both instructors and students. The package includes new items that have been carefully prepared and reviewed and previously available materials that have been extensively revised.

Available to Instructors

Solutions Manual. This manual contains the answers to all end-of-chapter questions, exercises, and problems.

Solutions Transparencies. Transparencies of solutions for all end-of-chapter exercises and problems are available with the eighth edition of the text.

Instructor's Manual. Part 1 provides summaries and outlines for each chapter to facilitate development of classroom presentations and homework assignments. Part 2 contains a test bank of multiple choice questions and problems for each chapter, accompanied by solutions. Part 3 contains end-of-chapter problem check figures which may be reproduced and distributed to students at the discretion of the instructor.

MicroSWAT II. A microcomputer version of the printed test bank in the Instructor's Manual is available for either Apple or IBM computers. MicroSWAT II enables the user to select, mix, edit, and add questions or problems to create the type of test or problem set needed.

Achievement Tests. Six preprinted tests consisting of objective questions and short problems are available to adopters. Each test covers one or two chapters of text material.

Practice Set Solutions. Solutions for both the manual practice set, Judson Manufacturing Corporation, and the computerized practice set, Liberty Electronics, are available to adopters.

Available to Students

Study Guide and Working Papers. This new item includes both a study guide and working papers bound in a single volume, with perforated pages for easy removal. The study guide provides a review summary for each chapter and questions and problems to test comprehension of chapter material. Solutions for all questions and problems are included in a separate section at the end of the study guide. The working papers include printed forms for use in solving the problems at the end of each chapter of the textbook.

The Judson Manufacturing Corporation Practice Set. This job order practice set is designed for use with the textbook after Chapter 5 has been completed. The revised practice set has been shortened by minimizing repetitive transactions.

Liberty Electronics, Inc.: A Computerized Job Order Simulation. This computerized job order practice set with individual diskette is available for use with either Apple or IBM microcomputers.

ORGANIZATION OF THE EIGHTH EDITION

PRINCIPLES OF COST ACCOUNTING takes a logical approach to the fundamentals of cost accounting and the uses of cost data in planning and controlling operations. Principles and procedures of cost systems are presented first in an overview, then discussed and illustrated in detail. Each chapter builds on the terminology, concepts, and procedures introduced in previous chapters. The elements of manufacturing cost and the related accounting principles are described and illustrated first in the context of a job order cost system. The more complex systems of process cost and standard cost are presented after the basic terminology and principles have been mastered by the student. The concluding chapter of the text deals with some of the problems that may be encountered by management and techniques to aid in management's decision-making process.

The organization of the eighth edition of PRINCIPLES OF COST ACCOUNTING is briefly summarized in the following paragraphs.

Introduction to Cost Accounting

Chapter One is a general overview of subjects that are examined in detail in the subsequent chapters. The chapter introduces the elements of cost and the cost accounting systems used by manufacturing enterprises, including job order, process, and standard cost. The flow of manufacturing costs through the production process is illustrated and explained. This overview of manufacturing costs and accounting procedures gives students a "big picture"of how costs are accumulated and the importance of cost information in planning and controlling operations.

Accounting for Materials, Labor, and Factory Overhead

Chapters Two, Three, and Four detail the principles and procedures relating to the elements of manufacturing cost. Chapter Two focuses on controlling and accounting for materials. The chapter discusses the need for effective control of materials and the techniques used to establish both physical control and control of the investment in materials. Important aspects of ordering and maintaining the materials inventory are discussed, and the economic order quantity technique is described and illustrated. Procedures involved in accounting for materials are explained and illustrated, along with fifo, lifo, moving average, and other inventory costing methods. In addition, the procedures and problems relating to accounting for scrap, spoiled goods, and defective work are discussed and illustrated.

Chapter Three focuses on controlling and accounting for labor costs. The chapter describes various types of wage plans encountered in manufacturing environments and illustrates how payroll is computed under the different plans. The activities and records necessary for controlling and accounting for labor costs are introduced, followed by a discussion and illustration of the procedures applied in accounting for labor costs. The discussion of FICA and unemployment taxes has been updated to reflect recent changes in legislation.

Chapter Four is an in-depth study of factory overhead. The discussions include identifying cost behavior patterns, budgeting factory overhead, and accounting for the actual factory overhead costs incurred. Special attention is given to establishing predetermined factory overhead rates and applying factory overhead to production using these rates. The chapter concludes with a discussion and illustration of budget and volume variances.

Job Order Cost Accounting — Application of Principles

Chapter Five is a review of the principles of job order costing. Application of the principles and procedures introduced in previous chapters is illustrated for a manufacturing company. The illustration includes transactions for one month of operations and demonstrates how manufacturing costs are recorded and summarized. The financial statements generally prepared for a manufacturing company are also shown.

Process Cost Accounting

Chapters Six and Seven are devoted to process cost accounting. Chapter Six discusses the general procedures applicable to a process cost system. Included are comparisons of basic cost systems and work in process inventories. A detailed discussion of the average cost method is presented which includes calculating equivalent units of production and determining unit costs for the originating and subsequent departments. Chapter Seven covers additional procedures that are used in process costing and the first-in, first-out method. The procedures discussed in the chapter include calculating equivalent units of production when materials, labor, and factory overhead are not uniformly applied and accounting for units lost or gained during the production process.

Standard Cost Accounting

Chapters Eight and Nine discuss the principles and procedures related to a standard cost system. Chapter Eight discusses the different types of standards and the standard cost procedures applicable to materials and labor costs. How to determine material and labor variances is examined as well as the analysis of the calculated variances. Mix and yield variances for labor and material are also discussed and illustrated. Chapter Nine is devoted to factory overhead and standard costing. How to calculate factory overhead variances by using the two-variance and three-variance analytical methods is discussed in detail. A section of the chapter is devoted to the principles of budgeting.

Cost Analysis for Management Decision Making

Chapter Ten addresses selected topics that are directly related to management decision making. The subjects covered are: direct costing, segment reporting, cost-volume-profit analysis, discontinuing a division or department, differential cost analysis, and distribution costs.

We wish to thank the American Institute of Certified Public Accountants and the National Association of Accountants for their permission to use their materials in this publication. We also wish to express our gratitude to the many users of previous editions who offered helpful suggestions.

Robert E. Schmiedicke
Charles F. Nagy
Edward VanDerbeck

CONTENTS IN BRIEF

CONTENTS

INTRODUCTION TO COST ACCOUNTING

LEARNING OBJECTIVES

In studying this chapter, you will learn about the:

- Uses of cost accounting data
- Relationship of cost accounting to financial accounting
- Three basic elements of manufacturing costs
- Two basic types of cost accounting systems
- Organizations that influence cost accounting principles

Inflation has been a fact of life in the United States and most other countries of the world for over 50 years. The Consumer Price Index published by the U.S. Department of Labor, for example, shows that average prices of goods and services in this country rose by over 750% from 1940 to 1985. In some parts of the world, the rate of inflation has been much higher than in our country. Some South American countries, for example, have experienced price increases in a single year of over 1,000%.

Inflation results from a combination of many factors, and even economists do not totally understand or agree on the cause of changing price levels. One important factor, however, is the cost incurred to manufacture goods. For many years, there has been a continuing, significant increase in the costs of materials, labor, and other manufacturing needs. Historically, U.S. manufacturers have tended to pass on the higher costs of their prod-

1

ucts by increasing the prices charged to consumers. In recent years, however, many companies have been forced to limit price increases due to intense domestic and foreign competition. Some U.S. industries, in particular, are faced with serious problems as a result of competition from foreign manufacturers. Automobiles and electronic equipment from Japan, shoes from Brazil, and clothing from Taiwan are just a few examples of foreign-made products that have provided stiff competition to American manufacturers both at home and abroad.

As a result of these pressures, many companies today are placing more emphasis than ever before on controlling costs in an attempt to keep their prices competitive with those of other manufacturers. In addition, changing consumer demands and new technologies require the development of new products and production methods as well as more effective methods of marketing and servicing products. In order to remain competitive today, manufacturers must have control of costs and be ready to exploit new opportunities. Otherwise, they can be forced into declining economic growth and a vicious downward spiral of reduced capital expansion, decreasing profits, a declining work force, loss of markets, and eventual oblivion.

The importance of sound financial information, including specific cost data, has always been recognized, but in the current economic environment, such information is crucial to the survival of business and industry. The function of cost accounting is to provide the detailed cost data which are essential to management in controlling current operations and planning for the future. It provides the information that management needs in order to allocate resources to the most efficient and profitable areas of operation.

All types of business entities — manufacturing, merchandising, and service businesses — require information systems which provide the necessary financial data. Because of the nature of the manufacturing process, the information systems of manufacturing entities must be designed to accumulate detailed cost data relating to the production process. Thus, it is common today for small, medium, and large manufacturing companies to have structured cost accounting systems. Simply stated, these systems show what costs were incurred and where and how these costs were utilized. While cost accounting principles and procedures discussed in this text are used primarily by the manufacturing industry, many of the basic principles of control are also used by merchandising and service businesses. Cost accounting today is recognized as being essential to efficient operation of business and industry.

THE MANUFACTURING PROCESS

In order to appreciate the importance of an efficient cost system, it is necessary to understand the nature of the manufacturing process. In many ways, the activities of a manufacturing organization are similar to those of a merchandising business. Both are concerned with purchasing, storing, and selling goods; both must have efficient management and adequate sources of capital; both may employ hundreds or thousands of workers. In the manufacturing process itself, we see the distinction between the two: merchandisers, such as Sears Roebuck & Co., buy items in marketable form to be resold to their customers; manufacturers, such as RCA Corporation, must make the goods they sell. Once the merchandising organization has acquired and stored goods, it is ready to carry out the marketing function. The purchase of materials by a manufacturer, however, is only the beginning of a long, and sometimes complex, chain of events that will eventually produce a finished article ready for sale.

The manufacturing process involves the conversion of raw materials into finished goods through the application of labor and the incurrence of various factory expenses. The manufacturer must make a major investment in physical facilities, such as factory buildings and warehouses, and acquire many specialized types of machinery and equipment. In order to carry out the manufacturing process, the manufacturer must purchase appropriate quantities of raw materials, supplies and parts, and build up a work force to convert these resources into finished goods.

In addition to the cost of materials and labor, the manufacturer incurs other expenses in the production process. Many of these costs, such as depreciation, taxes, insurance, and utilities, are similar to those incurred by a merchandising concern. Other costs, such as machine maintenance and repair, materials handling, and inspection, are peculiar to the manufacturing industry.

Once the goods have been manufactured and are ready for sale, the manufacturer performs basically the same functions as the merchandiser in storing and marketing the goods. The methods of accounting for sales, cost of goods sold, and selling and administrative expenses are also similar to those of the merchandising organization.

USES OF COST ACCOUNTING DATA

Principles of cost accounting have been developed which enable the manufacturer to process the many different costs associated with manufacturing and to provide built-in control features. The information produced by a cost accounting system provides a basis for determining product costs and aids management in planning and controlling operations.

Determining Product Costs

Cost accounting procedures provide the means to gather the data needed to determine product costs and thus to generate meaningful financial statements and other reports, schedules, and analyses that are relevant to management. Cost procedures must be designed to permit the determination of **unit costs** as well as total product costs. For example, the fact that a manufacturer spent $10,000 for labor in a certain month is not, in itself, significant information; but if this labor produced 5,000 finished units, the fact that the cost of labor was $2 per unit is significant, because this figure can be compared to the unit labor cost of other periods and the trends analyzed.

Unit cost information is also useful in making a variety of important marketing decisions:

1. **Determining the selling price of a product.** A knowledge of the cost of manufacturing a unit of product aids in setting the selling price. This price should be high enough to cover the cost of producing the item, pay a portion of marketing and administrative expenses, and provide a profit.

2. **Meeting competition.** If a product is being undersold by a competitor, detailed information regarding unit costs can be used to determine whether the problem can be resolved by a reduction in selling price, a reduction of manufacturing costs, or the elimination of the product.

3. **Bidding on contracts.** Many manufacturing organizations must submit competitive bids in order to be awarded manufacturing contracts from government, business, and industry. An analysis of the unit costs relating to the manufacture of a particular product is of great importance in determining the bid price.

4. **Analyzing profitability.** Unit cost information enables management to determine the amount of profit that each product earns and possibly eliminate those that are least profitable, thereby concentrating

efforts on those items that are most profitable. It is not uncommon, however, for some companies to retain a certain line of goods yielding a very low profit, or even a loss, in order to provide the variety of products that will attract customers who also purchase the more profitable items.

Planning and Control

The ultimate value of cost accounting lies in the use of the data accumulated and reported. One of the most important functions of cost accounting is the development of information which can be used by management in planning and controlling operations.

Planning is the process of establishing objectives or goals for the firm and determining the means by which the firm will attain them. Effective planning is facilitated by the following:

1. **Clearly defined objectives of the manufacturing operation.** These objectives may be expressed in terms of the number of units to be produced, the quality desired, the estimated cost per unit, and the timing necessary to meet customer demand while avoiding the financial strain of being overstocked.

2. **The development of a production plan that will assist and guide the company in reaching its objectives.** This detailed plan includes a description of necessary manufacturing operations to be performed, a projection of personnel needs for the period, and the coordination of the timely acquisition of materials and facilities.

Cost accounting aids in the development of plans by providing historical costs that serve as a basis for projecting data for planning. Management can analyze trends and relationships among such data as an aid in estimating future costs and operating results and in making decisions regarding the acquisition of additional facilities, changes in marketing strategies, and obtaining additional capital.

The word "control" is used in many different ways, but from the viewpoint of the manufacturing concern, **control** is the process of monitoring the company's operations and determining whether the objectives identified in the planning process are being accomplished. Effective control is achieved through:

1. Assigning responsibility
2. Periodically measuring and comparing results

3. Taking necessary corrective action
4. Searching for ways to reduce costs

Assigning Responsibility.   Responsibility should be assigned for each detail of the production plan. All managers and supervisors should know precisely what their responsibilities are in terms of efficiency, operations, production, and costs. The key to proper control involves the use of responsibility accounting and cost centers.

The essence of **responsibility accounting** is the assignment of accountability for costs or production results to those individuals who have the authority to influence costs or production. It involves an information system that traces the data to the managers who are responsible for them.

A **cost center** is a unit of activity within the factory to which costs may be practically and equitably assigned. A cost center may be a department or a group of workers; it could represent one job, one process, or one manufacturing operation. The criteria for a cost center are (1) a reasonable basis on which manufacturing costs can be allocated, and (2) a person who has control over and is accountable for many of the costs charged to that center.

It is important to recognize that with responsibility accounting the manager of a cost center is accountable only for those costs that are controllable by that manager. For example, the costs of labor and materials will be charged to the cost center, but the manager may be responsible only for the quantity of materials used and the number of labor hours worked. This person would probably not be accountable for the unit cost of raw materials or the hourly rate paid to employees because these are normally beyond the manager's control and are the responsibility of the purchasing and personnel departments respectively. The manager may be responsible for the cost of machinery maintenance and repair due to misuse in the cost center, but would not be responsible for the costs of depreciation, taxes, and insurance on the machinery if the decision to purchase the machinery was made at a higher level in the organization. If production in the cost center for a given period is lower than planned, this could be due to poor supervision, which is the manager's responsibility; or, it may be that less-skilled workers are being hired—a factor that is usually beyond the control of the manager.

Cost and production reports for a cost center reflect all costs charged to that center and the related production information. In a responsibility accounting system, the specific data for which the manager is responsible would be highlighted or segregated for the purpose of evaluating that manager's performance and initiating action to correct deficiencies. Quite often, however, both a cost and production report and a separate performance report will be prepared for a cost center; the performance report will include only those costs and production data that are controllable by the center's manager.

It is imperative that these reports be furnished at regular intervals (monthly, weekly, or daily) on a timely basis. In order for the reports to provide the maximum benefit, they must be available as soon as possible after the end of the period being reported. Reports that are not produced in a timely fashion will lose their effectiveness as a control device.

Periodically Measuring and Comparing Results.   Actual operating results should be measured periodically and compared with the objectives established in the planning process. This analysis, which might be made monthly, weekly, or even on a daily basis, is a major part of cost control because it points out how current performance compares with the overall plan. The actual results in terms of dollars, units produced, hours worked, or materials used are compared with the budget, which is management's operating plan expressed in quantitative terms (units and dollars). This comparison is a primary feature of cost analysis. The number of dollars expended or the quantity of units produced have little significance until compared with the budgeted amounts. Comparisons may also be made with actual results of prior periods, thus serving to point out meaningful trends.

Taking Necessary Corrective Action.   The reports produced by the measurement and analysis of operating results may identify problem areas and deviations from the plan. Appropriate corrective action should be implemented where necessary. A significant variation from the plan is a signal for attention. An investigation may reveal an area of weakness or may indicate an area of strength where an especially efficient condition may be better utilized.

Management wants to know not only the results of operations, but how the results — whether favorable or unfavorable — compare with the plan, why things happened, and who was responsible. Management must be prepared to improve or change existing conditions; otherwise the periodic measurement of activity has little value.

Searching for Ways to Reduce Costs. Management has the responsibility not only to control costs, but also to reduce them in every possible way consistent with the type of operation and quality of product. There must be a continuing search for less expensive materials, for more efficient methods of operating, and for improved usage of materials and labor.

RELATIONSHIP OF COST ACCOUNTING TO FINANCIAL ACCOUNTING

The objective of accounting in general is the accumulation of financial information that is useful in making economic decisions. Financial accounting focuses on the gathering of information to be used in the preparation of financial statements that meet the needs of investors, creditors, and other external users of financial information. The statements include a balance sheet, income statement, and statement of cash flows. Although these financial statements are useful to management as well as external users, additional reports, schedules, and analyses are required for internal use in planning and control. Cost accounting provides the additional information required by management, and also provides data necessary for the preparation of external financial statements. For example, cost accounting procedures are necessary for the determination of cost of goods sold on the income statement and the valuation of inventories on the balance sheet.

Cost of Goods Sold

For the merchandising concern, the cost of goods sold is computed as follows:

> Beginning merchandise inventory
> Plus purchases (merchandise)
>
> Merchandise available for sale
> Less Ending merchandise inventory
>
> Cost of goods sold

The amount of purchases represents the cost of the goods which were acquired during the period for resale.

Since the manufacturing concern *makes* rather than *buys* the products it has available for sale, the term "finished goods inventory" replaces "merchandise inventory" and the term "cost of goods manufactured" replaces "purchases" in determining the cost of goods sold:

Beginning finished goods inventory
Plus cost of goods manufactured
Finished goods available for sale
Less ending finished goods inventory
Cost of goods sold

[handwritten: 2nd step of the Income Statement]
[handwritten: from Statement of]
[handwritten: date]
[handwritten: date]
*[handwritten: * Cost of Good manufactured Pg 21+35]*
[handwritten: (Summary of Finished Goods Inv Ad)]

The cost of goods manufactured amount is supported by a schedule detailing the costs of materials, labor, and the expenses of maintaining and operating a factory.

The format of the income statement for a manufacturer is not significantly different from that for a merchandiser. However, the cost accounting procedures involved in gathering the data for determining the cost of goods manufactured are considerably more complex than the recording of merchandise purchased in finished form. These procedures are introduced in this chapter and discussed in detail in subsequent chapters.

Inventories

If a merchandiser has unsold items of merchandise on hand at the end of an accounting period, the cost of the merchandise is reflected in the current asset section of the balance sheet in the following manner:

Current assets:
  Cash
  Accounts receivable
  Merchandise inventory

On the balance sheet of a manufacturing concern, the current asset section is expanded as follows:

Current assets:
  Cash
  Accounts receivable
  Inventories:
    Finished goods
    Work in process
    Materials

The balance in the finished goods account represents the total cost incurred in manufacturing goods that are complete but still on hand at the end of the period. The balance of the work in process account includes all manufacturing costs incurred to date for goods that are in various stages of production, but not yet completed. The balance of the materials account represents the cost of all materials purchased and on hand to be used in the manufacturing process, including raw materials, prefabricated parts, and other factory materials and supplies. Raw materials for one company are often the finished product of another company. For example, plastic to be used in the formation of office machine cases would be the finished product of a plastics manufacturer. Prefabricated parts would include units, such as electric motors, assembled by another manufacturer to be used in the manufacture of a product such as office machines. Other materials and supplies might include screws, nails, rivets, lubricants, and solvents.

Valuation of Inventories.   Although many procedures used to gather costs are unique to manufacturers, their inventories are valued for external financial reporting purposes using inventory costing methods such as first-in, first-out (FIFO), last-in, first-out (LIFO), and moving average, which are also used by merchandisers. Most manufacturers maintain a perpetual inventory system that provides a continuous record of purchases, issues, and balances of all goods in stock. Generally these data are verified by periodic counts of selected items throughout the year. Under the perpetual system, inventory valuation data for financial statement purposes are available at any time, as distinguished from a periodic inventory system that requires estimating inventory during the year for interim statements and shutting down operations to count all inventory items at the end of the year.

In addition to providing inventory valuation data for the financial statements, the detailed cost data and perpetual inventory records provide the information necessary to control inventory levels, to ensure the timely availability of materials for production, and to detect pilferage, waste, and spoilage. Inventory valuation and control are discussed in detail in Chapter 2.

Inventory Ledgers.   Generally both merchandisers and manufacturers maintain various subsidiary ledgers, such as that for accounts receivable. In addition, manufacturers usually maintain subsidiary ledgers for the general ledger inventory control accounts, Finished Goods, Work in Process, and Materials. These subsidiary ledgers are necessary for a perpetual inventory and provide the detailed balances and information to support the balances in the control accounts.

Some manufacturers, especially those that are decentralized, use a **factory ledger** which contains all of the accounts relating to manufacturing, including the inventory accounts. This ledger, which is maintained at the factory, is tied in to the general ledger at the main office through the use of a special account for the factory on the main office books and a special account for the main office on the factory books.

ELEMENTS OF MANUFACTURING COST

Manufacturing or production costs are classified into three basic elements: (1) direct materials, (2) direct labor, and (3) factory overhead.

Direct Materials

The costs of materials which become part of the product being manufactured and which can be readily identified with a certain product are classified as **direct materials**. Examples are: lumber used in making furniture, fabric used in the production of clothing, iron ore used in the manufacture of steel products, and rubber used in the production of tires.

There are many types of materials and supplies necessary for the manufacturing process that cannot be readily identified with any particular item manufactured or whose relative cost is too insignificant to measure. The costs of items such as sandpaper used in sanding furniture, lubricants used on machinery, and other items for general factory use are classified as **indirect materials** and are included in factory overhead. Similarly classified are materials that actually become part of the finished product but whose costs are relatively insignificant, such as thread, screws, rivets, nails, and glue.

Direct Labor

The cost of labor for those employees who work directly on the product manufactured, such as machine operators or assembly line workers, is classified as **direct labor**. The wages and salaries of employees who are required for the manufacturing process but who do not work directly on the units being manufactured are considered indirect labor and are included in factory overhead. This classification would include the wages and salaries of department heads, inspectors, materials handlers, and maintenance personnel.

Payroll related costs, such as payroll taxes, group insurance, sick pay, vacation and holiday pay, retirement program contributions, and other fringe benefits can be considered as part of direct labor costs, but are usually included in factory overhead.

Factory Overhead

Factory overhead is known by various names — *factory burden, manufacturing expenses, indirect costs, overhead,* and *factory expenses* — and includes all costs related to the manufacturing of a product <u>except direct materials and direct labor</u>. Thus factory overhead includes indirect materials, indirect labor, and other manufacturing expenses, such as depreciation on the factory building and machinery and equipment, supplies, heat, light, power, maintenance, insurance, and taxes.

Summary of Manufacturing Costs

The costs of direct materials and direct labor are sometimes combined and described as the **prime cost** of manufacturing a product. Prime cost plus factory overhead equals total cost of manufacturing. Direct labor cost and factory overhead, which are necessary to convert the direct materials into finished goods, can be combined and described as **conversion cost.**

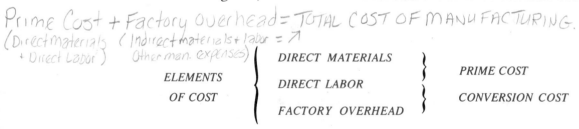

Prime Cost + Factory Overhead = TOTAL COST OF MANUFACTURING.
(Direct materials   (Indirect materials + labor = ↗
 + Direct Labor)   Other man. expenses)

	DIRECT MATERIALS	PRIME COST
ELEMENTS	DIRECT LABOR	
OF COST		CONVERSION COST
	FACTORY OVERHEAD	

Marketing or selling expenses, general administrative costs, and other nonfactory expenditures are not included in the costs of manufacturing. However, some costs incurred by a manufacturer may benefit both factory and nonfactory operations. An example is depreciation, insurance, and property taxes on a building that houses both the factory and the administrative offices. In this situation an allocation of cost must be made to each operation.

FLOW OF COSTS

All three elements of manufacturing cost flow through the <u>work in process inventory account</u>. The cost of direct materials used in production

Direct materials
Direct Labor

and direct labor costs incurred are charged (<u>debited</u>) directly to <u>Work in Process</u>. All other factory costs — indirect labor, indirect materials, and other factory expenses — are charged to the factory overhead account and later transferred to Work in Process. When goods are completed, the total costs incurred in producing the goods are transferred from Work in Process to the finished goods inventory account. The flow of manufacturing costs can be illustrated very simply as follows:

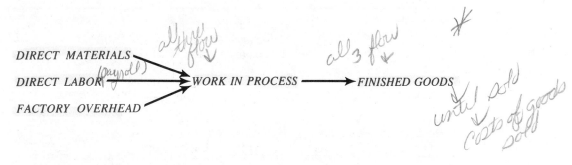

all 3 flow

all 3 flow

until sold

Costs of goods sold

When goods are sold, the costs incurred to manufacture the goods are transferred from the finished goods inventory account to the cost of goods sold account.

FINISHED GOODS ⟶ *COST OF GOODS SOLD*

A more detailed illustration of cost flow is presented in T-account form on page 24.

ILLUSTRATION OF ACCOUNTING FOR MANUFACTURING COSTS

Cost accounting procedures are used to accumulate and allocate all elements of manufacturing cost in a manner that will produce meaningful data for the internal use of management and for the preparation of external financial statements. The following example illustrates basic cost accounting procedures, utilizing the terminology and principles that have been discussed previously.

The Graymoore Products Company is a small, newly organized corporation that manufactures kitchen tables and chairs. The firm's products are sold to jobbers or wholesale distributors, who in turn sell them to retailers. The basic steps in the company's manufacturing process are as follows:

1. Lumber is cut to size for table tops, seats, legs, arms, and backs.
2. The individual pieces of cut lumber are painted in various bright colors.
3. The pieces are assembled into tables and chairs.

The beginning balance sheet for the company on January 1 of the current year is presented below.

Graymoore Products Company
Balance Sheet
January 1, 19--

Assets		Liabilities and Stockholders' Equity	
Cash	$ 40,000	Liabilities	$ –0–
Building	250,000		
Machinery and equipment	75,000	Capital stock	$365,000
		Total liabilities and	
Total assets	$365,000	stockholders' equity	$365,000

Assume, for the purpose of simplification, that in January the company makes only one style of table and no chairs. During January the following transactions are completed and recorded, in summary form, as follows:

1. Materials (lumber, paint, screws, lubricants, and solvents) are purchased at a cost of $25,000.

Materials	25,000	
Vouchers Payable (or Accounts Payable)		25,000

The cost of materials purchased is charged to the inventory control account, Materials. This treatment is based on the assumption that the company uses a perpetual inventory system.

2. During the month, direct materials (lumber and paint) costing $20,000 and indirect materials (screws, lubricants for machines, and solvents for cleaning) costing $995 are issued to the factory.

Work in Process	20,000	
Factory Overhead (Indirect Materials)	995	
Materials		20,995

Direct materials issued are charged directly to the work in process control account, but the indirect materials are charged to the factory overhead account. The factory overhead account will be used to accumulate various factory expenses that will later be transferred to Work in Process.

3. Total gross wages and salaries earned for the month were: factory employees working on the product, $10,000; factory supervision, maintenance, and custodial employees, $3,500; sales and administrative employees, $4,500. The entries to record the payroll and the payments to employees (ignoring payroll deductions) would be:

Payroll	18,000	
Vouchers Payable (or Wages Payable)		18,000
Vouchers Payable	18,000	
Cash		18,000

4. The entry to distribute or allocate the payroll to the appropriate accounts would be:

Work in Process	10,000	
Factory Overhead (Indirect Labor)	3,500	
Selling and Administrative Expenses (Salaries)	4,500	
Payroll		18,000

The wages earned by employees working directly on the product are charged to Work in Process, while the salaries and wages of the factory supervisor and the maintenance and custodial personnel, who do not work directly on the product, are charged to Factory Overhead as indirect labor. The salaries of nonfactory employees are debited to a separate expense account.

In order to focus on specific cost accounting procedures as distinguished from general accounting procedures, the general ledger account Selling and Administrative Expenses will be used to accumulate all nonmanufacturing expenses. In the usual situation, there would be a general ledger account for each type of nonmanufacturing expense.

5. Depreciation expense for the building is 6% of cost per year. The office occupies one-tenth of the total building, and the factory operation is contained in the other nine-tenths. The expense for one month is recorded as follows:

Factory Overhead (Depreciation of Building)	1,125	
Selling and Administrative Expenses (Depreciation of Building)	125	
Accumulated Depreciation — Building		1,250

($250,000 × .06 × 1/12 = $1,250; $1,250 × .90 = $1,125; $1,250 × .10 = $125)

The cost accounting principle illustrated here is that only those costs directly related to production should be charged to Factory Overhead. Depreciation on the portion of the building used as office space is an administrative expense and should not be treated as an element of production cost.

6. Depreciation expense for machinery and equipment is 20% of cost per year.

Factory Overhead (Depreciation of Machinery and Equipment).......... *Man*..	1,250	
Accumulated Depreciation—Machinery and Equipment)...		1,250

$$(\$75,000 \times .20 \times \frac{1}{12} = \$1,250)$$

All machinery and equipment is used in the factory for production purposes, so the depreciation expense, which generally cannot be traced to a certain unit of product, is properly charged to Factory Overhead.

7. The cost of heat, light, and power for the month was $1,500.

Factory Overhead (Utilities) .... *factory*	1,350	
Selling and Administrative Expenses (Utilities) .. *office*..	150	
Vouchers Payable...		1,500

Because one-tenth of the building is used for office purposes, 10% of the total utilities cost is allocated to Selling and Administrative Expenses.

8. Miscellaneous expenses for telephone, office supplies, travel, and rental of office furniture and equipment totaled $750.

Selling and Administrative Expenses *Misc.*	750	
Vouchers Payable..		750

Many other expenses may be incurred by a manufacturing organization, but for purposes of simplicity, it is assumed there are no other expenses during the month. After posting the journal entries to the appropriate ledger accounts, the factory overhead account will reflect the following debits:

Transaction	Description	Amount
(2)	Indirect materials	$ 995
(4)	Indirect labor...	3,500
(5)	Depreciation of building	1,125
(6)	Depreciation of machinery and equipment	1,250
(7)	Utilities...	1,350
	Total	$8,220

9. The balance in Factory Overhead is transferred to Work in Process by the following entry:

Work in Process	8,220	
Factory Overhead		8,220

The three elements of manufacturing cost — direct materials, direct labor, and factory overhead — are now accumulated in Work in Process, and the debits in the account are as follows:

Transaction	Description	Amount
(2)	Direct materials	$20,000
(4)	Direct labor	10,000
(9)	Factory overhead	8,220
	Total	$38,220

Work in Process

The fact that indirect factory expenses are first accumulated in Factory Overhead and subsequently transferred by journal entry to Work in Process rather than being charged directly to Work in Process may be perplexing. However, justification for this procedure will be offered in subsequent chapters when a more complete discussion of the allocation of factory overhead to jobs, processes, and departments is presented.

10. Assuming that all goods started in process have been finished, the following entry is recorded:

Finished Goods	38,220	
Work in Process		38,220

goods started finished

Assuming that 1,000 tables were produced during the month, the unit cost is $38.22 ($38,220 ÷ 1,000). The unit cost for each element of manufacturing cost is calculated as follows:

	Total	Units Produced	Unit Cost
Direct materials	$20,000	1,000	$20.00
Direct labor	10,000	1,000	10.00
Factory overhead	8,220	1,000	8.22
	$38,220		$38.22

If the same type of table is produced in future periods, the unit costs of those periods can be compared with the unit costs determined above, and any differences can be analyzed so that management might take appropriate action.

The unit cost also serves as a basis for establishing the selling price of the tables. After considering the anticipated selling and administrative expenses, a selling price can be established that should provide a reasonable profit. If management determines that a 33⅓% gross profit percentage (also known as a mark-on percentage) is necessary to cover the product's share of selling and administrative expenses and to earn a satisfactory profit, the selling price per unit, rounded to the nearest cent, would be determined as follows:

[handwritten margin note: Man. Cost + Gross Profit % / Selling Price]

Manufacturing cost	$38.22
Gross profit percentage (33⅓%)	12.74
Selling price	$50.96

In later periods, it might be found that this particular item cannot be sold at a price high enough to provide a reasonable profit. Through analysis of the unit costs, management might effect a cost-cutting measure, or perhaps even discontinue production of the item.

From this example, it is apparent that an accurate picture of cost for inventory valuation purposes is available. At any given time, the cost of each item in inventory is available. It should be reemphasized that one function of cost accounting is the accurate determination of the cost of manufacturing a unit of product. This knowledge of unit cost aids management in planning and controlling operations and in making marketing decisions.

To continue with the example, assume that the following transactions take place in January in addition to those already recorded:

[handwritten margin note: Vouchers being paid]

11.   Vouchers of $17,000, representing costs of materials, utilities, and selling and administrative expenses, are paid.

Vouchers Payable	17,000	
Cash		17,000

[handwritten margin note: Sales 2 entries]

12.   800 tables are sold to jobbers at a net price of $50.96 each.

Accounts Receivable (800 × $50.96) *[handwritten: (# of units sold × price per unit)]*	40,768	
Sales		40,768
Cost of Goods Sold (800 × $38.22) *[handwritten: (# of items sold × cost per unit)]*	30,576	
Finished Goods		30,576

Because the unit cost of each item is known, the cost of goods sold can be determined without a physical inventory or cost estimate.

13.   Cash totaling $27,500 is collected on accounts receivable.

Cash 27,500
    Accounts Receivable....................................   27,500

The accounts in the general ledger will reflect the entries as follows:

D   **Cash**   *C*

1/1 Bal.	40,000	(3)	18,000
(13)	27,500	(11)	17,000
	67,500		*35,000*
	32,500		

Accounts Receivable

(12)	40,768	(13)	27,500
	13,268		

Finished Goods

(10)	38,220	(12)	30,576
	7,644		

Work In Process

(2) Direct materials	20,000	(10)	38,220
(4) Direct labor	10,000		
(9) Factory overhead	8,220		
	38,220		

Materials

(1)	25,000	(2)	20,995
	4,005		

Building

1/1 Bal.	250,000	

Accumulated Depreciation — Building

	(5)	1,250

Machinery and Equipment

1/1 Bal.	75,000	

Accumulated Depreciation — Machinery and Equipment

	(6)	1,250

Vouchers Payable

(3)	18,000	(1)	25,000
(11)	17,000	(3)	18,000
	35,000	(7)	1,500
		(8)	750
			45,250
			10,250

Payroll

(3)	18,000	(4)	18,000
	0		

Capital Stock

	1/1 Bal.	365,000

Sales

	(12)	40,768

Cost of Goods Sold

(12)	30,576	

Factory Overhead

(2) Indirect materials	995	(9)	8,220
(4) Indirect labor	3,500		
(5) Depreciation of building	1,125		
(6) Depreciation of machinery & equip.	1,250		
(7) Utilities	1,350		
	8,220		

Selling and Administrative Expenses

(4) Salaries	4,500
(5) Depreciation of building	125
(7) Utilities	150
(8) Other	750
	5,525

After determining the balance of each general ledger account, the equality of the debits and credits is proven by preparing a trial balance as follows:

Graymoore Products Company
Trial Balance
January 31, 19--

Cash	$ 32,500	
Accounts Receivable	13,268	
Finished Goods	7,644	
Work in Process	–0–	
Materials	4,005	
Building	250,000	
Accumulated Depreciation — Building		$ 1,250
Machinery and Equipment	75,000	
Accumulated Depreciation — Machinery and Equipment		1,250
Vouchers Payable		10,250
Payroll		–0–
Capital Stock		365,000
Sales		40,768
Cost of Goods Sold	30,576	
Factory Overhead	–0–	
Selling and Administrative Expenses	5,525	
	$418,518	$418,518

Note that the finished goods control account reflects the cost of the 200 units still on hand — 200 × $38.22 = $7,644.

From an analysis of the general ledger accounts and the trial balance, financial statements for the period are prepared as follows.

④

no begin
:
ending balance

Graymoore Products Company
Statement of Cost of Goods Manufactured
For the Month Ended January 31, 19--

Direct materials:		
Inventory, January 1	$ –0–	
Purchases	25,000	
Total cost of available materials...............................	$25,000	
Less inventory, January 31	4,005	
Cost of materials used	$20,995	
Less indirect materials used	995	
Cost of direct materials used in production.................		$20,000
Direct labor..		10,000
Factory overhead:		
Indirect materials	$ 995	
Indirect labor...	3,500	
Depreciation of building	1,125	
Depreciation of machinery and equipment	1,250	
Utilities..	1,350	
Total factory overhead		8,220
Cost of goods manufactured during the month..............		$38,220

⑤

Graymoore Products Company
Income Statement
For the Month Ended January 31, 19--

Net sales..		$40,768
Cost of goods sold:		
Finished goods inventory, January 1........................	$ –0–	
Add cost of goods manufactured............................	38,220	
Goods available for sale.......................................	$38,220	
Less finished goods inventory, January 31	7,644	30,576
Gross profit on sales		$10,192
Selling and administrative expenses:		
Selling and administrative salaries	$ 4,500	
Depreciation of building...	125	
Utilities...	150	
Miscellaneous	750	5,525
Net income..		$ 4,667

whats left in inventory

Graymoore Products Company
Balance Sheet
January 31, 19--

Assets

Current assets:			
Cash..			$ 32,500
Accounts receivable......................................			13,268
Inventories:			
Finished goods..		$ 7,644	
Work in process...		–0–	
Materials		4,005	11,649
Total current assets..,.................................			$ 57,417
Plant and equipment:			
Building.......................................	$250,000		
Less accumulated depreciation.......	1,250	$248,750	
Machinery and equipment.................	$ 75,000		
Less accumulated depreciation.......	1,250	73,750	
Total plant and equipment.....................................			322,500
Total assets...			$379,917

Liabilities and Stockholders' Equity

Current liabilities:			
Vouchers payable			$ 10,250
Stockholders' equity:			
Capital stock...		$365,000	
Retained earnings...		4,667	
Total stockholders' equity			369,667
Total liabilities and stockholders' equity...........			$379,917

The figures in the cost of goods manufactured statement were obtained by analyzing the appropriate general ledger accounts. The materials inventory account had no beginning balance but has an ending balance of $4,005. The amount of purchases during the period was determined by analysis of the debits to the materials account. The cost of direct materials used of $20,000 and the direct labor cost of $10,000 were obtained from the work in process account. All other items in the statement of cost of goods manufactured represent factory overhead and are determined from the factory overhead account in the general ledger. These costs could also be accumulated in separate accounts before they are transferred to the factory overhead account and then to the work in process account, thus making available the amount incurred for each expense and eliminating the need to analyze the factory overhead account. As more advanced cost accounting procedures are presented in subsequent chapters, the common practice of maintaining a subsidiary ledger with an account for each type of factory overhead expense will be discussed. Following this procedure, the factory overhead account acts as a control account with its balance supported by the sum of the balances recorded in separate accounts in a subsidiary factory overhead ledger.

A complete cycle in cost accounting procedures has been presented. Before proceeding, a careful review of the basic elements of terminology and flow of costs is recommended. A firm grasp of the fundamentals already covered is necessary to comprehend the more complex material in subsequent chapters. A graphic illustration of the flow of costs is presented on page 24. You should study this illustration carefully, following each line to trace the flow of costs. This diagram should be compared with the journal entries and the ledger accounts illustrated on pages 14 to 20.

COST ACCOUNTING SYSTEMS

In the previous example, the basic foundation of a cost accounting system was presented. In that illustration, costs were accumulated for one month, and at the end of the month the costs were divided by the total units produced to determine the unit cost. This accomplished one function of cost accounting, the determination of product costs — both total costs for the period and cost per unit. However, another important objective of a cost accounting system — cost control — could not be satisfactorily achieved using the described procedure. The statement was made that the unit costs could be compared with similar costs in future periods to see if costs were increasing. Assuming that in a subsequent month the cost of direct labor had risen to $11.00 per unit, it is necessary to investigate and determine whether something can be done to correct the situation. The described accounting procedure restricts any investigation, because it is not known exactly where in the factory this increase has occurred. Labor costs went up; but did they go up because of a general rise in wages or because of inefficiency? Did labor costs increase throughout the manufacturing process or for a particular department or job? Answers to such questions are not readily available using the procedures described in the earlier example.

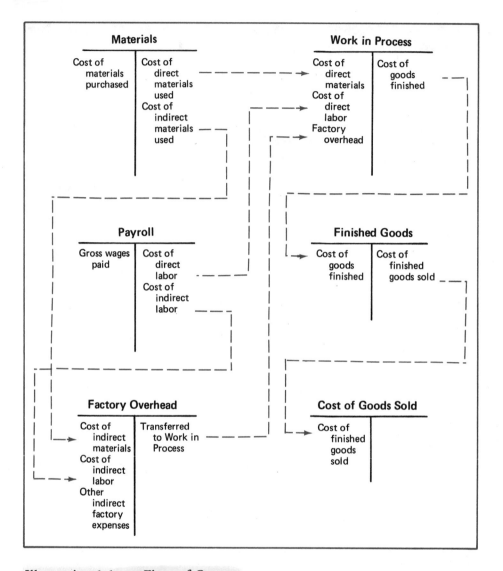

Illustration 1-1   Flow of Costs

To provide management with the data needed for effective cost control, two basic types of cost accounting systems have been developed—the process cost system and the job order cost system. These two systems are introduced in this chapter and discussed in greater detail in subsequent chapters.

Both systems are used to gather cost data and to allocate costs to goods manufactured. The selection of one method or the other depends on the type of manufacturing operation of a given company. For purposes of determining the appropriate method, manufacturing operations may be classified into two types — continuous or mass production and special order.

Continuous or Mass Production

In this type of operation, there is a continuous output of homogeneous products. Such an enterprise may produce a single product, such as an automobile, or many different products, such as breakfast cereals or patent medicines. The factory generally is departmentally organized. Industries of this type include those manufacturing automobiles, tires, cement, chemicals, canned goods, lumber, paper, candy, foodstuffs, flour, glass, soap, toothpaste, chewing gum, petroleum products, textiles, plastics, and paints, and firms engaged in such processes as rubber compounding and vulcanizing. A process cost system is normally used by this type of manufacturing enterprise.

Process cost accounting is suitable in manufacturing situations where all units of the final product are substantially identical. Finished units are placed in stock and removed, as needed, to fill customer orders. There are no separate jobs presenting substantially different characteristics; rather, the company (or a department within the company) produces large numbers of virtually identical items that are sold (or transferred to other departments) as orders are received.

Special Order

In this type of operation, the output consists of special or custom-made products; in other words, each product is made to order. An order may be of external or internal origin; that is, it may represent either a customer order or an internal order for a predetermined quantity of products. Industries of this type include those manufacturing or producing locomotives, ships, aircraft, machine tools, engines, structural steel, books and magazines, directories and catalogs; and specialty shops producing custom-made products such as clothing, shoes, and hats. A job order cost system is appropriate in these circumstances.

Illustration of Process Costing

With a process cost system, costs are allocated by departments (or processes). To illustrate this allocation, the Graymoore Products Company example will be revised, with certain transactions recorded as they would be when a departmentalized process cost system is used.

The main change from the previous example is that all factory costs will be charged to the various departments. The names of these departments or cost centers reflect their processing functions — Cutting, Painting, and Assembly. Only the transactions affecting the work in process accounts will be presented; the other entries would be recorded in the same way as previously described.

To record the issue of materials to the factory, entry 2 was:

Work in Process	20,000	
Factory Overhead	995	
Materials		20,995

Assume that certain materials records show that materials were issued as follows:

Cutting Department (lumber)	$18,500
Painting Department (paint)	1,500
Miscellaneous materials and supplies	995

With a process cost system, the entry would be recorded as follows:

Work in Process — Cutting Department	18,500	
Work in Process — Painting Department	1,500	
Factory Overhead	995	
Materials		20,995

Instead of charging the direct materials to one work in process account, the materials have been charged to the departments that will use them. This is the first indication that costs will be accumulated by departments, a basic procedure in a process cost system. For indirect materials, nothing has changed; the items that cannot be specifically identified with the product are still charged to the factory overhead account.

The next applicable entry is 4, which illustrates the distribution of the payroll for the month by the following entry:

Work in Process	10,000	
Factory Overhead	3,500	
Selling and Administrative Expenses	4,500	
Payroll		18,000

Assume that an analysis of factory labor costs disclosed the following data:

Cutting Department	$ 3,200
Painting Department	3,000
Assembly Department	3,800
	$10,000

The labor costs would be recorded in general journal form as follows:

Work in Process — Cutting Department	3,200	
Work in Process — Painting Department	3,000	
Work in Process — Assembly Department	3,800	
Factory Overhead	3,500	
Selling and Administrative Expenses	4,500	
Payroll		18,000

Entries 5, 6, and 7, recording factory overhead for depreciation of the building, depreciation of machinery and equipment, and utilities; and entry 8, for selling and administrative expenses, would be recorded in the same way as in the first example.

Now that the costs for direct materials and direct labor have been recorded in the work in process accounts for each department, only the distribution of factory overhead to these departments remains to be completed; this is one of the more complex problems of cost accounting. As has been illustrated, it is relatively easy to allocate direct materials and direct labor to a specific department, but this is not true for the other manufacturing expenses. Some method must be devised to distribute factory overhead to the departments on an equitable basis. Two common approaches to distributing factory overhead are: (1) the allocation or apportionment method and (2) the predetermined rate method. Both methods will be discussed in Chapter 4.

For simplicity, assume that the following distribution of factory overhead expenses has been prepared for the company.

Schedule of Factory Overhead Distribution				
Costs	Cutting	Painting	Assembly	Total
Indirect materials	$ 240	$ 480	$ 275	$ 995
Indirect labor	1,150	1,350	1,000	3,500
Depreciation — building	210	500	415	1,125
Depreciation — machinery and equipment	750	375	125	1,250
Utilities	720	455	175	1,350
Total	$3,070	$3,160	$1,990	$8,220

The schedule provides the basis for making the following entry to distribute factory overhead to the departments.

Work in Process — Cutting Department	3,070	
Work in Process — Painting Department	3,160	
Work in Process — Assembly Department	1,990	
Factory Overhead		8,220

The departmental work in process accounts appear as follows:

Work in Process — Cutting Dept.

(2) Direct materials	18,500
(4) Direct labor	3,200
(9) Factory overhead	3,070
	24,770

Work in Process — Painting Dept.

(2) Direct materials	1,500
(4) Direct labor	3,000
(9) Factory overhead	3,160
	7,660

Work in Process — Assembly Dept.

(4) Direct labor	3,800
(9) Factory overhead	1,990
	5,790

From this information, a summary of production costs is prepared. The summary, presented on page 29, provides a detailed breakdown of each element of cost by department. As unit costs are determined in subsequent months, a comparison can be made on a month-to-month basis of each cost element for each department. Any unexpected fluctuations in costs can be referred to the department supervisor for accountability. At the same time, the data necessary for inventory valuation are available.

Final entries can now be made to transfer the costs from each department to the next, following the flow of goods through the factory.

Work in Process — Painting Department	24,770	
Work in Process — Cutting Department		24,770
Work in Process — Assembly Department	32,430	
Work in Process — Painting Department		32,430
Finished Goods	38,220	
Work in Process — Assembly Department		38,220

Graymoore Products Company
Summary of Production Costs
For the Month Ended January 31, 19--

	Cutting	Painting	Assembly	Total
Total costs:				
Direct materials	$18,500	$1,500	–0–	$20,000
Direct labor.......................	3,200	3,000	$3,800	10,000
Factory overhead..............	3,070	3,160	1,990	8,220
Total	$24,770	$7,660	$5,790	$38,220
Number of units produced.......	1,000	1,000	1,000	1,000
Unit costs:				
Direct materials	$18.50	$1.50	$–0–	$20.00
Direct labor.......................	3.20	3.00	3.80	10.00
Factory overhead..............	3.07	3.16	1.99	8.22
Total	$24.77	$7.66	$5.79	$38.22

After these entries have been recorded, the work in process accounts
and the finished goods account will appear as follows:

Work in Process — Cutting Dept.

(2) Direct materials	18,500	To transfer costs		
(4) Direct labor	3,200	to Painting Dept.		24,770
(9) Factory overhead	3,070			

Work in Process — Painting Dept.

(2) Direct materials	1,500	To transfer costs		
(4) Direct labor	3,000	to Assembly Dept.		32,430
(9) Factory overhead	3,160			
From Cutting Dept.	24,770			

Work in Process — Assembly Dept.

(4) Direct labor	3,800	To transfer costs		
(9) Factory overhead	1,990	to Finished Goods		38,220
From Painting Dept.	32,430			

Finished Goods

(10) From Assembly Dept.	38,220	

The cost of the goods manufactured has now been transferred through the various departments to the inventory control account, Finished Goods. Additional entries, such as those for sales and cost of goods sold, will be the same as in the first example.

Illustration of Job Order Costing

With a job order cost system, costs are accumulated by *job* (or *lot*), rather than by department as was illustrated for the process cost system. One advantage of a job order cost system is that the accumulation of costs for a particular job facilitates the determination of its selling price; or, if a job is done under contract with a set price, the profit or loss on the job is readily determinable by comparing cost with contract price. At the same time, those costs that have been accumulated for a certain type of work will assist management in preparing bids for similar jobs in the future.

To illustrate the use of the job order cost accounting system, assume that the Graymoore Products Company accepts two orders to manufacture certain items during the month of February. These special orders are as follows:

1. From the Planetary Distributing Co.: to manufacture 1,000 chairs to their specifications; contract price, $26,000.
2. From the General Merchandising Center: to manufacture 500 tables to their specifications; contract price, $19,650.

After accepting these orders and planning the manufacturing requirements as to materials, labor, and overhead, the cost accounting department sets up a job cost sheet for each job. An example of this form is shown in Illustration 1-2 for the Planetary Distributing Co. order. All costs applicable to each job will be accumulated on these forms. Job numbers 101 and 102, respectively, are assigned to these orders.

Transactions and journal entries for the month of February are presented on pages 31 to 34. In order to highlight job order cost accounting procedures, only those entries relating to the manufacture of goods will be illustrated. Routine entries, such as those for purchases of materials, for recording of nonmanufacturing expenses, or for payment of vouchers, will be ignored, as these entries are made in the same way as previously illustrated, regardless of the cost system used.

GRAYMOORE PRODUCTS COMPANY
Job Cost Sheet

Customer Name: Planetary Dist. Co.   Job No: 101

Address: 5525 Skyway Dr.   Date Started: 2/24

Houston, TX 77057

Date Completed: 2/28

Quantity: 1,000

Product: chairs

Description: wooden kitchen

DIRECT MATERIALS			DIRECT LABOR			FACTORY OVERHEAD		
Date	Mat'l. Req. No.	Amount	Date	Time Tkt. No.	Amount	Date	Basis Applied	Amount
2/24	5505	8,200	2/25	2101	2,500			
2/26	6211	4,000	2/27	2826	1,500		60% of	
			2/28	3902	2,000	2/28	total	5,007
Total		12,200			6,000			5,007

SUMMARY:

				Remarks:
Direct materials . . .	$ 12,200	Selling price.	$ 26,000	
Direct labor.	6,000	Mfg. cost.	23,207	
Factory overhead . .	5,007	Gross profit	$ 2,793	
Total cost	$ 23,207			
Unit cost	$ 23.21			

Illustration 1-2   Job Cost Sheet

1. Indirect materials with a cost of $2,620 are issued to the factory, and direct materials are issued as follows:

	Job 101	Job 102
Lumber	$11,000	$8,000
Paint	1,200	1,000
	$12,200	$9,000

The entry to record the issues of materials is:

Work in Process — 101	12,200	
Work in Process — 102	9,000	
Factory Overhead (Indirect Materials)	2,620	
Materials		23,820

If the indirect materials were directly traceable to a specific job, the cost could be charged to that job; however, it is often difficult to determine which job benefited from use of the various supplies. Thus, indirect materials costs are usually charged to Factory Overhead and later distributed among the various jobs.

2. Indirect labor costs of $2,180 are incurred, and direct labor costs are incurred as follows:

	Job 101	Job 102
Direct Labor	$6,000	$3,750

The entry to distribute these costs is:

Work in Process — 101	6,000	
Work in Process — 102	3,750	
Factory Overhead (Indirect Labor)	2,180	
Payroll		11,930

3. Monthly depreciation expense for the building is recorded as follows:

Factory Overhead (Depreciation of Building)	1,125	
Selling and Administrative Expenses (Depreciation of Building)	125	
Accumulated Depreciation — Building		1,250

4. The entry to record monthly depreciation for machinery and equipment is:

Factory Overhead (Depreciation of Machinery and Equipment)	1,250	
Accumulated Depreciation — Machinery and Equipment		1,250

5. The cost of utilities for the month of February is $1,300 and is recorded as follows:

Factory Overhead (Utilities)	1,170	
Selling and Administrative Expenses (Utilities)	130	
Vouchers Payable		1,300

6. Total charges to Factory Overhead for the month are shown at the top of page 33.

Indirect materials	$2,620
Indirect labor	2,180
Depreciation of building	1,125
Depreciation of machinery and equipment	1,250
Utilities	1,170
Total	$8,345

Assume that factory overhead is allocated as follows: 60% to Job 101, 40% to Job 102.

Total Factory Overhead	60% Job 101	40% Job 102
$8,345	$5,007	$3,338

The distribution of factory overhead would be recorded as follows:

Work in Process — 101	5,007	
Work in Process — 102	3,338	
Factory Overhead		8,345

At the end of the month, the work in process and factory overhead accounts would appear as follows:

Work in Process — 101

(1) Direct materials	12,200	
(2) Direct labor	6,000	
(6) Factory overhead	5,007	
	23,207	

Work in Process — 102

(1) Direct materials	9,000	
(2) Direct labor	3,750	
(6) Factory overhead	3,338	
	16,088	

Factory Overhead

(1) Indirect materials	2,620	(6) Transfer to work in process	8,345
(2) Indirect labor	2,180		
(3) Depr. — building	1,125		
(4) Depr. — mach. and equip.	1,250		
(5) Utilities	1,170		
	8,345		

The costs shown in the work in process accounts are the result of summary entries for the month. These same costs are shown in more detail on job cost sheets such as the one illustrated previously.

7. Assuming both jobs were completed by the end of the month, the costs of the completed jobs would be transferred to the finished goods inventory control account:

Finished Goods...	39,295	
Work in Process — 101.....................................		23,207
Work in Process — 102.....................................		16,088

8. When the goods are shipped to the customers and billed, the following entries are made to record the sales and the cost of the jobs:

Accounts Receivable...	45,650	
Sales..		45,650
Cost of Goods Sold..	39,295	
Finished Goods..		39,295

The costs of producing the two jobs can be summarized as follows:

	Job 101 (1,000 Units)		Job 102 (500 Units)	
	Total Cost	Unit Cost	Total Cost	Unit Cost
Direct materials.....................	$12,200	$12.20	$ 9,000	$18.00
Direct labor	6,000	6.00	3,750	7.50
Factory overhead..................	5,007	5.01	3,338	6.68
Total...............................	$23,207	$23.21	$16,088	$32.18

The gross profit realized on each job is determined as follows:

	Job 101 (1,000 Units)		Job 102 (500 Units)	
		Per		Per
	Total	Unit	Total	Unit
Selling price	$26,000	$26.00	$19,650	$39.30
Cost...................................	23,207	23.21	16,088	32.18
Gross profit	$ 2,793	$ 2.79	$ 3,562	$ 7.12

[handwritten margin note: SP − Cost Gross Profit]

The job cost sheets would reflect the above information in more detail, so that a short time after each job is completed, the gross profit can be determined. In addition, if management should have an opportunity to bid on similar jobs in the future, an accurate record of all costs would be available to assist in determining contract prices.

Some companies use both a job order cost and a process cost system. A situation where this might occur would be one in which the company manufactures goods on specific order but also produces on a continuous basis a number of small parts that can be used in most job orders. The costs of making these small parts would be accumulated on a process cost basis, while the costs for each job would be gathered on a job cost sheet.

Work in Process Control Account

When jobs or departments become too numerous to maintain a separate work in process account for each, a work in process control account in the general ledger will be used. In a job order cost system, the details on the job cost sheets in the subsidiary job cost ledger support the balance in Work in Process in the general ledger. If a process cost system is used, the balance in the work in process control account will be supported by detailed departmental cost analysis sheets. The use of the control accounts and supporting data will be discussed in more depth in subsequent chapters.

Work in Process in the Manufacturing Statement

If there is work in process at the beginning and at the end of the month, it will be shown as follows in the statement of cost of goods manufactured (note that this statement is more condensed than the one on page 21 and reflects management's interest in summary data):

Short

Giant Manufacturing Company Statement of Cost of Goods Manufactured For the Month Ended June 30, 19--	
Direct materials used	$290,000
Direct labor	240,000
Factory overhead	130,000
Total manufacturing cost	$660,000
Add work in process inventory, June 1	85,000
	$745,000
Less work in process inventory, June 30	125,000
Cost of goods manufactured during the month	$620,000

The total manufacturing cost of $660,000 represents the cost of direct materials, direct labor, and factory overhead incurred during the month of June. $85,000 is the cost of materials, labor, and overhead incurred the previous month for goods that were not completed at the end of that month. The total of $745,000, therefore, represents manufacturing cost that must be accounted for. Work in Process at the end of June is $125,000, which represents the cost incurred for items that were not finished at the end of June. Therefore, the cost of goods completed in June, of which some were started in production the previous month, is $620,000. The work in process ledger account, in T-account form, would appear as follows at the end of the month:

Work in Process			
6/1 Balance	85,000	To Finished Goods	620,000
Direct materials	290,000		
Direct labor	240,000		
Factory overhead	130,000		
	745,000		
125,000			

If a job order cost system is being used, the balance of $125,000 in the account represents the manufacturing cost incurred to date on jobs that have not yet been completed. If a process system is in use, the balance represents the cost to date, in one or more departments, of goods still to be finished.

STANDARD COST SYSTEM

The job order and process cost accounting systems are the principal systems used by manufacturing organizations; however, as useful as they are in providing cost data, there is still a limitation with these systems with regard to the control of costs. These systems make it possible to determine what a product actually cost but not what it *should* have cost. A standard cost accounting system, which is not a third system but may be used with either a job order or a process cost system, is designed to furnish management with a measurement that will help in making decisions regarding the efficiency of operations.

Standard costs are those costs that would be incurred under efficient operating conditions and are forecast before the manufacturing process begins. During operations, comparisons are made between the actual costs incurred and these predetermined standard costs, and "variances", or differences, are calculated. These variances will reveal performances which deviate from standard and thus give management a basis on which they can take appropriate action to eliminate inefficient operating conditions. Standard cost accounting will be discussed in depth and illustrated in Chapters 8 and 9.

ORGANIZATIONS INFLUENCING COST ACCOUNTING

Cost accounting principles and procedures have developed because of the need of managers for the information provided. Certain professional organizations and governmental agencies have significantly affected this development. Most of these organizations are more directly concerned with general accounting principles and external financial reporting rather than with cost accounting. However, cost accounting principles and procedures are an extension of general accounting and are thus influenced by these organizations.

Private Organizations

The **American Institute of Certified Public Accountants (AICPA)** is the national professional organization for certified public accountants. The Institute is involved in a wide range of activities relating to the practice of public accounting including professional certification, continuing education and professional development, and professional ethics. The AICPA also establishes auditing standards, and until 1973 was responsible for establishing generally accepted accounting principles (GAAP). The Institute conducts extensive research in accounting and auditing and publishes the *Journal of Accountancy,* a monthly publication which addresses contemporary accounting and reporting issues and professional responsibilities.

The **American Accounting Association (AAA)** is primarily an organization of accounting educators, but its members include practicing accountants and others as well. The AAA encourages and sponsors research in accounting theory and publishes selected research projects and a quarterly journal, *The Accounting Review.*

The **National Association of Accountants (NAA)** is primarily an organization for management accountants in industry and is thus directly concerned with cost accounting and internal information systems. The NAA publishes a monthly journal, *Management Accounting,* which deals mainly with cost accounting and the uses of internal information. However, since information systems within an enterprise generate data for both internal and external reporting purposes, the NAA is also concerned with principles of accounting in general.

The **Financial Accounting Standards Board (FASB),** established in 1973 by the AICPA-sponsored Financial Accounting Foundation, is responsible for developing and issuing standards of financial reporting for businesses and other organizations. The Board issues *Statements of Financial Accounting Standards* which are recognized as generally accepted accounting principles and must be followed unless unusual circumstances justify departure from a standard. The FASB also issues *Statements of Financial Accounting Concepts,* which deal with the fundamental objectives and concepts of accounting and are intended to guide organizations in financial accounting and reporting, but are not accounting principles which must be followed.

Governmental Agencies

The **Securities and Exchange Commission (SEC)** was created by an Act of Congress in 1934 to regulate the public trading of securities. The SEC does not attempt to prohibit the trading of risky securities, but attempts to ensure full and fair disclosure of information so that buyers and sellers of securities can make informed investment decisions. Since much of the information disclosed is financial information, the SEC is vitally concerned with accounting and reporting practices.

The **Internal Revenue Service (IRS)** administers the provisions of the federal income tax law and issues regulations which require or permit certain methods of accounting for tax purposes. In most cases, the accounting methods required for tax purposes do not have to be used for financial reporting purposes. Nevertheless, the IRS has been influential in the development of financial accounting principles, particularly in the areas of depreciation and inventories.

no longer exist: FASB

The **Cost Accounting Standards Board (CASB)** was created by the U.S. Congress in 1970 for the purpose of establishing standards for cost accounting procedures to be followed by firms dealing with the federal government on certain contracts. Pronouncements of the Board are of considerable importance in accounting for nongovernmental contracts and other noncontractual manufacturing activities as well. Although the CASB was dissolved in 1980, due to a lack of funding, its rules and regulations remain in force.

KEY TERMS

Budget (7)
Control (5)
Conversion costs (12)
Cost accounting (2)
Cost accounting systems (2)
Cost and production report (6)
Cost center (6)
Direct labor (11)
Direct materials (11)
Factory ledger (11)
Factory overhead (12)
Factory overhead ledger (23)
Financial accounting (8)
Finished goods (9)
Gross profit (or mark-on)
  percentage (18)
Indirect labor (11)
Indirect materials (11)
Information systems (2)

Job cost ledger (35)
Job cost sheet (30)
Job order cost system (25)
Manufacturing (or production)
  costs (11)
Manufacturing process (3)
Materials (10)
Performance report (7)
Periodic inventory system (10)
Perpetual inventory system (10)
Planning (5)
Prime cost (12)
Process cost system (25)
Responsibility accounting (6)
Standard cost accounting
  system (36)
Standard costs (36)
Unit costs (4)
Work in process (10)

QUESTIONS

1. How does the cost accounting function assist in the management of a business?
2. In what ways does a typical manufacturing business differ from a merchandising concern? In what ways are they similar?
3. How are cost accounting data used by management?
4. Why is unit cost information important to management?
5. For a manufacturer, what does the planning process involve and how are cost accounting data used in planning?
6. How is effective control achieved in a manufacturing concern?
7. Define responsibility accounting.
8. What are the criteria which must be met for a unit of activity within the factory to qualify as a cost center?
9. How is cost accounting related to financial accounting?
10. How does the computation of cost of goods sold for a manufacturer differ from that of a merchandiser?
11. Describe the following accounts: Finished Goods, Work in Process, and Materials.
12. Distinguish between a perpetual inventory system and a periodic inventory system.
13. What are the basic elements of production cost?
14. Define the following costs: direct materials, indirect materials, direct labor, indirect labor, and factory overhead.
15. Define prime cost and conversion cost. Does prime cost plus conversion cost equal the cost of manufacturing?
16. In what way does the accounting treatment of factory overhead differ from that of direct materials and direct labor costs?
17. Distinguish between cost of goods sold and cost of goods manufactured.
18. How are nonfactory costs and costs which benefit both factory and nonfactory operations accounted for?
19. What is a mark-on percentage?
20. When is process costing appropriate, and how are costs accumulated in a process cost system?
21. When is job order costing appropriate, and how are costs accumulated in a job order cost system?
22. What are the advantages of accumulating costs by departments or jobs rather than for the factory as a whole?
23. What is a job cost sheet and why is it useful?
24. What are standard costs, and what is the purpose of a standard cost system?
25. Why was the Cost Accounting Standards Board created?

Exercise 1-1 Cost classification.

Classify the following as direct materials, direct labor, or factory overhead.
(a) Lumber used in a furniture factory.
(b) Cloth used in a shirt factory.
(c) Fiberglass used by a sailboat builder.
(d) Lubricating oils used on machines in a tool factory.
(e) Wages of a press operator employed in a printing plant.
(f) Insurance on factory machines.
(g) Rent paid for factory buildings.
(h) Wages of fork-lift operators employed in a factory.
(i) Leather used in a shoe factory.
(j) Wages of a factory janitor.
(k) Electric power consumed in operating factory machines.
(l) Depreciation on factory machinery.
(m) Fuel used in heating a factory.
(n) Paint used in the manufacture of automobiles.
(o) Wages of an ironworker in the construction business.
(p) Electricity used in lighting a factory.

Exercise 1-2 Cost flow.

Explain in narrative form the flow of direct materials, direct labor, and factory overhead costs through the accounts.

Exercise 1-3 Journal entries.

The following is a list of manufacturing costs incurred by Sequoia Products Co. during the month of May:

Direct materials used	$15,000
Indirect materials used	3,000
Direct labor employed	21,000
Indirect labor employed	5,000
Rent expense	4,000
Utilities	1,200
Insurance	500
Depreciation expense (machinery and equipment)	1,500

Prepare the journal entries necessary to record the preceding information and the entry transferring Factory Overhead to Work in Process.

Exercise 1-4 Statement of cost of goods manufactured; cost of goods sold.

The following data are taken from the general ledger and other records of the Murray Manufacturing Co. at January 31, the end of the first month of operations in the current fiscal year.

Sales.	$75,000
Materials inventory (January 1)	22,000
Work in process inventory (January 1)	24,000
Finished goods inventory (January 1)	32,000
Materials purchased	21,000
Direct labor cost	18,000
Factory overhead (including $1,000 of indirect materials used and $3,000 of indirect labor cost)	12,000
Selling and administrative expense.	10,000
Inventories at January 31:	
Materials.	25,000
Work in process	20,000
Finished goods	30,000

(a) Prepare a statement of cost of goods manufactured.
(b) Determine the cost of goods sold for the month.

Exercise 1-5 Unit manufacturing costs; cost analysis.

Akita Manufacturing Co. is engaged in the manufacture of candy bars and uses a process cost accounting system. At the end of April, the cost accountant obtains the following information from the cost records:

	No. 1 Bar	No. 2 Bar
Direct materials used	$18,750	$25,000
Direct labor cost	9,000	15,000
Factory overhead	6,000	11,600
Total manufacturing costs	$33,750	$51,600
Number of boxes produced	12,500	20,000

The records of Akita Manufacturing Co. disclose the following data for the month of May:

	No. 1 Bar	No. 2 Bar
Direct materials used	$15,000	$18,000
Direct labor cost	7,500	12,000
Factory overhead	5,000	9,000
Total manufacturing costs	$27,500	$39,000
Number of boxes produced	10,000	15,000

(a)   Prepare a comparative statement showing the costs of materials, direct labor, and factory overhead applicable to each box (there are 24 bars per box) and the total cost per box for each product for the months of April and May.

(b)   Give possible reasons for the changes in unit costs and each element of cost.

Exercise 1-6   Journal entries for process costing.

The Beech Company manufactures a single product and uses the process cost system. There are two production departments. During the month, the following transactions took place for Department 1:

Direct materials issued	$65,000
Direct labor incurred	90,000
Factory overhead allocated	63,000

Work in process for Department 1 at the beginning of the period was $18,000 and at the end of the period, $15,000.

Prepare journal entries to record:

(a)   the flow of costs into Department 1

(b)   the transfer of manufacturing costs to Department 2.

Exercise 1-7   Journal entries for job order costing; total and unit cost computation.

Becker Supply Inc. uses the job order cost system of accounting. The following information was taken from the books of the company after all posting had been completed at the end of May:

Jobs Completed	Direct Materials Cost	Direct Labor Cost	Factory Overhead	Units Completed
501	$3,600	$4,000	$1,600	400
502	2,380	2,500	1,000	240
503	1,800	1,700	680	200

(a)   Prepare the journal entries to allocate the costs of materials, labor, and factory overhead to each job and to transfer the costs of jobs completed to Finished Goods.

(b)   Compute the total production cost of each job.

(c)   Compute the unit cost of each job.

(d)   Compute the selling price per unit for each job, assuming a gross profit percentage of 50%.

Exercise 1-8   Journal entries for job order costing.

Star Warp Products Co. manufactures goods on a job order basis. During the month of April, three jobs were started in process. (There was no work in process at the beginning of the month.) Jobs 727 and 737 were completed and sold during the month (Selling prices: Job 727, $22,000; Job 737, $27,000); Job 747 was still in process at the end of April.

Shown below are data from the job cost sheets for each job. These costs include a total of $900 of indirect materials and $1,200 of indirect labor. One work in process control account is used. / w/p acct in general ledger.

no sep. job ledger.

	Job 727	Job 737	Job 747
Direct materials	$5,000	$6,000	$3,500
Direct labor	4,000	5,000	2,500
Factory overhead	2,000	2,500	1,250

(a)   (d)

Prepare journal entries to record:
(a) materials used
(b) factory wages and salaries earned
(c) Factory Overhead transferred to Work in Process
(d) jobs completed
(e) jobs sold.

Exercise 1-9   Determining materials, labor, and cost of goods sold.

The following inventory data relate to Benjamin Corp.

	Inventories	
	Ending	Beginning
Finished goods	$110,000	$90,000
Work in process	70,000	80,000
Direct materials	90,000	95,000

Revenues and Costs for the Period

Sales	$900,000
Cost of goods available for sale	775,000
Total manufacturing costs	675,000
Factory overhead	175,000
Direct materials used	205,000

Calculate the following for the year:
(a) direct materials purchased
(b) direct labor costs incurred
(c) cost of goods sold
(d) gross profit.

(AICPA adapted)

PROBLEMS

Problem 1-1   Basic cost system; journal entries; financial statements.

The post-closing trial balance of Mammoth Manufacturing Co. at September 30 is reproduced below.

Mammoth Manufacturing Co.
Post-Closing Trial Balance
September 30, 19--

Cash	15,000	
Accounts Receivable	18,000	
Finished Goods	25,000	
Work in Process	4,000	
Materials	8,000	
Building	156,000	
Accumulated Depreciation — Building		23,400
Factory Equipment	108,000	
Accumulated Depreciation — Factory Equipment		54,000
Office Equipment	12,000	
Accumulated Depreciation — Office Equipment		2,000
Vouchers Payable		30,000
Capital Stock		175,000
Retained Earnings		61,600
	346,000	346,000

During the month of October, the following transactions took place:

(a) Raw materials at a cost of $50,000 and general factory supplies at a cost of $8,000 were purchased and vouchers prepared (materials and supplies are recorded in the materials account).

(b) Raw materials to be used in production costing $41,000 and miscellaneous factory supplies costing $5,500 were issued.

(c) A voucher was prepared for wages and salaries earned for the month as follows: factory wages (including $2,500 indirect labor), $34,000 and selling and administrative salaries $5,000. (Ignore payroll withholdings and deductions.)

(d) Depreciation was recorded for the month at an annual rate of 5% on the building and 20% on the factory equipment and office equipment. The sales and administrative staff uses approximately one fifth of the building for its offices.

(e)   During the month, various other expenses totaling $5,200 were incurred
      and the vouchers prepared. It is determined that one fourth of this
      amount is allocable to the office function.
(f)   Total factory overhead costs were transferred to Work in Process.
(g)   During the month, goods with a total cost of $79,000 were completed
      and transferred to the finished goods storeroom.
(h)   Sales for the month totaled $128,000 for goods costing $87,000. (As-
      sume all sales were made on account.)
(i)   Accounts receivable in the amount of $105,000 were collected.
(j)   Vouchers totaling $94,000 were paid.

Required:
1.   Prepare journal entries to record the transactions.
2.   Set up T-accounts. Post the beginning trial balance and the journal
      entries prepared for (1) above to the accounts and determine the bal-
      ances in the accounts on October 31.
3.   Prepare a statement of cost of goods manufactured, an income state-
      ment, and a balance sheet.

Problem 1-2   Process cost; two departments; work in process.

   Assuming the same transactions as presented in Problem 1-1, also assume that Mammoth Manufacturing Co. has two production departments, A
and B, and uses a process cost system. Additional data are as follows:

1.   Materials are processed first in department A and are then transferred to
      department B for finishing goods
2.   Materials, labor, and factory overhead costs are incurred in the ratio
      of three to one in departments A and B, respectively.
3.   Work in process inventories were as follows:

	October 1	October 31
Department A	$3,000	$2,000
Department B	1,000	9,720

Required:
Prepare the journal entries to record the transactions which affect the work in
process accounts. (All other entries would be the same as in Problem 1-1.)

Problem 1-3   Job order cost; journal entries; profit analysis.

   Prince Manufacturing Co. obtains the following information from its
records for the month of August:

	Jobs Completed and Sold		
	Job 1610	Job 1620	Job 1630
Direct materials cost	$15,000	$10,000	$25,000
Direct labor cost	50,000	50,000	50,000
Factory overhead	30,000	30,000	30,000
Units manufactured	5,000	4,000	10,000
Gross profit or selling price................	25%	$80,000	20%

Required:
1. Prepare, in summary form, the journal entries that would have been made during the month to record the above.
2. Prepare schedules showing the gross profit or loss for August:
   (a) For the business as a whole.
   (b) For each job completed and sold.
   (c) For each unit manufactured and sold.
3. Explain the significant facts and possible causes brought out by the analysis in 2. above.

Problem 1-4   Job cost; journal entries; inventory analysis; manufacturing statement.

Reston Manufacturing Co. is engaged in the manufacture of engines which are made only on customers' orders and to their specifications. During January, the company worked on Jobs 901, 902, 903, and 904. The following figures summarize the cost records for the month.

	Job 901 (100 units)	Job 902 (60 units)	Job 903 (25 units)	Job 904 (100 units)
Direct materials put into process:				
Jan. 2	$15,000	$ 5,000	—	—
18	20,000	16,000	$ 5,000	—
22	15,000	1,000	10,000	$ 6,000
28	—	—	3,500	2,000
Direct labor cost: week ending				
Jan. 2	$ 1,000	$ 1,000	—	—
9	27,000	9,000	—	—
16	32,000	27,000	—	—
23	20,000	3,000	$ 5,000	$ 500
30	—	—	18,000	11,500
Factory overhead	$60,000	$32,000	$17,500	$ 9,000
Engines completed	100	60	25	—

Jobs 901 and 902 have been completed and delivered to the customer at a total selling price of $350,000. Job 903 is finished but has not yet been delivered. Job 904 is still in process. There was no work in process at the beginning of the month.

Required:

1. Prepare the summary journal entries for the month to record the preceding information. (Assume a work in process account is maintained for each job.)
2. Prepare a summary showing the total cost of each job completed during the month or in process at the end of month. Also determine the valuation of the inventories of completed engines and engines in process at end of month.
3. Prepare a statement of cost of goods manufactured.

Problem 1-5 Job order cost; journal entries; ending work in process; inventory analysis.

The Blackstar Company manufactures goods to special order and uses a job order cost system. During its first month of operations, the following selected transactions took place:

(a)	Materials purchased on account..	$37,000
(b)	Materials issued to the factory:	
	Job 101	$ 2,200
	Job 102	5,700
	Job 103	7,100
	Job 104	1,700
	For general use in the factory..	1,350
(c)	Factory wages and salaries earned:	
	Job 101	$ 2,700
	Job 102	6,800
	Job 103	9,200
	Job 104	2,100
	For general work in the factory......................................	2,250
(d)	Miscellaneous factory overhead costs vouchered..............	$ 2,400
(e)	Depreciation of $2,000 on the factory machinery was recorded.	
(f)	Factory overhead allocated as follows:	
	Job 101	$ 1,200
	Job 102	2,000
	Job 103	3,800
	Job 104	1,000
(g)	Jobs 101, 102, and 103 were completed.	
(h)	Jobs 101 and 102 were shipped to the customer and billed at $30,900.	

Required:

1. Prepare a schedule reflecting the cost of each of the four jobs.
2. Prepare entries to record the transactions above. (One control account is used for Work in Process.)

3. Compute the ending balance in Work in Process.
4. Compute the ending balance in Finished Goods.

Problem 1-6   Cash flow; journal entries; account analysis.

Selected account balances and transactions of The Larkin Manufacturing Co. are as shown below.

	Account Balances	
	May 1	May 31
Materials:		
Raw Materials........*direct*	$ 6,500	$ 5,000
Factory Supplies ......*indirect*	900	800
Work in Process..	5,300	6,000
Finished Goods...	13,200	12,000

May Transactions

(a) Purchases of raw materials and factory supplies were made on account at costs of $45,000 and $5,000 respectively. (One inventory account is maintained.) *materials*.

(b) Wages earned during the month totaled $65,000 of which $10,000 was for indirect labor.

(c) Factory overhead costs in the amount of $12,000 were vouchered.

(d) Adjusting entries to record $7,000 of factory overhead were made in the general journal.

Required:
Prepare the entries necessary to show the flow of all costs through the accounts. (Hint: Be certain to consider the beginning and ending account balances in determining the amounts of the debits to work in process, finished goods, and cost of goods sold.)

Problem 1-7 Data analysis; manufacturing statement.

Finder Corporation manufactures one product and accounts for costs by a job order cost system. You have obtained the following information for the year ended December 31 from the corporation's books and records:

(a) Total manufacturing cost during the year was $1,000,000, including direct materials, direct labor, and factory overhead.

(b) Cost of goods manufactured during the year was $970,000.

(c) Factory overhead charged to work in process was 75% of direct labor cost and 27% of the total manufacturing cost. *270,000*

(d) Beginning work in process inventory, January 1, was 60% of ending work in process inventory, December 31.

Required:
Prepare a statement of cost of goods manufactured for the year ended December 31 for Finder Corporation.

(AICPA adapted)

Problem 1-8   Data analysis, manufacturing statement, cost terminology.

Mat Company's cost of goods sold for the month ended March 31 was $345,000. Ending work in process inventory was 90% of beginning work in process inventory. Factory overhead was 50% of direct labor cost. Other information pertaining to Mat Company's inventories and production for the month of March is as follows:

Beginning inventories, March 1:	
Direct materials...	$ 20,000
Work in process, ...	40,000
Finished goods..	102,000
Purchases of direct materials during March	110,000
Ending inventories, March 31:	
Direct materials...	26,000
Work in process...	?
Finished goods..	105,000

Required:
1. Prepare a statement of cost of goods manufactured for the month of March. (Hint: Set up a statement of cost of goods manufactured, putting the given information in the appropriate spaces and solving for the unknown information.)
2. Prepare a schedule to compute the prime cost incurred during March.
3. Prepare a schedule to compute the conversion cost charged to work in process during March.

(AICPA adapted)

2

ACCOUNTING FOR MATERIALS

LEARNING OBJECTIVES

In studying the chapter, you will learn about the:

- Elements of an effective cost control system
- Two basic aspects of materials control
- Specific internal control procedures for material
- Accounting system for materials and how it is interrelated with the general ledger
- Accounting procedures for scrap materials, spoiled goods, and defective work

The total cost of a finished product is composed of the expenditures made for the raw materials used, the direct labor incurred, and the factory overhead generated by the manufacturing activities. The principles and procedures for controlling and accounting for these cost elements are the major subjects of Chapters 2, 3, and 4. In each chapter, the specific controls and accounting procedures that apply to each particular element will be discussed. However, there are common controls and practices that pertain to all cost control systems. The major function, in general, of any cost control system is to keep expenditures within the limits prescribed by a preconceived plan. The control system should also encourage cost reductions by eliminating waste and operational inefficiencies. An effective system of cost control is designed to control the people responsible for the expenditures because people control costs, costs do not control themselves.

An effective cost control system should include:

1. A specific assignment of duties and responsibilities.
2. A list of individuals who are authorized to approve expenditures.
3. An established plan of objectives and goals to be achieved.
4. Regular reports showing the differences between goals and actual performance.
5. A plan of corrective action to be taken to prevent a recurrence of unfavorable differences.
6. Follow-up procedures for corrective measures.

Responsibility accounting is an integral part of a cost control system because it focuses attention on specific individuals who have been designated to achieve the established goals. Of the three major objectives of cost accounting — cost control, product costing, and inventory pricing — cost control is often the most difficult to achieve. A weakness in cost control can often be overcome by placing more emphasis on responsibility accounting.

MATERIALS CONTROL

There are two basic aspects of materials control: (1) physical control or safeguarding of materials and (2) control of the investment in materials. Physical control is necessary to protect materials from misuse or misappropriation. Controlling the investment in materials is necessary for maintaining appropriate quantities of materials in inventory.

Physical Control of Materials

Every business requires a system of internal control that includes procedures for the safeguarding of assets. Highly liquid assets, such as cash and marketable securities, are particularly susceptible to misappropriation, and the protection provided for such assets is usually more than adequate. However, other assets, including inventories, must also be protected from unauthorized use or theft.

Because inventories usually represent a significant portion of a manufacturer's current assets, materials must be controlled from the time they are ordered until the time they are shipped to customers in the form of finished goods. In general, effective control of materials involves:

1. Limited access
2. Segregation of duties
3. Accuracy in recording

Limited Access.   Only authorized personnel should have access to materials storage areas. Materials should be issued for use in production only if requisitions for materials are properly documented and approved. Finished goods should also be safeguarded in limited access storage areas and not released for shipment in the absence of appropriate documentation and authorization. Procedures should be established within each production area or department for safeguarding work in process.

Segregation of Duties.   A basic principle of internal control is the segregation of duties to minimize opportunities for misappropriation of assets. With respect to materials control, the following functions should be segregated: purchasing, receiving, storage, use, and recording. The independence of personnel assigned to these functions does not eliminate the danger of misappropriation or misuse since the possibility of collusion still exists. However, appropriate segregation of duties limits an individual employee's opportunities for misappropriation and concealment. In smaller organizations, it is frequently not possible to achieve optimum segregation due to limited resources and personnel. In such cases, specially designed control procedures must be relied upon to compensate for the lack of independence of assigned functions.

Accuracy in Recording.   An effective materials control system requires accurate recording of purchases and issuances of materials. Inventory records should permit the determination of inventory quantities on hand upon request, and cost records should provide the data for the valuation of inventories for preparation of financial statements. Periodically, recorded inventories should be compared with a physical inventory count. Significant discrepancies between recorded and actual amounts should be investigated. Differences may be due to recording errors or may result from inventory losses through theft or spoilage. Once the cause has been determined, corrective action should be taken when appropriate.

Controlling the Investment in Materials

Maintaining the proper balance of materials on hand is one of the most important objectives of materials control. An inventory of sufficient size and diversity for efficient operations must be maintained, but the size should not be excessive in relation to scheduled production needs.

Since funds invested in inventories are unavailable for other uses, management must consider other working capital needs in determining the amount of funds to be invested in inventories and alternative uses of these funds which might yield a greater return. In addition to the usage of funds, consideration should be given to the costs of materials handling, storage, and insurance against fire, theft, or other casualty. Also, higher than needed inventory levels could increase the possibility of loss from damage, deterioration, and obsolescence. The planning and control of the materials inventory investment requires careful study of all these factors in determining (1) when orders should be placed and (2) how many units should be ordered.

Order Point.   A minimum level of inventory should be determined for each article of raw material, and inventory records should indicate how much of each article is on hand. This requires the establishment of a subsidiary ledger in which a separate account is maintained for each individual item of raw material used in the manufacturing process.

The point at which an item should be ordered, called the order point, occurs when the predetermined minimum level of inventory on hand is reached. Calculation of the order point is based on the following data:

1.   Usage — the anticipated rate at which the material will be used.
2.   Lead time — the estimated time interval between the placement of an order and receipt of the material.
3.   Safety stock — the estimated minimum level of inventory needed to protect against stockouts (running out of stock). Stockouts may occur due to inaccurate estimates of usage or lead time or various other unforeseen events, such as the receipt of damaged or inferior materials from the supplier.

Assume that the expected daily usage of an item of material is 100 units, the anticipated lead time is 5 days, and it is estimated that a safety stock of 1,000 units is needed. The following calculation shows that the order point is reached when the inventory on hand reaches 1,500 units:

100 units (daily usage) × 5 days (lead time)	500 units
Safety stock required	1,000 units
Order point	1,500 units

If estimates of usage and lead time are accurate, the level of inventory when the new order is received would be equal to the safety stock of 1,000 units. If, however, a 3-day delay is encountered in receiving the new order, it would be necessary to issue 300 units of material from the safety stock in order to maintain the production level.

Economic Order Quantity.   The order point establishes the time when an order is to be placed, but does not indicate the most economical number of units that should be ordered. In determining the quantity to be ordered, the cost of placing an order and the cost of carrying inventory must be considered. Order costs generally include such factors as:

1. Salaries and wages of employees engaged in purchasing, receiving, and inspecting materials.
2. Communications costs associated with ordering, such as telephone, postage, and forms or stationery.
3. Materials accounting and record keeping.

Factors to be considered in determining carrying costs typically include:

1. Materials storage and handling costs.
2. Interest, insurance, and property taxes.
3. Loss due to theft, deterioration, or obsolescence.
4. Records and supplies associated with the carrying of inventories.

Order costs and carrying costs move in opposite directions — order costs decrease when order size increases, while carrying costs increase with increases in order size. The optimal quantity to order at one time, called the economic order quantity, is the order size which minimizes total order and carrying costs over a period of time, e.g., one year.

The factors to be considered in determining order and carrying costs for a particular company vary with the nature of operations and the organizational structure. Special analyses are usually required to identify relevant costs, since these data are not normally accumulated in an accounting system. Care must be exercised in determining which costs are relevant. For example, a company may have adequate warehouse space to carry a large additional quantity of inventory. If the space cannot be used for some other profitable purpose, the cost of the space is not a relevant factor in determining carrying costs. If, however, the space in the company warehouse could be used for a more profitable purpose, or if additional warehouse space must be leased or rented to accommodate increased inventories, then the costs associated with the additional space are relevant in determining carrying costs.

The interest cost associated with carrying an inventory in stock should be considered whether or not funds are borrowed to purchase the inventory. If these funds were not used for inventory, they could have been profitably applied to some alternate use. The rate of interest to be used in the computations will vary depending upon the cost of borrowing, the average cost of capital, or the rate that could be earned by the funds if they were used for some other purpose.

Quantitative models or formulas have been developed for calculating the economic order quantity. One formula that can be used is:

$$EOQ = \sqrt{\frac{2CN}{K}}$$

where:
EOQ = economic order quantity
C = cost of placing an order
N = number of units required annually
K = carrying cost per unit of inventory

To illustrate application of the formula, assume that the following data have been determined by analysis of the factors relevant to materials inventory:

Number of units of material required annually   10,000
Cost of placing an order. \$10.00
Annual carrying cost per unit of inventory. . . . .   \$.80

Using the EOQ formula:

$$EOQ = \sqrt{\frac{2(\text{cost of order})(\text{number of units required annually})}{(\text{carrying cost per unit})}}$$

$$= \sqrt{\frac{2(\$10)(10,000)}{\$.80}}$$

$$= \sqrt{\frac{\$200,000}{\$.80}}$$

$$= \sqrt{250,000}$$

$$= \quad 500 \text{ units}$$

The EOQ can also be determined by constructing a table using a range of order sizes. A tabular presentation of the data from the previous example follows:

1 Order Size	2 Number of Orders	3 Total Order Cost	4 Average Inventory	5 Total Carrying Cost	6 Total Order & Carrying Cost
100	100	$1,000	50	$ 40	$1,040
200	50	500	100	80	580
300	33	330	150	120	450
400	25	250	200	160	410
500	20	200	250	200	400
600	17	170	300	240	410
700	14	140	350	280	420
800	13	130	400	320	450
900	11	110	450	360	470
1,000	10	100	500	400	500

1. Number of units per order
2. 10,000 annual units ÷ order size
3. Number of orders × $10 per order
4. Order size ÷ 2 = average inventory on hand during the year
5. Average inventory × $.80 per unit carrying cost for one year
6. Total order cost + total carrying cost

The data presented graphically (Illustration 2-1) show the order cost decreasing as the order size increases. Meanwhile, the carrying costs are

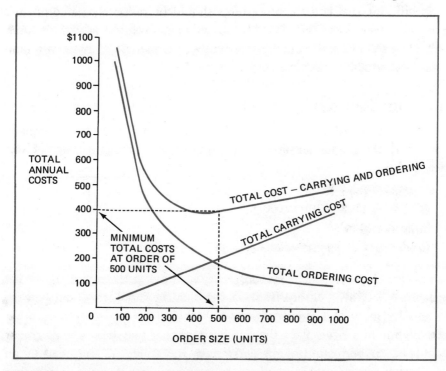

Illustration 2-1   Costs of Ordering and Carrying Inventory

increasing as the order size increases because of the necessity to maintain a large quantity of inventory in stock. At the 500-unit level, the carrying and order costs are at their minimum point.

Limitations of Order Point and EOQ Calculations.   The techniques illustrated for determining when to order (order point) and how much to order (EOQ) may give a false impression of exactness. However, because these calculations are based on estimates of factors such as production volume, lead time, and order and carrying costs, they are really approximations that serve as a guide to planning and controlling the investment in materials.

In addition, other factors may influence the time for ordering or the quantity ordered. Such factors include the availability of materials from suppliers, fluctuations in the purchase price of materials, and trade (volume) discounts offered by suppliers.

MATERIALS CONTROL PROCEDURES

Specific internal control procedures should be tailored to a company's needs. However, materials control generally involves the following functions: (1) purchase and receipt of materials, (2) storage of materials, and (3) requisition and consumption of materials.

Materials Control Personnel

Although actual job titles and duties may vary from one company to another, the personnel involved in materials control usually include the following:

1. Purchasing agent
2. Receiving clerk
3. Storeroom keeper
4. Production department supervisors

Purchasing Agent.   The responsibility for buying the materials needed for the manufacturing enterprise should rest on the shoulders of one person. In a small plant the employee who does the buying may also perform other duties, while in a large plant the purchasing agent may head a department established to perform buying activities. Regardless of the size of an organization, it is important that the responsibility for the purchasing function be assigned to one individual. The duties of a purchasing agent may include the following:

1. Working with the production manager to prevent delays in production caused by the lack of materials.
2. Compiling and maintaining information on sources from which the desired materials can be obtained at the most economical price.
3. Placing purchase orders.
4. Supervising the order process until the materials are received.
5. Verifying purchase invoices and approving them for payments.

Receiving Clerk.   The receiving clerk is charged with the responsibility of supervising the receipt of incoming shipments. All incoming materials must be checked as to quantity and quality and sometimes as to price.

Storeroom Keeper.   The storeroom keeper, who has charge of the materials after they have been received, must see that the materials are properly stored and maintained. The materials must be placed in stock and issued only on properly authorized requisitions. The purchasing agent should be informed of the quantities on hand as a guide to the purchasing of additional materials.

Production Department Supervisor.   Each production department has a person who is responsible for supervising the operational functions within the department. This individual may be given the title of the department supervisor or another similar designation. One of the assigned duties of a department supervisor is to prepare or approve the requisitions designating the quantities and kinds of material needed for the work to be done in the department.

Control During Procurement

Materials are ordered to maintain adequate levels of inventory to meet scheduled production needs. The storeroom keeper is responsible for monitoring quantities of materials on hand. When the order point is reached for a particular item of raw material, the procurement process is initiated. In many companies, electronic data processing (EDP) equipment is used to store data pertaining to inventories on hand, predetermined order points, and economic order quantities. The use of EDP equipment can simplify the task of maintaining appropriate inventory levels when the equipment is properly programmed, and the purchasing agent is adequately informed.

Supporting documents are essential to maintaining control during the procurement process. In general, the documents should be prenumbered and protected from unauthorized use. The documents commonly used in procuring materials include: (1) purchase requisitions, (2) purchase orders, (3) vendor's invoices, (4) receiving reports, and (5) debit-credit memoranda.

Purchase Requisitions.   The form used to notify the purchasing agent that additional materials are needed is known as a purchase requisition. This requisition is an important part of the materials control process because it is the agent's authority to buy. Purchase requisitions should originate with the storeroom keeper or some other individual with similar authority and responsibility.

Purchase requisitions should be prenumbered serially to help detect the loss or misuse of any of these forms. They are generally prepared in duplicate. The first copy goes to the purchasing agent; the second copy is retained by the storeroom keeper. A purchase requisition form is shown in Illustration 2-2 on page 61.

Purchase Order.   The purchase requisition gives the purchasing agent authority to order the materials described in the requisition. The purchasing agent should maintain or have access to an up-to-date list of vendors, which includes prices, available discounts, estimated delivery time, and any other relevant information. From this list, a vendor is selected from whom the materials can be obtained at the lowest cost and with the least delay. If this information is not available from the list for a particular item of material, the purchasing agent may communicate with several prospective vendors and request quotations on the materials needed.

A purchase order, as shown in Illustration 2-3, is then completed and addressed to the chosen vendor, describing the materials wanted, stating price and terms, and fixing the date and method of delivery. This purchase order should be prenumbered serially and prepared in quadruplicate. The first copy goes to the vendor, one copy is sent to the accounting department, one copy goes to the receiving clerk, and a copy is retained by the purchasing agent.

The purchasing agent's copy of the order should be placed in an unfilled orders file. Before the order is filed, the purchase requisition on which it is based should be attached to the order. This last step is important, for it is the beginning of the assembly of a complete set of all the forms pertaining

```
┌─────────────────────────────────────────────────────────────────┐
│                                                                   │
│   BLOOMINGTON        PURCHASE REQUISITION        No. 3246         │
│   MFG.                                                            │
│                                                                   │
│   Date ___January 3, 19--_____                             │
│                                                                   │
│   Date wanted __February 1, 19--____                             │
│                               ┌ Job No.   300                     │
│                        For  {                                     │
│                               └ Account No.  1482                 │
│                                                                   │
│                                   Authorization No.   3313        │
│  ┌──────────────────┬────────────────────────────────────────┐   │
│  │    QUANTITY      │              DESCRIPTION               │   │
│  ├──────────────────┼────────────────────────────────────────┤   │
│  │   20,000 Gal.    │   Adhesive Compound -- Grade A102       │   │
│  │                  │                                         │   │
│  │                  │                                         │   │
│  │                  │                                         │   │
│  │                  │                                         │   │
│  └──────────────────┴────────────────────────────────────────┘   │
│                                                                   │
│   Approved by _L. Merz_____   Signed by _G. Thomas_____        │
│  ─────────────────────────────────────────────────────────────   │
│   Purchase order No. _1131_____   Date ordered _January 6, 19--   │
│   Ordered from _____Piefer Corporation_____          │
│                                                                   │
└─────────────────────────────────────────────────────────────────┘
```

Illustration 2-2   Purchase Requisition (Notifies purchasing agent that additional materials should be ordered)

to the purchase transaction. In order to identify each document relating to a transaction with all others of the same set, the purchase order number should be shown on each of the documents. The sets can then be compiled according to the respective purchase order numbers.

3 **Vendor's Invoice.** The vendor's invoice should be received before the materials arrive at the factory. As soon as it is received, it goes to the purchasing agent, who compares it with the purchase order, noting particularly that the description of the materials is the same, that the price and the terms agree, and that the method of shipment and the date of delivery conform to the instructions on the purchase order. When satisfied that the invoice is

```
┌─────────────────────────────────────────────────────────────────────┐
│                                                                       │
│   BLOOMINGTON        PURCHASE ORDER        Order No. 1982             │
│   MFG.                                                                 │
│                                            Mark Order No. on invoice  │
│                                            and on all packages        │
│                                                                       │
│   To: Piefer Corporation        Date January 6, 19--                 │
│        Cleveland, Ohio 44115                                          │
│                                 Terms 3/10 eom n/60                   │
│                                                                       │
│                                 Ship Via Truck (to arrive            │
│                                          January 25, 19--)           │
│  ┌──────────────┬─────────────────────────┬──────────────┐          │
│  │   QUANTITY   │      DESCRIPTION         │    PRICE     │          │
│  ├──────────────┼─────────────────────────┼──────────────┤          │
│  │ 20,000 Gal.  │  Adhesive Compound--     │ $31,300  00  │          │
│  │              │  Grade A102              │              │          │
│  │              │                          │              │          │
│  │              │                          │              │          │
│  │              │                          │              │          │
│  │              │                          │              │          │
│  └──────────────┴─────────────────────────┴──────────────┘          │
│                                                                       │
│                    By A. Lauren                                       │
│                                            Purchasing Agent           │
└─────────────────────────────────────────────────────────────────────┘
```

Illustration 2-3   Purchase Order (Prepared by purchasing agent and sent to vendor to order materials)

correct, the purchasing agent initials or stamps the invoice indicating that it has been reviewed and agrees with the purchase order. The invoice is then filed together with the purchase order and the purchase requisition in the unfilled orders file until the materials are received.

An objection may be made to the practice of leaving the invoice in the hands of the purchasing agent until the goods are received, because it delays the recording of this liability in the books of the buyer. However, the benefit of a complete file of the transaction more than offsets this disadvantage, if the delay is not too prolonged. Also, if any adjustment is needed because of a discrepancy between the materials received and those ordered, there will not be a problem with correcting or rewriting the voucher for the order. However, care must be exercised at the end of the accounting period to add the invoices held by the purchasing agent to the accounts payable in order not to understate the liabilities. Invoices received for goods in transit are classified as current liabilities if title to the goods passes to the purchaser at the time of shipment. An adjusting entry, debiting the appropriate accounts and crediting accounts payable for the total of the goods-in-transit invoices for which title has passed, should be made at the end of the period.

Receiving Report.   As noted previously, a copy of the purchase order is sent to the receiving clerk to give advance notice of the arrival of the materials ordered. This is done to facilitate planning and allotting space to incoming materials. The receiving clerk is in charge of the receiving department where all incoming materials are received, opened, counted or weighed, and tested for conformity with the order. If the materials received are of too technical a nature to be tested by the receiving clerk, the inspection may be undertaken by an engineer from the production manager's office, or the materials may be sent to the plant laboratory for testing.

The receiving clerk counts and identifies the materials received and prepares a receiving report similar to the one reproduced in Illustration 2-4. Each report is numbered serially and shows from whom the materials were received, when they were received, what the shipment contained, and the number of the purchase order that identifies the shipment. The report should be prepared in quadruplicate. Two copies go to the purchasing agent; one copy goes with the materials or supplies to the storeroom keeper to ensure that all of the materials that come to the receiving department are put into the storeroom; and one copy is retained by the receiving clerk. In some plants, the receiving clerk is given a copy of the purchase order with the quantity ordered omitted. This omission of the quantity assures that the items received will be counted.

The purchasing agent compares the receiving report with the vendor's invoice and the purchase order to determine that the materials received are those ordered and billed. If the documents agree, the purchasing agent initials or stamps the two copies of the receiving report. One copy is then attached to the other forms already in the file, and the entire set of forms is sent to the accounting department, where a voucher is prepared and recorded in the voucher register. The other copy of the receiving report is sent to the person in the accounting department who maintains inventory records. The procedures for recording materials purchases are discussed in a subsequent section of this chapter.

```
┌─────────────────────────────────────────────────────────────────┐
│  BLOOMINGTON          RECEIVING REPORT           No. 496          │
│  MFG.                                                             │
│                                  Date ___January 21, 19--_____   │
│                                                                   │
│  To the purchasing agent:                                         │
│                                                                   │
│      RECEIVED FROM    __Piefer Corporation_____   │
│                                                                   │
│      Via __Ace Trucking___   Transportation Charges _$210.85___   │
│                                                                   │
├───────────────────────────┬───────────────────────────────────────│
│       QUANTITY            │            DESCRIPTION                 │
├───────────────────────────┼───────────────────────────────────────│
│      20,000 Gal.          │   Adhesive Compound -- Grade A102      │
│                           │                                        │
│                           │                                        │
│                           │                                        │
│                           │                                        │
│                           │                                        │
├───────────────────────────┴────────────────────────────────────────│
│   Counted by R.S._____      Inspected by B.P._____    │
│   Purchase order No. __1982_____           │
└─────────────────────────────────────────────────────────────────┘
```

Illustration 2-4   Receiving Report (incoming materials opened, counted, weighed, or tested for conformity with purchase order)

Debit-Credit Memorandum.   Occasionally, a shipment of materials does not match the order and the invoice. When this situation occurs, comparing the receiving report with the purchase order and the invoice will disclose the discrepancy to the purchasing agent. Whatever the cause of the difference, it will lead to correspondence with the vendor, and copies of the letters should be a part of the file of forms relating to the transaction. If a larger quantity has been received than has been ordered and the excess is to be kept for future use, a credit memorandum is prepared notifying the vendor of the amount of the increase in the invoice. One form of the debit-credit memorandum is shown in Illustration 2-5. This memo shows that the vendor has delivered materials that do not meet the buyer's

```
┌─────────────────────────────────────────────────────────────────┐
│  BLOOMINGTON      (DEBIT) MEMORANDUM                              │
│  MFG.             CREDIT                                          │
│                                                                   │
│                         Date ___January 3, 19--___                │
│                                                                   │
│  To: The Iron and Brass Machine Company                          │
│       Cleveland, Ohio 44118                                      │
│                                                                   │
│  We have today (Debited)     your account for the following:     │
│                 Credited                                          │
│                                                                   │
│  Explanation __wrong size_____        │
│                                                                   │
│  ─────────────────────────────────────────────────────          │
│                                                                   │
│  QUANTITY │    DESCRIPTION       │ UNIT PRICE │ AMOUNT           │
│  5 boxes  │ Brass machine screws,│  $27.50    │ $137 │ 50        │
│           │ 8/32" x 1", flat head│            │                  │
│                                                                   │
│  Purchase order No. ____1029_____                            │
│  Your invoice date __December 27, 19--__                         │
│                                                                   │
│                    By  A. Lauren                                 │
│                        Purchasing Agent                          │
└─────────────────────────────────────────────────────────────────┘
```

Illustration 2-5   Debit-Credit Memorandum (Discrepancy between order, shipment, and vendor invoice. Price adjustment request shown on debit-credit memo)

specifications. The purchasing agent will prepare a return shipping order and return the materials to the vendor.

If, on the other hand, the shipment is short, one of two courses of action may be taken. If the materials received can be used, they may be retained and a debit memorandum prepared notifying the vendor of the amount of the shortage. If the materials received cannot be used, a return shipping order is prepared and the materials are returned. A return shipping order form is shown in Illustration 2-6.

The return shipping order is usually made out in triplicate. The first copy goes to the vendor, the second copy goes to the receiving or shipping

```
┌─────────────────────────────────────────────────────────────────┐
│  BLOOMINGTON      RETURN SHIPPING ORDER                           │
│  MFG.                                                             │
│                                                                   │
│                            Date ___January 4, 19--___             │
│                                                                   │
│  To the shipping clerk:                                           │
│    Send the following to:  Smart Manufacturing Company            │
│                            Grand Rapids, Michigan 49501           │
│                                                                   │
├──────────┬────────────────────────┬────────────┬─────────────────┤
│ QUANTITY │      DESCRIPTION        │ UNIT PRICE │     AMOUNT      │
├──────────┼────────────────────────┼────────────┼─────────────────┤
│   100    │ Laminated plywood       │   $12.15   │ $1,215    00    │
│          │ boards, 4 x 8 x 3/4     │            │                 │
│          │                         │            │                 │
├──────────┴────────────────────────┴────────────┴─────────────────┤
│  Shipper's invoice date ___December 14, 19--___                   │
│  Purchase order No. __1992___                                     │
│                                                                   │
│                          By  A. Lauren                            │
│                              ─────────────────────                │
│                                       Purchasing Agent            │
└─────────────────────────────────────────────────────────────────┘
```

Illustration 2-6   Return Shipping Order (When material shipment is returned to vendor)

clerk, and the third copy is filed with other forms relating to the transaction. Debit or credit memorandums should be prepared in duplicate. The first copy goes to the vendor and the second copy is filed with other documents relating to the transaction.

Not until all differences have been resolved will the transaction be complete. When they are resolved, the purchasing agent sends the documents to the accounting department for recording.

Control During Storage and Issuance

The preceding discussion centered on the control of materials during the process of procurement. The procedures and forms described are necessary for control of the ordering and receiving functions and the transfer of incoming materials to the storeroom. The next problem to be considered is the storage and issuance of materials and supplies.

1. **Materials Requisition.** As discussed earlier, materials should be protected from unauthorized use. No materials should be issued from the storeroom except on written authorization so that there is less chance of theft, carelessness, or misuse. The form used to provide this control is known as the materials requisition or stores requisition (see Illustration 2-7) and is prepared by factory personnel who are authorized to withdraw materials from the storeroom. The individuals who are authorized to perform this function may differ from company to company, but such

BLOOMINGTON MFG.	MATERIALS REQUISITION		
Date January 19, 19--		No. **632**	
To: D. Graham			

QUANTITY	DESCRIPTION	UNIT PRICE	AMOUNT	
100 Gal.	Adhesive Compound--Grade A102	$1.565	$156	50

Approved by _E. B._   Issued by _B. W._

Received by _L. M._

Charge to Job/Dept. _300_   Factory Overhead Expense Account _____

Illustration 2-7 Materials Requisition (Authorization to withdraw materials from storeroom)

authority must be given to someone of responsibility. The most satisfactory arrangement would be to have the production manager prepare all materials requisitions, but this is usually not feasible. Another arrangement is to require that the department supervisors approve (sign) all materials requisitions for their respective departments. When a properly signed requisition is presented to the storeroom keeper, the requisitioned materials are released. Both the storeroom keeper and the employee to whom materials are issued should be required to sign the requisition.

The materials requisition is usually prepared in quadruplicate. Two copies are sent to the accounting department for recording; one copy is forwarded to the storeroom keeper and serves as authorization for issuing the materials; and one copy is retained by the production manager or department supervisor who prepared it.

Identification is an important factor in the control of materials. For this reason, the materials requisition should indicate the job number (job order costing) or department (process costing) for which the materials are issued. When indirect materials, such as cleaning materials, lubricants, and paint are issued, the requisition will indicate the name or number of the factory overhead account to be charged.

Returned Materials Report.   After materials are requisitioned, occasionally some or all of the materials must be returned to the storeroom. Perhaps more materials were requested than were needed, or the wrong type of materials were issued. Whatever the reason, a written report describing the materials and the reason for the return must accompany the materials to the storeroom.

Assume that after an order is started in the factory, it is discovered that more materials were taken out of the storeroom than were needed. The excess materials should be returned at once, accompanied by a returned materials report (Illustration 2-8). The report, except for price data, should be prepared by the supervisor of the department returning the materials. One copy is sent to the storeroom keeper along with the returned materials. A second copy is forwarded to the accounting department, where the unit price and the total cost are entered. The return of the materials to the storeroom is then recorded in the appropriate accounting records as discussed in the following section. A third copy of the report is retained by the production supervisor who prepared it.

```
BLOOMINGTON              RETURNED                No. 232
MFG.                  MATERIALS REPORT

                            Date    January 21, 19--

   To:   D. Graham


The following excess materials are being returned to the storeroom from Job  300

| QUANTITY  |      DESCRIPTION       | UNIT PRICE | AMOUNT    |
| 100 Gal.  | Adhesive Compound--    |  $1.565    | $156  50  |
|           | Grade A102             |            |           |

Date of original issue          Returned by:
  January 19, 19--                H. Beatley
                                          Department Supervisor
Posted to:                      Reason:  Production cutback

Stores ledger by  F. E. N.      Received by:
                                 D. Graham
Job cost ledger by  J. A.                 Storeroom Keeper
```

Illustration 2-8   Returned Materials Report (Materials requisitioned but unused by production and returned to storeroom)

ACCOUNTING FOR MATERIALS

A company's inventory records should show (1) the number of units of each kind of materials on hand and (2) their cost. The most desirable method of achieving this result is to integrate the materials accounting system with the general ledger accounts. All purchases of materials are recorded through the voucher register as a debit to Materials in the general ledger (the corresponding credit is to Vouchers Payable). The materials account is a control account supported by a subsidiary stores or materials ledger in which there is an individual account for each item of material carried in stock. Periodically the balance of the control account and the total of the individual accounts are compared, and any significant variation between the two investigated.

Each of the individual materials accounts in the subsidiary stores ledger shows (1) the quantity on hand and (2) the cost of the materials. In order to keep this information current, it is necessary to record in each individual account the quantity and the cost of materials received, issued, and on hand. The stores ledger accounts are usually maintained on cards similar in design to the one shown in Illustration 2-9.

As explained previously, copies of the purchase order and receiving report are approved by the purchasing agent and sent to the accounting department. Upon receipt of the purchase order, the stores ledger accountant enters the quantity in the "On Order" columns of the appropriate stores ledger card. When materials are delivered, the accounting department's copy of the receiving report serves as the basis for posting the receipt of the materials to the stores ledger card. The posting shows the date of receipt, the number of the receiving report, and the number of units received and their cost. The cost may be expressed in terms of both unit cost and total cost or in totals only.

When materials are issued, two copies of the materials requisition are sent to the accounting department. One copy is used in posting the cost of requisitioned materials to the appropriate accounts in the job cost and factory overhead ledgers. Direct materials are charged to the job (or department), and indirect materials are charged to the appropriate factory overhead accounts. The other copy of the requistion is sent to the stores ledger accountant and becomes the basis for posting to the ledger cards. The posting shows the date of issue, the number of the requisition, and the number of units issued and their cost.

When materials are returned to the storeroom, a copy of the returned materials report is sent to the accounting department. The cost of the returned materials is entered on the report and posted to the appropriate stores ledger card. The cost assigned to the returned materials should be the same as that recorded when the materials were issued to the factory.

The copy of the returned materials report is then routed to the cost accountant in charge of the job cost and factory overhead ledgers. Direct materials returned are credited to the job or department, and indirect materials returned are credited to the appropriate factory overhead account.

When receipts and issues of materials are posted to the stores ledger cards, the balance is extended after each entry. These extensions could be made at the end of the accounting period when inventories are to be

| Description | White Lead | | Location in Storeroom | Bin 8 |
| Maximum | 15,000 lbs. | Minimum | 1,000 lbs. | Stores Ledger Acct. No. | 1411 |

	ON ORDER	RECEIVED				ISSUED				BALANCE		
Date	Purchase Order No.	Quantity	Receiving Report No./ (Returned Shipping Order No.)	Quantity	Unit Price	Amount	Materials Requisition/ (Returned Materials Report No.)	Quantity	Unit Price	Amount	Quantity	Unit Price	Amount

Illustration 2-9   **Stores Ledger Card**

determined. However, to wait until that time would defeat one of the advantages of this method of materials control, because it would not be possible to determine from the stores ledger when stock is falling below the minimum requirements.

Determining the Cost of Materials Issued

An important area of materials accounting is the costing of materials requisitioned from the storeroom for factory use. The unit cost of incoming materials is known at the time of purchase. The date of each purchase is also known, but the materials on hand typically include items purchased on different dates and at different prices. Items which are alike in appearance usually are commingled in the storeroom. As a result, it may be difficult or impossible to identify an issue of materials with a specific purchase when determining what unit cost should be assigned to the materials being issued.

Several practical methods of solving this problem are available. In selecting the method to be employed, the accounting policies of the firm and the federal and state income tax regulations are important factors to be considered. As the methods are discussed, it is important to remember that the flow of materials does not dictate the flow of costs. The flow of materials is the order in which materials are actually issued for use in the factory. The flow of costs is the order in which unit costs are assigned to materials issued.

First-In, First-Out Method.   The first-in, first-out (fifo) method of costing has the advantages of simplicity and wide adoption. The fifo method is based on the assumption that materials issued are taken from the oldest materials in stock. Therefore, the materials are costed at the prices paid for the oldest materials. In many companies the flow of costs using fifo closely parallels the physical flow of materials. For example, if materials have a tendency to deteriorate in storage, the oldest materials would be issued first. However, as noted previously, the flow of costs does not have to be determined on the basis of the flow of materials. As a result, fifo may be used by any organization.

Application of the fifo method can be illustrated using the following data:

Dec. 1   Balance, 1,000 units @ $20.
      10   Issued 500 units.
      15   Purchased 1,000 units @ $24.

20   Issued 250 units.
26   Issued 500 units.
28   Purchased 500 units @ $26.
30   Issued 500 units.
31   Balance, 750 units.

Using fifo, costs would be assigned to materials issued during the month and to materials on hand at the end of the month as follows:

Dec. 10   Issued from the December 1 balance: 500 units @ $20, total cost, $10,000.
20   Issued from the December 1 balance: 250 units @ $20, total cost, $5,000.
26   Issued from the December 1 balance: 250 units @ $20, total cost, $5,000.
Issued from the December 15 purchase: 250 units @ $24, total cost, $6,000.
Total cost of materials issued: $5,000 + $6,000 = $11,000.
30   Issued from the December 15 purchase: 500 units @ $24, total cost, $12,000.
31   The ending inventory of materials, 750 units, consists of the following:

Date of Purchase	Units	Unit Cost	Total Cost
December 15	250	$24	$ 6,000
December 28	500	26	13,000
	750		$19,000

As illustrated in the example, ending inventories using fifo are costed at the prices paid for the most recent purchases. Thus, 500 of the units on hand are assigned a unit cost of $26, the unit cost of the December 28 purchase. The remaining 250 units on hand are costed at $24 per unit, reflecting the unit cost of the next most recent purchase on December 15.

Last-In, First-Out Method.   The last-in, first-out (lifo) method of costing materials, as the name implies, is based on the assumption that materials issued for use in manufacturing are the most recently purchased materials. Thus, materials issued are costed at the most recent purchase prices, and inventories on hand at the end of the period are costed at prices paid for the earliest purchases. The lifo method of costing closely approximates the physical flow of materials in some industries. For example, in the smelting of iron ore, the raw material is stored in mountainous piles. As ore is needed for production, it is drawn from the pile in such a way that the material being used is the last ore to have been received. As emphasized previously, however, physical flow does not determine the costing method used.

Using the same data given to illustrate the fifo method, costs under the lifo method would be determined as follows:

Dec. 10 Issued from the December 1 balance: 500 units @ $20, total cost, $10,000.
　　20 Issued from the December 15 purchase: 250 units @ $24, total cost, $6,000.
　　26 Issued from the December 15 purchase: 500 units @ $24, total cost, $12,000.
　　30 Issued from the December 28 purchase: 500 units @ $26, total cost, $13,000.
　　31 The ending inventory of materials, 750 units, consists of the following:

Date of Purchase	Units	Unit Cost	Total Cost
Balance, December 1	500	$20	$10,000
December 15	250	24	6,000
	750		$16,000

Moving Average Method.   The moving average method is based on the assumption that the materials issued at any time are simply withdrawn from a mixed group of like materials in the storeroom, and no attempt is made to identify the materials as being from the earliest or the latest purchases. This method has the disadvantage of requiring more frequent computations than the other methods. However, with the availability of computers, this disadvantage has been overcome and many firms are adopting this method. A basic requirement of the moving average method is that an average unit price be computed every time a new lot of materials is received and that this average unit price be used to cost all issues of materials until another lot is purchased. Thus, the issues in the illustration would be computed as follows:

Dec. 10 Issued from the December 1 balance: 500 units @ $20, total cost, $10,000.
　　15 The balance of materials on hand on December 15 consists of 500 units from December 1 and 1,000 units acquired on December 15, for a total of 1,500 units which cost $34,000. The average cost is $22.66⅔ per unit ($34,000 ÷ 1,500).
　　20 Issued 250 units @ $22.66⅔, total cost, $5,666.67.
　　26 Issued 500 units @ 22.66⅔, total cost, $11,333.33.
　　28 The balance of materials on hand on December 28 consists of 750 units which cost $17,000 (purchased prior to December 28) and 500 units @ $26 (purchased on December 28) costing $13,000. The total cost is $30,000 for 1,250 units, representing an average cost of $24 per unit ($30,000 ÷ 1,250).
　　30 Issued 500 units @ $24, total cost, $12,000.
　　31 The ending inventory of materials consists of:

Units	Unit Cost	Total Cost
750	$24	$18,000

4 **Analysis of Fifo, Lifo, and Moving Average.** Fifo, lifo, and moving average are the most commonly used methods of inventory costing. Any of these methods may be adopted for use in the keeping of the stores ledger as shown in Illustration 2–10.

First-In, First-Out Method

Date	Received Quantity	Unit Price	Amount	Issued Quantity	Unit Price	Amount	Balance Quantity	Unit Price	Amount
Dec. 1							1,000	20 00	20,000 00
10				500	20 00	10,000 00	500	20 00	10,000 00
15	1,000	24 00	24,000 00				500	20 00 ⎱	34,000 00
							1,000	24 00 ⎰	
20				250	20 00	5,000 00	250	20 00 ⎱	29,000 00
							1,000	24 00 ⎰	
26				250	20 00 ⎱	11,000 00	750	24 00	18,000 00
				250	24 00 ⎰				
28	500	26 00	13,000 00				750	24 00 ⎱	31,000 00
							500	26 00 ⎰	
30				500	24 00	12,000 00	250	24 00 ⎱	19,000 00
							500	26 00 ⎰	

Last-In, First-Out Method

Date	Received Quantity	Unit Price	Amount	Issued Quantity	Unit Price	Amount	Balance Quantity	Unit Price	Amount
Dec. 1							1,000	20 00	20,000 00
10				500	20 00	10,000 00	500	20 00	10,000 00
15	1,000	24 00	24,000 00				500	20 00 ⎱	34,000 00
							1,000	24 00 ⎰	
20				250	24 00	6,000 00	500	20 00 ⎱	28,000 00
							750	24 00 ⎰	
26				500	24 00	12,000 00	500	20 00 ⎱	16,000 00
							250	24 00 ⎰	
28	500	26 00	13,000 00				500	20 00 ⎱	
							250	24 00 ⎬	29,000 00
							500	26 00 ⎰	
30				500	26 00	13,000 00	500	20 00 ⎱	16,000 00
							250	24 00 ⎰	

Illustration 2-10   Comparison of Inventory Valuation Methods

Moving Average Method

Date	Received Quantity	Unit Price	Amount	Issued Quantity	Unit Price	Amount	Balance Quantity	Unit Price	Amount
Dec. 1							1,000	20 00	20,000 00
10				500	20 00	10,000 00	500	20 00	10,000 00
15	1,000	24 00	24,000 00				1,500	22 66⅔	34,000 00
20				250	22 66⅔	5,666 67	1,250	22 66⅔	28,333 33
26				500	22 66⅔	11,333 33	750	22 66⅔	17,000 00
28	500	26 00	13,000 00				1,250	24 00	30,000 00
30				500	24 00	12,000 00	750	24 00	18,000 00

Illustration 2-10   Continued

Since no one method is best suited to all manufacturing situations, the method chosen should be the one that most accurately reflects the income for the period in terms of the current economic conditions. One factor to be considered is the effect the costing method has on reported net income. Overstating net income will cause a firm to be subject to higher taxes than those of a competitor who is using a different costing method.

In an economic environment with constantly rising prices, lifo is sometimes adopted so that the higher prices of materials may be charged against the increasingly higher sales revenue. The resulting gross margin, under these conditions, is assumed to reflect a more accurate picture of earnings. Also, the lower gross margin, brought about by use of the lifo method, results in a smaller tax liability for the firm. This lifo benefit, however, does not mean that all companies should adopt lifo.

Before selecting any method for costing materials, a firm should consider the size and dollar valuation of the inventory to be maintained, the inventory turnover rate, and the frequency, direction, and magnitude of price changes. If the manufacturing operations require only a small inventory that turns over rapidly, the materials costing method may have only a small effect on the profit margin, because the price changes are quickly absorbed in the current cost of goods sold. For such firms, the fifo method would be the most appropriate, because it is the method which usually minimizes the clerical costs associated with inventory accounting.

To illustrate the effects that the different costing methods have on profit determination, assume that A, B, and C are competing companies that use

fifo, moving average, and lifo, respectively. The companies have no beginning inventories, and they purchase identical materials at the same time as
follows (assume also that each purchase is for one unit):

Purchase No. 1 @ $.10
Purchase No. 2 @ $.50
Purchase No. 3 @ $.90

Assume that one unit of materials is used and sold at a price of $1.00
after the last purchase has been made. The net income is determined as
follows:

	Co. A Fifo (Per Unit)	Co. B Moving Avg. (Per Unit)	Co. C Lifo (Per Unit)
Net Sales	$1.00	$1.00	$1.00
Less cost of goods sold	.10	.50*	.90
Gross margin on sales	$ .90	$ .50	$ .10
Operating expenses	.08	.08	.08
Income before income taxes	$ .82	$ .42	$ .02
Less income taxes (50%)	.41	.21	.01
Net income	$ .41	$ .21	$ .01

*$.10 + $.50 + $.90 = $1.50/3 units = $.50 per unit.

Under conditions of rapidly rising prices, as shown in the example,
Company C has a definite advantage over its competitors. It reports a profit
of only $.01 on each unit of sales and pays $.01 per unit for taxes, whereas
Company A pays $.41 and Company B, $.21 per unit in taxes. Income taxes
represent money that is leaving the company. On the other hand
Company C retains $.99 of each dollar of sales by charging $.98 to costs and
expenses and reporting $.01 profit per unit. Company A retains $.59 and
Company B, $.79. However, since replacing each unit of material used will
now cost $.90 per unit, Company A will require an additional $.31 and
Company B, $.11 which must be obtained from some source before replace-
ment can be made. Only Company C can replace the materials used, pay
operating expenses, and retain its $.01 profit per unit.

The companies, using their respective costing methods, have the following ending materials inventory balances:

Company A (fifo) .... $1.40 ($.50 + $.90)
Company B (moving average) ... $1.00 ($.50 + $.50)
Company C (lifo) .... $ .60 ($.10 + $.50)

Company C has the most conservatively valued inventory at $.60, and Company A shows the highest inventory value at $1.40. The Company A inventory value ($1.40) also may be detrimental because it is subject to state and local property taxes. Company C will avoid some of these taxes because of its lower inventory valuation.

Many companies have adopted the lifo method in order to match current materials costs with current revenue as well as to minimize the effect of income taxes in periods of rising prices. For companies that are considering the adoption of the lifo method, however, it is important to carefully analyze economic conditions and to examine the tax regulations that pertain to lifo. If there should be a downward trend of prices, these companies would probably desire to change to the fifo method in order to have the same competitive advantages that were gained by using lifo when prices were rising. However, the lifo election cannot be rescinded unless authorized or required by the Internal Revenue Service.

Other Inventory Costing Methods.   There are other inventory methods in addition to those previously discussed which are used for pricing inventory and costing materials issued. However, these methods are less frequently used because the firm's operational requirements must be carefully coordinated with the designed inventory system in order to make such methods feasible to use and to maintain.

Weighted or Month-End Average Method.   The weighted or month-end average method is used with a periodic inventory system where a periodic physical count of items establishes the quantity of units on hand at the end of a designated period. Then, the quantity of materials used is calculated by subtracting the ending quantity on hand from the total inventory that was available for use during the period. The unit cost of inventory is calculated by dividing the total inventory cost incurred for the period by the total units available.

To illustrate, assume the same transactions as on pages 72–73.

		Units	Unit Cost	Total Cost
Dec. 1	Balance	1,000	$20	$20,000
15	Purchase	1,000	24	24,000
28	Purchase	500	26	13,000
		2,500		$57,000

Weighted average cost per unit . . . . $57,000 ÷ 2,500 = $22.80
Cost of ending inventory. . . . . $22.80 × 750 units = $17,100

Cost of inventory used:

Total available, 2,500 units	$57,000
Less ending inventory, 750 units	17,100
Total inventory used, 1,750 units	$39,900

Market Price at Date of Issue.   The market price at date of issue can be used for costing materials traded on commodity exchanges, such as cotton, wheat, copper, and crude oil. This method substitutes replacement cost for the actual price paid for the material. Currently this method is used exclusively for internal reporting purposes. However, the popularity of using the market price at date of issue in costing materials can be expected to grow because the interest in current-value and replacement-value costing is increasing.

Standard Cost Method.   A company that uses a standard cost system predetermines the cost of each unit of material, then charges production with the predetermined unit costs when materials are requisitioned. One advantage of this method is that only the quantity of materials is maintained in the records since all units of the same class of materials have the same price per unit. The details of standard costing are discussed in Chapters 8 and 9.

Accounting Procedures

The purpose of materials accounting is to provide a summary from the general ledger of the total cost of materials purchased and used in manufacturing. The forms commonly used in assembling the required data have already been discussed. The purchase invoices provide the information needed in preparing the vouchers. The vouchers should then be recorded in a voucher register where a special column is provided for recording materials purchased. At the end of the month, the total materials purchased during the month is posted by debiting Materials and by crediting Vouchers Payable or Accounts Payable. The materials account in the general ledger serves as a control account for the stores ledger.

All materials issued during the month and materials returned to stock are recorded on a summary of materials issued and returned form (see Illustration 2-11). When the summary is completed at the end of the month, the total cost of direct materials requisitioned is recorded by debiting Work in Process and by crediting Materials. The total of indirect materials requisitioned is recorded by debiting the appropriate factory over-

SUMMARY OF MATERIALS ISSUED AND RETURNED

Month Ending _____ 19____

| | | Materials Issued | | | | Materials Returned to Storeroom | | | | |
| | | Direct Materials | | Indirect Materials | | | Direct Materials | | Indirect Materials | |
Date	Req. No.	Job	Amount	Overhead Acct. No.	Amount	Report No.	Job	Amount	Overhead Acct. No.	Amount
Mar. 5	825	315	$2,150 00							
8	826	316	3,210 00	3121	$ 440 00					
11	827	317	280 00	3121	132 50					
14	828	316	415 00							
17	829	317	340 00							
17	830	318	820 00	3121	135 00					
18	831	319	290 00			232	319	$ 12 10	3121	$ 12 50
19	832	319	224 20							
20	833	320	975 90			233	320	448 90		
24	834	321	4,350 00	3121	432 00	234	321	318 20	3121	15 00
27	835	322	6,500 00							
29	836	321	550 00							
30	837	321	785 40							
31	838	320	870 00							
			$21,760 50		$1,139 50			$ 779 20		$ 27 50

Illustration 2-11   Summary of Materials Issued and Returned

head account and by crediting Materials. The work in process account in the general ledger serves as a control account for the factory cost ledger.

Any undamaged materials returned to the storeroom from the factory should also be recorded on the summary of materials issued and returned in order that the totals may be recorded at the end of the month. The entries required to record undamaged materials returned are the reverse of the entries required to record materials requisitioned. Thus, the total cost of direct materials returned to the storeroom is recorded by debiting Materials and by crediting Work in Process, while the total cost of indirect materials returned is recorded by debiting Materials and by crediting the proper factory overhead account.

Any materials returned to the vendors from whom they were originally purchased should be recorded by debiting Vouchers Payable or Accounts Payable and by crediting Materials. Unless a special journal is provided for recording such returns, the entries may be made in the general journal. All transactions relating to materials should be recorded so that the balance of the materials account in the general ledger will represent the cost of materials on hand at the end of a period. The balance of the materials account may be proved by listing the stores ledger account balances.

A summary of the procedures involved in accounting for materials is shown in Illustration 2-12. This is a presentation of the recordings required for the more typical materials transactions, both at the time of the transaction and at the end of the period. At the time of the transaction, the recordings to be made affect the subsidiary ledgers such as the stores ledger and the job cost ledger. At the end of the period, the recordings to be made affect the control accounts for materials, work in process, and factory overhead in the general ledger.

The Voucher System.   Throughout this discussion it has been assumed that the voucher system of accounting is in use. The voucher system, due to its many advantages, is more widely used than the simpler but less efficient purchases journal system, particularly in large manufacturing enterprises.

The two systems differ only in the effect they have on general accounting procedures. For example, when a purchase transaction is completed, the set of forms pertaining to the purchase is sent to the accounting department. If the voucher system is in use, a voucher is prepared, entered in the voucher register, and filed in the unpaid vouchers file. If the purchases journal system is in use, the invoice is entered in the purchases journal, posted to the accounts payable ledger, and filed under the vendor's name.

Transaction	Entry at Time of Transaction			Entry at End of Accounting Period		
	Source of Data	Book of Original Entry	Subsidiary Ledger Posting	Source of Data	Book of Original Entry	General Ledger Posting
Purchase of materials	Vendor's Invoice Receiving Report	Voucher Register	Stores Ledger	Voucher Register	None	Materials Vouchers Payable
Materials returned to vendor	Return Shipping Order	General Journal	Stores Ledger	General Journal	None	Vouchers Payable Materials
Payment of invoices	Approved Voucher	Check Register	None	Check Register	None	Vouchers Payable Cash
Direct materials issued	Materials Requisitions	None	Stores Ledger Job Cost Ledger	Materials Summary	General Journal	Work in Process Materials
Indirect materials issued	Materials Requisitions	None	Stores Ledger Factory Overhead Ledger	Materials Summary	General Journal	Factory Overhead Materials
Direct materials returned from factory to storeroom	Returned Materials Report	None	Stores Ledger Job Cost Ledger	Materials Summary	General Journal	Materials Work in Process
Indirect materials returned from factory to storeroom	Returned Materials Report	None	Stores Ledger Factory Overhead Ledger	Materials Summary	General Journal	Materials Factory Overhead
Inventory adjustment: (a) Materials on hand less than stores ledger balance	Inventory Report	General Journal	Factory Overhead Ledger Stores Ledger	General Journal	None	Factory Overhead Materials
(b) Materials on hand more than stores ledger balance	Inventory Report	General Journal	Factory Overhead Ledger Stores Ledger	General Journal	None	Materials Factory Overhead

Illustration 2-12   Summary of Materials Transactions

2 **Inventory Verification.**   The stores ledger contains an account for each material used in the manufacturing process. Each account shows the number of units on hand and their cost. In other words, the stores ledger provides a perpetual inventory of the individual items of material in the storeroom. From the information in the store ledger, the necessary materials inventory data can be obtained for preparation of a balance sheet, an income statement, and a manufacturing statement.

However, it is always possible that errors may occur in recording receipts or issues of materials in the stores ledger accounts. Such errors affect the reliability of the inventory totals. To guard against error, the materials on hand should be periodically checked against the figures shown in the individual stores ledger accounts. The usual practice is to count one lot of materials at a time, spacing the time of the counts so that a complete check of all inventories in the storeroom can be made within a fixed period of time, such as three months. These periodic checks have the advantage of eliminating the costly and time consuming task of counting all the materials at one time. To guard against carelessness or dishonesty, the count should be made by someone other than the storeroom keeper or the stores ledger clerk.

The person making the count should prepare an inventory report similar to the one shown in Illustration 2-13. If the total indicated in the report differs from the balance in the stores ledger account, an immediate correcting entry should be made in the proper stores ledger account. The entries in the general ledger accounts may be made in total at the end of the month. If the materials on hand exceed the balance in the control account, the balance in that account should be increased by the following entry:

Materials..	xxx	
Factory Overhead (Inventory Over and Short)........		xxx

If the amount of materials on hand is less than the control account balance, the balance should be decreased by the following entry:

Factory Overhead (Inventory Over and Short)..........	xxx	
Materials..		xxx

Such inventory differences are almost always a shortage and may arise from carelessness in handling materials, shrinkage in goods as a result of handling, or issuing excess quantities of materials to production. Such shortages are considered unavoidable and constitute part of the cost of operating a manufacturing plant. Shortages (or overages) are recorded in a

```
BLOOMINGTON      INVENTORY REPORT
MFG.

     Material _____        3/4" valves         ____
     Location in storeroom __ Bin L123            ____
     Stores ledger acct. No. _12345               ____
     Date of verification ___ January 27, 19--    ____

     Units in storeroom ___590___
     Units in receiving
          department ___300___
     Total number units on hand  890   ____
     Balance per stores ledger   910   ____
     Difference                   20   ____

     Counted by  P. Valence       ____
     Supervised by  W. Cox        ____
     Variance entered in stores ledger
          By  A. Nieman           ____
```

Illustration 2-13   Inventory Report (Compares book inventory and physical inventory quantities)

factory overhead account, usually entitled Inventory Over and Short, as indicated in the preceding entries.

Visual Aid.   If a cost accounting system is to function properly, it is important that each employee has a clear understanding of assigned duties and the function of each form to be prepared and of each record to be kept. Illustration 2-14 emphasizes the importance of internal control in the manufacturing operations. It shows the interrelationship of the accounts and how internal control procedures can be established.

SCRAP, SPOILED GOODS, AND DEFECTIVE WORK

Manufacturing operations usually produce some imperfect units that cannot be sold as regular items by the company. The controls over imperfect items and operations that waste materials are important elements of inventory control. Scrap or waste materials may result naturally from the produc-

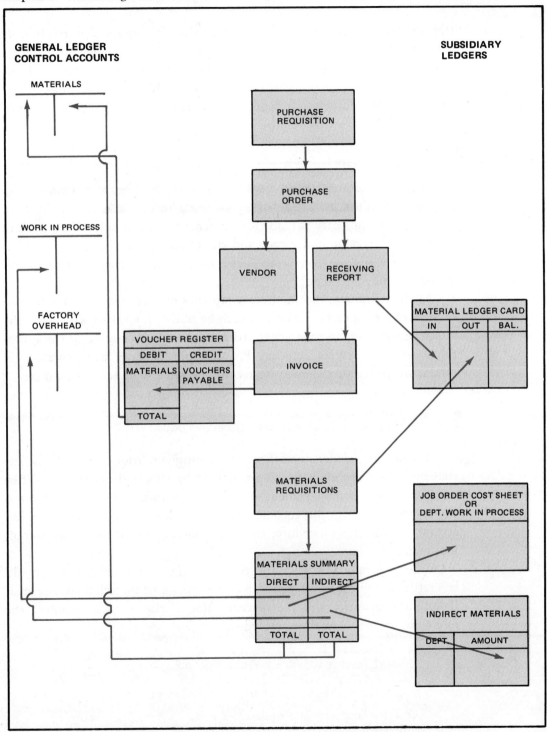

GENERAL LEDGER
CONTROL ACCOUNTS

SUBSIDIARY
LEDGERS

MATERIALS

WORK IN PROCESS

FACTORY
OVERHEAD

PURCHASE
REQUISITION

PURCHASE
ORDER

VENDOR

RECEIVING
REPORT

MATERIAL LEDGER CARD

IN	OUT	BAL.

VOUCHER REGISTER

DEBIT	CREDIT
MATERIALS	VOUCHERS PAYABLE
TOTAL	

INVOICE

MATERIALS
REQUISITIONS

JOB ORDER COST SHEET
OR
DEPT. WORK IN PROCESS

MATERIALS SUMMARY

DIRECT	INDIRECT
TOTAL	TOTAL

INDIRECT MATERIALS

DEPT.	AMOUNT

Illustration 2-14   Interrelationship of Materials Documents and Accounts

tion process, or they may be spoiled or defective units that result from avoidable or unavoidable mistakes during production. Quality control techniques are usually introduced by a company so that imperfect items will not be sold, thereby damaging the reputation of the company. Since scrap, spoiled goods, and defective work usually have some value, each is treated separately in accounting for their costs.

Scrap Materials

The expected sales value of the **scrap** produced by the manufacturing process determines the accounting procedures to be used. When the scrap value is small, no entry is made for the scrap until it is sold. Then Cash or Accounts Receivable is debited, and an account such as Scrap Revenue is credited. The income from scrap sales is usually reported as "Other income" in the income statement.

As an alternative, income from scrap sales may be treated as a reduction in manufacturing costs. If the scrap can be readily identified with a specific job or department, income generated from the sale is credited to the appropriate work in process account. For example, if scrap was generated in producing Job 100, the entry to record the sale of the scrap would be:

```
Cash (or Accounts Receivable) . . . . . . . . . . . . . . . . . . . . . .   xxx
    Work in Process — Job 100 . . . . . . . . . . . . . . . . . . . . . . .        xxx
        To record the sale of scrap generated by Job 100.
```

Realistically, under normal manufacturing conditions, it would be extremely difficult to identify scrap materials by jobs or departments. When that is the case, if management wishes to treat income from scrap sales as a reduction in cost, the income may be credited to a factory overhead account. Using this procedure, the cost reduction would be spread over all jobs or departments.

When the value of the scrap is relatively high, an inventory card should be prepared, and the scrap transferred to a controlled materials storage area. If both the quantity and the market value of the scrap are known, the following journal entries are recorded:

```
Scrap Materials . . . . . . . . . . . . . . . . . . . . . . . . . . . . . . . . .   xxx
    Scrap Revenue (or Work in Process or Factory
    Overhead) . . . . . . . . . . . . . . . . . . . . . . . . . . . . . . . . . . .        xxx
        To record the value of scrap transferred to inventory.

Cash (or Accounts Receivable) . . . . . . . . . . . . . . . . . . . . . .   xxx
    Scrap Materials . . . . . . . . . . . . . . . . . . . . . . . . . . . . . . . .        xxx
        To record the sale of scrap.
```

If the market value of the scrap is not known, no journal entry is made until the scrap is sold. At the time of sale, the following entry is then recorded:

```
Cash (or Accounts Receivable)......................    xxx
    Scrap Revenue (or Work in Process or Factory
    Overhead)........................................         xxx
        To record the sale of scrap.
```

Spoiled and Defective Work

Scrap is an expected by-product that results from the production of the primary product. Spoiled or defective goods are not by-products, but imperfect units of the primary product. Spoiled units have imperfections that cannot be economically corrected. They are sold as items of inferior quality or "seconds." Defective units have imperfections that are considered correctable, because the market value of the corrected unit will be greater than the total cost incurred for the unit.

Spoiled Work.   The loss associated with spoiled goods may be treated as part of the cost of the job or department which produced the spoiled units, or the loss may be charged to Factory Overhead and allocated among all jobs or departments. Generally, Factory Overhead is charged unless the loss results from a specific job that is a special order and the spoilage is due to the type of work required on that particular order. In both cases, the spoiled goods are recorded in a spoiled goods inventory account at the expected sales price.

To illustrate, assume a garment manufacturer using job order costing completes an order for 1,000 sport jackets (Job 350) at the following unit costs:

```
Materials ...............    $20
Labor ..................     20
Factory overhead .......     10
Total cost per unit ........    $50
```

The journal entry to record the costs of production is:

```
Work in process — Job 350 ...........................    50,000
    Materials.........................................         20,000
    Payroll...........................................         20,000
    Factory Overhead .................................         10,000
        To record the production costs for Job 350.
```

At the point of final inspection, 50 jackets are found to be inferior and are classified as irregulars or seconds. They are expected to sell for $10 each. If the unrecovered costs of spoilage are to be charged to Factory Overhead, the following entry is recorded:

Spoiled Goods Inventory..............................	500	
Factory Overhead...................................	2,000	
Work in Process—Job 350		2,500
To record spoiled goods at market value (50 jackets		
@ $10, charge Factory Overhead for the loss of $40		
per unit, and reduce the cost of Job 350 (50 jackets		
@ $50).		

If the loss from spoilage is considered a cost of the specific job, the entry to record the market value is:

Spoiled Goods Inventory..............................	500	
Work in Process—Job 350		500
To record spoiled goods at market value.		

When spoilage costs are charged to Factory Overhead, the costs are allocated among all jobs in production. When spoilage is attributed to a specific job, however, the entire cost of spoilage is reflected in the cost of that job. In the example, Job 350 will be charged with only a portion of the $2,000 loss from spoilage when Factory Overhead is allocated to the various jobs. When Factory Overhead is not charged for the spoilage costs, however, the entire $2,000 loss is included in the total cost of Job 350.

Defective Work.   The procedures for recording the cost associated with defective work are similar to those employed in accounting for spoiled work. There are, however, additional costs for correcting the imperfections on defective units. If these costs are incurred on orders regularly produced by the company, they are charged to Factory Overhead. For special orders, the additional costs are charged to the job. An inventory account is not established for goods that are classified as defective, because the defects are corrected and the units become first-quality merchandise.

As in the previous illustration, assume it costs $50 to manufacture each jacket. Upon final inspection of the 1,000 jackets completed, 50 jackets are considered defective because one sleeve on each jacket is a slightly different shade of blue than the other parts of the jacket. Management decides to recut the sleeves from a bolt of material that is identical in color to the rest of the jacket. The costs of correcting the defects are $500 for materials, $400 for labor, and $300 for factory overhead, representing a total cost of $1,200.

If the additional costs are charged to Factory Overhead, the cost of correcting defective work is spread over all jobs that go through the production cycle. The journal entry is:

Factory Overhead (Costs to Correct Defective Work)............	1,200	
Materials...		500
Payroll...		400
Factory Overhead..		300
To record costs of correcting defective units.		

If the order for 1,000 jackets was a special order and the defects resulted from the specifications of the order, the additional costs would be charged to the job as follows:

Work in Process—Job 350	1,200	
Materials...		500
Payroll...		400
Factory Overhead..		300
To charge Job 350 with the cost of correcting defective work.		

The total cost of Job 350 will be higher because the additional costs to correct the defects were charged to the order rather than to the factory overhead account. The unit cost of each completed jacket is increased from $50 ($50,000/1,000) to $51.20 ($51,200/1,000) because of the additional costs charged to the work in process account.

Classifying Imperfect Units as Spoiled or Defective.   The amount of net revenue that can be obtained from an irregular versus a perfected unit determines whether the item will be classified as spoiled or defective. For example, assume that if the 50 jackets are classified as spoiled, they can then be sold as seconds for $10 per jacket. However, if the defects are corrected at a cost of $1,200, these same jackets can be sold for $50 per jacket.

	Spoiled	Defective
Revenue from sales (50 units)......................	$500	$2,500
Cost to correct defects...........................		1,200
Net revenue	$500	$1,300

In this situation, the correction of the imperfections appears warranted because the net revenue is $1,300 when the goods are classified as defective, and only $500 when they are considered spoiled and are sold as seconds.

SUMMARY

The costs incurred for materials used by a manufacturing company are usually of such magnitude that they must be carefully controlled. The accounting control system for materials should provide for both physical control of materials and control of the investment in materials. The physical control of materials requires that access to the materials be limited, that the duties of employees be segregated, and that purchases and issuances of materials be recorded accurately. Controlling the investment in materials includes establishing an inventory of sufficient size and diversity for efficient manufacturing operations. A minimum level of inventory for each type of raw material should be determined as well as an order point and an economic order quantity.

Effective materials control requires procedures for controlling the procurement process, including documentation in the form of purchase requisitions, purchase orders, vendors' invoices, receiving reports, and debit-credit memoranda. After ordered goods are received, the control procedures include properly storing and issuing the storeroom materials. Included in these controls should be proper authorization for materials requisitions and the accounting for returned materials.

Accounting for materials requires maintaining inventory records which show the number of units of each kind of materials on hand and their cost. An important area of materials accounting is the costing of materials that are requisitioned by production. Since the flow of materials does not have to coincide with the flow of costs, several methods of costing are available. The most commonly used methods include first-in, first-out (fifo); last-in, first-out (lifo); and moving average. The selection of a costing method depends on the type of enterprise, economic conditions, the size of inventory, and the frequency of inventory turnover.

Scrap, spoiled goods, and defective work are frequently encountered by manufacturing organizations; therefore, control over these imperfect products is an important element of inventory control. The proper classification of an imperfect item is important if the revenue from such units is to be maximized.

KEY TERMS

Carrying costs (55)   Defective units (87)
Debit-credit memorandum (64)   Economic order quantity (55)

First-in, first-out (fifo) (72)
Flow of costs (72)
Flow of materials (72)
Inventory report (83)
Last-in, first-out (lifo) (73)
Lead time (54)
Materials control (52)
Materials ledger (69)
Materials (or stores) requisition (67)
Moving average (74)
Order costs (55)
Order point (54)
Production department supervisor (59)
Purchasing agent (58)
Purchase order (60)
Purchase requisition (60)

Receiving clerk (59)
Receiving report (63)
Return shipping order (65)
Returned materials report (68)
Safety stock (54)
Scrap materials (86)
Spoiled units (87)
Stockout (54)
Storeroom keeper (59)
Stores ledger (69)
Summary of materials issued and
    returned (79)
Usage (54)
Vendor's invoice (61)
Voucher system (81)
Weighted or month-end average (78)

QUESTIONS

1. What are the two major objectives of materials control?
2. Materials often represent a substantial portion of a company's assets; therefore, they should be controlled from the time orders are placed to the time that finished goods are shipped to the customer. Describe the control procedures for safeguarding materials.
3. What factors should management consider in determining the amount of investment in materials?
4. Maintaining and replenishing the stock of materials used in manufacturing operations is an important aspect of the procurement process. What is the meaning of the term "order point"?
5. What kind of information and data are needed to calculate an order point?
6. Define the term "economic order quantity."
7. What are the factors to be considered when determining the cost of an order?
8. What are the costs of carrying materials in stock?
9. Briefly, discuss the duties of the following employees:
   (a) Purchasing agent
   (b) Receiving clerk
   (c) Storeroom keeper
   (d) Production supervisor
10. Proper authorization is required before orders for new materials can be placed. Distinguish between a purchase requisition and a purchase order.
11. Purchasing agents are responsible for contacting vendors from which to purchase materials required by production. Why is the purchasing agent

also responsible for reviewing and approving incoming vendors' invoices?

12. Illustrations of forms for requisitioning, ordering, and accounting for materials are presented in the chapter. Would you expect these forms, as shown, to be used by all manufacturers? Discuss.

13. What internal control procedures should be established for incoming shipments of materials purchased?

14. What is the purpose of a debit-credit memorandum?

15. Who is the originator of each of the following forms?
    (a) Purchase requisition
    (b) Purchase order
    (c) Receiving report
    (d) Return shipping order
    (e) Materials requisition
    (f) Returned materials report

16. Normally a manufacturer maintains an accounting system which includes a stores ledger and a general ledger account for Materials. Describe the relationship between the stores ledger and the materials account.

17. A company may select an inventory costing method from a number of commonly used procedures. Briefly describe each of the following methods:
    (a) First-in, first-out
    (b) Last-in, first-out
    (c) Moving average

18. Why do companies adopt the lifo method of inventory costing? Your discussion should include the effects on both the income statement and balance sheet.

19. Referring to the forms shown in the chapter, which forms are the source for the following entries to subsidiary ledger accounts?
    (a) Debits to record materials purchased in stores ledger.
    (b) Credits to record materials requisitioned in stores ledger.
    (c) Debits to record materials placed in process in job cost ledger.
    (d) Credits to record materials returned to storeroom in job cost ledger.
    (e) Debits to record materials returned to storeroom in stores ledger.
    (f) Credits to record materials returned to vendor in stores ledger.

20. Which book of original entry is the source for each of the following entries in the general ledger, assuming that a general journal, voucher register, and check register are used?
    (a) Debits to materials account to record materials purchased.
    (b) Credits to materials account to record materials placed in production.
    (c) Debits to vouchers payable account to record vouchers paid.
    (d) Debits to work in process account to record materials placed in production.
    (e) Credits to work in process account to record materials returned to storeroom.

21. A manufacturing process may produce a considerable quantity of scrap material because of the nature of the product. What methods can be used to account for the sale value of the scrap material?
22. After inspection of a product, some units are classfied as spoiled and others as defective. What distinguishes a product as being spoiled or defective?

EXERCISES

Exercise 2-1   Economic order quantity.

The Mets Company predicts that 8,000 units of material will be used during the year. The material is expected to cost $4 per unit. It is anticipated that it will cost $40 to place each order. The annual carrying cost is $.25 per unit. Determine:
(a) the most economical order quantity by use of the formula
(b) the total cost of ordering and carrying at the EOQ point

Exercise 2-2   Journalizing materials requisitions.   *issuance*

The Betta Corporation records the following use of materials during the month of November:

| | | | Materials Requisitions | |
| | | | Direct Materials | Indirect Materials F/O |
Date	Req. No.	Use		
1	110	Material A, Job 10	$20,000	
5	111	Material B, Job 11	18,000	
9	112	Material B, Job 12	16,000	
12	113	Factory supplies F/O		$ 800
18	114	Material C, Job 10	3,000	
21	115	Material D, Job 10	9,000	
23	116	Material E, Job 13	2,000	
28	117	Factory supplies F/O		1,300
30	118	Factory supplies		1,700

Prepare a summary journal entry for the materials requisitions.

Exercise 2-3   Computing direct materials cost.

The Hytech Electric Motor Company manufactures small electric motors used in windshield wiper assemblies. Selected accounts from their general ledger show the following balances for September:

Finished Goods, September 1	$ 80,500
Work in Process, September 1	161,200
Raw Materials, September 1	35,500
Raw Materials Purchases	540,250
Direct Labor	315,200
Indirect Materials	30,600
Repairs and Maintenance	40,150
Utilities	18,210
Indirect Labor	33,330
Supervisors' Salaries and Wages	62,250
Finished Goods, September 30	70,200
Work in Process, September 30	142,200
Raw Materials, September 30	25,150

Compute the cost of direct materials used during the month of September.

Exercise 2-4   Recording materials transactions.

Prepare a journal entry to record each of the following materials transactions:

(a) The voucher register shows that the total materials purchased during the month amounted to $200,000.
(b) Direct materials requisitioned for the month totaled $175,000.
(c) Indirect materials requisitioned during the month totaled $12,000.
(d) Direct materials returned to the storeroom from the factory amounted to $2,500.
(e) Total materials returned to vendor during the month amounted to $800.
(f) Vouchers paid during the month for materials purchases only totaled $80,000 less 2% discount.

Exercise 2-5   Fifo costing.

Using first-in, first-out and perpetual inventory costing, determine the cost of materials used and the cost of the May 31 inventory from the following information:

May 1   Balance on hand, 1,000 units (bearings, $4 each).
      3   Issued 250 units.
      5   Received 500 units at $4.50 each.
      6   Issued 150 units.
     10   Issued 110 units.
     11   Factory returned 10 units to the storeroom that were issued on the 10th.
     15   Received 500 units at $5.00 each.
     20   Returned 300 units to vendor from May 15th purchase.
     26   Issued 100 units.

Exercise 2-6   Lifo costing.

Using last-in, first-out and perpetual inventory costing, determine the cost of materials used and cost of the May 31 inventory, based on the information presented in Exercise 5.

Exercise 2-7   Moving average costing.

Using the moving average method of inventory costing, determine the cost of materials used and the cost of the May 31 inventory, based on the information presented in Exercise 5.

Exercise 2-8   Comparison of fifo, lifo, and moving average methods.

In tabular form, compare the total cost transferred to Work in Process and the cost of the ending inventory for each method used in Exercises 5, 6, and 7.

Exercise 2-9   Impact of costing methods on net income.

The New Company was franchised on January 1, 19A1. At the end of its third year of operations, December 31, 19A3, management requested a study to determine what effect different materials inventory costing methods would have had on its reported net income over the three-year period.

The materials inventory account, using lifo, fifo, and moving average, would have had the following ending balances:

	Materials Inventory Balances		
December 31	Lifo	Fifo	Average
19A1	$20,000	$22,000	$21,000
19A2	22,000	24,000	23,000
19A3	26,000	30,000	28,000

(a) Were material costs rising or falling from 19A1 to 19A3?
(b) Which costing method would show the highest net income for 19A1?
(c) Which method would show the highest net income for 19A3?
(d) Which method would show the lowest net income for the three years combined?
(e) For the year 19A2, how would the profit using lifo compare to the profit if average cost was used?

Exercise 2-10   Recording materials transactions.

Mark Manufacturing Company maintains the following accounts in the general ledger: Materials, Work in Process, Factory Overhead, and Vouchers

Payable. On June 1, the materials account had a debit balance of $20,000. Following is a summary of material transactions for the month of June:

1. Materials purchased, per voucher register, $66,750.
2. Direct materials requisitioned, $53,250.
3. Direct materials returned to storeroom, $1,400.
4. Indirect materials requisitioned, $1,975.
5. Indirect materials returned to storeroom, $185.

(a) Prepare journal entries to record the materials transactions.
(b) Post the journal entries to ledger accounts (in T-account form).
(c) What is the balance of the materials inventory account at the end of the month?

Exercise 2-11   Scrap materials.

A machine shop manufactures a stainless steel part that is used in an assembled product. Materials charged to a particular job amounted to $600. It was discovered at the point of final inspection that the material used was inferior to the specifications required by the engineering department; therefore, all units had to be scrapped.
Record the entries required for scrap under each of the following conditions:
(a) The revenue received for scrap is to be spread over all jobs. The value of stainless steel scrap is stable. The scrap is sold two months later for $125.
(b) Revenue received for scrap is to be spread over all jobs. A firm price is not determinable for the scrap until it is sold. It is sold eventually for $75.
(c) The production job is a special job and the $85 received for the scrap is credited to the job.
(d) Only $40 was received for the scrap when it was sold in the following fiscal period.

Exercise 2-12   Spoiled work.

The SporTee Company is a manufacturer of golf clothing. During the month, the company cut and assembled 8,000 golf jackets. One hundred of the golf jackets did not meet specifications and were considered "seconds". Seconds are sold for $8 per jacket, whereas first quality jackets sell for $39.95. During the month Work in Process was charged $132,000: $36,000 for materials, $48,000 for labor, and $48,000 for factory overhead.
Record the entries required for each of the following conditions:
(a) The loss due to spoiled work is spread over all jobs in the department.
(b) The loss due to spoiled work is charged to this job because it is a special order.

Exercise 2-13   Defective Work

The X-T-Y Company manufactures an integrated transistor circuit board for repeat customers but also accepts special orders for the same product. Job No. 10A1 incurred the following unit costs for 1,000 circuit boards manufactured:

Materials	$5.00
Labor	2.00
Factory Overhead	2.00
Total cost per unit	$9.00

When the completed products were tested, 20 circuit boards were found to be defective, and the costs per unit of correcting the defects were as follows:

Materials	$3.00
Labor	1.00
Factory Overhead	1.00

Record the journal entry required:
(a)   if the cost of the defective work is charged to factory overhead
(b)   if the cost of the defective work is charged to the job

PROBLEMS

Problem 2-1   Economic order quantities.

The Tenkotte Corporation has made several forecasts concerning the number of units of material that will be purchased in the coming fiscal period. The price to be paid for materials is directly related to the quantity purchased; therefore, the study group has decided that costs should be determined for three different usage levels. The company anticipates that it will cost $30 for each order placed, and the carrying cost will be $.80 per unit.

Required:
    Determine the most economical order quantity under each of the following conditions:
1.   the expected annual usage of material is 5,000 units
2.   the expected annual usage of material is 10,000 units
3.   the expected annual usage of material is 15,000 units

Problem 2-2   Inventory costing methods.

The purchases and issues of materials as shown in the records of the Arondo Corporation for the month of April were as follows:

		Units	Unit Price
April 1	Beginning balance	30,000	$3.00
4	Received, Rec. Report No. 11	10,000	3.10
5	Issued, Mat. Req. No. 115	30,000	
8	Received, Rec. Report No. 12	50,000	3.30
15	Issued, Mat. Req. No. 116	20,000	
22	Received, Rec. Report No. 13	25,000	3.50
28	Issued, Mat. Req. No. 117	50,000	

Required:

1. Using the above data, complete a stores ledger card similar to the one illustrated on page 71 (the "on order" columns may be omitted) for each of the following inventory costing methods:
   (a) Fifo
   (b) Lifo
   (c) Moving average
2. For each method, prepare a schedule which shows the total cost of materials transferred to Work in Process and cost of the ending inventory.
3. If prices continue to increase, would you favor adopting the fifo or lifo method? Explain.
4. When prices continue to rise, what is the effect of fifo versus lifo on the inventory balance reported in the balance sheet? Discuss.

Problem 2-3   Inventory costing methods.

The following transactions affecting materials occurred in December:

Dec. 1 Balance on hand, 1,200 units @ $2.76, $3,312.00 (copper wire, 100 feet per unit).
      5 Issued 60 units on Materials Requisition No. 108.
     11 Issued 200 units on Materials Requisition No. 210.
     14 Received 800 units, Receiving Report No. 634, price $2.8035 per unit.
     15 Issued 400 units, Materials Requisition No. 274.
     16 Returned for credit 90 units purchased on December 14 which were found to be defective.
     18 Received 1,000 units, Receiving Report No. 712, price $2.82712 per unit.
     21 Issued 640 units, Materials Requisition No. 318.

Required:

Using the inventory methods listed below, record the above transactions on stores ledger cards similar to the one illustrated on page 71 (the "on order" column may be omitted).
1. Fifo
2. Lifo
3. Moving average

Problem 2-4   Inventory costing methods.

The Raphael Corporation began operations on December 1, 19A. The following information was recorded in the materials inventory records:

	Units	Unit Cost
January 1, 19B, beginning inventory...........	1,000	$10
Purchases:		
January 5, 19B.........................	1,500	12
January 25, 19B	1,200	13
February 16, 19B.......................	600	14
March 26, 19B.........................	700	15

A physical inventory on March 31, 19B shows 1,600 units on hand.

Required:

Prepare schedules to compute the ending inventory at March 31, 19B, under each of the following inventory methods:
1. Fifo
2. Lifo
3. Weighted average

Problem 2-5   Comparison of inventory costing methods.

The controller of the Sneltor Corporation, a retail company, prepared three different schedules of gross margin for the quarter ended September 30. These schedules appear below.

	Sales ($10 per unit)	Cost of Goods Sold	Gross Margin
Schedule A........	$280,000	$116,000	$164,000
Schedule B........	280,000	115,600	164,400
Schedule C........	280,000	115,200	164,800

The computation of cost of goods sold in each schedule is based on the following data:

	Units	Cost per Unit	Total Cost
Beginning inventory, July 1.....	10,000	$4.00	$40,000
Purchase, July 25.............	8,000	4.20	33,600
Purchase, August 15..........	5,000	4.10	20,500
Purchase, September 5........	7,000	4.30	30,100
Purchase, September 25.......	12,000	4.05	48,600

The president of the corporation cannot understand how three different gross margins can be computed from the same set of data. As controller, you have explained that the three schedules are based on three different assumptions concerning the flow of inventory costs; first-in, first-out; last-in, first-out; and weighted average. Schedules A, B, and C were not necessarily prepared in the sequence of cost-flow assumptions.

Required:

Prepare three separate schedules computing cost of goods sold and supporting schedules showing the composition of the ending inventory under each of the three cost-flow assumptions.   (AICPA adapted)

Problem 2-6   Journalizing materials transactions.

The Turnbuckle Tool Company uses a job order cost system. A partial list of the accounts being maintained by the company, with their balances as of November 1, is shown below:

Cash	$32,250
Materials...	29,500
Work in Process...	27,000
Vouchers Payable (credit).................................	21,000
Factory Overhead..	none

The following transactions were completed during the month of November:

(a) Materials purchases during the month, per voucher register, $30,000.
(b) Materials requisitioned during the month:
    (1) Direct materials, $25,000.
    (2) Indirect materials, $2,000.
(c) Direct materials returned by factory to storeroom during the month, $1,500.
(d) Materials returned to vendors during the month, $800.
(e) Vouchers paid during the month, $27,000.

Required:

1. Prepare general journal entries for each of the above transactions.
2. Post the general journal entries to "T" accounts.
3. Balance the accounts and report the balances of November 30 for:
   (a) Cash
   (b) Materials
   (c) Vouchers Payable

Problem 2-7 Analyzing materials and other transactions.

The Ahmer Manufacturing Company uses a job order cost system. The following accounts have been taken from the books of the company:

Materials

19--			19--		
Oct. 1 Inventory		7,000	Oct. 31 Requisitions for month	23,000	
31 Purchases for month		20,000			

Work in Process

19--			19--		
Oct. 1 Inventory		3,600	Oct. 31 To finished goods	50,000	
31 Material requisitions		23,000			
31 Direct labor		17,000			
31 Factory overhead		12,000			

Finished Goods

19--			19--		
Oct. 1 Inventory		11,650	Oct. 31 Cost of goods sold	55,000	
31 Goods finished		50,000			

Required:

1. Analyze the accounts and describe in narrative form what transactions took place.
2. List the supporting documents or forms, if any, required for each transaction.
3. Determine the balances, as of October 31, for Materials, Work in Process, and Finished Goods.

Problem 2-8 Comprehensive analysis of materials accounting procedures.

The decisions and transactions made by the Bay Sheet Metal Company in accounting for materials costs for April are shown on page 102.

Mar. 31

The storeroom keeper is notified by the factory manager that for the month of April 2,000 sheets of aluminum will be required. A check of the stock shows 500 aluminum sheets, costing $23 each, on hand. A minimum stock of 300 sheets must be maintained and the purchasing agent is notified of the need for 1,800 sheets. This quantity will cover the April production requirements and, at the same time, maintain the minimum inventory level.

Apr. 1

After checking with a number of different vendors, the purchasing agent orders the requested number of sheets at $30 each.

6   The shipment of aluminum sheets is received, inspected, and found to be in good condition. However, the order is short 200 sheets which are "back ordered" and are expected to be shipped in five days.

6   The invoice from the vendor covering the aluminum sheets is received and is approved for payment.

11   The aluminum sheets that were "back ordered" are received and approved.

11   The vendor's invoice for the back ordered shipment is received and approved for payment.

16   The April 6 invoice is paid, less a cash discount of 2%.

30   During the month, 1,900 sheets are issued to the factory. The company uses FIFO costing.

30   Twenty unused sheets are returned to stores from the factory. The returned sheets have a cost of $30 each.

30   At the end of the day, 398 sheets are on hand.

Required:
1. In tabular form, answer the following questions pertaining to *each* of the preceding decisions and transactions:
   (a) What forms, if any, were used?
   (b) What journal entries, if any, were made?
   (c) What books of original entry, if any, were used to record the data?
   (d) What subsidiary records were affected?
2. Calculate and show your computations for:
   (a) the material inventory balance as of April 30.
   (b) the cost of materials placed in production during April.

Problem 2-9 Materials inventory shortage; returns; scrap; spoiled goods.

An examination of Apeeco Corporation's records reveals the following transactions:

(a) On December 31, the physical inventory of raw material was 9,970 units.
The book quantity, using the moving average method, was 11,000 units
@ $.525 per unit.

(b) Materials worth $775 were returned to stores from production.

(c) Materials valued at $770 were charged to Factory Overhead (Repairs and
Maintenance) but should have been charged to Work in Process.

(d) Defective material was returned to vendor. The material returned cost
$234 and the shipping charges (our cost) of $35 were paid in cash.

(e) Goods sold to a customer for $5,000 (cost $2,500) were returned because of a misunderstanding of the quantity ordered. The customer
stated that the goods returned were in excess of the quantity needed.

(f) Materials requisitioned totaled $22,300, of which $2,100 represented
supplies used.

(g) Materials purchased totaled $25,500, of which $3,700 were supplies.
Freight on the direct materials purchased was $185.

(h) Direct materials returned to stores amounted to $950.

(i) Scrap materials sent to the storeroom valued at selling price: from direct
materials, $620; from supplies, $65.

(j) Spoiled work sent to the storeroom valued at sales price of $60 had
production costs of $200 charged to it.

(k) The scrap materials in (i) above were sold for $685 cash.

Required:
Record the entries, in general journal form, for each transaction.

**Problem 2-10   Spoiled goods: loss charged to factory overhead; loss
charged to job.**

The Wooster Company manufactures wallypods which sell for $.99 each.
The cost of each wallypod consists of:

Materials	$.35
Labor	.15
Factory Overhead	.20
Total	$.70

Job 100 produced 10,000 wallypods, of which 600 units were spoiled and
classified as seconds. Seconds are sold to department stores for $.50 each.

Required:
Using the following assumptions, record in general journal form the entries
when:

1. The loss from spoilage will be distributed to all jobs produced during the
current period.

2. The loss due to spoilage will be charged to Job 100. The entries should include:
   (a) putting spoiled goods into inventory
   (b) cash sale of the spoiled units

Problem 2-11   Spoiled goods and defective work.

The Centrax Company manufactures electrical equipment from specifications received from customers. Job X10 was for 1,000 motors to be used in a specially designed electrical complex. The following costs were determined for each motor:

Materials	$117
Labor	100
Factory Overhead	83
Total	$300

It was discovered at final inspection that 33 motors did not meet the specifications established by the customer. An examination indicated that 15 motors were beyond repair and should be sold as scrap for $55 each, and the remaining 18 motors, although defective, could be reconditioned as first quality units by the addition of $1,650 for materials, $1,500 for labor, and $1,200 for factory overhead.

Required:
   Prepare the journal entries to record:
   1. the scrapping of the units
   2. the correction of the defective units
   3. the additional cost of replacing the 15 scrapped motors
   4. the sale of the scrap motors

Problem 2-12   Review problem; transactions and statements.

The Link-to-Link Company manufactures chain hoists. The raw material inventories on hand January 1 were:

Chain.	12,000 pounds, $24,000
Pulleys.	4,000 sets, $20,000
Bolts and taps	10,000 sets, $5,000
Steel plates	4,000 units, $2,000

The balances in the ledger accounts on January 1 were:

Cash	$ 12,000	
Work in Process....................	15,000	
Materials	51,000	
Prepaid Insurance..................	3,000	
Machinery.........................	125,000	
Office Equipment	30,000	
Office Furniture	20,000	
Accounts Payable..................		$ 30,000
Capital Stock		200,000
Retained Earnings..................		26,000
	$256,000	$256,000

Transactions during January were:

(a) Payroll recorded during the month: direct labor, $28,000; indirect labor, $3,000.

(b) Factory supplies purchased for cash, $1,000.

(c) Materials purchased on account: chain—4,000 pounds, $8,800; pulleys—2,000 units, $10,200; steel plates—5,000 units, $3,000.

(d) Sales on account for the month, $126,375.

(e) Accounts receivable collected, $72,500.

(f) Materials used during January (fifo costing): chain, 14,000 pounds; pulleys, 4,400 units; bolts and taps, 4,000 sets; steel plates, 3,800 units.

(g) Payroll paid, $31,000.

(h) Factory supplies on hand, January 31, $350.

(i) Factory heat, light, and power costs for January $3,000 (not yet paid).

(j) Office salaries paid, $6,000.

(k) Advertising paid, $2,000.

(l) Factory superintendence paid, $1,800.

(m) Expired insurance—on office equipment, $100; on factory machinery, $300.

(n) Factory rent paid, $2,000.

(o) Depreciation on office equipment, $400; on office furniture, $180; on machinery, $1,200.

(p) Factory overhead charged to jobs, $11,950.

(q) Work in process, January 31, $11,000.

(r) Cost of goods sold during the month, $84,250.

(s) Accounts payable paid, $33,750.

Required:

1. Set up T-accounts and enter the balances as of January 1.
2. Prepare journal entries to record each of the above transactions.

3. Post the journal entries to the accounts, setting up any new ledger accounts necessary. Only controlling accounts are to be maintained; however, show the calculation for the cost of materials used.
4. Prepare a statement of cost of goods manufactured for January.
5. Prepare an income statement.
6. Prepare a balance sheet showing the classifications of current assets, plant and equipment, current liabilities, and stockholders' equity.

3

ACCOUNTING FOR LABOR

LEARNING OBJECTIVES

In studying this chapter, you will learn about the:

- Differences between direct and indirect labor costs
- Distinguishing features of hourly-rate and piece-rate plans
- Procedures for controlling labor costs
- Functions of timekeeping and payroll departments
- Procedures involved in accounting for labor costs
- Calculation and reporting of payroll taxes
- Special problems that are encountered in labor costing

Factory payroll costs are divided into two categories: direct labor and indirect labor. **Direct labor** represents payroll costs that are allocated directly to the product. The cost of direct labor is debited to the work in process account. **Indirect labor** consists of labor costs incurred for a variety of jobs that are related to the production process but are considered either too remote or too insignificant to be charged directly to production. Indirect labor costs include: salaries and wages of the factory superintendent, supervisors, janitors, clerks, factory accountants, and timekeepers. Indirect labor costs are charged to the factory overhead account.

The accounting system of a manufacturer must include the following procedures for recording payroll costs:

1. Recording the hours worked by employees in total and by job, process, or department; or recording the quantity of the employee's output.
2. Analyzing the hours worked by employees to determine how time is to be charged.
3. Allocating payroll costs to jobs, processes, departments, and factory overhead accounts.
4. Preparing the payroll, which involves computing and recording employee gross earnings, withholdings and deductions, and net earnings.

Most cost systems incorporate many of the procedures discussed in this chapter in accounting for labor costs. However, other procedures, which may be more or less elaborate, can also be used. Therefore, the illustrations, procedures, and forms as presented will apply to the majority of companies, while other manufacturers will find it necessary to make some modifications in order to meet their specific operational requirements.

WAGE PLANS

The wages paid to employees are based on plans that have been established by management, approved by the unions, and comply with the regulations of governmental agencies. There are advantages and disadvantages to all plans. However, the plan selected for a particular organization is generally the one management believes to be the most productive and profitable for the company. There are many variations of wage plans that may be used by a manufacturing organization. The plans discussed in this chapter are those that are most frequently encountered and include hourly-rate, piece-rate, and modified wage plans.

Hourly-Rate Plan

An hourly-rate plan establishes a definite rate per hour for each employee. An employee's wages are calculated by multiplying the established rate per hour times the number of hours worked by the employee in the wage period. The hourly-rate plan is widely used and is simple to apply. It has a serious limitation in that it provides no incentive for the employee to maintain or achieve a high level of productivity. An employee is paid for merely "being on the job" for an established period of time. The plan gives no recognition or reward for extra effort or for being a conscientious employee. However, since productivity is not an important factor of such a plan, employees will not be tempted to sacrifice the quality of the product by speeding up production to earn a higher wage.

To illustrate the hourly-rate plan, assume an employee earns $10 per hour and works 40 hours per week. The employee's gross earnings would be $400 (40 × $10 per hour).

Piece-Rate Plan

A company that gives a high priority to the quantity produced by each worker will give serious consideration to using a piece-rate plan. Under a piece-rate plan, earnings are based on the employee's quantity of production. To illustrate, assume a machine operator will earn $.20 for each part (or "piece") finished. If, in a week, 2,000 parts are finished, the operator will earn $400 ($.20 × 2,000 parts). The plan provides an incentive for the employee to produce a high level of output, thereby maximizing earnings and also increasing the company's net income. However, a serious shortcoming of such plans is that they encourage employees to sacrifice quality in order to maximize their earnings. Usually, in order to overcome this limitation, additional expense is incurred for supervision to maintain quality. The plan also requires more recordkeeping and constant review to update piece rates.

Modified Wage Plans

Modified wage plans combine some features of the hourly-rate and piece-rate plans. An example of a modified wage plan would be to set a minimum hourly wage that will be paid by the company even if an established quota of production is not attained by an employee. If the established quota is exceeded, an additional payment per piece would be added to the minimum wage level. This type of plan directs management's attention to the employee who is unable to meet the established quotas.

The process of management and union negotiations creates many variations of the hourly-rate and piece-rate plans. These variations occur because management wishes to minimize costs and maximize profits, while the labor union attempts to maximize the employee's earnings.

To illustrate a modified wage plan, assume an employee earns $.40 for each finished unit. The employee is guaranteed $5 per hour as a minimum wage. If the daily quota of 100 units is not attained, the employee will still be paid $40 (8 hours × $5 per hour) for the day's work. When less than 100 units are produced, the difference, often referred to as a make-up guarantee, will be charged to Factory Overhead.

Assume production and earnings for one week were as follows:

	Hours Worked	Pieces Finished (Quota 100)	Earnings @ $5 per Hour	Earnings @ $.40 per Unit	Make-Up Guarantee	Payroll Earnings
Mon.	8	120	$ 40	$ 48		$ 48
Tues.	8	90	40	36	$ 4	40
Wed.	8	80	40	32	8	40
Thurs.	8	110	40	44		44
Fri.	8	80	40	32	8	40
	40		$200	$192	$20	$212

The employee earned $192 on the piece-rate basis, but the daily guarantee of $40 per day compensated for the days when the quota was not reached. A make-up guarantee of $20 is charged to Factory Overhead because the quota was not met on Tuesday ($4), Wednesday ($8), and Friday ($8). The payroll distribution for the week would be:

Work in Process	192	
Factory Overhead	20	
Payroll		212
To distribute payroll earned.		

Another type of modified wage plan includes an incentive wage that encourages employees to work harder and earn bonuses for meeting or exceeding quotas. These plans are introduced by management, frequently in opposition to union wishes, to increase output and thereby increase profits.

To illustrate an incentive-wage plan, assume a production quota has been set that requires each employee to produce 100 units per hour. The regular hourly wage for the employees is $5 per hour. The incentive-wage schedule established for bonus earnings is as follows:

Units per Hour	Wage per Hour	Bonus Rate	Total Wage per Hour
Less than 100	$5.00	—	$5.00
100	5.00	$1.00	6.00
110	5.00	1.10	6.10
120	5.00	1.20	6.20

The significance of the incentive-wage plan for the employee is that if the quota is met for a 40-hour week, the worker can earn $240 (40 hours

@ $6) rather than $200 (40 hours @ $5) for the week. If an even higher level of output can be attained by the worker, the weekly wage will again increase. The potential benefit to the employer from an incentive-wage plan is a decrease in product cost. Some costs, such as straight-line depreciation on factory equipment, are fixed; that is, they remain the same in total regardless of the number of units produced. Thus, as output increases, the fixed costs will be spread over a greater number of units, resulting in a lower fixed cost per unit of product. To illustrate, assume a manufacturer can produce either 1,000 units for a given period or 2,000 units for that period. Total fixed costs for the period amount to $10,000 regardless of how many units are produced. The fixed cost per unit for the two levels of production would be as follows:

Units Produced	Fixed Costs	Fixed Cost per Unit
1,000	$10,000	$10
2,000	10,000	5

When total fixed costs remain fairly stable but the units of production can be increased, the effect is a decrease in the amount of fixed costs assigned to each unit. Wages paid for production represent variable costs; that is, they increase or decrease as output increases or decreases. Therefore, for an incentive-wage plan to be beneficial to the employer, the decrease in fixed cost per unit must be more than the increase in variable cost per unit created by the incentive wages paid to the employees. For example, if wages increase by $1 per hour when an established quota is attained, but fixed costs are reduced by $1.25 at that level of output, total unit cost would decrease by $.25. The saving in unit cost would benefit the company by increasing its profitability.

CONTROLLING LABOR COST

Maintaining labor records is the responsibility of the timekeeping and payroll departments. The timekeeping and payroll functions may be established as separate departments or organized as subdivisions of a single department. In either case, they should function as independent units to provide an internal check on the accuracy of computing and recording labor costs.

The timekeeping department accounts for the time spent by the hourly employees in the factory. The overall objective of the department is to determine the number of hours that should be paid for and the type of work performed by the employees during the working day.

The payroll department computes each employee's gross earnings, the amount of withholdings and deductions, and the net earnings to be paid to the employee.

The departmental responsibilities of timekeeping and payroll are carried out by completing and maintaining the following forms and records:

Timekeeping	Payroll
Clock cards	Payroll records
Time tickets	Employees earnings records
Production reports	Payroll summaries

Clock Cards and Time Tickets

A clock card is provided for each company employee who is required to punch a time clock. The card is used to record the total amount of time the employee spends in the plant. The preprinted card contains such information as the employee's name, clock number, and the week or pay period. The clock number is also used to identify the employee in the payroll records. An example of a clock card is shown in Illustration 3-1.

Each entrance to the factory may be a clock card station with time clocks and a rack of clock cards for the employees assigned to that entrance. The clock card should show the time of each employee's entrance and exit.

The employee, upon reporting to a work station, is given a time ticket (Illustration 3-2) for recording the hours worked on specific assignments. The time spent on each assignment may be entered on the time ticket by an individual from the timekeeping department or by a mechanical time-recording device. The labor hours recorded on the time ticket should be approved by a supervisor, because the ticket is the source document for allocating the cost of labor to jobs or departments in the cost ledger and factory overhead ledger.

The time ticket shows the employee's starting and stopping time on each job, the rate of pay, and the amount of earnings. When job transfers occur during a working day, the times of the transfers to and from different jobs are recorded on the ticket. The preparation of separate or unit time tickets for each job or operation on which an employee works may be required by the established accounting system (Illustration 3-3). Different colors may be selected for these time tickets to facilitate the sorting of the tickets into direct labor and indirect labor categories.

DAY	IN	OUT	IN	OUT	TOTAL	FOR PAYROLL USE ONLY

NAME   David A. Dressler

SOCIAL SEC. NO.   410-80-7865

DEPT. NO.	CLOCK NO.
04	2316

WEEK ENDING   2/16

AUTHORIZED   *Helene Johnson*

DAY	IN	OUT	IN	OUT	TOTAL	FOR PAYROLL USE ONLY
M	7:56	12:01	12:59	5:03	8	60.00
T	8:28	12:03	12:58	5:07	7½	56.25
W	7:54	12:01	12:57	5:00	8	60.00
TH	7:58	12:05	1:00	5:05	8	60.00
F	7:55	12:00	12:55	5:02	8	60.00
S						
S						

	RATE			HOURS	AMOUNT
REGULAR	7.50/hr.	REGULAR		39½	296.25
OVERTIME		OVERTIME			

Illustration 3-1   Employee Clock Card

After employees are clocked in, the timekeeper collects the preceding day's time tickets from supervisors and compares the time tickets and clock cards. The purpose of the comparison is to determine that all time spent in the factory by the employee is accounted for. Total time worked as shown on the employee's clock card should correspond to the time reported on the time ticket. Discrepancies should be investigated immediately.

The employer must compensate the employee for the time spent on assigned jobs. When time is not fully utilized, the employer suffers a loss just as if a theft of some tangible good had occurred. Therefore, if time spent in the factory has been unproductive, the idle time, along with the reason for it, should be recorded.

After the clock cards and time tickets have been compared, the cards are returned to the racks and the time tickets are forwarded to payroll. The pay rates are entered, and the employee's gross earnings are calculated and

Name David A. Dressler					Clock No. 2316		
Dept. Grinding (04)							

Job or Type of Work	Time Started	Time Stopped	Hours Worked		Payroll Use Only		
					Rate		Amount Earned
			Reg.	O.T.	Reg.	O.T.	
402	8:00	12:00	4		7.50		30 00
437	1:00	4:00	3		7.50		22 50
Machine repair	4:00	5:00	1		7.50		7 50

Date 2/14   Signed David A. Dressler
                                                  Employee
                  Approved Sharon Chapman
                                                  Supervisor

Illustration 3-2   Time Ticket (Daily)

DEPT. 04	CLOCK NO. 2316	NAME David A. Dressler
JOB 402	DESCRIPTION OF WORK 3 HP gear Semi-finishing housings	

			HOURS	AMOUNT	TOTAL
STOP	12:00	OVERTIME		PAYROLL USE ONLY	
START	8:00	REGULAR	4	7.50	30.00

Date 2/14

Signed David A. Dressler
                                                  Employee
Approved Sharon Chapman
                                                  Supervisor

Illustration 3-3   Time Ticket (Unit)

recorded on the time tickets. At the end of the week, the clock cards are removed from the rack, and the total hours worked by the employee are calculated and recorded. The cards are then forwarded to payroll, where the pay rate and gross earnings are entered on the clock cards and recorded in the payroll records. The cards are then filed by employee name or number.

Piece-Rate System Production Reports

Individual production reports (Illustration 3-4) are used instead of time tickets when labor costs are calculated using piece rates. A daily report is prepared for each employee that shows work assignments by job number or type of work performed and the total number of units completed. After approval by the supervisor, the report is forwarded to payroll for earnings computation.

Payroll Department

The payroll department's primary responsibility is to compute the wages and salaries earned by the employees. It involves combining the daily wages,

BLOOMINGTON MFG.   INDIVIDUAL
                                 PRODUCTION REPORT

Employee's Name __Marion Laurion__

Clock No. __1070__ Dept. __Finishing__ Date __February 3, 19--__

Job or Type of Work Performed	Number of Units Completed	Rate	Amount
3149	40	.50	20.00
3152	60	.55	33.00
Total			53.00

Signed __Marion Laurion__

                                            Employee

Approved __L. N. F.__

                                            Supervisor

Illustration 3-4   Individual Production Report

determining the total earnings, and calculating deductions and with-holdings for each employee.

The department must maintain current information concerning regulatory requirements regarding wages and salaries, because a stipulated amount of the employees' wages are subject to social security and income tax deductions. Additional deductions, approved by the employee, can be taken for group insurance premiums, union dues, U.S. Savings Bonds, and so on.

Payroll Records.   Forms used to record earnings information may vary considerably from company to company; however, all forms possess some common characteristics. The payroll record, as shown in Illustration 3-5, provides the following information about each employee:

(a)   Marital status
(b)   Number of withholding allowances for income tax purposes
(c)   Rate of pay
(d)   Hours worked per day
(e)   Regular earnings — hours and amount
(f)   Overtime earnings — hours and amount
(g)   Total earnings
(h)   FICA taxable earnings
(i)   Withholdings and deductions — FICA tax, income tax, union dues, etc.
(j)   Net earnings paid — check number and amount

Employee Earnings Records.   In addition to the payroll record, a record is also kept of the earnings for each employee. The employee earnings record (Illustration 3-6) provides the following information:

(a)   Name and social security number
(b)   Sex, date of birth, marital status, and withholding allowances
(c)   Clock number, department, and occupation
(d)   Hourly rate of pay
(e)   Regular hours and amount earned each pay period
(f)   Overtime hours, if any, and amount earned each pay period
(g)   Total regular and overtime earnings each pay period
(h)   Accumulated earnings for the current year
(i)   Amounts withheld each pay period for FICA tax and federal, state, and local income taxes
(j)   Deductions such as health insurance premiums
(k)   Net amount paid to the employee each period and the check number

FOR PERIOD ENDING February 16

19 --

NAME	Clock No.	Marital Status	No. of Allow.	Rate	TIME RECORD M	T	W	T	F	S	S	EARNINGS Regular Hours	AMOUNT	Overtime Hours	AMOUNT	TOTAL EARNINGS
Donovan, P.	1987	M	0	7.00	8	8	8	8	8			40	280 00			280 00
Frey, R.	2403	M	2	8.00	8	8	9	9	8			40	320 00	2	24 00	344 00
Bressler, D.	2316	S	1	7.50	8	7½	8	8	8			39½	296 25			296 25

WITHHOLDINGS FICA Taxable Earnings	FICA Tax	INCOME TAXES Federal	State	Local	DEDUCTIONS Health Insurance	OTHER Item	Amount	NET PAID Check No.	Amount	REMARKS
280 00	22 40	28 00	11 30	5 60	5 00			8441	207 70	
344 00	27 52	25 00	12 40	7 10	5 00	advance	25 00	8442	241 98	
296 25	23 70	35 00	12 00	6 00	5 00			8443	214 55	

Summary of payroll period
on end of

Illustration 3-5   Payroll Record

	19— Period Ending	Regular Rate	Regular Hours	Regular Amount	Overtime Hours	Overtime Amount	Total Earnings	Accum. Total	FICA Tax	Income Taxes Federal	Income Taxes State	Income Taxes Local	Health Ins.	Other	Check No.	Net Paid Amount
1	1/5	7.20	40	288 00			288 00	288 00	23 04	33 70	7 20	4 32	5 00		7911	214 74
2	1/12	7.20	40	288 00	4	43 20	331 20	619 20	26 50	41 00	8 28	4 97			8046	250 45
3	1/19	7.20	40	288 00	4	43 20	331 20	950 40	26 50	41 00	8 28	4 97	5 00		8129	245 45
4	1/26	7.20	40	288 00			288 00	1238 40	23 04	33 70	7 20	4 32		18 75	8203	200 99
5	2/2	7.50	40	300 00	6	67 50	367 50	1605 90	29 40	47 50	9 19	5 51	5 00		8298	270 90
6	2/9	7.50	40	300 00			300 00	1905 90	24 00	35 60	7 50	4 50			8371	228 40
7	2/16	7.50	39½	296 25			296 25	2202 15	23 70	35 00	12 00	6 00	5 00		8443	214 55
8																
9																
10																
11																
12																
13																
Quarter Total																

Sex	Department	Occupation	Social Security No.	Marital Status	No. of Allow.	Name	Clock No.
Ⓜ F	Grinding	Machinist	410-80-7865	S	1	David A. Dressler Date of Birth 4/4/47	2316

Illustration 3-6   Employee Earnings Record

Payroll Summary.   A schedule summarizing gross earnings, the amount of withholdings and deductions, and net earnings is prepared for each payroll period. The schedule, frequently referred to as a payroll summary, is sent to accounting where it serves as the basis for recording the payroll in the voucher register.

Payment of Net Earnings.   The payroll record (Illustration 3-5) prepared by Payroll is sent to the treasurer's department, which is responsible for making the payments to the employees. The earnings may be paid in cash or by check. In either case, a check for the total amount to be paid is drawn to create a special payroll fund from which the employees will be paid.

When checks are to be issued to employees, the check drawn by the company for the total payroll net earnings is deposited in a separate payroll account in the bank. The special account is used only for payroll, and the individual payroll checks, when cashed, are charged to the special account. A new payroll account may be established for each payroll period, numbering the accounts sequentially. The checks drawn for each payroll period can then be identified as belonging to a specific payroll period. This system facilitates the reconciliation of bank statements.

When cash is used to pay the employees, a check is cashed for the total amount of net earnings. The cash is then divided into the amounts earned by individual employees. These cash amounts are placed in envelopes and distributed to the employees. A receipt or signature from the employee acknowledges the payment.

ACCOUNTING FOR LABOR COSTS

For all regular hourly employees, the hours worked should be recorded on a time ticket or individual production report. The time tickets and production reports are sent to payroll on a daily basis. The pay rates and gross earnings are entered, and the reports are forwarded to accounting. Cost accountants sort the time tickets and production reports and charge the labor costs to the appropriate jobs or department and factory overhead. This analysis of labor costs is recorded on a labor cost summary (Illustration 3-7), in the job cost ledger, and in the factory overhead ledger.

Salaried employees, such as department supervisors, are not required to punch time clocks or prepare daily time tickets. A list of salaried employees is sent by payroll to accounting showing the names of employees, the nature

LABOR COST SUMMARY

Dept. *Grinding* _____ Month Ending *May 31, 19--*

Date	Dr. Work in Process (Direct labor-regular time)		Dr. Factory Overhead (Indirect labor and overtime premium)		Cr. Payroll (Total)	
5/14	11,050	00	1,950	00	13,000	00
5/28	13,000	00	2,600	00	15,600	00
5/31	3,900	00	780	00	4,680	00

Illustration 3-7   Labor Cost Summary

of work performed, and the salary. The accounting department records the earnings in factory overhead ledger accounts and on the labor cost summary.

The labor cost summary is used as the source for making a general journal entry to distribute payroll to the appropriate accounts. The entry is then posted to the control accounts, Work in Process and Factory Overhead, in the general ledger. The time tickets and individual production reports have been used to record the labor costs in the subsidiary job cost and factory overhead ledgers and in the labor cost summary. Therefore, the debit to the work in process control account must equal the direct labor cost charged to the jobs, and the charge to the factory overhead control account must equal the labor costs recorded in the factory overhead ledger.

In preparing the labor cost summary from the time tickets, it is important to separate any overtime from an employee's regular time, because the accounting treatment may be different for each type of pay. Regular time worked is charged to jobs. Overtime pay may be charged to jobs, to factory overhead, or allocated partly to jobs and partly to overhead. Overtime distribution depends upon the conditions creating the need for overtime hours.

If an employee works beyond the regularly scheduled time but the employee is paid at the regular hourly rate, the extra pay is called overtime pay. If an additional rate is allowed for the extra hours worked, the additional rate earned is referred to as overtime premium. The premium pay rate is added to the employee's regular rate for the additional hours worked. The premium rate is frequently one-half the regular rate, resulting in a total hourly rate for overtime that is 150 percent of the regular rate. Under these circumstances, overtime pay is often referred to as "time-and-a-half" pay. In some cases, the overtime premium may be equal to or even twice the regular rate, resulting in "double-time" or "triple-time" pay. The double or triple-time pay rates are not as common as the time-and-a-half pay rate.

To illustrate how a payroll is calculated where overtime premium is a factor, assume an employee regularly earns $10 per hour for an 8-hour day. If called upon to work more than 8 hours in a working day, the company pays time-and-a-half for overtime hours. Assuming the employee works 12 hours on Monday, the earnings would be calculated as follows:

Direct labor—8 hours @ $10		$ 80
Direct labor—4 hours @ $10	$40	
Factory overhead (overtime premium)—4 hours @ $5	20	60
Total earnings		$140

If the above employee is paid double-time for the extra hours, the earnings would be:

Direct labor—8 hours @ $10		$ 80
Direct labor—4 hours @ $10	$40	
Factory overhead (overtime premium)—4 hours @ $10	40	80
Total earnings		$160

The preceding analysis shows the regular rate of pay was used to charge Work in Process for the direct labor. The additional rate was used to determine the cost of the overtime hours, and the overtime premium was charged to Factory Overhead. By charging the overtime premium to the factory overhead account, all jobs worked on during the period share the cost of overtime premiums paid. If the job contract stipulated that it was a rush order and the overtime premium resulted from the time limitation in the contract, it would be appropriate to charge the premium pay to the job instead of to a factory overhead account.

Decisions as to charging overtime premiums to jobs or factory overhead should not be made without first considering the consequences. For example, assume that a product requires four hours to finish. During a 12-hour work day, 2 units are completed during the regular 8-hour period at a labor rate of $10 per hour, and 1 unit is completed during the 4-hour overtime period at a labor rate of $15, one-and-a-half times the regular rate of pay.

If the overtime premium is charged to the third unit, the first two units would be charged $40 each for labor, whereas the third unit would be charged with $60 for labor. The conditions creating the need for overtime should be studied to determine the fairness of the labor costs assigned to the completed units. Questions to be answered may include: Was production inefficiency the cause of the overtime? Do all units require the same labor time and skills? Did scheduling require more output for the day than could be produced? Was the third unit a rush order, due to an emergency demand from a customer? If analysis indicates that the overtime is not directly attributable to the third unit, the overtime premium should be charged to the factory overhead account. Otherwise, the cost of the third unit will be overstated.

Employers' Payroll Taxes

Payroll taxes imposed on employers include social security tax and federal and state unemployment taxes. Employers are responsible for periodically reporting and paying the taxes to the appropriate government agencies. Employers who fail to file required reports or pay taxes due are subject to civil, and in some cases, criminal penalties.

The Federal Insurance Contributions Act (FICA) requires employers to pay social security taxes on wages and salaries equal to the amount withheld from employees' earnings. The employers and employees, therefore, share equally in the cost of the social security program. The legislation that governs FICA is frequently amended. These amendments change the wage base subject to FICA and the percentage rate of tax to be charged. For example, in 1980 the tax rate for the employer was 6.13% and the wage base was $25,900. By 1987, the rate had been raised to 7.15% and the base to $43,800. Due to the uncertainty that surrounds both the rate and the base wage, an arbitrary FICA tax rate of 8% will be applied to the first $50,000 of earnings in all discussions, examples, and problems in this text. The selected arbitrary rate and wage base will simplify the tax calculations related to FICA, but they are not predictive of future legislation which may alter the social security system.

The Federal Unemployment Tax Act (FUTA) requires employers to pay an established rate of tax on wages and salaries to provide for compensation to employees if they are laid off from their regular employment. For 1987, employers were subject, under FUTA, to a tax of 6.2% on the first $7,000 of wages or salaries paid to each employee during the calendar year.

Unemployment benefits, however, are actually paid by individual states and not the federal government. The employer's contributions under FUTA are apportioned between the federal and state governments as follows: (a) 0.8% goes to the federal government for administration costs relating to the program and (b) 5.4% goes to the state government to accumulate funds for paying unemployment compensation. Each state has its own unemployment tax laws, although such laws must conform to certain requirements established under FUTA . Both tax rates and wage bases vary among states, and the actual amount of combined federal and state unemployment taxes paid depends on a number of factors. Because of the variation among states and because FUTA taxes are subject to amendments, the examples, exercises, and problems in the text will assume a 4% rate for state taxes and a 1% rate for federal taxes. These tax rates will be applied to the first $8,000 of an employee's annual earnings.

The employer's payroll taxes are directly related to the costs of direct labor and indirect labor, and theoretically should be charged to these categories of labor cost. However, due to the additional expense and time such allocations would require, it is usually more practical to record all factory-related payroll taxes as factory overhead.

Illustration of Accounting for Labor Costs

The Brown Manufacturing Company pays employees every two weeks. Monday, May 1, is the beginning of a new payroll period. The following records are maintained by the company:

(a) Payroll record
(b) Employee earnings records
(c) Voucher register
(d) Check register

(e)   General journal
(f)   General ledger
(g)   Job cost ledger
(h)   Factory overhead ledger

The following general ledger accounts are used in accounting for labor costs:

(a)   Cash
(b)   Work in Process
(c)   Vouchers Payable
(d)   FICA Tax Payable
(e)   Employees Income Tax Payable
(f)   Federal Unemployment Tax Payable
(g)   State Unemployment Tax Payable
(h)   Health Insurance Premiums Payable
(i)   Accrued Payroll
(j)   Payroll
(k)   Factory Overhead
(l)   Administrative Salaries
(m)   Sales Salaries
(n)   Payroll Tax Expense — Administrative Salaries
(o)   Payroll Tax Expense — Sales Salaries

Applicable withholding and payroll tax rates and wage bases are as follows:

| | Rates | | Annual |
	Employee Withholdings	Employer Payroll Taxes	Wages/Salaries Subject to Tax
Federal income tax	Graduated*		100%
FICA	8%	8%	$50,000
Federal unemployment ..		1%	$ 8,000
State unemployment		4%	$ 8,000

*Federal income tax withholdings are determined from tables. State and local income taxes are not shown in this example.

The following payroll summary is prepared by the payroll department and forwarded to accounting for recording:

| | Payroll Summary For the Period May 1–14 | | |
	Factory Employees	Sales and Administrative Employees	Total
Gross earnings...........	$100,000	$30,000	$130,000
Withholdings and deductions:			
FICA tax..............	$ 8,000	$ 2,400	$ 10,400
Income tax............	11,250	3,500	14,750
Health insurance premiums.............	2,100	700	2,800
Total...............	$ 21,350	$ 6,600	$ 27,950
Net earnings	$ 78,650	$23,400	$102,050

After the data are verified, a payroll voucher is authorized and recorded in the voucher register as follows:

```
May 14  Payroll .....................................Gross 130,000
            FICA Tax Payable.......................          10,400
            Employees Income Tax Payable ...........          14,750
            Health Insurance Premiums Payable ........           2,800
            Vouchers Payable.......................         102,050 Net
               To record payroll for the period ending
               May 14.
```

To record the payment of the net earnings to employees, the following entry is required:

```
May 14  Vouchers Payable..........................   102,050
            Cash ..................................              102,050
               To record payment of payroll for the period
               ending May 14.
```

The following schedule provides the information necessary to distribute the total payroll of $130,000 to the appropriate accounts and to record the employer's payroll taxes for the period.

Schedule of Earnings and Payroll Taxes
For Payroll Period, May 1–14

Nonfactory Employees	Gross Earnings	FICA 8%	Unemployment Taxes Federal 1%	Unemployment Taxes State 4%	Total Payroll Taxes
Sales	$ 20,000	$ 1,600	$ 200	$ 800	$ 2,600
Administrative.......	10,000	800	100	400	1,300
	$ 30,000	$ 2,400	$ 300	$1,200	$ 3,900
Factory Employees					
Direct labor:					
Regular	$ 85,000	$ 6,800	$ 850	$3,400	$11,050
Overtime					
Premium	10,000	800	100	400	1,300
Indirect labor	5,000	400	50	200	650
	$100,000	$ 8,000	$1,000	$4,000	$13,000
Total	$130,000	$10,400	$1,300	$5,200	$16,900

The distribution of the payroll and the employer's payroll taxes are recorded as follows:

May 14	Work in Process............................	85,000	
	Factory Overhead..........................	15,000*	
	Sales Salaries.............................	20,000	
	Administrative Salaries.....................	10,000	
	Payroll		130,000
	To distribute payroll for the period ending May 14.		

*Overtime premium ($10,000) + indirect factory labor ($5,000)

May 14	Factory Overhead...........................	13,000	
	Payroll Tax Expense—Sales Salaries..........	2,600	
	Payroll Tax Expense—Administrative Salaries..	1,300	
	FICA Tax Payable.........................		10,400
	Federal Unemployment Tax Payable		1,300
	State Unemployment Tax Payable...........		5,200
	To record employer's payroll taxes for the period ending May 14.		

The general ledger accounts that reflect the entries related to the May 1–14 payroll period are shown on page 127.

Payroll				FICA Tax Payable		
(1)	130,000	(3)	130,000		(1)	10,400
					(4)	10,400

Employees Income Tax Payable				Health Insurance Premiums Payable		
		(1)	14,750		(1)	2,800

Vouchers Payable				Cash		
(2)	102,050	(1)	102,050		(2)	102,050

Work in Process				Factory Overhead		
(3)	85,000			(3)	15,000	
				(4)	13,000	

Sales Salaries				Administrative Salaries		
(3)	20,000			(3)	10,000	

Payroll Tax Expense — Sales Salaries				Payroll Tax Expense — Admin. Salaries		
(4)	2,600			(4)	1,300	

Federal Unemployment Tax Payable				State Unemployment Tax Payable		
		(4)	1,300		(4)	5,200

1. To record payroll
2. To record payment of payroll
3. To record distribution of payroll
4. To record employer's payroll taxes

The next payroll period is May 15 to May 28. At the end of the two-week period, the following schedule for payroll is prepared:

Payroll Summary For the Period May 15–28			
	Factory Employees	Sales and Administrative Employees	Total
Gross earnings..............	$120,000	$30,000	$150,000
Withholdings and deductions:			
FICA tax...................	$ 9,600	$ 2,400	$ 12,000
Income tax................	13,000	3,500	16,500
Health insurance premiums .	2,300	700	3,000
Total	$ 24,900	$ 6,600	$ 31,500
Net earnings	$ 95,100	$23,400	$118,500

The payroll data are verified, and authorization is given for a payroll voucher to be recorded in the voucher register as follows:

```
May 28   Payroll ...................................   150,000
              FICA Tax Payable.........................            12,000
              Employees Income Tax Payable ............            16,500
              Health Insurance Premiums Payable ........             3,000
              Vouchers Payable.........................           118,500
              To record payroll for the period ending
              May 28.
```

To record the payment of the net earnings to employees, the following entry is required:

```
May 28   Vouchers Payable.........................   118,500
              Cash ....................................           118,500
              To record payment of payroll for the period
              ending May 28.
```

The following schedule provides the information necessary to distribute the total payroll of $150,000 to the appropriate accounts and to record the employer's payroll taxes for the period.

Schedule of Earnings and Payroll Taxes
For Payroll Period May 15–28

Nonfactory Employees	Gross Earnings	FICA 8%	Unemployment Taxes Federal 1%	Unemployment Taxes State 4%	Total Payroll Taxes
Sales	$ 20,000	$ 1,600	$ 200	$ 800	$2,600
Administrative.......	10,000	800	100	400	1,300
	$ 30,000	$ 2,400	$ 300	$1,200	$3,900
Factory Employees					
Direct labor:					
Regular............	$100,000	$ 8,000	$1,000	$4,000	$13,000
Overtime premium ..	12,000	960	120	480	1,560
Indirect labor	$ 8,000	640	80	320	1,040
	$120,000	$ 9,600	$1,200	$4,800	$15,600
Total	$150,000	$12,000	$1,500	$6,000	$19,500

The distribution of the payroll and the employer's payroll taxes are recorded as follows:

May 28	Work in Process..........................	100,000	
	Factory Overhead........................	20,000*	
	Sales Salaries...........................	20,000	
	Administrative Salaries...................	10,000	
	Payroll...............................		150,000
	To distribute payroll for the period ending		
	May 28.		

*Overtime premium ($12,000) + indirect factory labor ($8,000)

May 28	Factory Overhead........................	15,600	
	Payroll Tax Expense—Sales		
	Salaries................................	2,600	
	Payroll Tax Expense—		
	Administrative Salaries...................	1,300	
	FICA Tax Payable......................		12,000
	Federal Unemployment Tax		
	Payable..............................		1,500
	State Unemployment Tax		
	Payable..............................		6,000
	To record employer's payroll taxes for the		
	period ending May 28.		

PAYROLL ACCRUAL

When the financial statement date does not coincide with the ending date for a payroll period, an accrual for payroll earnings and payroll tax expense should be made. The accrual computations will not include the employees' withholdings because they do not affect the employer's income or total liabilities to be reported. However, the employer's payroll taxes are accrued to avoid understating the expenses and liabilities for the period.

The next payroll period for the Brown Manufacturing Company begins on May 29 and ends June 11. However, the financial statements to be prepared for May will require an accrual of payroll earnings and taxes for the period May 29–31. The employee earnings and the payroll taxes for the accrual period are shown on page 130, followed by the journal entries required to record and distribute the accrued payroll and to record the employer's payroll taxes.

Schedule of Earnings and Payroll Taxes
For Payroll Period May 29–31

			Unemployment Taxes		
Nonfactory Employees	Gross Earnings	FICA 8%	Federal 1%	State 4%	Total Payroll Taxes
Sales	$ 6,000	$ 480	$ 60	$ 240	$ 780
Administrative.	3,000	240	30	120	390
	$ 9,000	$ 720	$ 90	$ 360	$1,170
Factory Employees					
Direct labor:					
Regular	$30,000	$2,400	$300	$1,200	$3,900
Overtime premium	4,000	320	40	160	520
Indirect labor	2,000	160	20	80	260
	$36,000	$2,880	$360	$1,440	$4,680
Total	$45,000	$3,600	$450	$1,800	$5,850

May 31	Payroll	45,000	
	Accrued Payroll.		45,000
	To record the accrued payroll for May 29–31.		
	Work in Process.	30,000	
	Factory Overhead	6,000*	
	Sales Salaries.	6,000	
	Administrative Salaries.	3,000	
	Payroll		45,000
	To distribute accrued payroll for the period May 29–31.		

*Overtime premium ($4,000) + indirect labor ($2,000)

May 31	Factory Overhead	4,680	
	Payroll Tax Expense—Sales Salaries.	780	
	Payroll Tax Expense—Administrative Salaries. .	390	
	FICA Tax Payable		3,600
	Federal Unemployment Tax Payable		450
	State Unemployment Tax Payable.		1,800
	To record employer's payroll taxes for the period May 29–31.		

Before June transactions are recorded, the entry for accruing payroll should be reversed:

June 1	Accrued Payroll	45,000	
	Payroll.		45,000
	To reverse May 31 adjusting entry for accrued payroll.		

The amount earned by the employees during the May 29–31 period is a portion of the total costs and expenses for production, sales, and administration for the month of May. However, the employees will not be paid until June 11 for the payroll period from May 29 to June 11. The credit balance in the payroll account, created by the reversing entry, will assure that only the payroll costs accumulated during the June 1 to June 11 period will be included in the June production, sales, and administrative costs.

Payroll					FICA Tax Payable	
May 14	130,000	May 14	130,000		May 14	10,400
28	150,000	28	150,000		14	10,400
31	45,000	31	45,000		28	12,000
	325,000	June 1	45,000		28	12,000
			370,000		31	3,600
			45,000			*48,400*

Employees Income Tax Payable			Health Insurance Premiums Payable	
	May 14	14,750	May 1	2,800
	28	16,500	28	3,000
		31,250		*5,800*

Vouchers Payable				Cash	
May 14	102,050	May 14	102,050	May 14	102,050
28	118,500	28	118,500	28	118,500

Work in Process			Factory Overhead	
May 14	85,000		May 14	15,000
28	100,000		14	13,000
31	30,000		28	20,000
	215,000		28	15,600
			31	6,000
			31	4,680
				74,280

	Accrued Payroll		
June 1	45,000	May 31	45,000

	Administrative Salaries	
May 14	10,000	
28	10,000	
31	3,000	
	23,000	

	Sales Salaries	
May 14	20,000	
28	20,000	
31	6,000	
	46,000	

Payroll Tax Expense— Administrative Salaries		
May 14	1,300	
28	1,300	
31	390	
	2,990	

Payroll Tax Expense—Sales Salaries		
May 14	2,600	
28	2,600	
31	780	
	5,980	

	State Unemployment Tax Payable	
		May 14	5,200
		28	6,000
		31	1,800
			13,000

Federal Unemployment Tax Payable		
		May 14	1,300
		28	1,500
		31	450
			3,250

Summary of Labor Costing Procedures

Illustrations 3-8 and 3-9 summarize the labor cost accounting procedures and forms which are commonly used in payroll systems. These brief summaries are useful to recall when a specific technique or form should be used in reporting payroll costs.

SPECIAL LABOR COST PROBLEMS

An employer may be required to account for a variety of labor-related costs that do not fall into the normal routine of accounting for payroll costs. These special labor-related cost problems may include shift premiums, pensions, guaranteed annual wages, bonuses, and vacation and holiday pay. If encountered, each of these costs should be systematically recorded and recognized as a cost of the production process.

Shift Premium

A work shift is defined as a regularly scheduled work period for a designated number of hours. If a company divides each work day into two

Transaction	Source of Data	Book of Original Entry	General Ledger Entry
Recording wages and salaries	Payroll summary	Voucher register	Payroll (gross earnings for payroll.) FICA Tax Payable Employees Income Tax Payable Health Insurance Premiums Payable Vouchers Payable (net amount payable to employees)
Paying wages and salaries	Voucher	Check register	Vouchers Payable Cash
Distributing wages and salaries	Labor cost summary	General journal	Work in Process (direct labor) Factory Overhead (indirect labor and overtime premium) Administrative Salaries Sales Salaries Payroll
Recording payroll taxes imposed on the employer	Schedule of earnings and payroll taxes	General journal	Factory Overhead (taxes on factory labor) Payroll Tax Expense—Administrative Salaries Payroll Tax Expense—Sales Salaries FICA Tax Payable Federal Unemployment Tax Payable State Unemployment Tax Payable

Illustration 3-8   Summary of Payroll Transactions

or three 8-hour shifts, the employees working on shifts other than the regular daytime shift may receive additional pay, which is called a **shift premium.** For example, assume the company operates three shifts: day shift, 8 a.m. to 4 p.m.; evening shift, 4 p.m. to 12 p.m.; night shift, 12 p.m. to 8 a.m. The company pays an additional $1.00 per hour to employees who work the evening shift and an additional $1.50 per hour to workers on the night shift. The additional payroll costs for the shift premiums do not increase the productivity of the shifts but are paid because of the social and other life-style adjustments required of the late shift workers. The "other-than-normal" sleep and work schedules deprive the workers from participating in the normal, established social activities and routines. The shift premiums are designed to attract workers to the later shifts

Name of Form and Illustration Number	When Prepared	By Whom Prepared	Purpose	How Used
Clock Card Illus. 3-1	On entering and leaving factory.	Employees	Shows length of time, regular and overtime, spent in factory or office.	Provides a check on the accuracy of the number of hours reported on time tickets and as a means of employee control. Used by payroll clerk for computing employees' earnings and recording the data in the payroll record and employee earnings record.
Time Ticket Illus. 3-2 or 3-3 Individual Production Report Illus. 3-4	During each working day.	Timekeeper or employees under supervisor	Shows how employee spends time in factory.	Timekeeper reconciles with hours shown on clock card. Payroll clerk enters pay rates and gross earnings. Cost accountant uses as source of data for labor cost summary and for posting to the job cost ledger and factory overhead ledger.
Schedule of Fixed Salaries (for factory employees)	Usually once a year (unless salaries are changed during year).	Payroll clerk	Provides a ready source of the amount payable to those employees who do not prepare time tickets and clock cards.	Source of data on fixed salaries to be entered in the payroll record and in the employee earnings record. Cost accountant uses as source of data for labor cost summary and for posting to the factory overhead ledger.
Payroll Record Illus. 3-5	At end of payroll period from clock cards and schedule of fixed salaries.	Payroll clerk	Shows by payroll periods, amounts earned, deductions, and net amounts payable.	Source of information for preparing payroll vouchers. Basis for preparing individual payroll checks or pay envelopes.
Employee Earnings Record Illus. 3-6	At end of payroll period from payroll record.	Payroll clerk	Shows for each employee a permanent, continuous record of earnings while with company.	Provides permanent record of each employee's earnings. Satisfies requirement of FICA and income tax laws as to record keeping. Basis for preparing payroll tax returns.
Labor Cost Summary Illus. 3-7	Daily from time tickets and at end of payroll period from schedule of fixed salaries.	Cost accountants	Classifies total factory wages between regular time and overtime and between direct and indirect.	Source of amounts to be charged to Work in Process and Factory Overhead in the general ledger.

Illustration 3-9   Summary of Labor Cost Accounting Forms

scheduled by a company. In reality, even though later shift workers are paid at higher rates, the productivity level of the day workers usually exceeds the productivity of the higher paid, late-shift employees. In order to avoid a distortion in worker productivity, shift premiums are usually charged to Factory Overhead. However, due to the unproductive nature of shift premiums, they may instead be charged to a separate nonfactory account which is closed to Income Summary.

Shift premiums that are charged to Factory Overhead become a part of the cost assigned to a manufactured product. Therefore, if inventories remain at the end of an accounting period, the cost of such inventories, including the shift premium, is deferred as a product cost to the next period. The deferral of the cost will increase the reported net income of the current period. If the shift premium is charged instead to a separate nonfactory account that is then closed into Income Summary, the total cost for shift premiums is charged to the period in which the shift premiums were incurred. All premium costs are charged to the current period and the product cost remains unaffected by the shift premiums paid. The method chosen to classify the additional costs for shift premiums will directly affect the net income reported. However, if such costs are negligible, they may be deemed immaterial and not given any special consideration. It is generally considered acceptable to charge shift premiums to Factory Overhead on the premise that such costs result directly from manufacturing activities and are somewhat similar to overtime premium payments.

Employee Pension Costs

Pension costs originate from an agreement between a company and its employee group whereby the company promises to provide income to employees after they retire. The amount of pension benefits paid to a retired employee is commonly based on the employee's past level of earnings and length of service with the company. Some plans are completely funded (paid for) by the company, while others require a partial contribution from the employee. When a pension plan is initiated by a company, the plan is usually retroactive and recognizes the previous years of each employee's service with the company.

A basic provision of all plans is to systematically accrue, over the period of active service, the total estimated pension cost from the beginning date of the pension plan to the employee's retirement date. The pension costs related to the factory employees could be charged to general or administrative expenses under the premise that the cost of pensions is beneficial to the company as a whole. However, it is also considered appropriate to charge pension costs directly to the individual employee's department or to apportion the cost of pensions, using a percentage of total payroll, to all departments within the company. A percentage allocation plan would seem to be the most desirable to avoid charging the highest pension costs to those departments that employ the oldest workers.

Guaranteed Annual Wage

Guaranteed annual wage (GAW) plans assure the employees a guaranteed level of earnings over a stipulated period of weeks or months, even though the company experiences a shutdown. Companies with such a plan usually feel that sometime in the future, they will experience a layoff situation and be required to pay wages under the GAW plan. Therefore, recognition of this contingency can be made by establishing a GAW liability account for accumulating the anticipated cost of such an occurrence. A plan may be established which requires that a stipulated amount be set aside for each hour worked by an employee. The factory overhead account is debited for the hourly cost and a GAW liability account is credited.

To illustrate, assume a weekly payroll for 2,000 hours amounts to $15,000. If a GAW plan requires $.50 per hour to be recognized as a liability, the entry would be:

Work in Process	15,000	
Factory Overhead	1,000	
Payroll		15,000
GAW Liability		1,000
To distribute payroll and record the GAW liability for 2,000 hours @ $.50 per hour.		

Assume the company accumulated the GAW liability for 10 years and the liability total was $5,000,000 when a layoff occurred. If payment for one week under the GAW plan is $50,000, the following entry would be made:

GAW Liability	50,000	
Cash		50,000
Payment to employees under GAW agreement.		

Bonuses

Employees may receive bonus pay for a variety of reasons, such as higher-than-usual company profits, exceeding departmental quotas for selling or production, or for any other achievement that the company feels merits additional pay. Bonus plans may include some or all employees. The cost of bonuses is generally charged to the department in which the employee works. Therefore, factory workers' bonuses are charged to factory overhead and sales employees' bonuses are charged to selling expense.

Vacation and Holiday Pay

All permanent employees of a company expect a vacation period each year that will be paid for by their employer. Usually the vacation pay is earned gradually by the employee for daily service on the job.

Vacation plans generally stipulate that an employee will be granted a specified period of paid vacation time each year for services rendered during the year. The vacation cost is accrued throughout the year and assigned to the employee's department. For example, assume an employee earns $600 per week and is entitled to a 4-week vacation. The total cost of the vacation to the company would be $2,400. Each week, the employee's department would be charged $50 ($2,400/48 weeks) for vacation pay expense.

Holiday pay is based on an agreement between management and company employees which stipulates that certain holidays during the year will be paid for by the company but are nonworking days for the employees.

Accounting for Bonuses, Vacations, and Holiday Pay

To illustrate accounting for bonuses, vacations, and holiday pay, assume a factory worker earns $700 each week. In addition, the worker will receive a $1,000 bonus at year end, a 4-week paid vacation, and 10 paid holidays. The entry to record the weekly payroll and the costs and liabilities related to the bonus, vacation, and holiday pay would be as follows:

Work in Process	700.00	
Factory Overhead (Bonus)*	19.23	
Factory Overhead (Vacation)**	58.33	
Factory Overhead (Holiday)***	26.92	
Payroll		700.00
Bonus Liability		19.23
Vacation Pay Liability		58.33
Holiday Pay Liability		26.92

*Bonus—$1,000/52 weeks = $19.23 per week.
**Vacation Pay—$700 × 4 weeks = $2,800/48 = $58.33 per week.
***Holiday Pay—$700/5 = $140 per day × 10 = $1,400
$1,400/52 weeks = $26.92 per week.

KEY TERMS

Bonus pay (136)
Clock card (112)
Direct labor (107)
Employee earnings record (116)
Federal Insurance Contributions
   Act (FICA) (122)
Federal Unemployment Tax Act
   (FUTA) (123)
Guaranteed annual wage (GAW)
   (136)
Holiday pay (137)
Hourly-rate plan (108)
Incentive wage (110)
Indirect labor (107)
Individual production report (115)
Labor cost summary (119)

Make-up guarantee (110)
Modified wage plan (109)
Overtime pay (121)
Overtime premium (121)
Payroll department (112)
Payroll record (116)
Payroll summary (119)
Payroll taxes (122)
Pension costs (135)
Piece-rate plan (109)
Shift premium (133)
Timekeeping department (111)
Time ticket (112)
Vacation pay (137)
Work shift (132)

QUESTIONS

1. Distinguish between direct and indirect labor.
2. State briefly the advantages and disadvantages of (a) the hourly-rate wage plan and (b) the piece-rate wage plan.
3. What is an incentive-wage plan?
4. What are the functions of the timekeeping and payroll departments?
5. The timekeeping and payroll departments are expected to operate, to a degree, independently of each other. Discuss why this independence is important.
6. (a) In a payroll system, what purpose is served by the clock card and time ticket? (b) How is the information recorded on clock cards and time tickets used?
7. How do the clock cards and time tickets complement each other?
8. Although payroll records may vary in design, what types of employee data would be found in the payroll records of most manufacturing companies?
9. What is the source for posting direct labor cost to (a) individual accounts in the job cost ledger and (b) the work in process account in the general ledger?
10. What is the source for posting indirect labor cost to the indirect labor account in the factory overhead ledger?
11. In accounting for labor costs, what is the distinction between regular pay and overtime premium pay?

12. Maintaining internal control over labor cost is necessary for a cost accounting system to function effectively. What are the internal control procedures regarding the charge to the work in process account and the credit to the payroll account in the general ledger?

13. What accounts are used to record employees' withholdings and the employer's payroll taxes?

14. Summarize the procedures involved in accounting for labor cost, and name the supporting forms used for each procedure.

15. For each of the following, identify the sources of data and the books of original entry:
    (a) recording the wages and salaries earned during the payroll period.
    (b) paying the wages and salaries earned.
    (c) recording the payroll taxes imposed on the employer.

16. What is a shift premium?

17. What is a basic requirement in all pension plans?

18. What is the major purpose of a guaranteed annual wage plan?

19. What accounting treatments do factory bonuses, vacation pay, and holiday pay for employees have in common?

EXERCISES

NOTE: For the exercises and problems in this chapter, use the following tax rates:
FICA—Employer and employee, 8% of the first $50,000 of earnings per employee per calendar year.
State unemployment—4% of the first $8,000 of earnings per employee per calendar year.
FUTA—1% of the first $8,000 of earnings per employee per calendar year.
Federal income tax withholding—10% of each employee's gross earnings, unless otherwise stated.

Exercise 3-1   Payroll taxes.

The Lavendor Company paid wages to its employees during the year as follows:

Brooks	$11,400
Coombs	12,700
Durkins	9,000
Evans	19,300
Hull	29,200
Massey	32,100
Oliver	62,700
Sanders	75,000

(a) How much of the total payroll is exempt from FICA tax?
(b) How much of the total payroll is exempt from federal and state unem-
     ployment taxes?

Exercise 3-2 Computing payroll earnings and taxes.

  J. Blum of the Chelsa Manufacturing Co., is paid at the rate of $10 an hour
for an 8-hour day, with time and a half for overtime and double time for Sundays
and holidays. Regular employment is on the basis of 40 hours a week — five
days a week. The regular workday is from 7:00 a.m. to 12:00 noon and from
12:30 p.m. to 3:30 p.m. At the end of a week the clock card shows:

	A. M.		P. M.		Overtime	
	In	Out	In	Out	In	Out
Sunday	8:00	12:00				
Monday	6:58	12:01	12:25	3:35		
Tuesday	7:00	12:03	12:28	3:32		
Wednesday	6:56	12:02	12:30	3:33		
Thursday	6:55	12:05	12:28	3:35	6:00	9:30
Friday	6:55	12:01	12:29			6:32
Saturday	6:55			1:30		

  On Monday through Friday night, Blum worked on the production line. The
hours worked on Saturday and Sunday were used to repair machinery.
(a) Compute Blum's total earnings for the week. (Ignore odd minutes).
(b) Present the journal entry to distribute Blum's total earnings.

Exercise 3-3 Computing payroll taxes.

  Using the earnings data developed in Exercise 2, and assuming that this
was the first week of employment for J. Blum with the Chelsa Manufacturing
Co., prepare the journal entries to:
(a) record the week's payroll.
(b) record payment of the payroll.
(c) record the employer's payroll taxes.

Note: These single journal entries are for the purpose of illustrating the principle involved. Normally the entries would be made for the total factory payroll plus the administrative and sales payroll.

Exercise 3-4 Computing payroll taxes.

  Using the earnings data developed in Exercise 2, and assuming that this
was the tenth week of employment for Blum and that the previous earnings to
date were $7,900, prepare the journal entries to:

(a)   record the week's payroll.
(b)   record payment of the payroll.
(c)   record the employer's payroll taxes.

Exercise 3-5   Computing payroll taxes.

Using the earnings data developed in Exercise 2, and assuming that this was the fiftieth week of employment for Blum and that the previous earnings to date were $49,800 prepare the journal entries to:
(a)   record the week's payroll.
(b)   record payment of the payroll.
(c)   record the employer's payroll taxes.

Exercise 3-6   Determining payroll earnings.

The J. T. Street Co. requires all factory workers to record the time of arrival and departure by means of a time clock. The company operates on a forty-hour basis, time and a half allowed for overtime. The regular work day is from 8:30 a.m. to 12:00 noon and from 1:00 p.m. to 5:00 p.m., Monday through Friday, and from 8:30 a.m. to 11:50 a.m. on Saturday.

The clock card record of a group of employees for Monday, is as follows:

Employee No.	Morning In	Noon Out	Noon In	Night Out	Extra In	Extra Out
51	8:19	12:10	12:51	4:57		
52	8:30	12:01	12:56	4:58		
53	8:21	12:05				
54	8:20	12:02	12:57	4:53		
55	8:24	12:04	12:57	4:50		
56	8:29	12:04	12:53	4:57		
57	8:25	12:04				
58	8:27	12:00	12:48	4:56		
59	8:28	12:01	12:57			6:50
60	8:26	12:03	12:56			5:20
61	8:26	12:05	12:59	4:58		
62	8:23	12:00	12:52	4:59	5:30	9:30

(a)   Compute the regular and overtime hours for each employee for the day. (Ignore odd minutes).
(b)   Assuming that all of the above employees are paid at the rate of $9.20 an hour, compute the amount of each employee's earnings for the day.

Exercise 3-7 Payroll distribution.

The total wages and salaries earned by all employees of The Hogue Manufacturing Co. during the month of June as shown in the labor cost summary and the schedule of fixed administrative and sales salaries are classified as follows:

Direct labor..	$625,125
Indirect labor...	62,120
Administrative salaries................................	140,200
Sales salaries..	172,500
Total wages earned	$999,945

(a) Prepare a journal entry to distribute the wages earned during June.
(b) What is the total amount of payroll taxes that will be imposed on the employer for the above payroll, assuming that none of the employees has achieved the maximums for FICA and unemployment taxes?

Exercise 3-8 Overtime allocation.

The Robbins Machine Tool Co. produces tools on a job order basis. During May, two jobs were completed, and the following costs were incurred:

	Job 401	Job 402
Direct materials	$28,000	$37,000
Direct labor: regular.........................	18,000	23,000
overtime premium	—	6,000

Other factory costs for the month totaled $16,800. Factory overhead costs are allocated one-third to Job 401 and two-thirds to Job 402.
(a) Describe two alternative methods for assigning costs to Jobs 401 and 402 and explain how the appropriate method would be determined.
(b) Compute the cost of Job 401 and Job 402 under each of the two methods described in (a).

Exercise 3-9 Employees' earnings and taxes.

A weekly payroll summary made from time tickets shows the following data:

		Hourly	Hours	
Employee	Classification	Rate	Regular	Overtime
Abbott, A.	Direct	$12	40	2
Hacker, B.	Direct	12	40	3
Smythe, C.	Direct	15	40	4
Tomas, D.	Indirect	6	40	
Walters, E.	Indirect	6	40	

Overtime is payable at one-and-a-half times the regular rate of pay for an employee.
(a) Determine the net pay of each employee. The income taxes withheld for each employee amount to 15% of the gross wages.
(b) Prepare journal entries for:
1. recording the payroll.
2. payment of the payroll.
3. distribution of the payroll.
4. the employer's payroll taxes. Assume that none of the employees has achieved the maximum wage bases for FICA and unemployment taxes.

Exercise 3-10   Employees' earnings using hourly and piece-rate methods.

The payroll records of Great Northern Manufacturing Co. show the following information for the week ended August 17:

Employee	Classification	Hours Worked	Production (Units)	Hourly Rate	Piece Rate	Weekly Rate	Income Tax Withheld
Charles, A.	Direct	42		$9.00			$40
Donn, B.	Direct	48		8.80			42
Johns, C.	Direct	39	2,000		$.22		55
Peter, D.	Direct	40	1,800		.22		50
Pope, E.	Indirect	40				$200	25
Swen, F.	Indirect	40				400	60
Wojo, G.	Indirect	40				350	30

Hourly workers are paid time-and-a-half for overtime.
(a) Determine the net earnings of each employee.
(b) Prepare the journal entries for:
1. recording the payroll.
2. paying the payroll.
3. distributing the payroll.
4. recording the employer's payroll taxes. Assume that none of the employees has achieved the maximum wage bases for FICA and unemployment taxes.

Exercise 3-11   Journal entries for payroll.

A partial summary of the payroll data for The Vaporaire Manufacturing Co. for each week of June is as follows:

	June 7	June 14	June 21	June 28
Total earnings	$36,500	$34,200	$37,300	$38,400
Deductions:				
FICA tax, 8%	$?	$?	$?	$?
Income tax	4,215	4,120	4,320	4,410
Health insurance..	600	600	600	600
Total deductions	$?	$?	$?	$?
Net earnings........	$?	$?	$?	$?

(a) Compute the missing amounts in the summary.
(b) For each payroll perod, prepare journal entries to (1) record the payroll and (2) record the payments to employees.

PROBLEMS

Problem 3-1 Computing and journalizing employer's payroll taxes.

The following form is used by The Westville Manufacturing Co. to compute payroll taxes incurred during the month of June.

Classification of Wages and Salaries	Total Earnings for Month	FICA Tax 8%	Unemployment Taxes		Total Payroll Taxes Imposed on Employer
			Federal Tax 1%	State Tax 4%	
Direct labor.........	88,180				
Indirect labor	16,220				
Total taxes on factory wages					
Administrative salaries	12,000				
Sales salaries.......	11,500				
Total payroll taxes...					

Required:
1. Using the above form, calculate the employer's payroll taxes for June. Assume that none of the employees has achieved the maximums for FICA and unemployment taxes.
2. Assuming that the payroll taxes imposed on the employer covering factory wages are treated as factory overhead, the taxes covering administrative salaries as an administrative expense, and the taxes covering sales salaries as a selling expense, prepare a general journal entry to record the employer's liability for the June payroll taxes.

Problem 3-2 Payroll for piece-rate wage system.

The Georgia Manufacturing Company operates on a piece-rate wage system. During one week's operation, the following direct labor costs were incurred.

Employee	Piece Rate per 100 Units	Units Completed				
		M	T	W	T	F
A. Boye	$.45	6,800	7,100	6,500	8,000	4,800
B. Cool	.55	6,300	6,400	2,900	2,800	7,000
C. Smith	.65	6,200	6,100	7,100	6,000	2,800

The above employees are machine operators. Piece rates vary with the kind of product being produced. A minimum of $30 per day is guaranteed each employee by union contract.

Required:
1. Compute Boye's, Cool's, and Smith's earnings for the week.
2. Prepare journal entries to:
   (a) Record the week's payroll.
   (b) Record payment of the payroll.
   (c) Record the employer's share of payroll taxes, assuming none of the employees have achieved the maximum base wage for FICA or unemployment taxes.

Problem 3-3 Payment and distribution of payroll.

The general ledger of the Allerton Manufacturing Company showed the following credit balances on July 15.

FICA Tax Payable	$ 336
Employees Income Tax Payable	1,750
FUTA Tax Payable.	42
State Unemployment Tax Payable.	168

Direct labor earnings amounted to $5,100 from July 16 to July 31. Income tax of $1,285 was withheld from the wages. The sales and administrative salaries for the same period amounted to $1,500, from which $200 was withheld for income taxes.

Required:
1. Prepare the journal entries to:
    (a) record the payroll voucher.
    (b) pay the payroll voucher.
    (c) record the employer's payroll tax liability.
    (d) distribute the payroll for July 16 to 31.
2. Prepare the journal entries to record the payment of the amounts due for the month for FICA and income tax withholdings.
3. Calculate the amount of total earnings for the period from July 1 to July 15.

Problem 3-4   Payroll computation with incentive bonus.

Fifteen workers are assigned to a group project. The production standard calls for 500 units to be completed each hour to meet a customer's set deadline for the products. If the required units can be delivered before the target date on the order, a substantial premium for early delivery will be paid by the customer. The company, wishing to encourage the workers to produce beyond the established standard, has offered a bonus that will be added to each project employee's pay for excess production. The bonus is to be computed as follows:

(a) $\dfrac{\text{Group's excess production over standard}}{\text{Standard units for week}} \times 50\% = \text{bonus percentage}$

(b) Individual's hourly wage rate × bonus percentage = hourly bonus rate
(c) Hourly wage rate + hourly bonus rate = new hourly rate for week
(d) Total hours worked × new hourly rate = earnings for week

The average wage rate for the project workers is $8 per hour. The production record for the week shows:

	Hours Worked	Production (Units)
Monday	112	61,040
Tuesday	112	60,032
Wednesday	112	60,480
Thursday	112	65,632
Friday	108	57,344
Saturday	60	26,000
	616	330,528

Required:
1. Determine the rate and the total amount of the bonus for the week.
2. What are the total wages of S. Bassett, who worked 40 hours at a base rate of $8 per hour?
3. What are the total wages of M. Beth, who worked 35 hours at a base rate of $9 per hour?

Problem 3-5   Payroll work sheet and journal entries.

The payroll records of the Ridgefarm Corporation for the week ending October 7, the fortieth week in the year, show the following:

Employee	Classification	Pay Rate per 40-Hour Week	Hours Worked	Income Tax Withheld	Gross Earnings up to Fortieth Week
Coster	President	$1,500	40	$300	$58,500
Davis	Vice-President	1,275	40	240	49,725
Evans	Supervisor	700	40	180	27,300
Frank	Factory—Direct	500	48	150	19,820
Gregg	Factory—Direct	400	46	160	17,200
Haynes	Factory—Direct	400	44	110	16,600
Porter	Factory—Direct	380	42	120	15,200
Revoz	Factory—Indirect	300	42	80	13,200
Stover	Factory—Indirect	300	42	60	12,950

Required:
1. Complete a work sheet with the following column headings:
    Employee
    3 columns for Earnings for Week:
       Use one for Regular Pay
       Use one for Overtime Premium Pay
       Use one for Total for Week
    Total Earnings through Fortieth Week
    FICA Taxable Earnings
    FICA—8%
    Income Tax Withheld
    Net Earnings
2. Prepare journal entries for:
    (a) payroll for fortieth week.
    (b) payment of payroll for week.
    (c) distribution of the payroll.
    (d) employer's payroll tax liability.

3. The company carries a disability insurance policy for the employees at a cost of $7.80 per week for each employee. Journalize the employer's cost of insurance premiums for the week.

Problem 3-6   Piece-rate and incentive-wage plans.

The Rigwood Company employs seven workers in its factory. The union contract provides that the minimum wage for a worker is the base rate, which is also paid for any "down time" when the worker's machine is under repair. The standard work week is 40 hours. The union contract also provides that workers be paid time and a half for overtime. In addition to these provisions, the following incentive wage plans are in effect:

(a)   Straight piece-rate. The worker is paid at the rate of $.80 per unit produced.
(b)   Percentage bonus plan. Standard quantities of production per hour are established by the engineering department. The worker's average hourly production, determined from total hours worked and production, is divided by the standard hourly production to determine a percentage. This percentage (if greater than 100%) is then applied to the worker's base rate to determine hourly earnings for the period.
(c)   Efficiency bonus. A minimum wage is paid for production up to 66⅔% of the standard output or "efficiency." When the worker's production exceeds 66⅔% of the standard output, a bonus rate is paid. The bonus is determined from the following table:

Efficiency	Bonus
Under 66⅔%	0%
66⅔%–79%	10%
80%–99%	20%
100%–125%	45%

A weekly payroll for the workers shows the following:

Worker	Incentive Wage Plan	Total Hours	Down Time Hours	Units Produced	Standard Units	Base Rate
James	Straight piece-rate	40	5	400	—	$3.50
Lang	Straight piece-rate	46	—	455(1)	—	3.50
Briggs	Straight piece-rate	44	4	420(2)	—	3.50
Bando	Percentage bonus	40	—	250	200	4.00
Johnson	Percentage bonus	40	—	180	200	3.80
O'Toole	Efficiency bonus	40	—	240	300	3.90
Spang	Efficiency bonus	40	2	590	600(3)	3.70

(1)   Includes 45 pieces produced during the 6 overtime hours.
(2)   Includes 50 pieces produced during the 4 overtime hours. The overtime, which was brought about by the "down time," was necessary to meet a production deadline.
(3)   Standard units for 40 hours production.

Required:

Compute each individual's gross wages, applying the contract provisions and incentive wage plans.   *(AICPA adapted)*

Problem 3-7   Payroll calculation and distribution; overtime and idle time.

A rush order was accepted by the Ty-Nee Trailer Company for five trailers. The time tickets and clock cards for the week ended March 27 show the following:

Time Tickets — Hour Distribution

Employees	Clock Hours	Trailer #1	Trailer #2	Trailer #3	Trailer #4	Trailer #5
Amos (Supervisor)	42					
Brown	45	10	10	10	10	5
Calvin	48	24	24			
Davis	48			24	24	
Sweet	45	15	15	15		
Thomas	42	24	8			
Vendor	40	20	10			

All employees are paid $10.00 per hour, except Amos, who receives $15 per hour. All overtime premium pay except Amos' is chargeable to the job and all employees, including Amos, receive time and a half for overtime hours.

Required:

1. Calculate the total payroll and total net earnings for the week. Assume that an 18% deduction for federal income tax is required in addition to FICA deductions. Assume that none of the employees has achieved the maximums for FICA and unemployment taxes. Hours not worked on trailers are idle time and are not charged to the job.
2. Prepare the journal entries to record and pay the payroll.
3. Prepare the journal entry to distribute the payroll to the appropriate accounts.
4. Determine the dollar amount of labor that is chargeable to each trailer, assuming the overtime costs are proportionate to the regular hours used on the trailers.

Problem 3-8   Allocating overtime premium and bonus costs.

The Medina Manufacturing Company uses a job order cost system to cost its products. It recently signed a new contract with the union that calls for time and a half for all work over 40 hours a week and double time for Saturday and Sunday. Also, a bonus of 1% of the employees' earnings for the year is to be paid to the employees at the end of the fiscal year. The controller, the plant manager, and the sales manager disagree as to how the overtime pay and the bonus should be allocated.

An examination of the first month's payroll under the new union contract provisions shows the following:

Direct labor:		
Regular — 40,200 hours @ '$10		$402,000
Overtime:		
Weekdays — 1,700 hours @ $15	$25,500	
Saturdays — 400 hours @ $20	8,000	
Sundays — 300 hours @ $20	6,000	39,500
Indirect labor		14,800
		$456,300

Analysis of the payroll supporting documents revealed:
(a) More production was scheduled each day than could be handled in a regular work day, resulting in the need for overtime.
(b) The Saturday and Sunday hours resulted from rush orders with special contract arrangements with the customers.

The controller believes that the overtime premiums and the bonus should be charged to factory overhead and spread over all production of the accounting period, regardless of when the jobs were completed.

The plant manager favors charging the overtime premiums directly to the jobs worked on during overtime hours and the bonus to administrative expense.

The sales manager states that the overtime premiums and bonus are not factory costs chargeable to regular production but are costs created from administrative policies and, therefore, should be charged only to administrative expense.

Required:
1. Evaluate each position — the controller's, the plant manager's, and the sales manager's. If you disagree with all of the positions taken, present your view of the appropriate allocation.
2. Prepare the journal entries to illustrate the position you support.

Problem 3-9   Calculating payroll and correcting payroll and tax accounts.

A company's controller has requested a review of the financial statements regarding wage and salary tax computations. The company's general ledger accounts for salary and payroll taxes are as follows:

Employees FICA and Income Taxes Payable	
	19A Jan. 1 Balance forward 6,200

Employers FICA and Unemployment Taxes Payable	
	19A Jan. 1 Balance forward 1,900

Wages and Salary Expense	
19A Dec. 31 Total of 12 monthly summary entries 65,980	

Payroll Taxes Expense	
19A Jan. 10 Quarterly payment 7,348 Apr. 20 Quarterly payment 10,896 July 14 Quarterly payment 10,340 Oct. 18 Quarterly payment 10,128	

An investigation reveals the following additional data:

(a)   Copies of the quarterly tax returns are not available, because the typist did not understand that the returns were to be typed in duplicate. The pencil drafts of the tax returns were discarded.

(b)   The payroll records reveal that the payroll clerk properly computed the payroll tax deductions and the amounts of quarterly remittances. The following summary is developed:

Quarter	Gross Wages and Salaries	Taxes Withheld FICA 8%	Taxes Withheld Income Tax	Net Wages and Salaries
First	$23,600	$1,888	$6,200	$15,512
Second	22,000	1,760	6,100	14,140
Third	22,800	1,824	6,000	14,976
Fourth	28,700	1,200	6,900	20,600

(c)   The company did not make monthly deposits of taxes withheld. The following remittances were made with respect to 19A payrolls:

	Apr. 20, 19A	July 14, 19A	Oct. 18, 19A	Jan. 12, 19B
FICA — 16%	$ 3,776	$ 3,520	$ 3,648	$2,400
Income tax	6,200	6,100	6,000	6,900
State unemployment tax — 4.0%	920	720	480	240
Total................	$10,896	$10,340	$10,128	$9,540

(d)   The federal unemployment tax rate for 19A is 1.0% on salaries and wages up to a maximum of $8,000.

Required:

1. Prepare a work sheet to determine the correct balances at December 31, 19A, for the general ledger accounts, Wages and Salary Expense, Payroll Taxes Expense, Employees' FICA and Income Taxes Payable, and Employer's FICA and Unemployment Taxes Payable. (Disregard accrued wages and salaries at year-end.)
2. Prepare an adjusting entry to correct the accounts at December 31, 19A.

(AICPA adapted)

Problem 3-10   Estimating labor costs for bids.

The Maree Manufacturing Company prepares cost estimates for projects on which it will bid. In order to anticipate the labor cost to be included in a request to bid on a contract for 1,200,000 units which will be delivered to the customer at the rate of 100,000 units per month, the company has compiled the following data related to labor:

(a) The first 100,000 units will require 5 hours per unit.
(b) The second 100,000 units will require less labor due to the skills learned on the first 100,000 units finished. It is expected that labor time will be reduced by 10% if an incentive bonus of one-half of the labor savings is paid to the employees.
(c) For the remaining 1,000,000 it is expected that the labor time will be reduced 15% from the original estimate (the first 100,000 units) if the same incentive bonus (½ of the savings) is paid to the employees.
(d) Overtime premiums are to be excluded when savings are computed.

The contract will require 2,500 employees at a base rate of $10.00 per hour with time and a half for overtime. The plant operates on a 5-day, 40-hour-per-week basis. Employees are paid for a two-week vacation in August and for eight holidays.

The scheduled production for the 50-week work-year shows:

> January—June: 26 weeks with 4 holidays
> July—December: 24 weeks with 4 holidays

Required:

Prepare cost estimates for direct labor and labor related costs for the contract showing:

1. wages paid at the regular rate.
2. overtime premium payments.
3. incentive bonus payments.
4. vacation and holiday pay.
5. employer's payroll taxes (13% of wages).

Problem 3-11   Summary of payroll procedures.

An analysis of the time tickets for the month of November of the Stratton Manufacturing Co. reveals the information shown:

Employee Name	Gross Earnings* — Week Ending			
	11/8	11/15	11/22	11/29
A. Arthur	$ 300	$ 280	$ 290	$ 320
B. Bennett.	280	270	260	280
C. Carletto	320	300	340	280
D. Davenport	1,200	1,200	1,200	1,200
E. Evans	800	760	850	870

*All regular time

Arthur, Bennett, and Carletto are production workers, and Davenport is the supervisor of the group. Evans is in charge of the office.

Cumulative earnings paid (before deductions) in this calendar year prior to the payroll period ending November 8 were as follows: Arthur, $12,000; Bennett, $11,800; Carletto, $11,500; Davenport, $48,000; and Evans, $32,800.

Required:

The solution to this problem requires the following forms, using the indicated column headings:

Employee Earnings Record
Week Ending
Weekly Gross Earnings
Accumulated Gross Earnings
Weekly Earnings Subject to FICA
Withholdings (2 columns):
  FICA Tax
  Income Tax
Net Amount Paid

Payroll Record
Employee's Name
Gross Earnings
Withholdings (2 columns):
  FICA Tax
  Income Tax (10%)
Net Amount Paid

Labor Cost Summary
Week Ending
Dr. Work in Process (Direct Labor)
Dr. Factory Overhead (Indirect Labor)
Dr. Administrative Salaries (Office)
Cr. Payroll (Total)

1. Prepare an employee earnings record for each of the five employees.
2. Prepare a payroll record for each of the four weeks.
3. Prepare a labor cost summary for the month.
4. Prepare journal entries to record:
    (a) the payroll for each of the four weeks.
    (b) the payment of wages for each of the four payrolls.
    (c) the distribution of the monthly labor costs per the labor cost summary.
    (d) the company's payroll taxes covering the four payroll periods.

Problem 3-12   Summary of payroll procedures.

The Shaker Construction Co. uses the job order cost system. In recording payroll transactions, the following accounts are used:

Cash	Administrative Salaries
Vouchers Payable	Miscellaneous Administrative
FICA Tax Payable	Expense
Federal Unemployment Tax Payable	Sales Salaries
State Unemployment Tax Payable	Miscellaneous Selling Expense
Employees Income Tax Payable	Factory Overhead
Payroll — *expense*	Work in Process

Factory employees are paid weekly, while all other employees are paid semimonthly on the fifteenth and the last day of each month. Amounts withheld from the earnings of the employees, income taxes and FICA taxes, are recorded in special columns of the voucher register at the time of recording the payroll vouchers. All salaries and wages are subject to all taxes. — *employees FICA, FUTA, SUTA*

Following is a narrative of transactions completed during the month of March:

FICA 8%

Mar. 7 Issued payroll voucher for the total earnings of factory employees amounting to $68,200 less deductions for employees' income taxes and FICA taxes.
      7 Issued check for payment of the payroll voucher.
     14 Issued payroll voucher for the total earnings of factory employees amounting to $66,300 less deductions for employees' income taxes and FICA taxes.
     14 Issued check for payment of the payroll voucher.
     15 Issued voucher covering administrative salaries, $9,000, and sales salaries, $17,000, less deductions for employees' income taxes and FICA taxes.
     15 Issued check for payment of the salary voucher.
     21 Issued payroll voucher for the total earnings of factory employees amounting to $72,500 less deductions for employees' income taxes and FICA taxes.
     21 Issued check for payment of the payroll voucher.
     28 Issued payroll voucher for the total earnings of factory employees amounting to $74,200 less deductions for employees' income taxes and FICA taxes.
     28 Issued check for payment of the payroll voucher.
     31 Issued voucher covering administrative salaries, $9,000, and sales salaries, $17,000 less deductions for employees' income taxes and FICA taxes.
     31 Issued check for payment of the salary voucher.

end FICA 8%

31 The following wages and salaries were earned or accrued during March:

Direct labor.............................. $302,500
Indirect labor 22,500
Administrative salaries 18,000
Sales salaries............................ 34,000
Total..................................... $377,000

The following form is used by The Shaker Construction Co. to compute the amount of payroll taxes incurred:

Items	Taxable Earnings		FICA	FUTA	State Unemployment Tax	Total Taxes Imposed on Employer
	FICA	FUTA				
Factory wages ...... Administrative salaries............. Sales salaries	325,000 00	325,000 00				
Total	377,000 00	377,000 00				

Required:

1. Complete the above form to show the payroll taxes imposed on the employer for the month of March.
2. Prepare the journal entries to record the foregoing transactions and payroll taxes, assuming that the payroll taxes imposed on the employer for factory wages are to be charged to Factory Overhead; the taxes for administrative salaries are to be charged to Miscellaneous Administrative Expense; and the taxes for sales salaries are to be charged to Miscellaneous Selling Expense.
3. Assume the factory employees worked on March 29, 30, and 31. What was the amount of accrued wages on March 31?

employers payroll taxes

ACCOUNTING FOR FACTORY OVERHEAD

LEARNING OBJECTIVES

In studying this chapter, you will learn about the:

■ Identification of cost behavior patterns
■ Techniques used to separate semivariable costs into variable and fixed components
■ Budgeting of factory overhead costs
■ Accounting for actual factory overhead costs
■ Methods for distributing service department factory overhead costs to production departments
■ Application of factory overhead using predetermined rates
■ Calculation of budget and volume variances for factory overhead deviations

All costs incurred in the factory that are not chargeable directly to the finished product are generally termed factory overhead. These operating costs of the factory cannot be traced specifically to a unit of production. A variety of terms have been used to describe this type of cost, such as *supplementary costs, indirect expenses, indirect manufacturing costs, factory overhead expenses,* or *factory burden.* These costs are also referred to simply as "overhead" or "burden."

One method to determine whether a factory expenditure is a factory overhead item is to compare it to the classification standards established for direct materials and direct labor costs. If the expenditure cannot be charged to either of these two "direct" factory accounts, it is classified as factory overhead. Thus, all "indirect" expenditures are factory overhead items. Generally, factory overhead accounts include (1) indirect materials consumed, such as cleaning materials and lubricants required for production; (2) indirect labor, such as wages of janitors, elevator operators, and supervisors, and overtime premiums paid to all factory workers; and (3) other indirect manufacturing expenses, such as rent, insurance, property taxes, depreciation, heat, light, and water.

Accounting for factory overhead involves the following procedures:

1.   Identifying cost behavior patterns
2.   Budgeting factory overhead costs
3.   Accumulating actual factory overhead costs
4.   Applying factory overhead estimates to production
5.   Calculating and analyzing differences between actual and applied factory overhead

IDENTIFYING COST BEHAVIOR PATTERNS

Direct materials and direct labor are classified as variable costs. Variable costs are costs that vary in proportion to volume changes. In direct contrast are those costs that remain constant when production levels increase or decrease. These unchanging costs are referred to as fixed costs. A third type of cost is one that is erratic or irregular and does not respond in a predictable way to a change in volume. These costs, which are difficult to predict, are called semivariable costs.

Factory overhead expenses include costs that may be classified as variable, fixed, or semivariable. Therefore, factory overhead creates a difficult problem for most companies because it is essential to predict costs that will be incurred at various levels of production. The factory overhead costs that behave in the same pattern as direct material costs and direct labor costs are considered variable costs and are readily forecast because they move up or down proportionately with production changes. The factory overhead charges deemed to be fixed costs remain unchanged when production varies; therefore, they are also considered predictable. The factory overhead costs that are semivariable require additional analysis and attention because they are not readily predictable. In many companies, semivariable costs consti-

tute a substantial portion of the factory overhead charges, and the method
used to forecast these costs must be carefully selected.

Illustration 4-1 shows the basic patterns of factory overhead costs as
volume changes are encountered.

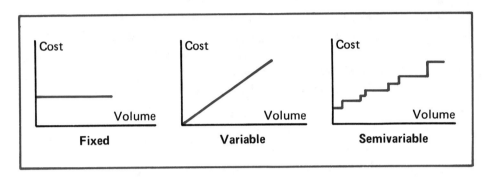

Illustration 4-1   Cost Behavior Patterns

Examples of variable, fixed, and semivariable factory overhead costs are:

Variable: Power costs directly associated with production, deprecia-
             tion expense computed on the basis of hours equipment is
             used, repairs directly related to usage, supplies, spoilage,
             small tools expense.

Fixed: Factory property taxes, depreciation of equipment com-
             puted on a straight-line basis, periodic rent payments, pro-
             duction executives' salaries, insurance.

Semivariable:

Type A: Changes as various levels of production are reached. This
             type of cost will remain constant over a range of production,
             then abruptly change. The increases are not continuous and
             costs will plateau before another cost change occurs. Ex-
             amples are: inspection and handling costs, factory super-
             vision and other indirect labor costs, indirect materials.

Type B: Varies continuously but not in direct proportion (ratio) to
             volume changes. Examples are: fuel costs, power costs,
             maintenance of factory equipment.

The composition of the different semivariable factory overhead costs
makes the prediction of a specific amount of overhead cost for a given level

of production very difficult. Mathematical techniques can be used to establish fixed and variable components that comprise semivariable costs and, to a degree, remove some of the uncertainty. The forecasting of overhead costs for production levels within the usual operating (relevant) range can be markedly improved through behavioral cost studies and the application of statistical techniques.

ANALYZING SEMIVARIABLE FACTORY OVERHEAD COSTS

There are many different techniques and theories regarding the prediction of future events. Most mathematical techniques attempt to establish a pattern from the historic evidence available, then use the pattern as a model for predicting future outcomes. If history repeats itself, the model will satisfactorily simulate the future events and the predictions will be beneficial to the decision-making process.

The mathematical (statistical) techniques to be discussed use the relationships of historic costs to isolate variable and fixed elements that can then be used to determine future costs. The nonmathematical (observation) method is to a degree based on intuition.

Observation Method

The observation method relies heavily on the ability of an observer to detect a pattern of cost behavior by reviewing past cost and volume data. A minimal amount of mathematical expertise is required. The reaction of a semivariable expense to past changes in production is analyzed, and the relationship of the expense change to the production change is observed. A decision is made, subjectively, that the observed semivariable cost will be treated as either a variable item or a fixed item, depending on which type of cost behavior it more closely resembles. The analyzed overhead item will thereafter be treated like any other variable or fixed cost until another study is considered necessary. Companies that use this method believe that the discrepancy between the actual costs and the forecast costs will be insignificant and will not affect management strategies or operations.

The observation method probably remains the most popular method for many companies; however, due to an increasing emphasis on quantifying business data, statistical methods can be expected to increase in popularity. Two of these methods are discussed in the following sections: (1) the high-low method and (2) the least squares method. Both of these methods isolate an element of a semivariable cost, then suggest the remainder of the cost is the other element.

High-Low Method

The high-low method compares a high volume and its related cost to a low volume with its related cost. The difference in volume between the two points is compared to the difference in costs. It is assumed that all costs between the two points being compared are linear and will fall along a straight line.

To illustrate, assume the following overhead costs were incurred at two different levels of production:

	1,000 Units	2,000 Units
Depreciation (fixed)	$2,000	$2,000
Inspection costs (semivariable)	3,000	5,000
Factory supplies (variable)	1,000	2,000

Depreciation is a fixed cost and remained unchanged. Factory supplies varied proportionately with the change in volume, but the unit cost remained constant at $1 per unit. Inspection costs, however, were neither fixed nor did they change proportionately with volume. By using the high-low technique, part of the inspection cost will be considered variable and the remaining part fixed:

Variable element:

	Units	Costs
High volume	2,000	$5,000
Low volume	1,000	3,000
Difference	1,000	$2,000

Variable cost per unit ($2,000 ÷ 1,000 units) = $2

Fixed element:

	1,000 Units	2,000 Units
Cost	$3,000	$5,000
Variable @ $2 per unit	2,000	4,000
Fixed cost (remainder)	$1,000	$1,000

Inspection costs at various levels of production can be estimated using the following formula:

Inspection costs = $1,000 + $2(number of units produced)

Assume that management wishes to estimate total factory overhead costs for one month at a production level of 4,000 units. Using the data on page 160 and the formula for the semivariable cost, projected factory overhead costs for the month would be $15,000, calculated as follows:

Depreciation (fixed)..	$ 2,000
Inspection costs [semivariable, $1,000 + $2(4,000)]...............	9,000
Factory supplies (variable, $1 × 4,000)	4,000
Total estimated factory overhead at 4,000 units	$15,000

Least Squares Method

The least squares method is a more refined statistical technique from which a more reliable separation of the variable and fixed elements can be expected. The least squares method is conceptually similar to a scatter-diagram method of estimating a straight line along which the semivariable costs will fall. With the scatter-graph method the observations of cost and production data are plotted on graph paper and, based on intuitive judgment, a line is drawn that will divide the observation points, with an equal number on each side. Then from two points selected on the line, the variable and fixed elements can be determined using the high-low technique.

However, the least squares method uses a mathematical procedure, rather than intuitive judgment, to determine the line placement. As shown in Illustration 4-2, a straight line (regression line) is mathematically fitted to the observed data. The line is positioned at the points that minimize the sum of the squared deviations between the observed data and the line.

The term *least squares* is derived from the process of minimizing the sum of the squares of the deviations. The line is fitted to calculated points and represents an equation in which the sum of the squared deviations is a minimum.

One method of calculating the regression line is to solve two simultaneous equations to determine the fixed cost and the variable cost elements for each unit of production.

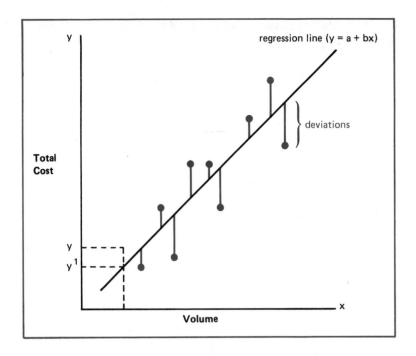

Illustration 4-2   Least Squares Method

The equations to be used are:

$$\Sigma y = na + b\Sigma x$$
$$\Sigma xy = a\Sigma x + b\Sigma x^2$$

x = number of units
y = total cost at a given production level
n = number of observations
a = fixed cost
b = variable cost per unit of production
Σ = the sum of

Assume the following cost data for a four-month period:

Month	Units of Production	Semivariable Cost
1	100	$100
2	200	200
3	400	300
4	500	400

Using the assumed cost data, the calculations are:

Month	x Units	y Cost	xy	x^2
1	100	$ 100	$ 10,000	10,000
2	200	200	40,000	40,000
3	400	300	120,000	160,000
4	500	400	200,000	250,000
	1,200	$1,000	$370,000	460,000

Substitute for the x and y factors in the equations:

$\Sigma y = na + b\Sigma x$ $\$1,000 = 4a + 1,200b$ Equation 1

$\Sigma xy = a\Sigma x + b\Sigma x^2$ $\$370,000 = 1,200a + 460,000b$ Equation 2

To eliminate a:
multiply Eq. 1 by 300
to get Eq. 3, then $\$300,000 = 1,200a + 360,000b$ Equation 3

subtract Eq. 3 from
Eq. 2 $\$ 70,000 = \underline{\quad -0- \quad} + 100,000b$ Equation 4

Solve Eq. 4 for b: $100,000b = \$70,000$

                 b = $.70 variable cost per unit of production

Solve for a:
Substitute $.70 for b in either Eq. 1 or 2

         $\$1,000 = 4a + 1,200b$ Equation 1
         $\$1,000 = 4a + 1,200(\$.70)$
         $\$1,000 = 4a + \$840$
           $4a = \$1,000 - \$840$
           $4a = \$160$
            a = $40 fixed cost

The value of $.70 for the variable cost and $40 for the fixed cost are the variable and fixed components in the semivariable cost. Using these values, the composition of the semivariable cost could be shown as follows:

       1,200 units @ $.70 per unit = $ 840 variable cost
       4 months @ $40 per month =   160 fixed cost
           Total semivariable cost = $1,000

Using the same cost data, the fixed and variable components can be calculated without equations as follows:

Column 1	Column 2	Column 3	Column 4	Column 5	Column 6
	Deviations		Deviations		
Units	from		from		
(volume)	Average of		Average of		Column 2
	x in	Cost	y in	Column 2	times
x	Column 1	y	Column 3	Squared	Column 4
100	−200	$ 100	$−150	40,000	$30,000
200	−100	200	− 50	10,000	5,000
400	+100	300	+ 50	10,000	5,000
500	+200	400	+150	40,000	30,000
Total 1,200	−0−	$1,000	−0−	100,000	$70,000
Average 300		250			

$$\text{Variable cost } b = \frac{\text{Column 6}}{\text{Column 5}} = \frac{\$70,000}{100,000}$$

$$b = \$.70 \text{ variable cost per unit}$$

To determine the fixed component, substitute the average of x (Column 1) and the average of y (Column 3) in the equation for a straight line, y = a + bx, as follows:

$$y = a + bx$$
$$\$250 = a + (\$.70)300$$
$$a = \$250 - \$210$$
$$a = \$40 \text{ fixed cost}$$

Limitations of High-Low and Least Squares Methods

The high-low and least squares methods both use historic cost patterns to predict future costs and are, therefore, subject to the limitations that apply to all forecasting techniques. The use of mathematical techniques does not insure accurate forecasts. The accuracy of a forecast, to a great extent, depends on the validity of the data used with the chosen method.

Cost analysis is more useful for decision making when all costs are segregated into two categories: variable and fixed. Therefore, the semi-variable costs should be analyzed and subdivided into the two categories. The high-low method bases its solution on two observations and assumes that all other unanalyzed relationships will fall along a straight line between these selected observations. Such an assumption may prove to be highly unrealistic because the two observations used may not be representative of the group from which the data was selected. The method may be considered reliable, however, if additional pairs of data are analyzed and the results approximate those obtained from the first observations.

The least squares method uses a larger sample of data and applies a statistical methodology to fit a line to any set of cost data. However, caution should be exercised before accepting the results as being reliable. The equations used for calculations give an impression of accuracy that may not be justifiable. If invalid data are used, no known mathematical technique will produce a reliable solution.

Both methods stress the importance of the relationship of cost factors to volume; however, many other factors may affect cost behavior and should not be ignored. For example, consideration should also be given to price changes and changes in technology. Generalizations about cost patterns should be avoided because only a few costs have inherent characteristics. Most costs are directly influenced by management policies.

BUDGETING FACTORY OVERHEAD COSTS

Budgets are management's operating plans expressed in quantitative terms, such as units of production and related costs. After factory overhead costs have been classified as either fixed or variable, budgets can be prepared for expected levels of production. The segregation of fixed and variable cost components permits the company to prepare a flexible budget. A flexible budget is a budget that shows estimated costs at different production volumes.

Assume management desires to budget factory overhead costs at three levels of production — 10,000, 20,000 and 40,000 units. Variable factory overhead cost is $5 per unit, and fixed cost totals $50,000. The budgeted costs at these volumes are:

	10,000 units	20,000 units	40,000 units
Variable cost @ $5 per unit	$ 50,000	$100,000	$200,000
Fixed cost	50,000	50,000	50,000
Total factory overhead...........	$100,000	$150,000	$250,000
Factory overhead per unit	$10.00	$7.50	$6.25

As the volume increases the factory overhead cost per unit decreases because the total fixed cost, $50,000, is spread over a larger number of units. For example, the fixed cost per unit will add $5 ($50,000 ÷ 10,000 units) at the 10,000-unit level but only $1.25 ($50,000 ÷ 40,000 units) when 40,000 units are produced. The variable cost remains constant at $5 per unit for the entire range of production.

Budgeting is a valuable management tool for planning and controlling costs. A flexible budget aids management in establishing realistic production goals and in comparing actual costs with budgeted costs. Differences (variances) between actual and budgeted costs are discussed in a later section of this chapter.

ACCOUNTING FOR ACTUAL FACTORY OVERHEAD

Cost accounting systems are designed to accumulate, classify, and summarize the factory overhead costs actually incurred. The specific procedures used to account for actual factory overhead costs depend on the nature and organization of the manufacturing firm.

In a small manufacturing company having only one production department, factory overhead may be accounted for in much the same manner as selling and administrative expenses. All the factory overhead accounts may be kept in the general ledger. However, separate accounts should be kept for indirect materials, indirect labor, and for each of the indirect manufacturing expenses.

Indirect materials and indirect labor costs are recorded first in the general journal. These entries are made from the summary of materials issued and returned and from the labor cost summary. If a voucher system is used, other factory overhead expenses are recorded in the voucher register from which they are posted to the appropriate accounts in the general ledger. The invoices that have been received are the sources for these entries. Schedules of fixed costs should be prepared and used as the source for general journal adjusting entries to record the amount of taxes, depreciation, insurance, and other similar expenses for the period.

A substantial modification must be made in the accounting system when the number of factory overhead accounts becomes sizeable. A factory overhead subsidiary ledger should be created and maintained, along with a control account in the general ledger. The subsidiary ledger is known as the factory overhead ledger and the control account is entitled "Factory Overhead." A column is established in the voucher register for recording factory overhead expenses. When the column is totaled, the amount is posted to the debit side of the factory overhead control account. All entries in the voucher register for factory overhead are posted either individually or in total to the appropriate accounts in the subsidiary factory overhead ledger. At the end of each accounting period, the balance of the factory overhead control account is proved by comparing its balance to the total of the account balances in the subsidiary factory overhead ledger.

Accounts in the factory overhead ledger should have titles that are clearly descriptive of the nature of the expenditure. Examples of typical factory overhead accounts are:

Defective work	Plant security
Depreciation	Power
Fuel	Property tax
Heat and light	Rent
Indirect labor	Repairs
Indirect materials	Small tools
Insurance	Spoilage
Janitorial service	Supplies
Lubricants	Telephone
Maintenance	Water
Materials handling	Workers' compensation insurance
Overtime premium	

In addition to the expenses related to factory operations and the manufacturing process are employee fringe benefit costs. Examples of these benefits include paid vacations and holidays, paid sick leave, pensions, bonuses, profit-sharing plans, group life and medical insurance, group medical and hospitalization insurance, credit unions, free physical examinations, payment of tuition for education, recreational activities, and other services. Fringe benefits may also include the employer's cost for FICA, state unemployment taxes, and federal unemployment taxes.

Departmentalizing Factory Overhead

In manufacturing companies with several departments, the accounting system is designed to accumulate costs by department. Separate budgets are generally prepared for each department and then combined into a master budget for the company. The actual costs incurred can thus be readily compared with budgeted costs for each department.

Factory overhead expenses must be carefully analyzed before the expenses are assigned to departments. For example, total factory depreciation is analyzed to determine the distribution of depreciation charges among the departments. The accounting system should be designed to provide the necessary data promptly and accurately.

Departmental Accounts in the Factory Overhead Ledger.   The required analysis of factory overhead can be accomplished by any one of several methods. One approach is to expand the factory overhead ledger to include a separate account for each department's share of different expenses. For example, instead of maintaining one account for indirect materials, the ledger could be expanded to include the following accounts: Indirect Materials — Department A, Indirect Materials — Department B, Indirect Materials — Building Maintenance Department, and so on, for every department that uses indirect materials. This system requires establishing a total number of accounts equal to the number of types of expenses multiplied by the number of departments. Consequently, this method is appropriate for a moderate-size company with relatively few expense accounts and three or four departments.

In a very large enterprise, this method of recording factory overhead would be unwieldy. Several hundred accounts would require analysis at the end of each accounting period, making statement preparation both slow and costly.

Factory Overhead Analysis Sheets.   Instead of departmental ledger accounts, factory overhead analysis sheets may be used to keep a subsidiary record of factory overhead expense. A separate analysis sheet may be used to record each type of expense, with individual columns for the departmental classification of the expense. Alternatively, a separate analysis sheet can be used for each department, with individual columns for the expense classification.

An example of an analysis sheet used to keep individual records for each kind of factory overhead expense is shown in Illustration 4-3. The expense-type analysis sheet provides a separate amount column for each department that makes it possible to distribute charges among departments as expenses are recorded. Each column represents a department; therefore, each analysis sheet replaces as many separate accounts as there are departments in the factory. In Illustration 4-3, which illustrates the distribution of one month's depreciation to departments, the depreciation cost assignable to the various

	DEPARTMENTAL ANALYSIS									
Account No. *3111*				Distribution Base: *Valuation of Plant and Equipment*						
Account	*Depreciation*									
Dept. A	Dept. B	Dept. C	Dept. D	Date	Description	Post. Ref.	Debit	Credit		Balance
3 0 0 00	2 0 0 00	1 5 0 00	5 0 0 00	Jan. 31	*Depreciation for January*	GJ	1 1 5 0 00			1 1 5 0 00

Illustration 4-3   Factory Overhead Analysis Sheet — Expense Type

departments was determined by multiplying the plant and equipment valuation in each department (A: $36,000; B: $24,000; C: $18,000; D: $60,000) by the annual rate of depreciation (10%) applicable to the property. The estimated monthly depreciation (1/12 of the annual depreciation) was recorded in the general journal and became the source of posting to the analysis sheet.

The department-type analysis sheet (Illustration 4-4) provides a separate amount column for each kind of expense, making it possible to distribute expenses on a departmental basis as they are recorded. Each column represents a different expense; therefore, each analysis sheet replaces as many separate accounts as there are types of expenses in the factory. All expenses incurred during January for department A are shown in Illustration 4-4. Only the totals are entered. Vouchered expenses are posted from the books of original entry either in total or as of the date they are incurred, and the fixed expenses are posted from the general journal at the end of the month.

Factory overhead analysis sheets, both expense and department types, serve as subsidiary ledgers and are controlled by the factory overhead account in the general ledger. The advantage of using an analysis sheet for each expense, classified by departments, is that it provides only as many amount columns as there are departments within the factory (see Illustration 4-3). However, a summary should be prepared at the end of an accounting period to determine the total expenses incurred for each department.

The advantage of using an analysis sheet for each department, classified by expense, is that fewer sheets are required and the preparation of a summary is not required at the end of an accounting period (see Illustration 4-4). When a factory is departmentalized, the factory overhead must

FACTORY OVERHEAD - DEPARTMENT A						
Indirect Materials No. 311.1	Indirect Labor No. 311.12	Power No. 311.13	Depreciation No. 311.18	Factory Property Tax No. 311.20	Insurance No. 311.30	General Factory Expenses No. 311.50
1 0 0 00	2 0 0 00	1 5 0 00	3 0 0 00	2 8 0 00	3 5 0 00	1 5 0 00

FACTORY OVERHEAD - DEPARTMENT A							
Misc. Factory Expenses		Date	Description	Post. Ref.	Debit	Credit	Balance
Account No.	Amount						
		Jan. 31	Total expenses-January		1 5 3 0 00		1 5 3 0 00

Illustration 4-4   Factory Overhead Analysis Sheet — Department Type

be recorded departmentally to determine the total cost of operating each department.

To illustrate the use of a departmental analysis sheet, assume the Village Manufacturing Company has four departments: A, B, C, and D. A factory overhead control account is maintained in the general ledger, and an overhead analysis sheet is prepared for each department at the beginning of a period. In the voucher register, a separate column is used to record factory overhead items.

By referring to Illustration 4-4, note that Indirect Materials (Account No. 311.1) was charged $100. This amount represents the cost of lubricating oil that was issued from the storeroom. The requisition indicated that department A was to be charged for the indirect material.

Department A shows a charge for indirect labor of $200. This is the result of idle time caused by the lack of work available to machine operators during part of a workday.

Each department would have an overhead analysis sheet similar to the one illustrated for department A. When the cost of work is allocated to a particular department, it is then classified as to the account to be charged.

If an invoice for $50 is received for the cost of repairing a machine in department B, a voucher is prepared for the indirect factory overhead expense. The voucher identifies the department to be charged and the amount is entered in the voucher register column, Factory Overhead. The voucher, or a memorandum, is then sent to the individual responsible for maintaining the factory overhead ledger who enters the expense in the appropriate column of the analysis sheet for department B.

Schedule of Fixed Costs. Fixed costs are assumed not to vary in amount from month to month. Some fixed costs, such as insurance and property taxes, are either prepaid or accrued expenses. Since these costs are considered very predictable, schedules for the periodic amount of fixed costs to be allocated to the various departments can be prepared in advance. A schedule of fixed costs similar to Illustration 4-5 can be prepared for several periods. By referring to the schedule at the end of a period, a journal entry can be prepared to record the total fixed costs. The schedule can also be used as the source from which fixed costs can be posted to the departmental factory overhead analysis sheets.

In Illustration 4-5, the schedule of fixed costs shows that for the month of January, the total depreciation expense for machinery, $1,150, is allocated to the departments as follows: A, $300; B, $200; C, $150; D, $500. The illustration also shows the monthly departmental fixed costs for property tax and insurance.

At the end of the month, the accountant would post the amounts from the schedule of fixed costs to each department's analysis sheet. For example, the following amounts would be posted to department A's analysis sheet:

Depreciation	$300
Property Tax	280
Insurance	350

A general journal entry would be prepared, summarizing the total fixed costs for the period, as follows:

Jan. 31	Factory Overhead	3,550	
	Accumulated Depreciation—Machinery		1,150
	Accrued Property Tax		1,000
	Prepaid Insurance		1,400
	Fixed expenses for January.		

General Factory Overhead Expenses. All factory overhead expenses are recorded in a regular, systematic manner so that at the end of an

Schedule of Fixed Costs

Item of Cost	January	February	March	April	May	June
Depreciation:						
Dept. A	$ 300.00	$ 300.00	$ 300.00	$ 300.00	$ 300.00	$ 300.00
Dept. B	200.00	200.00	200.00	200.00	200.00	200.00
Dept. C	150.00	150.00	150.00	150.00	150.00	150.00
Dept. D	500.00	500.00	500.00	500.00	500.00	500.00
Total	$1,150.00	$1,150.00	$1,150.00	$1,150.00	$1,150.00	$1,150.00
Property tax:						
Dept. A	$ 280.00	$ 280.00	$ 280.00	$ 280.00	$ 280.00	$ 280.00
Dept. B	270.00	270.00	270.00	270.00	270.00	270.00
Dept. C	250.00	250.00	250.00	250.00	250.00	250.00
Dept. D	200.00	200.00	200.00	200.00	200.00	200.00
Total	$1,000.00	$1,000.00	$1,000.00	$1,000.00	$1,000.00	$1,000.00
Insurance:						
Dept. A	$ 350.00	$ 350.00	$ 350.00	$ 350.00	$ 350.00	$ 350.00
Dept. B	325.00	325.00	325.00	325.00	325.00	325.00
Dept. C	300.00	300.00	300.00	300.00	300.00	300.00
Dept. D	425.00	425.00	425.00	425.00	425.00	425.00
Total	$1,400.00	$1,400.00	$1,400.00	$1,400.00	$1,400.00	$1,400.00
Grand Total.	$3,550.00	$3,550.00	$3,550.00	$3,550.00	$3,550.00	$3,550.00

Illustration 4-5   Schedule of Fixed Costs

accounting period, all expenses that are chargeable to the period have already been distributed to the factory departments. The allocation of overhead to departments would have been made in proportion to the measurable benefits received from such expenses. However, for some items of factory overhead, the benefits cannot be measured departmentally. Instead, the factory as a whole is the beneficiary. An example is the salary of the superintendent, who has the responsibility to oversee all factory operations. Another example would be the wages of the company security guards.

General factory overhead expenses not identified with a specific department are charged to departments by a process of allocation. This allocation is usually made on an arbitrary basis, such as proportional to each department's share of the total direct expenses. The allocation may be made for each item of expense at the time it is incurred and recorded, or expenses may be accumulated as they are incurred and the allocation of the total expenses made at the end of the accounting period. If the allocation is made at the end of the period, a separate analysis sheet is prepared to record each kind of general factory overhead expense incurred during the period. At the end of the period, the total is allocated and recorded on the departmental analysis sheets. The desirability of recording the overhead on a separate sheet depends on the frequency with which such expenses are incurred during the period.

Summary of Factory Overhead.   All factory overhead expenses incurred during the accounting period, both variable and fixed, are recorded on factory overhead analysis sheets and in the factory overhead control account in the general ledger. After the posting is completed at the end of an accounting period, the balance of the control account is proved by preparing a summary of factory overhead (Illustration 4-6) from the analysis sheets. This summary shows the items of expense by department and in total.

Distributing Service Department Expenses

All job order and process cost systems are designed to accumulate the total cost of each job or unit of product. In order to include factory overhead

---

Summary of Factory Overhead
For the Month Ended January 31, 19--

Expenses	Dept. A	Dept. B	Dept. C	Dept. D	Total
Indirect materials..............	$ 100	$ 50	$ 40	$ 30	$ 220
Indirect labor	200	150	140	160	650
Power........................	150	140	120	100	510
Depreciation...................	300	200	150	500	1,150
Factory property tax............	280	270	250	200	1,000
Insurance	350	325	300	425	1,400
General factory expenses.......	150	350	200	300	1,000
Total.......................	$1,530	$1,485	$1,200	$1,715	$5,930

Illustration 4-6   Summary of Factory Overhead

as part of the total cost, the amount of factory overhead incurred by each production department must be determined.

In a factory, the manufacturing process consists of a series of operations performed in departments or cost centers. Departments are divided into two classes, service departments and production departments. A service department is an essential part of the organization, but it does not work directly on the product. The function of a service department is to serve the needs of the production departments and other service departments. The product indirectly receives the benefit of the work performed by the service department. Examples of service departments are: a department that generates power for the factory; a building maintenance department that is responsible for maintaining the buildings; or the cost accounting department that maintains the factory accounting records.

A production department performs the actual manufacturing operations that physically change the units being processed. Since the production departments receive the benefit of the work performed by the service departments, the total cost of production must include not only the costs charged directly to the production departments but also a portion of the costs of operating the service departments. The total product costs should therefore include a share of service department costs.

The distribution of the service department costs to production departments involves an analysis of the service department's relationship to the other departments before an apportionment process can be developed. The cost of operating each service department should be distributed in proportion to the benefits received by the various departments. The apportionment of service department costs is complicated because some service departments render service to other service departments as well as to the production departments. For a distribution to be equitable, the cost of operating a service department should be divided among all departments that it serves, service and production alike.

The first requirement of the distribution process is to determine how a particular service department divides its services among the other departments. In some cases, the services performed for another department may be determined precisely; more often, however, the distribution must be based on approximations. For example, the power department may be furnishing power for the operation of the machines and for lighting the building and the surrounding grounds of the plant. If the power used in each department is metered, the meters can be read at the end of the period and the departments charged for the exact amount of power used. This type of charge to a department would be termed a direct charge.

On the other hand, a department such as building maintenance, which keeps the building clean and in repair, cannot measure exactly the benefits it provides to the other departments that it serves. The cost of operating the building maintenance department is therefore distributed on some equitable basis to the other departments.

Some common bases for distributing service department costs are:

Service Departments	Basis for Distribution
Building Maintenance	Floor space occupied by other departments
Inspection and Packing	Production volume
Machine Shop	Value of machinery and equipment
Personnel	Number of workers in departments served
Purchasing	Cost of materials used
Shipping	Floor space occupied by other departments
Stores	Units of materials requisitioned
Tool Room	Total direct labor hours in departments served

A distribution base should be selected for a service department that will increase or decrease in proportion to the increase or decrease in benefits rendered. For example, a suggested base for distributing the personnel department operating expense is the total number of workers in the departments served. This is based on the assumption that the more workers there are in a department, the more service must be rendered to the department by the personnel staff. For the tool room, the base suggested is the total direct labor hours in the departments served. The premise for this distribution base is that usually only those who work directly on the manufactured product use the inventory of tools maintained in the tool room. The cost of maintaining and repairing the tools used should therefore increase or decrease as the direct labor hours increase or decrease.

After the bases for distribution have been selected for the service departments, the next step is to distribute the total cost of each service department to the other departments. To illustrate the distribution process, assume the following conditions:

1. The maintenance department services the power plant building.
2. The power department furnishes power to the maintenance department for maintenance equipment.
3. The power department and the maintenance department service the personnel department facilities.

4. The personnel department services the power and maintenance departments through their functions of hiring personnel and maintaining the departments' personnel records.

Additional information:

1. Total maintenance department cost includes part of the total costs of the power department and the personnel department.
2. Total power department cost includes part of the total costs of the maintenance and personnel departments.
3. Total personnel department cost includes part of the total costs of the maintenance department and power department.

The first step is to compute the total cost of any one of these overlapping departments. Three different methods are available for use:

1. Distribute service department costs *directly* to production departments.
2. Distribute service department costs regressively to other service departments and then to production departments. The sequence of service departments is established on one of two bases:
    (a) Service to other departments, or
    (b) Magnitude of total costs in each service department.
3. Distribute by algebraic procedures recognizing the interrelationship of services rendered to each other.

In the direct distribution method, no attempt is made to determine the extent to which one service department renders service to another service department. Instead, the service department costs are allocated directly and only to the production departments. This method has the advantage of simplicity, but may produce less accurate results than the other methods. Use of the direct method is justified if the costs allocated to the production departments do not differ materially from the costs that would be allocated using another, more precise method.

The second method recognizes the interrelationship of the service departments. The power department costs are divided among the personnel, maintenance, and production departments. After the power department cost distribution, the personnel department total costs—which now include a portion of the power department costs—will be allocated to maintenance and the production departments. Finally, the maintenance department costs will be distributed to the production departments.

The distribution sequence for allocating service department costs is a high priority decision. The sequential procedure should first distribute the costs of the service department that renders the greatest amount of service to all other departments. Next, distribute the costs of the department that renders the second greatest amount of service to all other departments, and so on, until all service department costs have been distributed to the production departments. The sequential distribution method of distribution can be long and laborious, but it has the advantage of being more accurate if the sequence established is based on a sound analysis of services rendered by the various departments. If there is a substantial degree of uncertainty as to which department's cost should be distributed first to other departments, and such uncertainty cannot be resolved, the department with the largest total overhead should be distributed first. This order of distribution is based on the assumption that the departments render services in direct proportion to the amount of expense they incur.

The algebraic distribution method takes into consideration that some service departments not only may provide service to, but may also receive service from other service departments. If the power department provides power for the building maintenance department and the building maintenance department keeps the power department building in repair, the cost of the building maintenance department cannot be determined until part of the cost of the power department is added to it. Likewise, the cost of the power department cannot be determined until part of the cost of the building maintenance department is added to it. This type of distribution creates a circular flow of costs because two or more service departments render services to each other. When service department overhead distributions are made to other service departments on a reciprocal basis, the departments not included in the circle are distributed first. The method used may involve continued distribution back and forth among the service departments which service each other until the amount remaining for distribution is so infinitesimal that it does not merit another redistribution. Simultaneous equations can also be used to obtain the same results as continued distributions; however, the results are a direct factor of the equations, and therefore require less arithmetical effort. Since conditions rarely justify such an exact distribution, only a brief explanation of these methods is presented. The results obtained from the complicated arithmetical or mathematical calculations usually do not justify the effort.

The direct and sequential methods of distributing service department costs to production departments are shown in Illustration 4-7 (direct distribution to production departments only), Illustration 4-8 (sequential distribution to service departments and production departments based on service

	Power	Personnel	Maintenance	Dept. A	Dept. B	Dept. C	Dept. D	Total
Total from factory overhead analysis sheets........	30,000 00	10,000 00	20,000 00	50,000 00	40,000 00	60,000 00	90,000 00	300,000 00
Power distribution— (kw. hours)				3,600 00	5,400 00	6,000 00	15,000 00	
Personnel distribution (number of employees served)				3,000 00	1,000 00	2,000 00	4,000 00	
Maintenance distribution—(square feet)				5,000 00	6,000 00	4,000 00	5,000 00	
				61,600 00	52,400 00	72,000 00	114,000 00	300,000 00

Power distribution— (kw. hours)
A— 12,000 @ $.30*
B— 18,000 @ .30
C— 20,000 @ .30
D— 50,000 @ .30
   100,000

Personnel distribution (number of employees served)
A— 30 @ $100**
B— 10 @ $100
C— 20 @ $100
D— 40 @ $100
   100

Maintenance distribution—(square feet)
A— 5,000 @ $1.00***
B— 6,000 @ 1.00
C— 4,000 @ 1.00
D— 5,000 @ 1.00
   20,000

*$30,000 ÷ 100,000 (kilowatt hours) = $.30 per kilowatt hour
**$10,000 ÷ 100 (number of employees served) = $100 per employee
***$20,000 ÷ 20,000 (square feet) = $1.00 per square foot

Illustration 4-7   Method 1—Direct Distribution of Service Department Costs to Production Departments

	Power	Personnel	Main-tenance	Dept. A	Dept. B	Dept. C	Dept. D	Total
Total from factory overhead analysis sheets............	30,000 00	10,000 00	20,000 00	50,000 00	40,000 00	60,000 00	90,000 00	300,000 00
Power distribution (kilowatt hours)								
Personnel— 10,000 @ $.25* .		2,500 00	2,500 00	3,000 00	4,500 00	5,000 00	12,500 00	
Maintenance—								
A— 10,000 @ .25..								
B— 12,000 @ .25..								
C— 18,000 @ .25..								
D— 20,000 @ .25..								
50,000 @ .25..								
120,000		12,500 00						
Personnel distribution (number of employees served)								
Maintenance— 25 @ $100** ..			2,500 00	3,000 00	1,000 00	2,000 00	4,000 00	
A— 30 @ 100......								
B— 10 @ 100......								
C— 20 @ 100......								
D— 40 @ 100......								
125			25,000 00					
Maintenance distribution (square feet)								
A— 5,000 @ $1.25*** ..				6,250 00	7,500 00	5,000 00	6,250 00	
B— 6,000 @ 1.25..								
C— 4,000 @ 1.25..								
D— 5,000 @ 1.25..								
20,000				62,250 00	53,000 00	72,000 00	112,750 00	300,000 00

*$30,000 ÷ 120,000 (kilowatt hours) = $ .25 per kilowatt hour
**$12,500 ÷ 125(number of employees served) = $100 per employee
***$25,000 ÷ 20,000 (square feet) = $1.25 per square foot

Illustration 4-8   Method 2(a)—Sequential Distribution of Service Department Costs Based on Service to Other Departments

to other departments), and Illustration 4-9 (sequential distribution to service departments and production departments based on magnitude of total costs in service departments). The organization and operational structure of a company is the determinant of which distribution method should be selected and used. If the variation from one method to another is insignificant, the direct distribution method would be suitable because it saves time and effort.

A comparison of the results obtained from the various methods, based on information shown in Illustrations 4-7, 4-8, 4-9, is shown below:

	Dept. A	Dept. B	Dept. C	Dept. D	Total
Method 1	$61,600	$52,400	$72,000	$114,000	$300,000
Method 2(a)—based on service	62,250	53,000	72,000	112,750	300,000
Method 2(b)—based on total cost.	62,600	51,600	72,000	113,800	300,000
1 and 2(a) difference. .	$ −650	$ −600	$ −0−	$ +1,250	−0−
1 and 2(b) difference. .	$−1,000	$ +800	$ −0−	$ +200	−0−
2(a) and 2(b) difference.	$ −350	$+1,400	$ −0−	$ −1,050	−0−

The completed distribution worksheets are the basis for a series of general journal entries. The journal entries (below and on page 182) are based on the data shown in Illustration 4-9.

Factory Overhead — Power Department	30,000	
Factory Overhead — Maintenance Department	20,000	
Factory Overhead — Personnel Department	10,000	
Factory Overhead — Department A	50,000	
Factory Overhead — Department B	40,000	
Factory Overhead — Department C	60,000	
Factory Overhead — Department D	90,000	
Factory Overhead.		300,000
Factory overhead expenses closed to service and production departments.		

The allocation of service department costs would be journalized as follows:

Factory Overhead — Maintenance Department	2,500	
Factory Overhead — Personnel Department	2,500	
Factory Overhead — Department A	3,000	
Factory Overhead — Department B	4,500	
Factory Overhead — Department C	5,000	
Factory Overhead — Department D	12,500	
Factory Overhead — Power Department		30,000
Factory overhead expenses of power department closed to service and production departments.		

	Power	Main-tenance	Personnel	Dept. A	Dept. B	Dept. C	Dept. D	Total
Total from factory over-head analysis sheets.....	30,000 00	20,000 00	10,000 00	50,000 00	40,000 00	60,000 00	90,000 00	300,000 00
Power distribution (kw hours)								
Maintenance— 10,000 @ $.25*		2,500 00						
Personnel— 10,000 @ .25..			2,500 00					
A— 12,000 @ .25..				3,000 00				
B— 18,000 @ .25..					4,500 00			
C— 20,000 @ .25..						5,000 00		
D— 50,000 @ .25..							12,500 00	
120,000								
		22,500 00						
Maintenance distribution (square feet)								
Personnel— 5,000 @ $.90**			4,500 00					
A— 5,000 @ .90....				4,500 00				
B— 6,000 @ .90....					5,400 00			
C— 4,000 @ .90....						3,600 00		
D— 5,000 @ .90....							4,500 00	
25,000								
			17,000 00					
Personnel distribution (number of employees served)								
A— 30 @ $170***				5,100 00				
B— 10 @ 170......					1,700 00			
C— 20 @ 170......						3,400 00		
D— 40 @ 170......							6,800 00	
100								
				62,600 00	51,600 00	72,000 00	113,800 00	300,000 00

*$30,000 ÷ 120,000 (kilowatt hours) = $.25 per kilowatt hour
**$22,500 ÷ 25,000 (square feet) = $.90 per square foot
***$17,000 ÷ 100 (number of employees served) = $170 per employee

Illustration 4-9   Method 2(b)—Sequential Distribution of Service Department Costs Based on Magnitude of Total Costs in Service Departments

Factory Overhead — Personnel Department   4,500
Factory Overhead — Department A   4,500
Factory Overhead — Department B   5,400
Factory Overhead — Department C   3,600
Factory Overhead — Department D   4,500
   Factory Overhead — Maintenance Department   22,500
   Factory overhead expenses of maintenance department
   closed to service and production departments.

Factory Overhead — Department A   5,100
Factory Overhead — Department B   1,700
Factory Overhead — Department C   3,400
Factory Overhead — Department D   6,800
   Factory Overhead — Personnel Department   17,000
   Factory overhead expenses of personnel department
   closed to production departments.

The distribution work sheet can also be used to prepare a compound journal entry that combines the above entries to close the service department expenses to the production departments as follows:

Factory Overhead — Maintenance Department   2,500
Factory Overhead — Personnel Department   7,000
Factory Overhead — Department A   12,600
Factory Overhead — Department B   11,600
Factory Overhead — Department C   12,000
Factory Overhead — Department D   23,800
   Factory Overhead — Power Department   30,000
   Factory Overhead — Maintenance Department   22,500
   Factory Overhead — Personnel Department   17,000
   To close factory overhead expenses.

An accounting system can be designed to reduce the number of factory overhead accounts to be maintained for the service departments. In such a system, after the distribution work sheet in Illustration 4-9 has been completed, a journal entry can be made to close the factory overhead control account. The charges are made directly to the production departments as follows:

Factory Overhead — Department A   62,600
Factory Overhead — Department B   51,600
Factory Overhead — Department C   72,000
Factory Overhead — Department D   113,800
   Factory Overhead.   300,000
   Factory overhead closed to production departments.
   (The departmental totals include the apportioned
   costs of the service departments.)

After the journal entries are posted to the general ledger, the total balances of the departmental factory overhead accounts will equal the balance of the factory overhead control account before it was closed. The journal entries have not affected the total of the factory overhead expenses. However, the general ledger now shows the amount of factory overhead expense being allocated to each of the production departments.

APPLYING FACTORY OVERHEAD TO PRODUCTION

In previous discussions, the estimating and applying of factory overhead to production was avoided by charging the actual or incurred factory overhead costs to the work in process account. These procedures were used to emphasize the flow of costs and the basic techniques used in cost accounting without unduly complicating the basic fundamentals. However, factory overhead includes many different costs, some of which will not be known until the end of the accounting period. Since it is desirable to know the total cost of a job or process soon after completion, some method must be established for *estimating* the amount of factory overhead that should be applied to the finished product. Through the estimating procedure, a job or process will be charged an estimated amount of factory overhead expense. At the end of a period the actual or incurred factory overhead costs can be compared to the estimated factory overhead applied, and if a difference is encountered, an analysis and subsequent distribution can be made to the appropriate accounts.

The advantages of estimating and charging factory overhead include billing a customer on a more timely basis and preparing bids for new contracts more accurately. If it were not possible to bill a customer for a completed job until a month or more later because all factory overhead costs were not known, the extension of time in collecting such accounts would prove very costly to the company. Many companies rely heavily on a bidding process to obtain new jobs. If a company cannot include a fairly accurate factory overhead charge in the cost of a bid, the financial health of the enterprise can be detrimentally affected. If an awarded contract had been underbid because of understating the actual factory overhead expenses, there could be a loss of revenue to the company. Overstating factory overhead on bids may result in lack of new work. Therefore, the approximation of the overhead charges assigned to bids and to completed jobs is important to the financial well-being and continued growth of a company.

Establishing Predetermined Factory Overhead Rates

The flexible budget, which includes the expected departmental factory overhead costs at given levels of production, is used to establish predetermined factory overhead rates. The rates are computed by dividing the budgeted factory overhead cost by the budgeted production. The budgeted production may be expressed in terms of machine hours, direct labor hours, direct labor cost, units, and so on. The accuracy of the rate depends on the cost projections and production estimates forecast in the flexible budget. In budget projections, the fixed and variable cost components, historic cost behavior patterns, and possible future economic and operational differences must be considered carefully. Specifically, these factors include: the anticipated volume of production, the variability of expenses, the fixed costs relevant to the production levels, the activity of the industry as forecast, and the possible price changes that may occur. Because of the many unknowns, absolute accuracy cannot be expected. Nevertheless, management should give a high priority to attaining the most accurate rate possible.

In a departmentalized company, factory overhead should be budgeted for each department. The procedures for distributing the budgeted departmental expenses are identical to those used to allocate the actual factory overhead expenses. The departmental overhead budgets should also include an allotment of budgeted fixed expenses, such as depreciation and a portion of the budgeted service department expenses.

Upon completion of the factory overhead expense budget, the method to be used to apply the estimated expenses to the departments must be chosen. The usual application methods require that data from the period's production budgets be obtained. The production budgets will provide information as to: the estimated quantity of product, direct labor cost, direct labor hours, and machine hours.

From the production estimates for the plant or for each department, a method can be selected that will charge the product with a fair share of the factory overhead that is expected to be incurred by the company. The departmental composition of human labor versus machines will influence the method of applying factory overhead to the product. A department with little mechanization will usually apply overhead using either the direct labor cost or direct labor hour method, whereas a highly mechanized production department will normally use the machine hour method.

Direct Labor Cost Method

The direct labor cost method uses the amount of direct labor cost that has been charged to the product as the basis for applying factory overhead. The overhead rate to be used is predetermined by dividing the estimated (budgeted) factory overhead cost by the estimated (budgeted) direct labor cost. The relationship of the overhead to the direct labor cost is expressed as a percentage of direct labor cost (the base).

For example, assume the budgeted factory overhead cost for department A amounts to $100,000, and the estimated direct labor cost is expected to be $200,000. The predetermined rate would be 50% ($100,000 ÷ $200,000).

Also, assume that during the first month of operations, Job 100 incurred $1,000 for materials and $3,000 for direct labor. The job is completed and the total cost is determined as follows, using the predetermined rate to estimate factory overhead:

Job 100

Materials.	$1,000
Direct labor	3,000
Factory overhead (50% of direct labor).	1,500
Total cost of completed job	$5,500

The direct labor cost method is appropriate in departments that require mostly human labor and in which the direct labor cost charges are relatively stable from one product to another. If a labor force generates direct labor cost that varies widely due to the hourly-rate range of the employees or absenteeism, another method should be used. For example, a low-paid hourly employee could be replaced, due to absenteeism, with a higher-paid hourly employee. The higher paid employee would increase the direct labor cost and thereby increase the amount of factory overhead charged to the department. Such increases in factory overhead charges to a department are usually unwarranted because the higher paid employee does not normally increase the actual factory overhead expense incurred by the department. Any fluctuation in the departmental direct labor cost that is not accompanied by a proportional increase in actual factory overhead expenses will cause a distortion in the product's total cost which can be detrimental to the company's ability to control costs.

Direct Labor Hour Method

The direct labor hour method overcomes the problem of varying wage rates by applying factory overhead using the number of direct labor hours worked on a job or process. The predetermined rate is computed by dividing the budgeted factory overhead cost by the estimated direct labor hours to be worked. For example, assume the budgeted factory overhead cost was $100,000, and it is expected that 25,000 direct labor hours will be required by production. The predetermined rate would be $4 per direct labor hour ($100,000 ÷ 25,000 hours).

If factory overhead is applied to Job 100 using the direct labor hours method, the records would include the number of direct labor hours worked by the employees. Assume it took 500 direct labor hours to complete Job 100, and the materials and direct labor cost were $1,000 and $3,000, respectively:

Job 100

Materials...	$1,000
Direct labor (500 hours)	3,000
Factory overhead (500 hours @ $4)	2,000
Total cost of completed job	$6,000

An advantage of the direct labor hour method is that the amount of factory overhead applied is not affected by the mix of labor rates in the total direct labor cost. A disadvantage in using this method could be that the application base, the number of direct labor hours, could be substantially smaller than when direct labor cost is used and would thereby be more affected by slight deviations in direct labor hours. Such possibilities should be carefully examined and analyzed before adopting the direct labor hour method.

Machine Hour Method

A highly mechanized department is normally best served by the machine hour method. In such a department, the factory overhead cost should be more proportionate to the machine hours generated by the equipment than the direct labor hours or costs incurred by the employees operating the machinery. It is common in mechanized departments for one employee to operate more than one piece of equipment. Therefore, one direct labor hour may generate, possibly, five machine hours. It is a complex method that requires substantial preliminary study before installation and an additional quantity of records to be maintained. However, the advantages to be gained by a more dependable factory overhead application rate more than outweigh the additional effort and costs involved. The machine hour rate is determined by dividing the budgeted factory overhead cost by the estimated machine hours to be used by production.

For example, assume the factory overhead budget is $100,000, and it is expected that 10,000 machine hours will be required. The predetermined rate would be $10 per machine hour ($100,000 ÷ 10,000 hours).

Assume that Job 100, now completed, used $1,000 for materials, $3,000 for direct labor, and required 300 machine hours.

Job 100

Material.	$1,000
Direct labor	3,000
Factory overhead (300 hours @ $10)	3,000
Total cost of completed job	$7,000

Each of the preceding illustrations for direct labor cost, direct labor hours, and machine hours presents a different amount for the total cost of the completed job. Each illustration should be viewed independently based on the conditions stated. The purpose of the examples is to illustrate how each method can be used in applying factory overhead, not how the different methods will affect total cost in a particular factory environment.

Selecting the Proper Factory Overhead Application Method

Any of the factory overhead methods discussed can be used to apply the estimated factory overhead to production. However, the method selected should allocate the estimated factory overhead in proportion to the actual factory overhead being incurred by the department.

For example, assume two employees in a department use identical tools and machinery, do the same work, work at the same speed, and are equally proficient at their jobs. One employee, due to seniority, is paid $10 an hour while the other receives only $5 an hour. The $10-per-hour employee works on Job 200, while the $5-per-hour employee works on Job 201. Both employees work eight hours on their respective jobs. Job 200 is charged $80 (8 hours @ $10) for direct labor and Job 201 is charged $40 (8 hours @ $5).

The actual factory overhead incurred in the department for each job is identical. However, if the direct labor cost method is used (assume a 50% rate), Job 200 would be charged $40 for factory overhead and Job 201 would be charged only $20. The merit of using the direct labor cost method under such conditions should be questioned because there is no evidence that different amounts of expense should be charged when conditions clearly indicate both jobs should have similar charges.

Factory overhead will rarely change in direct proportion to changes in the pay rates of employees. An increase in an employee's wages seldom means that more light, heat, or power will be consumed in the performance of the job. Neither will a pay increase affect the depreciation expense for the machinery or tools used. Under conditions where factory overhead does not vary in proportion to direct labor costs, the direct labor cost method should not be adopted.

The acceptability of the direct labor hour method can be examined using the above data, since both employees worked the same number of hours under identical conditions. If the predetermined factory overhead rate is $4 per direct labor hour, each job would have a charge of $32 (8 hours × $4) for applied factory overhead. Therefore, the direct labor hour method would apply the same amount of overhead cost to both jobs, worked under identical conditions, and be an acceptable method.

The heat, light, and power consumed by workers is not a function of the amount of wages earned but is closely related to the length of time an employee works. Neither will total employee earnings affect the amount of depreciation, property taxes, rent, or most other factory overhead items. The payroll taxes, however, will increase in proportion to the increase in earnings because they are based on wages earned.

The machine hour method is favored in mechanized factories. To illustrate, assume a factory has two departments. Department A punches blanks on two high-cost machines, then transfers the blanks to department B. The two machines are automatic and require only an occasional inspection to determine operating efficiency. However, department B has no machines, and all work is performed manually. The production sheets for the two departments show department A incurred actual factory overhead costs of $3,000, consisting mostly of power, depreciation, property taxes, insurance, repairs, and maintenance. Department B incurred $2,000 of factory overhead for supervision, heat, light, property taxes, and depreciation.

If factory overhead were applied on a direct labor hour or direct labor cost basis, department A would not have a charge for factory overhead because no direct labor hours or cost had been charged to the department. Therefore, if any factory overhead is to be allocated to the jobs completed in department A, another more appropriate overhead method must be used, such as the machine hour method. The direct labor hour or cost method, however, could meet department B's requirements effectively.

The above example is extreme but does illustrate that under certain circumstances the direct labor methods do not provide an accurate application of factory overhead to the individual job cost. The machine hour method is most useful when the greater part of a department's production is mechanized, since the factory overhead will probably increase or decrease as the hours of operation of the machines increase or decrease. As automation increases in manufacturing operations, the use of the machine hour method will also increase in popularity.

Although the direct labor cost, direct labor hour, and machine hour methods have been emphasized, other methods can be developed that will be equally effective for applying factory overhead to the cost of production. For example, a company might use the units of production or the cost of material as the base for applying overhead. In addition, a factory may use a different method to apply factory overhead in each department.

Applying Factory Overhead at Predetermined Rates

After selecting the application method and calculating the predetermined rate that is to be used, all jobs or processes should be charged with the estimated overhead cost rather than the actual factory overhead costs being incurred. The estimated factory overhead is applied to production by a debit to Work in Process and a credit to an account entitled **Applied Factory Overhead.** Use of the applied factory overhead account avoids confusing the actual factory overhead charges, which are debited to the factory overhead control account, with the estimated charges that are debited to production. At the end of a period, the debit balance in Factory Overhead is compared to the credit balance in Applied Factory Overhead to determine the accuracy of predetermined rates.

To illustrate the use of a predetermined rate, assume a rate of $5 per direct labor hour has been estimated, and a production job required 1,000 direct labor hours to complete. Using the direct labor hour method, $5,000 of estimated factory overhead cost would be applied to the job as follows:

Work in Process	5,000	
Applied Factory Overhead.		5,000
Applied factory overhead to job (1,000 hours @ $5).		

At the end of the period, the applied factory overhead account is closed to the factory overhead control account:

```
Applied Factory Overhead..............................    5,000
    Factory Overhead.......................................            5,000
        Applied factory overhead account closed to control account.
```

After the above entries are posted, if a balance (debit or credit) remains in the factory overhead control account, it indicates that the actual factory overhead incurred did not equal the estimated factory overhead applied. A remaining debit balance in Factory Overhead indicates that a smaller amount of overhead was applied to production than was actually incurred during the period. The debit balance indicates technically that the factory overhead costs were underapplied or underabsorbed. In other words, the work in process account was undercharged for the costs of factory overhead incurred in the accounting period. If, on the other hand, a credit balance should remain after the applied factory overhead account is closed to the control account, the credit balance would represent overapplied or over-absorbed factory overhead, meaning that more overhead was applied to production than was actually incurred in the period. In order to begin each new accounting period with a zero balance in Factory Overhead, the debit or credit balance in the account is usually transferred to an account entitled Under- and Overapplied Factory Overhead, as follows:

```
Under- and Overapplied Factory Overhead......................    xx
    Factory Overhead..........................................            xx
        To close debit balance (underapplied) in factory overhead
        control account.

Factory Overhead...........................................    xx
    Under- and Overapplied Factory Overhead....................            xx
        To close credit balance (overapplied) in factory overhead
        control account.
```

An entry transferring the balance remaining in the factory overhead control account will be made each period, e.g., each month. The special account, Under- and Overapplied Factory Overhead, will accumulate the differences period-to-period. At the end of the calendar or fiscal year, the balance of the under- and overapplied account will be closed to Cost of Goods Sold or allocated on a prorata basis to Work in Process, Finished Goods, and Cost of Goods Sold. The remaining balance should be prorated if the magnitude of the balance would materially distort net income if it were charged entirely to Cost of Goods Sold. When interim statements are prepared, the balance in the under- and overapplied account can be shown in the income statement as a debit or credit adjustment to Cost of Goods Sold or in the balance sheet as a deferred charge (asset) or deferred credit (liability).

The following table illustrates how under- and overapplied factory overhead costs typically offset each other over a given period of time as seasonal demands and production levels change:

Under- and Overapplied Factory Overhead

Month	Underapplied	Overapplied	Dr(Cr) Balance
January	$1,200		$1,200
February	800		2,000
March		$3,500	(1,500)
April		2,000	(3,500)
May		1,000	(4,500)
June		500	(5,000)
July	700		(4,300)
August	1,100		(3,200)
September	2,500		(700)
October	1,000		300
November	500		800
December		1,000	(200)
	$7,800	$8,000	

If a small balance remains in Under- and Overapplied Factory Overhead at year-end, it may be closed directly to Cost of Goods Sold because it will not materially affect net income. A large remaining balance however, could distort the year's net income if it were closed entirely to Cost of Goods Sold; therefore, an adjustment is required to restate the balances of the Work in Process, Finished Goods, and Cost of Goods Sold accounts.

To illustrate the proration (adjusting) procedure, assume a debit balance of $10,000 (underapplied factory overhead) remained in the under- and overapplied factory overhead account. The year-end balances, before adjustment, of the following accounts were:

		Percent of Total
Work in Process	$ 10,000	10%
Finished Goods	30,000	30
Cost of Goods Sold	60,000	60
Total	$100,000	100%

The prorata amount chargeable to each account would be determined as follows:

Work in Process ($10,000 × 10%) .... $ 1,000
Finished Goods ($10,000 × 30%)   3,000
Cost of Goods Sold ($10,000 × 60%)   6,000
                                                             $10,000

The journal entry to close the debit balance in Under- and Overapplied Factory Overhead would be:

Work in Process   1,000
Finished Goods...   3,000
Cost of Goods Sold   6,000
   Under- and Overapplied Factory Overhead.............   10,000
      To close debit balance in Under- and Overapplied
      Factory Overhead.

The amount allocated to Cost of Goods Sold becomes a period cost that directly reduces the amount of net income for the current period. The amounts allocated to Work in Process and Finished Goods become part of the product cost of the inventories and will be deferred, along with the other inventory costs, to the next period.

Illustration of Actual and Applied Factory Overhead

The preceding sections of this chapter have discussed and illustrated the various aspects of accounting for factory overhead including: departmentalizing factory overhead costs, distributing service department costs, applying factory overhead to production using predetermined rates, and accounting for differences between actual and applied factory overhead. Illustrations 4-10 through 4-16 are presented here to tie together these various aspects and to show the flow of factory overhead costs through the accounting system.

Illustration 4-10 shows actual factory overhead costs, using the same data and service department cost distribution method presented in Illustration 4-9. Factory overhead was applied to the production department as follows:

Department A .... $ 66,000
Department B   56,000
Department C   70,000
Department D   110,000

	Power	Main-tenance	Personnel	Dept. A	Dept. B	Dept. C	Dept. D	Total
Total actual expenses from factory overhead analysis sheets	30,000 00	20,000 00	10,000 00	50,000 00	40,000 00	60,000 00	90,000 00	300,000 00
Power distribution (kw hours)								
Maintenance—								
10,000 @ $.25 ..		2,500 00						
Personnel—								
10,000 @ .25..			2,500 00					
A— 12,000 @ .25..				3,000 00				
B— 18,000 @ .25..					4,500 00			
C— 20,000 @ .25..						5,000 00		
D— 50,000 @ .25..							12,500 00	
120,000		22,500 00						
Maintenance distribution (square feet)								
Personnel—								
5,000 @ $.90..			4,500 00					
A— 5,000 @ .90..				4,500 00				
B— 6,000 @ .90..					5,400 00			
C— 4,000 @ .90..						3,600 00		
D— 5,000 @ .90..							4,500 00	
25,000			17,000 00					
Personnel distribution (number of employees served)								
A— 30 @ $170......				5,100 00				
B— 10 @ 170......					1,700 00			
C— 20 @ 170......						3,400 00		
D— 40 @ 170......							6,800 00	
100				62,600 00	51,600 00	72,000 00	113,800 00	300,000 00
Applied factory overhead				66,000 00	56,000 00	70,000 00	110,000 00	302,000 00
(Over-) or underapplied factory overhead........				(3,400 00)	(4,400 00)	2,000 00	3,800 00	(2,000 00)

Illustration 4-10   Summary of Actual and Applied Factory Overhead

Illustration 4-10 also shows the under- or overapplied factory overhead by department and in total as follows:

	Actual Costs	Applied	Under/(Over)
Department A	$ 62,600	$ 66,000	$(3,400)
Department B	51,600	56,000	(4,400)
Department C	72,000	70,000	2,000
Department D	113,800	110,000	3,800
Total............	$300,000	$302,000	$(2,000)

Illustration 4-11 shows the flow of actual factory overhead expenses through the accounting records. In the example, it is assumed that the amounts posted to the factory overhead control account were originally recorded as follows: general journal, $100,000; voucher register, $200,000. The total charge to the control account of $300,000 is equal to the sum of the actual factory overhead expenses incurred by the individual departments and recorded on the factory overhead analysis sheets.

In Illustration 4-12, the $300,000 balance in the factory overhead control account is transferred to the factory overhead accounts for the indi-

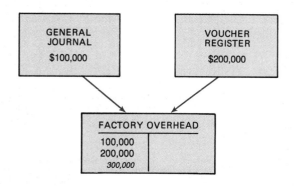

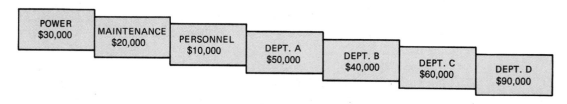

Illustration 4-11   Actual Factory Overhead Expenses

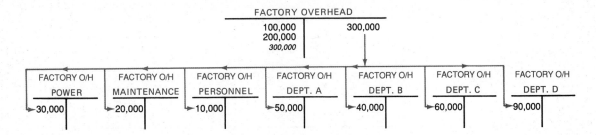

Illustration 4-12   Distribution of Actual Factory Overhead to Service and Production Departments

vidual departments, both service and production. The factory overhead analysis sheets provide the data necessary for the distribution.

Illustration 4-13 shows the distribution of service department costs to production department factory overhead accounts. Illustration 4-14 shows the application of factory overhead, based on predetermined rates, to the individual production departments. In Illustration 4-15, the applied factory overhead accounts are closed to the departmental factory overhead accounts. Finally, as shown in Illustration 4-16, the balances in the departmental factory overhead accounts are closed to Under- and Overapplied Factory Overhead. The net amount of overapplied factory overhead, $2,000, is relatively small and could be closed entirely to Cost of Goods Sold rather than allocated (prorated) among Cost of Goods Sold and the inventory accounts.

CALCULATING BUDGET AND VOLUME VARIANCES

Earlier in the chapter, it was stated that a company needs to forecast the factory overhead costs associated with different levels of production, or capacity. When costs are separated into fixed and variable components, a company can prepare a flexible budget for different levels of capacity. The budget can be used to analyze the over or underapplied factory overhead in terms of the budgeted overhead at the capacity attained compared to the actual overhead costs incurred. When a difference between the total budgeted overhead at the actual capacity attained and the actual costs incurred is computed, it is referred to as a budget or spending variance. The budget variance can be further analyzed to show the separate effects of the actual capacity on the fixed cost factor and the variable cost factor. The combination of these two factors results in the overall budget variance,

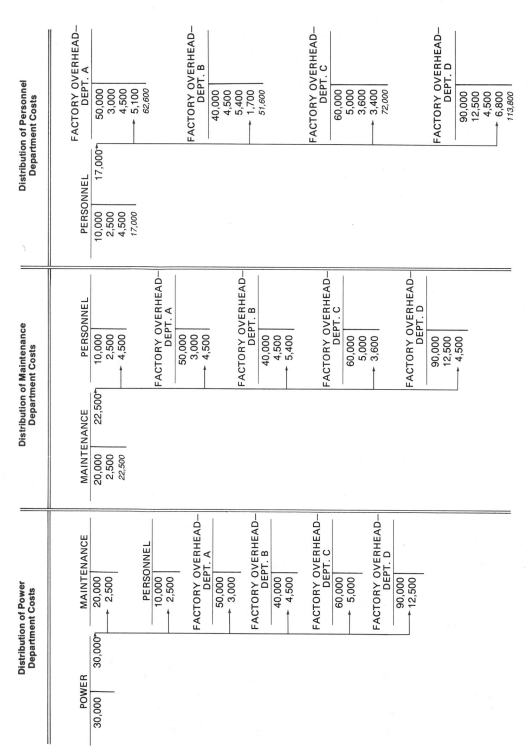

Illustration 4-13   Distribution of Service Department Costs

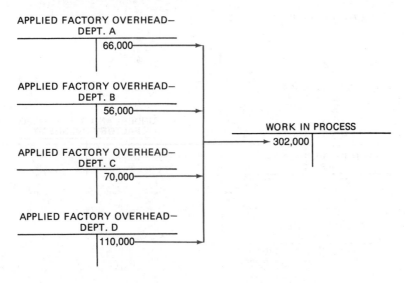

Illustration 4-14   Departmental Applied Factory Overhead

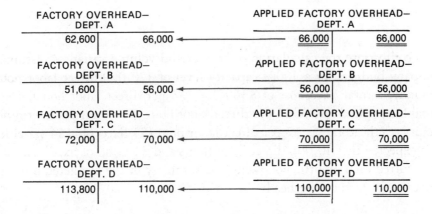

Illustration 4-15   Closing Applied Factory Overhead Accounts to Departmental Factory Overhead Accounts

which is favorable (credit) when the actual overhead costs are less than the budget, and unfavorable (debit) when the actual costs exceed the budget.

A second variance that can be calculated is referred to as a volume variance. This variance measures the effect of a change in the volume of production. The variance is calculated by comparing the total budgeted fixed overhead at the actual capacity to the fixed overhead applied at the actual capacity.

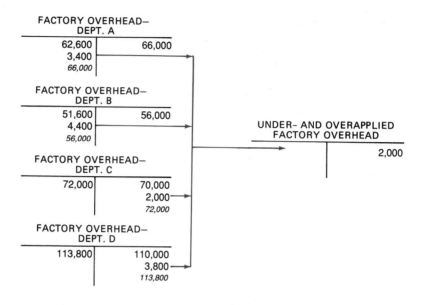

Illustration 4-16   Closing Balances in Departmental Factory Overhead
Accounts

To illustrate the calculation of budget and volume variances, assume a
company budgets for a 100% capacity level of 120,000 direct labor hours
annually, a total fixed cost of $360,000 ($3 per direct labor hour), and a
variable overhead rate of $4 per direct labor hour. The total predetermined
factory overhead rate is $7 per direct labor hour ($3 fixed plus $4 variable).
It is expected that 10,000 direct labor hours and $30,000 of fixed costs will
be incurred each month. Following is a summary of the budgeted monthly
amounts for factory overhead:

	Fixed Costs	Variable Costs	Total Factory Overhead
Budgeted monthly factory overhead:			
Budgeted overhead costs	$30,000	$40,000	$70,000
Budgeted capacity — labor hours...	10,000	10,000	10,000
Predetermined application rate	$3	$4	$7

Actual overhead costs, actual direct labor hours used (attained capacity),
and factory overhead applied for the first month of operations were as
follows:

Actual factory overhead:
Fixed costs....................................... $34,000
Variable costs 39,000 $73,000

Direct labor hours used—9,900
Applied factory overhead:
9,900 hours × $7.............................   69,300
Underapplied factory overhead.................... $ 3,700

At the end of the month, the under- and overapplied factory overhead account has a debit balance of $3,700, indicating that factory overhead has been underapplied. A more detailed analysis of the underapplied overhead balance is shown below:

	Fixed Costs	Variable Costs	Total Factory Overhead
Actual factory overhead	$34,000	$39,000	$73,000
Applied factory overhead:			
9,900 × $3........................	29,700		
9,900 × $4........................		39,600	
9,900 × $7........................			69,300
Underapplied overhead—debit	$ 4,300		
Overapplied overhead—(credit).......		$ (600)	
Net underapplied overhead—debit....			$ 3,700

The underapplied balance of $3,700 can be further analyzed by computing the budget and volume variances. The budget (spending) variance is the difference between actual and budgeted costs at the attained capacity, which in this example is 9,900 hours. This variance indicates the total amount of the overexpenditure (unfavorable variance — debit) or the saving (favorable variance — credit). Differences between actual and budgeted amounts for both fixed and variable costs are included in the budget variance, which is illustrated below:

Budget variance:
Total actual factory overhead costs $73,000
Budgeted overhead at attained capacity:
Budgeted fixed costs............................ $30,000
Budgeted variable costs (9,900 × $4) 39,600   69,600
Budget variance (unfavorable—debit) .... $ 3,400

The volume variance relates only to fixed costs and represents the difference between budgeted fixed costs and fixed costs applied to production at the predetermined rate. If attained capacity exceeds budgeted capacity, the volume variance will be favorable (credit). If attained capacity is less than budgeted capacity, the volume variance will be unfavorable (debit). The volume variance is computed as follows:

Volume variance:
Budgeted fixed costs at attained capacity	$30,000
Applied fixed costs (9,900 × $3)	29,700
Volume variance (unfavorable—debit)	$ 300

The following formula provides an alternative method for computing the volume variance:

$$\text{Volume variance} = (\text{budgeted hours} - \text{actual hours}) \times \text{fixed rate}$$
$$= (10{,}000 - 9{,}900) \times \$3$$
$$= \$300$$

The unfavorable budget variance ($3,400) plus the unfavorable volume variance ($300) equals the net amount of underapplied factory overhead ($3,700). A detailed analysis of the budget and volume variances is presented below.

	Fixed Costs	Variable Costs	Total Factory Overhead
Budget variance:			
Budgeted overhead at attained capacity (9,900 hours)	$30,000	$39,600	$69,600
Actual factory overhead	34,000	39,000	73,000
Unfavorable variance—debit	$ 4,000		
Favorable variance—(credit)		$ (600)	
Net budget variance—unfavorable/debit			$ 3,400
Volume variance:			
Budgeted overhead at attained capacity (9,900 hours)	$30,000	$39,600	$69,600
Applied factory overhead:			
9,900 × $3	29,700		
9,900 × $4		39,600	
9,900 × $7			69,300
Volume variance—unfavorable/debit	$ 300	–0–	$ 300
Net underapplied overhead—debit	$ 4,300	$ (600)	$ 3,700

The analysis shows that actual fixed costs exceeded budgeted fixed costs by $4,000, while variable cost expenditures were $600 less than budgeted at the attained level of production. The net result is an overexpenditure or unfavorable budget variance of $3,400. Fixed costs for the month should be analyzed carefully to determine the cause of the $4,000 difference between actual and budgeted amounts. If further study indicates that total annual fixed costs were underestimated, the budget and the predetermined rate should be revised accordingly.

The unfavorable volume variance of $300 results from fewer direct labor hours being used than expected. This variance is considered unfavorable because it reflects underutilization or inefficient use of capacity. On the other hand, when actual direct labor hours exceed the budget expectation, the resulting overapplication of factory overhead is deemed to be favorable. Due to the higher volume of production and hours worked, the fixed cost per unit of product is lower than has been budgeted. Therefore, at higher plant capacities a company realizes a higher net income because the total product cost is reduced due to lower fixed cost charges per unit.

The analysis of budget and volume variances provides management with information as to how well actual production met the standards established by the budget forecasts. The earlier management is informed regarding deviations from the budget and the direction of the deviations, the more time there is to correct an undesirable condition. When unfavorable deviations are not discovered until the end of a period, it is too late to make operational changes or revise the system. A control system that requires regular calculation of variances serves management by making them aware of conditions in a time-frame that makes corrective action possible.

APPLICATION OF PRINCIPLES

On April 1, the Merz Manufacturing Company found that Job 500 was completed on March 31, and there were no jobs in process in the plant. Prior to April 1, the predetermined overhead application rate for April was calculated from the following data, based on an estimate of 40,000 direct labor hours:

Estimated variable factory overhead	$10,000
Estimated fixed factory overhead	20,000
Total estimated factory overhead	$30,000

Estimated variable factory overhead per hour.....................		$.25
Estimated fixed factory overhead per hour.......................		.50
Predetermined overhead rate per direct labor hour..............		$.75

There is one production department in the factory, and the direct labor hour method is used to apply factory overhead.

Three jobs are started during the month and postings are made daily to the job cost sheets from the materials requisitions and time tickets. The following schedule shows the jobs and amounts posted to the job cost sheets:

Job	Date Started	Materials	Direct Labor	Direct Labor Hours
401	April 1	$10,000	$20,000	12,000
402	April 12	20,000	25,000	18,000
403	April 15	8,000	14,000	8,000
		$38,000	$59,000	38,000

On April 11, Job 401 was completed and factory overhead was applied as follows:

Job 401

Materials..	$10,000
Labor...	20,000
Applied factory overhead (12,000 hours × $.75)	9,000
Total cost	$39,000

On April 24, Job 402 was completed and factory overhead was applied:

Job 402

Materials..	$20,000
Labor...	25,000
Applied factory overhead (18,000 hours × $.75)................	13,500
Total cost	$58,500

On April 30, Job 403 is not completed; however, factory overhead is applied to the partially completed job to determine the total cost incurred during the month of April.

Job 403

Materials..	$ 8,000
Labor...	14,000
Applied factory overhead (8,000 hours × $.75).................	6,000
Total cost (for month of April)	$28,000

The total factory overhead applied to the three jobs during April was $28,500. The factory overhead control account was debited during the month for actual factory overhead expenses of $32,500. After the closing of Applied Factory Overhead to the factory overhead control account, a debit balance of $4,000 in the control account indicates an underapplication of overhead cost.

The general journal entries made on April 30 include the following:

```
April 30  Work in Process ............................  28,500
              Applied Factory Overhead..................          28,500
```

The applied factory overhead of $28,500 has already been recorded on the job cost sheets. The above general journal entry brings the work in process control account into agreement with the subsidiary job cost ledger. When there is more than one production department in a company, it is necessary to debit each departmental work in process account and credit each applied factory overhead account for the amount of overhead applied.

The next procedure is to close the applied factory overhead account to Factory Overhead, and then transfer any remaining balance to the under- and overapplied factory overhead account.

```
April 30  Applied Factory Overhead....................  28,500
              Factory Overhead.........................          28,500
                  To close applied factory overhead.

      30  Under- and Overapplied Factory Overhead......  4,000
              Factory Overhead.........................          4,000
                  To close factory overhead.
```

During April the following entries were made for the completed jobs:

```
Finished Goods......................................  97,500
    Work in Process ..................................          97,500
        Jobs 401 and 402 were completed and transferred to
        finished goods.

Accounts Receivable.................................  58,500
    Sales............................................          58,500
        Delivered Job 401 to customer and billed at 50% markup.

Cost of Goods Sold .................................  39,000
    Finished Goods...................................          39,000
        To record cost of Job 401 delivered to customer.
```

The following diagram shows the work in process account and the flow of factory overhead costs:

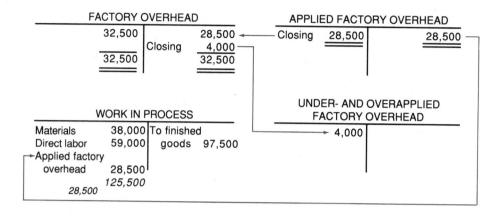

The analysis of the $4,000 debit balance in the under- and overapplied overhead account would show variances as follows:

Actual factory overhead incurred		$32,500
Budgeted overhead at attained capacity:		
Fixed costs.	$20,000	
Variable costs (38,000 × $.25)	9,500	29,500
Budget variance — unfavorable/debit.		$ 3,000
Budgeted overhead at attained capacity	$29,500	
Applied factory overhead	28,500	
Volume variance — unfavorable/debit.		1,000
Net underapplied factory overhead/debit		$ 4,000

Illustration 4-17 shows in summary form the transactions involved in accounting for factory overhead.

KEY TERMS

ACCOUNTING FOR FACTORY OVERHEAD

Transaction	Source of Data	Book of Original Entry	General Ledger Entry	Subsidiary Cost Records
Indirect materials requisitioned from storeroom for factory use	Materials issued summary	General Journal or Requisition Journal	Factory Overhead Materials	Factory overhead analysis ledger sheets Stores ledger cards
Indirect labor employed in factory	Labor cost summary	General Journal	Factory Overhead Payroll	Factory overhead analysis ledger sheets
Payroll taxes imposed on the employer	Payroll record	General journal	Factory Overhead FICA Tax Payable FUTA Tax Payable State Unemployment Tax Payable	Factory overhead analysis ledger sheets
Vouchering factory overhead such as rent, power, and repairs	Invoices	Voucher Register	Factory Overhead Vouchers Payable	Factory overhead analysis ledger sheets
Adjustments for factory overhead such as expired insurance, accrued property tax, and depreciation	Schedules	General Journal	Factory Overhead Prepaid Insurance Accrued Property Tax Payable Accumulated Depreciation	Factory overhead analysis ledger sheets
Distribution of factory overhead to service and production departments	Schedules	General Journal	Departmental Factory Overhead Accounts Factory Overhead	None
Distribution of service department expenses to production department expense accounts	Schedules	General Journal	Production Department Factory Overhead Accounts Service Department Expense Accounts	Factory overhead analysis ledger sheets
Application of factory overhead to jobs	Schedule of predetermined departmental application rates	General Journal	Work in Process Production Department Applied Factory Overhead Accounts	Job cost sheets
Close applied factory overhead accounts to factory overhead control	Applied factory overhead accounts	General Journal	Applied Factory Overhead Accounts Factory Overhead	None
Close factory overhead control balances to under- and overapplied factory overhead account	Factory overhead control accounts	General Journal	Under- and Overapplied Factory Overhead Factory Overhead (If underapplied) Factory Overhead Under- and Overapplied Factory Overhead (If overapplied)	None

Illustration 4-17   Summary of Factory Overhead Transactions

Flexible budget (165)
General factory overhead
    expenses (172)
High-low method (160)
Least squares method (161)
Machine hour method (186)
Observation method (159)
Overapplied factory overhead (190)
Period cost (192)
Predetermined factory overhead
    rate (184)
Product cost (192)

Production department (174)
Schedule of fixed costs (171)
Semivariable costs (157)
Sequential distribution method (177)
Service department (174)
Summary of factory overhead (173)
Under- and Overapplied Factory
    Overhead (190)
Underapplied factory overhead (190)
Variable costs (157)
Volume variance (197)

QUESTIONS

1. Define factory overhead expenses in a manner that distinguishes them from other manufacturing costs. What other terms are used to describe factory overhead expenses?

2. What are three categories of factory overhead expenses? Give examples of each.

3. What are the distinguishing characteristics of variable, fixed, and semivariable factory overhead costs?

4. When a product's cost is composed of both fixed and variable costs, what effect does the increase or decrease in production have on total unit costs?

5. Is an understanding of cost behavior essential in managerial accounting? Discuss.

6. What effect does a change in volume have on total variable, fixed, and semivariable costs?

7. What is the basic premise underlying the high-low method of analyzing semivariable costs?

8. Since the least squares method is a more sophisticated mathematical procedure, does it produce more accurate and reliable results?

9. How does accounting for factory overhead differ in small enterprises versus large enterprises?

10. How do the amounts posted in the factory overhead control account in the general ledger serve as a check on the amounts posted to the individual factory overhead analysis sheets?

11. What is the function and use of each of the two types of factory overhead analysis sheets?

12. What are two types of departments found in a factory? What is the function or purpose of each?

13. What are the two most frequently used methods of distributing service department costs to production departments?

14. What are the shortcomings of waiting until the actual factory overhead expenses are known before recording such costs on the job cost sheets?

15. What are the two types of budget data needed to calculate predetermined overhead rates?

16. What are three commonly used methods for applying factory overhead to jobs? Discuss each method.

17. What factory operating conditions and data are required for each of the commonly used methods for applying factory overhead to products? Discuss.

18. Under what conditions would it be desirable for a company to use more than one method to apply factory overhead to jobs or products?

19. If the factory overhead control account has a credit balance of $1,000 at the end of the first month of the fiscal year, has the overhead been under- or overapplied for the month? What are some probable causes for the credit balance?

20. What are two ways that an under- or overapplied factory overhead balance can be disposed of at the end of a fiscal period?

21. What two variances describe why an under- or overapplied factory overhead balance exists? How are they computed?

EXERCISES

Exercise 4-1   Classifying fixed and variable costs.

Classify each of the following items of factory overhead as either a fixed or a variable cost:

(a) Indirect labor
(b) Indirect material
(c) Insurance on building
(d) Overtime premium pay
(e) Depreciation on building (straight-line)
(f) Polishing compounds
(g) Depreciation on machinery (based on hours used)
(h) Employer's payroll taxes
(i) Property taxes
(j) Machine lubricants
(k) Employees' hospital insurance (paid by employer)
(l) Labor for machine repairs
(m) Vacation pay
(n) Patent amortization
(o) Janitor's wages
(p) Rent
(q) Small tools
(r) Plant manager's salary
(s) Receiving clerk's wages
(t) Product inspector's wages

Exercise 4-2   High-low and least squares methods.

The Aloza Company has accumulated the following data over a six-month period.

	Indirect Labor Hours	Indirect Labor Costs
January	400	$ 3,000
February	500	3,500
March	600	4,000
April	700	4,500
May	800	5,000
June	900	5,500
	3,900	$25,500

Separate the indirect labor into its fixed and variable components using:
(a)   the high-low method
(b)   the least squares method.

Exercise 4-3   Computing unit costs at different levels of production.

The Small Manufacturing Co. budgeted for 1,200 units of product X during the month of May. The unit cost of product X was $20, consisting of direct materials, $7; direct labor, $8; and factory overhead, $5 (fixed, $3 and variable, $2).
(a)   What would be the unit cost if 800 units were manufactured?
(b)   What would be the unit cost if 1,500 units were manufactured?
(c)   Explain why there is a difference in the unit costs.

Exercise 4-4   Identifying basis for distribution of overhead to departments.

What would be the appropriate basis for distributing each of the following factory overhead expenses to departments?
(a)   Depreciation on buildings   (g)   Indirect materials
(b)   Depreciation on machinery   (h)   Indirect labor
(c)   Taxes on the buildings   (i)   FICA taxes
(d)   Insurance on the machinery   (j)   Unemployment taxes
(e)   Heat   (k)   Repairs to machinery
(f)   Light

Exercise 4-5   Computing factory overhead application rates—direct labor hour method.

A manufacturing company has two service and two production departments. Building maintenance and factory office are the service departments.

The production departments are department A and department B. The following data have been estimated for next year's operations:

   Direct labor hours: department A, 80,000; department B, 40,000
   Floor space occupied: factory office 10%; department A, 50%; depart-
      ment B, 40%
   The direct charges expected to be made to the departments are:

Building maintenance.	$ 90,000
Factory office	171,000
Department A.	378,000
Department B.	328,000

The building maintenance department services all departments of the company, while factory office costs are allocable to departments A and B on the
basis of direct labor hours. Determine the departmental direct labor hour application rate for each production department.

Exercise 4-6   Determining job cost using direct labor cost, direct labor hour,
and machine hour methods.

(a) If the direct labor cost method is used in applying factory overhead and
     the predetermined rate is 120%, what amount should be charged to Job
     301 for factory overhead, assuming that the direct materials used totaled
     $5,000 and the direct labor cost totaled $3,200?

(b) If the direct labor hour method is used in applying factory overhead and
     the predetermined rate is $1.20 an hour, what amount should be charged
     to Job 301 for factory overhead, assuming that the direct materials used
     totaled $5,000, the direct labor cost totaled $3,200, and the number of
     direct labor hours totaled 2,500?

(c) If the machine hour method is used in applying factory overhead and the
     predetermined rate is $7.20 an hour, what amount should be charged to
     Job 301 for factory overhead, assuming that the direct materials used
     totaled $5,000, the direct labor cost totaled $3,200, and the number of
     machine hours totaled 295?

Exercise 4-7   Determining actual factory overhead.

The books of The Bronze Products Co. revealed that the following general
journal entry had been made at the end of the current accounting period:

Factory Overhead	2,000	
Under- and Overapplied Factory Overhead		2,000

The total direct materials cost for the period was $40,000. The total direct
labor cost, at an average rate of $7.50 per hour for direct labor, was one and
one-half times the direct materials cost. Factory overhead was applied on the

basis of $4.00 per direct labor hour. What was the total actual factory overhead incurred for the period?

Exercise 4-8   Determining labor and factory overhead costs.

The general ledger of The Trickie Manufacturing Co. contains the following control account:

Work in Process			
Materials	15,000	Finished goods	30,000
Labor	15,000		
Factory overhead	9,000		

If the materials charged to the one uncompleted job still in process amounted to $3,400, what amount of labor and factory overhead must have been charged to the job? (Assume overhead applied on the basis of direct labor cost.)

Exercise 4-9   General ledger account analysis.

The following form represents an account taken from the general ledger of The Suzy Manufacturing Co.:

F/O

Indirect materials	500	Work in Process	8,200
Supervisor's salary	1,200	(50% of $16,400 direct labor)	
Power	5,000		
Building expenses	1,000		
Miscellaneous overhead	1,400		

Actual F/O Cost   *applied F/O*

900 - under applied F/O

Answer the following questions:
(a)   What is the title of the account?
(b)   Is this a departmentalized factory? *NO*
(c)   What does the balance of the account represent?
(d)   How was the 50% rate determined?
(e)   What disposition should be made of the balance?

Exercise 4-10   Computing under- and overapplied overhead; budget and volume variances.

The Laurie Manufacturing Company estimated its factory overhead expenses as follows:

Fixed expenses. . *same*.	$20,000
Variable expenses. *Change*.	60,000
Estimated direct labor hours.	80,000

budgeted

The actual factory overhead expenses for the year amounted to $55,000 of which $14,500 were fixed costs. The production attained a capacity of 75% of that budgeted.   60,000
(a)   Compute the under- or overapplied factory overhead.
(b)   Determine the budget and volume variances.

Exercise 4-11   Computing under- and overapplied overhead; budget and volume variances.

The Wells Company applies factory overhead to production using a predetermined rate based on a predicted number of direct labor hours. The number of direct labor hours estimated for the year is 400,000, and the estimates for factory overhead are $240,000 for fixed expenses and $260,000 for variable expenses. The actual production statistics for the year show that only 368,000 direct labor hours were used and the actual factory expenses totaled $459,000, of which $208,400 was fixed cost.
   Determine the following:
(a)   the under- or overapplied expense for the year
(b)   the budget variance
(c)   the volume variance.

PROBLEMS

Problem 4-1   Variable and fixed cost analysis; high-low and least squares methods.

The Daycota Company manufactures a product which requires the use of a considerable amount of natural gas to heat it to a desired temperature. The process requires a constant level of heat, so the furnaces are maintained at a set temperature for 24 hours a day, although units are not continuously processed. Management desires that the variable cost be charged directly to the product and the fixed cost to the factory overhead. The following data have been collected for the year:

	Units	Cost		Units	Cost
January....	2,400	$4,400	July.........	2,200	$4,200
February...	2,300	4,300	August......	2,100	4,100
March.....	2,200	4,200	September...	2,000	4,000
April.......	2,000	4,000	October.....	1,400	3,400
May.......	1,800	3,800	November...	1,900	3,900
June.......	1,900	3,900	December...	1,800	3,800

Required:
1. Separate the variable and fixed elements using:
    (a) High-low method
    (b) Least squares method
2. Determine the cost to be charged to the product for the year.
3. Determine the cost to be charged to factory overhead for the year.

Problem 4-2   Variable and fixed cost pattern analysis.

The cost behavior patterns below are lettered A through L. The vertical axes of the graphs represent total dollars of expense and the horizontal axes represent production. In each case the zero point is at the intersection of the two axes. Each graph may be used more than once.

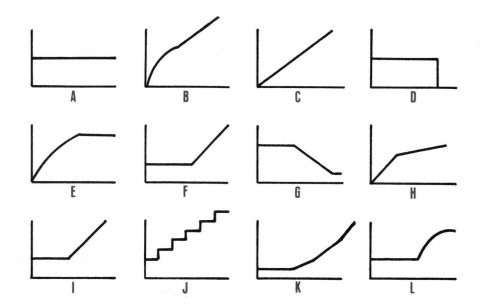

Required:
Select the graph that matches the lettered cost described below.
(a) Depreciation of equipment — the amount of depreciation charged is computed by the machine hour method.
(b) Electricity bill — flat fixed charge, plus a variable cost after a certain number of kilowatt hours are used.
(c) City water bill — computed as follows:

First 1,000,000 gallons or less . . . . $1,000 flat fee
Next 10,000 gallons . . . .   .003 per gallon used

Next 10,000 gallons . . . .   .006 per gallon used
Next 10,000 gallons . . . .   .009 per gallon used
and so on.

(d)   Cost of lubricant for machines — cost per unit decreases with each pound of lubricant used (for example, if one pound is used, the cost is $10.00; if two pounds are used, the cost is $19.98; if three pounds are used, the cost is $29.94; with a minimum cost per pound of $9.25).

(e)   Depreciation of equipment — the amount is computed by the straight-line method. When the depreciation rate was established, it was anticipated that the obsolescence factor would be greater than the wear-and-tear factor.

(f)   Rent on a factory building donated by the city — the agreement calls for a fixed fee payment unless 200,000 work-hours are worked, in which case no rent need be paid.

(g)   Salaries of repair workers — one repair worker is needed for every 1,000 hours of machine hours or less (i.e., 0 to 1,000 hours requires one repair worker, 1,001 to 2,000 hours requires two repair workers, etc.).

(h)   Federal unemployment compensation taxes for the year — labor force is constant in number throughout year (average annual salary is $6,000 per worker).

(i)   Cost of raw materials used.

(j)   Rent on a factory building donated by the county — agreement calls for rent of $100,000, less $1 for each direct labor hour worked in excess of 200,000 hours, but minimum rental payment of $20,000 must be paid.

(AICPA adapted)

Problem 4-3   General journal entries for factory overhead.

The Chapman Company uses a job order cost system. Selected transactions dealing with factory overhead for the month are as follows:

(a)   Requisitioned indirect materials from storeroom, $1,600.
(b)   Purchased factory supplies for future needs, $2,200.
(c)   Purchased parts for repairing a machine, $700.
(d)   Requisitioned factory supplies from storeroom, $450.
(e)   Returned defective factory supplies to vendor, $350.
(f)   Rent accrued for the month, $1,200.
(g)   Returned previously requisitioned factory supplies to storeroom, $175.
(h)   Depreciation of machinery and equipment, $1,400.
(i)   Payroll taxes liability for month, $1,600.
(j)   Heat, light, and power charges payable for the month, $3,200.
(k)   Expired insurance on inventories, $675.
(l)   Factory overhead applied to production, $18,200.
(m)   Indirect labor for the month, $1,300.

(n)   Goods completed and transferred to finished goods: materials, $7,200; labor, $20,200; factory overhead, $15,200.

Required:

Record the above transactions in general journal form assuming that the records include a control account and a subsidiary ledger for factory overhead to which the entries will be posted at some later date.

Problem 4-4   Distribution of service department costs to production departments.

The Elizabeth Manufacturing Co. is divided into five departments, A, B, C, D, and E. The first three departments are engaged in production work. Departments D and E are service departments. During the month of August, the following factory overhead was incurred for the various departments:

Department A......	$21,000	Department D	$9,000
Department B......	18,000	Department E.......	6,400
Department C	25,000		

The bases for distributing service department expenses to the other departments are as follows:

Department E—On the basis of floor space occupied by the other departments as follows: department A, 10,000 sq. ft.; department B, 4,500 sq. ft.; department C, 10,500 sq. ft.; and department D, 7,000 sq. ft.

Department D—Divided: dept. A—30%; dept. B—20%; dept. C—50%.

Required:

Prepare schedules showing the distribution of the service departments' expenses to:
1.   the other service department and the production departments.
2.   to the production departments only (see Illustrations 4-7 and 4-8). (It is advisable to arrange the schedules so that the service departments precede the production departments.)

Problem 4-5   Determining total job costs using predetermined overhead rate.

The Brasso Manufacturing Co. uses the job order cost system of accounting. Shown below is a list of the jobs completed during the month of March showing the charges for materials requisitioned and for direct labor.

Job	Materials Requisitioned	Direct Labor
317	$ 300.00	$ 600.00
318	1,080.00	940.00
319	720.00	1,400.00
320	4,200.00	5,120.00

Required:

Assuming that factory overhead is applied on the basis of direct labor costs and that the predetermined rate is 180%, compute:
1. the amount of overhead to be added to the cost of each job completed during the month.
2. the total cost of each job completed during the month.
3. the total cost of producing all the jobs finished during the month.

Problem 4-6   Determining job cost—calculation of predetermined rate for applying overhead by direct labor cost and direct labor hour methods.

The Blue Manufacturing Co. has its factory divided into three departments. In each department, all the operations are sufficiently alike for the department to be regarded as a cost center. The estimated monthly factory overhead for the departments are: Department A, $32,000; Department B, $18,000; and Department C, $5,040. The estimated production data are:

	Dept. A	Dept. B	Dept. C
Materials used	$20,000	$10,000	$10,000
Direct labor cost	$16,000	$15,000	$ 8,400
Direct labor hours	16,000	10,000	7,000

The job cost ledger shows the following data for Job 250, which was completed during the month:

	Dept. A	Dept. B	Dept. C
Materials used	$12.00	$14.00	$12.00
Direct labor cost	$13.00	$13.50	$12.50
Direct labor hours	11	9	10

Required:

Determine the cost of Job 250, assuming that the factory overhead is applied to production orders on the basis of:
1. Direct labor cost.
2. Direct labor hours.

Problem 4-7   Determining overhead rates using direct labor cost, direct labor hour, and machine hour methods.

The Klanco Manufacturing Company is studying the results of applying factory overhead to production. The following data have been used: estimated factory overhead, $60,000; estimated materials costs, $50,000; estimated labor costs, $60,000; estimated direct labor hours, 40,000; estimated machine hours, 25,000; work in process at the beginning of the month, none.

The actual factory overhead incurred for the month of November was $55,000, and the production statistics at November 30 are:

actual

Job	Materials Costs	Direct Labor Costs	Direct Labor Hours	Machine Hours	Date Jobs Completed
101	$ 5,000	$ 7,200	5,000	3,000	Nov. 10
102	7,000	10,000	6,000	3,200	Nov. 14
103	8,000	11,000	6,500	4,000	Nov. 20
104	9,000	9,000	5,600	3,400	In process
105	10,000	15,000	10,500	6,500	Nov. 26
106	11,000	4,200	3,000	1,500	In process
Total	$50,000	$56,400	36,600	21,600	

Required:

1. Calculate the predetermined rate based on:
   estimated (a) Direct labor cost
   (b) Direct labor hours
   (c) Machine hours   3/ *p/hr DL Applied —*
2. Using each of the methods, compute the total cost of each job at the end of the month.
3. Determine the under- or overapplied factory overhead at the end of the month under each of the methods.
4. Which method would you recommend? Why?

Problem 4-8   Determining overhead rate; using direct labor cost, direct labor hour, and machine hour methods.

The following information was taken from the books of Danko Company and represents the operations for the month of January:

actual

	Dept. A	Dept. B	Dept. C
Materials used	$20,000	$10,000	$10,000
Direct labor cost	$ 8,000	$ 5,000	$ 9,000
Direct labor hours	20,000	10,000	27,000
Machine hours.	4,000	5,000	2,025
Factory overhead	$10,000	$ 5,000	$ 8,100

The job cost system is used, and the February cost sheet for Job 100 shows the following:

actual

	Dept. A	Dept. B	Dept. C
Materials requisitions	$2.00	$4.00	$2.00
Direct labor cost	$3.60	$3.00	$2.10
Direct labor hours	8	6	6
Machine hours.	2	3	1

The following information was accumulated during February:

actual

	Dept. A	Dept. B	Dept. C
Direct labor hours	15,000	9,800	20,000
Factory overhead	$7,000	$5,000	$5,900

Required:

1. Using the January data, ascertain the factory overhead application rates to be used during February on the basis of:
   (a) Direct labor cost
   (b) Direct labor hours
   (c) Machine hours

3 elements 2. Prepare a schedule showing the total production cost of Job 100 under each method of applying factory overhead.

3. Draft in general journal form the entries required to record the following operations:
   (a) Payment of total factory overhead.
   (b) Distribution of factory overhead to the departments. *A B C*
   actual (c) Application of factory overhead to the jobs. (Use the predetermined rate calculated in (1) above.) *rate x actual*
   (d) Closing of the applied factory overhead accounts.
   (e) Recording under- and overapplied factory overhead. *(Closing out departmental)*

Problem 4-9 Determining the under- and overapplied overhead; budget variances; volume variances.

The Millbrooke Corporation has four departmental accounts: Building maintenance, General factory overhead, Department A, and Department B. The direct labor hours method is used to apply factory overhead to the jobs being worked on in departments A and B. The company expects each production department to use 30,000 direct labor hours during the year. The estimated overhead rates for the year are:

	Dept. A	Dept. B
Variable cost per hour	$1.10	$1.20
Fixed cost per hour	2.70	3.00
	$3.80	$4.20

7,000 *8,400*

During the year, both departments A and B used 28,000 direct labor hours in their departments. Factory overhead costs incurred during the year were as follows:

actual

Building maintenance	$30,000	
General factory overhead	75,400	→ *none* *DL hours*
Department A	45,800	→ *28,000*
Department B	68,800	→ *28,000*

refers to dist. service to prod.

In determining application rates at the beginning of the year, cost allocations were made as follows:

service

Building maintenance to general factory overhead, 10%; to department A, *production* 50%; to department B, 40%.

General factory overhead was distributed according to direct labor hours.

Required:

1. Determine the under- or overapplied overhead for each production department.
2. Calculate the budget variance and the volume variance for each production department.

Problem 4-10 Distribution of service department costs; reasons for allocations.

Given below are the details pertaining to the power service department.

Schedule of Horsepower Hours

	Production Departments		Service Departments	
	A	B	X	Y
Needed at capacity production	10,000	20,000	12,000	8,000
Used during the month of April	8,000	13,000	7,000	6,000

During the month of April, the expenses of operating the power service department amounted to $93,000; of this amount $25,000 was considered to be fixed costs.

Required:

1. What dollar amounts of the power service department expense should be allocated to each production and service department?
2. What are the reasons for allocating the costs of one service department to other service departments as well as to production departments?

(AICPA adapted)

Problem 4-11 Distributing service department costs; high-low method; budget and volume variances.

The Excello Casting Company manufactures zinc castings. The estimated factory overhead for the four production departments (including service department overhead) for two levels of activity was:

Estimated/Bud. Cost rates per hour   *VCPH*

Production Department	25,000 hours	30,000 hours		
Casting	16. $ 400,000	$ 450,000	50,000	10.
Break-off	16. 400,000	450,000	50,000	10.
Polishing	12. 300,000	350,000	50,000	10.
Plating	15.20 380,000	450,000	70,000	10.
Total	$1,480,000	$1,700,000		14

Bud. Capacity The predetermined departmental factory overhead rates are based on 25,000 direct labor hours at normal capacity. Depreciation of machinery is 10% annually. Machinery was recorded at the following costs:

Department	Cost of Machinery *Actual 10%*
Casting	$500,000
Break-off	100,000
Polishing	400,000
Plating	250,000
Pentagraph	150,000
Shipping	10,000
Art	10,000
General Factory	10,000

The actual operations for the year show the following:
1. Each of the four production departments worked 28,000 actual hours.
2. Actual departmental factory overhead costs incurred were as follows:

Nom   *act. Cost*

	Supervision	Indirect Labor	Insurance	Taxes	Machine Repairs	Supplies
General Factory	$50,000	$143,500	$ 4,500	$ 5,000	-0-	$ 6,000
Pentagraph	-0-	200,000	6,000	6,500	$ 1,000	1,000
Art	-0-	138,300	4,000	4,500	-0-	10,000
Shipping	-0-	100,000	3,000	4,000	1,000	5,000
Casting	60,000	5,000	12,500	15,000	11,000	12,000
Break-off	55,000	6,000	10,000	13,000	5,000	9,000
Polishing	-0-	18,200	9,500	10,000	6,000	8,000
Plating	65,000	-0-	8,500	9,000	4,000	11,000

3. The total cost of factory utilities amounted to $100,000 and is to be distributed as follows:

Actual

General Factory	5%	Casting	25%
Pentagraph	10%	Break-off	12%
Art	3%	Polishing	20%
Shipping	5%	Plating	20%

4. The fixed charges associated with the building (including taxes and depreciation) amounted to $300,000. The building's 20,000-square-feet area is occupied as follows:

Department	Square feet
General Factory	3,000
Pentagraph	1,500
Art	1,000
Shipping	1,000
Casting	3,000
Break-off	4,500
Polishing	2,500
Plating	3,500

Required:
1. Determine the direct labor hour rates to be used for each of the four production departments.
2. Compute the net amount of under- or overapplied factory overhead and the budget and volume variance for the year by:
   (a) transferring general factory overhead to the other departments using the following percentages: Pentagraph, 5%; Art, 2%; Shipping, 13%; and allocating the remainder equally among the production departments.
   (b) closing the Pentagraph Department costs to the Art Department.
   (c) closing the Art Department and Shipping Department costs to the production departments on an equal basis.

Problem 4-12   Using overhead to determine gross profit rates.

The Newzone Company sold 50 air conditioning units for $300 each in June. Costs included materials cost of $70 a unit and direct labor cost of $50 a unit. Factory overhead is computed at 100% of direct labor cost. Interest expense on a 12% bank loan is equivalent to $1 a unit. Federal income tax at a 30% rate is equivalent to $15 a unit.

Effective July 1, materials costs decreased 5% and direct labor costs increased 20%. Also effective July 1, the interest rate on the bank loan increased from 12% per annum to 18% per annum.

Required:
1. Assuming no change in the rate of overhead in relation to direct labor costs, compute the sales price per unit that will produce the same ratio of gross profit.
2. Assuming that $20 of the overhead consists of fixed costs, compute the sales price per unit that will produce the same ratio of gross profit.

(AICPA adapted)

5

JOB ORDER COST ACCOUNTING—

APPLICATION OF PRINCIPLES

LEARNING OBJECTIVES

In studying this chapter, you will learn about the:

■ Application of the principles and procedures involved in accounting for materials, labor, and factory overhead by a manufacturing firm using a job order cost system.

The principles and procedures involved in accounting for materials, labor, and factory overhead have been discussed in the preceding chapters. This chapter integrates the information previously developed and illustrates the application of cost accounting procedures to the operations of a hypothetical manufacturing concern. The procedures illustrated are typical of those encountered in firms using the job order cost system.

To derive the maximum benefit from the chapter, it should be read carefully and thoughtfully. Each transaction should be followed through the accounting process, and each figure in the general ledger accounts should be analyzed in order to understand the origin of the figure and how it flows into the ledger account.

COMPREHENSIVE ILLUSTRATION OF JOB ORDER COST ACCOUNTING

This comprehensive illustration covers the accounting procedures for the Judson Manufacturing Corporation for the month of May. Following a description of the company's factory organization and accounting system, a complete accounting cycle is presented—from beginning-of-the-month balances through the recording of transactions for the month and end-of-month procedures, including preparation of the trial balance, the work sheet, schedules, and financial statements.

Factory Organization

The Judson Manufacturing Corporation is engaged in the manufacture of commercial water softening equipment. The softeners are either built to order from customer specifications or manufactured according to standard specifications and carried in stock for sale in the usual course of business. Essentially, a water softening unit comprises two tanks: one contains the softening agent, the other rock salt. Rock salt provides the brine to rejuvenate the softening agent. Parts for softeners are also manufactured and carried in stock for sale or for use in the production of softeners. The job order cost system is used in accounting for the cost of production.

The factory is organized on a departmental basis. The departmentalization described here is not intended to be complete for a factory of this type. Two typical production departments and two typical service departments are used. The following is a brief description of the activities of each of these departments.

Department A — Welding.   The welding department fabricates the water softening unit tanks. First, prerolled and formed sheet steel purchased from a foundry is welded in a lengthwise direction to make the tank wall. Then the bottom and top plates, which have been cut in department B, are fitted and welded to the tank wall.

Department B — Cutting.   The cutting department cuts sheet steel into circular pieces for the bottom and top of the tank; it also cuts galvanized iron pipe used in the assembly into various required lengths. This department also assembles, tests, and inspects the softeners.

Service (handwritten in margin)

Department C — Maintenance. The maintenance department is responsible for the maintenance of the buildings, machinery, and other factory equipment as well as for the janitorial service and the heating and lighting of the factory. The expenses of this service department are apportioned to departments A, B, and D on the basis of the floor space that each occupies.

Department D — Engineering. The engineering department is responsible for preparing the detailed specifications and plans for all softeners manufactured. The expenses of this department are apportioned to departments A and B on a basis of two-thirds to A and one-third to B. This arbitrary allocation is based on the past experience of the company: in general, twice as much work is performed for department A as for department B and no services are rendered to department C.

Chart of Accounts

The chart of general ledger accounts for the Judson Manufacturing Corporation is reproduced below. Control accounts for subsidiary ledgers are maintained as described on pages 224 and 225.

THE JUDSON MANUFACTURING CORPORATION
CHART OF ACCOUNTS

Current Assets:

Cash
1110 Cash
1120 Petty Cash — *used to pay w/cash* (handwritten)

Temporary Investments — *short term* (handwritten)
1200 Marketable Securities

Receivables — *asset* (handwritten)
1310 Notes Receivable
1320 Interest Receivable
1330 Accounts Receivable
1331 Allowance for Doubtful
    Accounts — *Contra asset* (handwritten)

Inventories
1410 Finished Goods
1420 Work in Process
1430 Materials

Prepayments
1510 Prepaid Insurance

Property, Plant, and Equipment *fixed assets* (handwritten)
1610 Land
1620 Buildings
1621 Accumulated Depreciation —
    Buildings
1630 Machinery
1631 Accumulated Depreciation — *Contra asset* (handwritten)
    Machinery
1640 Furniture and Fixtures
1641 Accumulated Depreciation —
    Furniture and Fixtures
1650 Small Tools
1651 Accumulated Depreciation —
    Small Tools

Intangibles
1710 Goodwill — *amortize at end* (handwritten)

Current Liabilities — *1 yr. or less* (handwritten)
2210 Notes Payable
2220 Vouchers Payable
2230 FICA Tax Payable

2240 Federal Unemployment Tax
Payable
2250 State Unemployment Tax
Payable
2260 Employees Income Tax
Payable
2271 Property Tax Payable
2272 Estimated Income Tax
Payable
2273 Interest Payable
2274 Accrued Payroll — *unfinished payroll*

Long-Term Liabilities
2710 Bonds Payable — *issue a bond*

Stockholders' Equity
2910 Capital Stock
2980 Retained Earnings — *net income*
2990 Income Summary — *current run*

Factory Overhead — *temporary*
3100 Factory Overhead
3140 Factory Overhead —
Department A
3150 Factory Overhead —
Department B
3160 Factory Overhead —
Department C

3170 Factory Overhead —
Department D
3180 Under- and Overapplied — *end of year*
Overhead

Sales and Cost of Goods Sold
4100 Sales
4600 Cost of Goods Sold

Payroll and General Expenses
5000 Payroll
5100 Salaries
5200 Payroll Tax Expense —
Salaries
5300 Office Expense
5500 Public Relations Expense
5800 Doubtful Accounts Expense
5900 Miscellaneous General
Expense

Additions to and Deductions from
Operating Income
Additions to Income:
6110 Purchase Discounts *(cost of goods sold)*
6120 Interest Income
Deductions from Income:
6220 Interest Expense *(bond)*
6420 Provision for Income Tax *(extra funds)*

1330 Accounts Receivable.   Accounts Receivable is the control account for the accounts receivable ledger. The accounts receivable ledger is a loose-leaf ledger containing ledger sheets for the individual customer accounts. The accounts are kept in alphabetic order.

acct for each customer alphabetic

1410 Finished Goods.   Finished Goods is the control account for the finished goods ledger. An account for each standard softener or finished part is maintained on a card. Since most of the work done by the company is on specific orders received from customers, the only items that will be recorded in the finished goods ledger will be softeners of standard sizes for which there is a continuous demand, parts that may be either sold or used in the manufacture of softeners, and jobs completed and not delivered. During slack seasons, the employees and facilities of the company may be profitably employed in building up the stock of standard softeners and parts. The job cost sheets are the source of the information needed in recording the quan-

acct for each type of F/G

tities and manufacturing costs of all softeners and parts manufactured for stock.

1420 Work in Process.   Work in Process is the control account for the job cost ledger. The job cost ledger is a loose-leaf ledger in which a job cost sheet is used to keep an account of the cost of completing each job.

1430 Materials. *[General ledger]* Materials is the control account for the stores ledger. Cards are used to keep track of the various types of materials and factory supplies carried in stock. Purchase invoices and receiving reports are the sources of the information needed to record the quantities and costs of materials and factory supplies received, while materials requisitions provide the source of the information needed to record the quantities and costs of materials and factory supplies issued.

[separate acct for each type of material inflow + outflow FIFO, LIFO, AVE.]

2910 Capital Stock.   Capital Stock is the control account for the stockholders ledger. A separate account for each stockholder is kept in the stockholders ledger. The Judson Manufacturing Corporation has an authorized capital of $200,000 divided into 2,000 shares of common stock with par value of $100 per share. All stock has been issued and is outstanding.

[name, add, + # of shares of each stockholder]

3100 Factory Overhead.   Factory Overhead is the control account for the factory overhead ledger. The factory overhead ledger is a loose-leaf ledger in which analysis sheets, similar to those on pages 169 and 170, are used.

[expense type. head w/each dept]

Following is a list of the individual accounts kept in the factory overhead ledger.

Fixed Costs	Variable Costs
3111 Depreciation	**3121** Indirect Materials
3112 Property Tax	**3122** Indirect Labor
3113 Insurance	**3123** Fuel Consumed
	3124 Water
	3125 Light
	3126 Power
	3127 Payroll Tax Expense
	3128 Miscellaneous Factory Expense

Trial Balance *[end of the month]*

The company operates on a fiscal year ending April 30. Following is the post-closing trial balance as of April 30:

The Judson Manufacturing Corporation
Post-Closing Trial Balance
April 30, 19--

Cash	21,500.00	
Petty Cash	100.00	
Marketable Securities	16,050.00	
Notes Receivable	10,000.00	
Interest Receivable	101.66	
Accounts Receivable	36,000.00	
Allowance for Doubtful Accounts		1,800.00
Finished Goods	18,000.00	
Work in Process	10,000.00	
Materials	25,000.00	
Prepaid Insurance	2,000.00	
Land	25,100.00	
Buildings	80,000.00	
Accumulated Depreciation — Buildings		12,000.00
Machinery	120,000.00	
Accumulated Depreciation — Machinery		25,000.00
Furniture and Fixtures	14,000.00	
Accumulated Depreciation — Furniture and Fixtures		4,480.00
Small Tools	14,000.00	
Accumulated Depreciation — Small Tools		8,520.00
Goodwill	5,300.00	
Notes Payable		7,000.00
Vouchers Payable		15,000.00
FICA Tax Payable		1,800.00
Federal Unemployment Tax Payable		315.00
State Unemployment Tax Payable		1,215.00
Employees Income Tax Payable		1,500.00
Property Tax Payable		2,000.00
Estimated Income Tax Payable		16,200.00
Interest Payable		102.22
Bonds Payable		25,000.00
Capital Stock		200,000.00
Retained Earnings		75,219.44
	397,151.66	397,151.66

Books of Account

The Judson Manufacturing Corporation uses an accounting system in which separate journals and books of account are kept to record each type of transaction. The books of account and other records consist of the following:

books of original entry

LEDGERS
1. General ledger *accts.*
2. Subsidiary ledgers:
   (a) Accounts receivable ledger
   (b) Stores ledger
   (c) Job cost ledger
   (d) Factory overhead ledger
   (e) Finished goods ledger
   (f) Stockholders ledger

JOURNALS
1. General journal
2. Voucher register
3. Check register
4. Sales journal *on acct.*
5. Cash receipts journal

AUXILIARY RECORDS
1. Clock card
2. Time ticket
3. Materials requisition
4. Petty cash disbursements record

The voucher register and check register used by Judson Manufacturing Corporation appear as shown on the following page.

Narrative of Transactions

The following is a discussion of the transactions completed during May. The subsequent posting of the journal entries illustrated in each of the following transactions is presented on pages 242 to 248.

(a) **Materials Purchased.**   As each purchase transaction is completed, the purchase invoice is verified and a voucher is prepared. The voucher is recorded in the voucher register in the columns headed Materials and Vouchers Payable and is posted to the proper accounts in the stores ledger. Since the voucher system is used, the file of unpaid vouchers takes the place of a subsidiary accounts payable ledger.

At the end of the month, when the summary posting from the voucher register is completed, the total of the Materials column, $22,200, is posted as a debit to Materials (Account No. 1430). At the same time, the total of the Vouchers Payable column is posted as a credit to Vouchers Payable (Account No. 2220). The entry, in general journal form, to record these summary data appears as follows:

```
Materials......................................    22,200
    Vouchers Payable..............................              22,200
```

summary voucher reg.

(b) **Factory Overhead.**   Invoices for factory overhead expenses are verified and vouchered, recorded in the voucher register in the columns headed Factory Overhead and Vouchers Payable, and are posted to the proper

VOUCHER REGISTER FOR MONTH OF										19		PAGE			
	MATERIALS DR.	PAYROLL DR.	FACTORY OVERHEAD DR.	SUNDRY ACCOUNTS				DAY	VOU. NO.	TO WHOM ISSUED	TERMS	DISPOSITION		VOUCHERS PAYABLE CR.	
				ACCT. NO.	AMOUNT DR.	AMOUNT CR.	√					DATE	CK. NO.		
1										AMOUNTS FORWARDED					1
2															2
3															3
4															4
5															5
6															6

CHECK REGISTER FOR MONTH OF					19	PAGE		
	VOUCHERS PAY. DR.		DAY	DRAWN TO THE ORDER OF	PURCHASE DISCOUNTS CR.	CASH CR.		
	NO.	AMOUNT				CK. NO.	AMOUNT	
1								1
2								2
3								3
4								4
5								5
6								6

Illustration 5-1 Voucher register and check register

accounts in the factory overhead ledger. The factory overhead ledger contains individual accounts for each type of overhead expense, including indirect materials, indirect labor, and other indirect manufacturing expenses.

At the end of the month, the total of the Factory Overhead column is posted as a debit to Factory Overhead (Account No. 3100). The amounts recorded in the Vouchers Payable column are included in the column total, which is posted as a credit to Vouchers Payable. The entry, in general journal form, to record these summary data appears as follows:

```
Factory Overhead.....................................    4,664
    Vouchers Payable...................................            4,664
```

(c) **Payroll.**   The wages of factory employees are paid weekly, while the salaries of all other employees are paid semimonthly. On each payday, a voucher is prepared for the amount of the wages and salaries earned during the pay period. The source of this information is a summary of the time tickets and a schedule of the salaries.

The amounts to be withheld for FICA taxes and employees' income taxes and the net amount payable to all factory employees are indicated on the voucher. The payroll vouchers are recorded in the voucher register, where the total amount of the wages earned is entered in the column headed Payroll Dr. and the net amount of the total wages payable to employees is entered in the column headed Vouchers Payable Cr. The amounts credited to FICA Tax Payable and Employees Income Tax Payable are entered in the Sundry Accounts Cr. amount column and are posted individually to the proper general ledger accounts.

At the end of the month, the total of the voucher register column headed Payroll is posted as a debit to Payroll (Account No. 5000). The amounts recorded in the Vouchers Payable column are included in the column total, which is posted as a credit to Vouchers Payable. The entry, in general journal form, to record these summary data appears as follows:

```
Payroll.............................................   53,000
    FICA Tax Payable...................................            4,240
    Employees Income Tax Payable......................            7,950
    Vouchers Payable...................................           40,810
```

(d) **Payroll Checks.**   The checks issued in payment of the payroll vouchers are recorded in the check register. At the end of the month, the total of the check register column headed Vouchers Payable is posted as a debit to Vouchers Payable, and the total of the Cash column is posted as a credit to

Cash. These column totals include payments for materials, payroll, various factory overhead items, and all other expenditures made by check during the period. The entry, in general journal form, to record the payment of wages and salaries is:

Vouchers Payable.	40,810	
Cash		40,810

(e) **Materials Requisitioned.**   During the month, materials requisitions are posted to the proper accounts in the subsidiary stores ledger, job cost ledger, and factory overhead ledger. At the end of the month, a summary of the materials requisitions is prepared. The summary for May provides the following information:

Direct materials requisitioned:	
For Job 308	$ 2,900
For Job 309	4,500
For Job 310	4,000
For Job 311	5,500
For Job 312	4,800
For Job 313	3,000
Total direct materials requisitioned	$24,700
Indirect materials requisitioned	4,700
Total materials requisitioned.	$29,400

The entry, in general journal form, to record these summary data appears as follows:

Work in Process	24,700	
Factory Overhead.	4,700	
Materials.		29,400

Three control accounts are affected by this entry: Work in Process (Account No. 1420), the control account for the job cost ledger; Factory Overhead (Account No. 3100), the control account for the factory overhead ledger; and Materials (Account No. 1430), the control account for the stores ledger.

(f) **Wages and Salaries Earned.**   The time tickets and schedule of fixed salaries are the sources of individual postings to the proper accounts in the subsidiary job cost ledger and factory overhead ledger. At the end of the month, the labor cost summary is prepared from the time tickets, which show the amount of labor applied directly to jobs in process and the amount of indirect labor. The labor cost summary and a schedule of the fixed salaries provide the information for drafting a general journal entry to distribute the total wages and salaries earned during the month.

In distributing the total wages and salaries earned during the month, two control accounts are affected: Work in Process (Account No. 1420) is debited for the total of the direct labor cost, and Factory Overhead (Account No. 3100) is debited for the total indirect labor cost. Also, Salaries (Account No. 5100) is debited for the total of the salaries paid to all other employees. Payroll (Account No. 5000) is credited for the total wages and salaries earned during the month. The following general journal entry distributes the total wages and salaries earned during the month:

Work in Process	39,900	
Factory Overhead	7,000	
Salaries	10,000	
Payroll		56,900

In the subsidiary job cost ledger, the detail for the direct labor in Work in Process is as follows:

Job 303	$ 3,500
Job 308	4,200
Job 309	5,400
Job 310	6,850
Job 311	7,250
Job 312	6,600
Job 313	6,100
Total direct labor	$39,900

The total wages and salaries earned during the month will be the same as the total amount of the payroll vouchers issued during the month if all wages and salaries are paid on a monthly or semimonthly basis. However, since some of the wages are paid on a weekly basis and the last payday for the month does not fall on the last day of the month, Judson Manufacturing Corporation must account for accrued wages. The amount of the accrued wages for May is $3,900, which is the credit balance of the payroll account.

If the payroll account is debited for the total wages and salaries paid during the month and is credited for the total wages and salaries earned during the month, the credit balance of the account should always represent the total amount of the wages and salaries accrued at the end of the month.

This credit balance should be transferred to a liability account. Therefore, at the end of May, the following general journal entry is recorded:

Payroll...	3,900	
Accrued Payroll		3,900

(g) **Payroll Taxes Imposed on Employer.** The payroll records provide the information for the schedule of wages earned and payroll taxes shown below. At the end of each payroll period, the payroll taxes imposed on the employer for FICA and federal and state unemployment taxes are recorded. At the end of May, the employer's payroll taxes on the accrued payroll are recorded.

Schedule of Earnings and Payroll Taxes
For the Month Ended May 31, 19--

Classification of Wages and Salaries	Total Earnings	FICA 8%	Unemployment Taxes		Total Payroll Taxes
			Federal 1%	State 4%	
Direct labor......	$39,900.00	$3,192.00	$399.00	$1,596.00	$5,187.00
Indirect labor	7,000.00	560.00	70.00	280.00	910.00
Total taxes on wages		$3,752.00	$469.00	$1,876.00	$6,097.00
Salaries	10,000.00	800.00	100.00	400.00	1,300.00
Total	$56,900.00	$4,552.00	$569.00	$2,276.00	$7,397.00

The combined general journal entry to record these summary data for May is as follows:

Factory Overhead.......................................	6,097	
Payroll Tax Expense—Salaries.........................	1,300	
FICA Tax Payable.....................................		4,552
Federal Unemployment Tax Payable		569
State Unemployment Tax Payable		2,276

(h) **Fixed Expenses.** At the end of each month, the schedule of fixed costs is the source of a general journal entry debiting Factory Overhead

(Account No. 3100) for the amount of all fixed manufacturing expenses, such as depreciation, property tax, and insurance applicable to the month. The schedule of fixed expenses is also the source of the posting of the proper amounts to the individual accounts in the subsidiary factory overhead ledger.

The depreciation of factory property is computed at the following annual rates:

Buildings — 4.875%	Furniture and Fixtures — 10%
Machinery — 8.25%	Small Tools — 20%

It should be noted that small tools are depreciated at the rate of 20 percent. It is rather difficult to determine a satisfactory rate of depreciation on small tools because there are so many of them and their life is so unpredictable. Instead of using the depreciation method, many firms use the fixed-sum system. Under this system, a definite amount, representing the average value of the tools on hand at all times, is set up as a plant asset and the amount of all replacements is treated as factory overhead. Other firms use the inventory system, in which all replacements are charged to the asset account, and at the end of the period the tools on hand are inventoried. The difference between the inventory value and the balance of the small tools account is then charged to Factory Overhead. Regardless of which method is used, the amount consumed in each accounting period should be treated as factory overhead.

The following general journal entry records these fixed expenses:

fixed expenses

Factory Overhead.	1,850.00	
Accumulated Depreciation — Buildings		325.00
Accumulated Depreciation — Machinery		825.00
Accumulated Depreciation — Furniture and Fixtures . . .		116.67
Accumulated Depreciation — Small Tools		233.33
Property Tax Payable. . . . *not yet paid*		150.00
Prepaid Insurance		200.00

(i) Factory Overhead Distributed to Departments.   At the end of each month, a summary of factory overhead is prepared on a departmental basis. The summary for May is at the top of page 234.

The subsidiary factory overhead ledger accounts are the source of the information for this summary. The amounts charged to Payroll Taxes Ex-

actual

Summary of Factory Overhead
For the Month Ended May 31, 19--

Acct. No.	Account	Dept. A Welding	Dept. B Cutting	Dept. C Maintenance	Dept. D Engineering	Total
3111	Depreciation	$ 625.00	$ 585.00	$ 200.00	$ 90.00	$ 1,500.00
3112	Property tax.........	60.00	55.00	25.00	10.00	150.00
3113	Insurance...........	90.00	80.00	20.00	10.00	200.00
3121	Indirect materials	2,100.00	2,200.00	270.00	130.00	4,700.00
3122	Indirect labor........	2,000.00	2,200.00	2,400.00	400.00	7,000.00
3123	Fuel consumed......	300.00	250.00	150.00	50.00	750.00
3124	Water...............	20.00	50.00	32.00	222.00	324.00
3125	Light	500.00	400.00	200.00	100.00	1,200.00
3126	Power	900.00	500.00	150.00	200.00	1,750.00
3127	Payroll taxes	3,314.00	1,824.00	639.00	320.00	6,097.00
3128	Miscellaneous factory expenses	240.00	192.00	128.00	80.00	640.00
	Total..............	$10,149.00	$8,336.00	$4,214.00	$1,612.00	$24,311.00

pense (Account No. 3127) include the FICA tax of 8%, the federal unemployment tax of 1%, and the state unemployment tax of 4% imposed on employers. From the summary, a general journal entry is prepared as follows:

from F/O ledger

Factory Overhead — Department A	10,149	
Factory Overhead — Department B	8,336	
Factory Overhead — Department C	4,214	
Factory Overhead — Department D	1,612	
Factory Overhead.................................		24,311

After this entry is posted, the factory overhead control account has a zero balance. The individual accounts in the subsidiary factory overhead ledger are also assumed to have zero balances.

(j) Distribution of Maintenance Department Expenses.   At the end of each month, the service departments' expenses are distributed on the basis of service rendered to the other departments. There are two service departments: department C, the maintenance department; and department D, the engineering department. The work sheet on page 235 was prepared to distribute the expenses of both service departments. The maintenance de-

2 entries

Service Departments Expense Distribution Work Sheet
For the Month Ended May 31, 19--

Description	Dept. C Maintenance	Dept. D Engineering	Dept. A Welding	Dept. B Cutting	Total
Direct costs	$4,214.00	$1,612.00	$10,149.00	$8,336.00	$24,311.00
Department C—Distribution $.1404667 per sq. ft. Dept. D—6,500 sq. ft. . . . . . . Dept. A—16,000 sq. ft. . . . . . Dept. B—7,500 sq. ft.		913.03 $2,525.03	2,247.47	1,053.50	
Department D—Distribution basis arbitrary Dept. A—⅔ . . . . Dept. B—⅓			1,683.35	841.68	
Total			$14,079.82	$10,231.18	$24,311.00

partment expenses are distributed to the other departments on the basis of the number of square feet occupied by each department:

Department	Area Sq. Ft.	Rate per Sq. Ft.*	Amount
A	16,000	$.1404667	$2,247.47
B	7,500	.1404667	1,053.50
D	6,500	.1404667	913.03
	30,000		$4,214.00

*$4,214 ÷ 30,000 sq. ft. = $.1404667

The distribution is accomplished by the following general journal entry:

Factory Overhead — Department A 2,247.47
Factory Overhead — Department B 1,053.50
Factory Overhead — Department D 913.03
    Factory Overhead — Department C 4,214.00

(k) Distribution of Engineering Department Expenses. The engineering department expenses are distributed to the production departments on the basis of two-thirds to department A and one-third to department B.

This arbitrary distribution is based on the past experience of the company. The amount to be distributed includes both the direct expenses from department D and the apportioned expenses from department C. The apportioned amounts are calculated as follows:

$$\text{Dept. A} - \tfrac{2}{3} \times \$2{,}525.03 = \$1{,}683.35$$

$$\text{Dept. B} - \tfrac{1}{3} \times \$2{,}525.03 = \$\;\;841.68$$

The distribution is accomplished by the following general journal entry:

Factory Overhead — Department A	1,683.35	
Factory Overhead — Department B	841.68	
Factory Overhead — Department D		2,525.03

(l) Distribution of the Production Departments' Expenses.   During the month, direct materials and direct labor costs are charged to the proper accounts in the job cost ledger from the materials requisitions and time tickets. To ascertain the total cost of each job processed during the month, factory overhead must be added. The company has adopted the direct labor hour basis for applying factory overhead. To ascertain the current rates, the following annual estimates were prepared at the beginning of the fiscal year, May 1:

Department	Estimated Direct Labor Hours	Estimated Factory Overhead	Application Rate per Hour
A.	64,500	$145,125	$2.25
B.	36,600	109,800	3.00
	101,100	$254,925	

During the month, departmental overhead expenses are added to the cost of the jobs in process by applying the predetermined application rates to the actual number of direct labor hours used on each job. The amount of overhead applicable to each job finished during the month is recorded at the time of completion. The amount of overhead applicable to the jobs still in process at the end of the month is recorded on the last day of the month. To determine the amount of overhead applied to jobs processed during May, the following summary is prepared on May 31:

Summary of Applied Factory Overhead for May

Job	Dept. A — Welding			Dept. B — Cutting			Total Applied Factory Overhead
	Direct Labor Cost	Direct Labor Hours	Applied Factory Overhead	Direct Labor Cost	Direct Labor Hours	Applied Factory Overhead	
303				$ 3,500	350	$1,050.00	$ 1,050.00
308	$ 1,800	360	$ 810.00	2,400	390	1,170.00	1,980.00
309	3,400	500	1,125.00	2,000	250	750.00	1,875.00
310	3,350	1,350	3,037.50	3,500	1,050	3,150.00	6,187.50
311	5,000	1,750	3,937.50	2,250	800	2,400.00	6,337.50
312	5,200	775	1,743.75	1,400	175	525.00	2,268.75
313	6,100	1,250	2,812.50				2,812.50
	$24,850	5,985	$13,466.25	$15,050	3,015	$9,045.00	$22,511.25

The summary is the basis for the following general journal entry:

```
Work in Process ................................   22,511.25
    Factory Overhead — Department A ..............              13,466.25
    Factory Overhead — Department B ..............               9,045.00
      A — 5,985 DLH × $2.25 = $13,466.25
      B — 3,015 DLH × $3.00 = $ 9,045.00
```

On May 1, there were three jobs in process, represented in the general ledger by a debit balance of $10,000 in the work in process control account, with three subsidiary accounts to which materials and labor costs have been posted during April and factory overhead has been applied on April 30. Following is a summary of the jobs in process:

Work in Process, April 30

Job	Materials	Labor	Overhead	Total
303	$2,000	$1,500	$ 750	$ 4,250
308	500	1,000	500	2,000
309	1,500	1,500	750	3,750
	$4,000	$4,000	$2,000	$10,000

Job 303 is almost completed; the other two need considerable work before they will be completed. All three are worked on during May. In addition, work is started on Jobs 310, 311, 312, and 313. In all, seven jobs are being processed during May. In the case of the jobs in process on May 1, the costs incurred for their benefit during May are added to the costs already recorded in April. Following is a summary of the jobs in process during May.

Summary of Factory Operations for May

| Job | Charges to Work in Process During May | | | | Charges to Work in Process in Prior Periods | Total Charges to Work in Process |
	Materials	Labor	Applied Overhead	Total		
303		$ 3,500.00	$ 1,050.00	$ 4,550.00	$ 4,250.00	$ 8,800.00
308	$ 2,900.00	4,200.00	1,980.00	9,080.00	2,000.00	11,080.00
309	4,500.00	5,400.00	1,875.00	11,775.00	3,750.00	15,525.00
310	4,000.00	6,850.00	6,187.50	17,037.50		17,037.50
311	5,500.00	7,250.00	6,337.50	19,087.50		19,087.50
312	4,800.00	6,600.00	2,268.75	13,668.75		13,668.75
313	3,000.00	6,100.00	2,812.50	11,912.50		11,912.50
	$24,700.00	$39,900.00	$22,511.25	$87,111.25	$10,000.00	$97,111.25

The charges of $97,111.25 must be accounted for as costs assigned to jobs remaining to be completed and to completed jobs that have been transferred out of Work in Process.

(m) Under- and Overapplied Overhead.   After the departmental overhead expenses are applied to the costs of the jobs in process at the predetermined application rates, Factory Overhead — Department A has a debit balance of $613.57($14,079.82 − $13,466.25) and Factory Overhead — Department B has a debit balance of $1,186.18 ($10,231.18 − $9,045.00). The debit balances represent an underapplication of overhead to the jobs in process during the month. It is common practice to transfer the balances of the departmental factory overhead accounts to an account entitled Under- and Overapplied Overhead. At the end of the year, this account is usually closed into Cost of Goods Sold, unless the balance of the account is unusually large.

The following general journal entry closes the departmental factory overhead accounts:

Under- and Overapplied Overhead	1,799.75	
Factory Overhead — Department A		613.57
Factory Overhead — Department B		1,186.18

(n) Finished Goods.   Jobs 303, 308, 309, and 310 are completed during May. The following information is prepared from the summary on page 238.

Job	Total Cost	
303	$ 8,800.00	*Out of W/P*
308	11,080.00	
309	15,525.00	*into F/G*
310	17,037.50	
Total cost of goods finished during May	$52,442.50	

The following general journal entry transfers the cost applicable to jobs finished in May from Work in Process to Finished Goods:

| Finished Goods | 52,442.50 | |
| Work in Process | | 52,442.50 |

After Finished Goods is debited and Work in Process is credited for the total cost of the jobs completed during May, the balance of the work in process account, $44,668.75, represents the amount of work in process on May 31.

(o) Sales.   The sales for May are as follows:

Job	Manufacturing Cost	Selling Price
303	$ 8,800.00	$13,200.00
307	18,000.00	27,000.00
308	11,080.00	16,620.00
310	17,037.50	25,556.25
	$54,917.50	$82,376.25

Job 307 was completed during April at a total cost of $18,000, but it was not sold until May. Reference to the post-closing trial balance for April 30 shows that this amount was the inventory of finished goods and indicates that this job was the only job completed and not delivered by that date. The sales during May are recorded in a sales journal in which separate amount columns are provided for recording both the selling price and the cost of goods sold. At the end of the month, the amount of total sales is posted to the general ledger as a debit to Accounts Receivable (Account

No. 1330) and a credit to Sales (Account No. 4100). The total cost of goods sold is posted to the general ledger as a debit to Cost of Goods Sold (Account No. 4600) and a credit to Finished Goods (Account No. 1410).

The entries, in general journal form, to record these summary data appear as follows:

Accounts Receivable	82,376.25	
Sales		82,376.25
Cost of Goods Sold	54,917.50	
Finished Goods		54,917.50

After the posting is completed, the finished goods account has a balance of $15,525. This amount represents the cost of Job 309, which is the only job completed but undelivered at May 31.

(p) Receipts from Customers. Cash received from customers to apply on account is recorded in the cash receipts journal, in which a separate amount column is provided for recording credits to Accounts Receivable. At the end of May, the total of this column, $68,000, is posted to the general ledger as a credit to Accounts Receivable. At the same time, the amount of cash received is included in the total deposits, which is posted as a debit to Cash.

The entry, in general journal form, to record these summary data is:

Cash	68,000	
Accounts Receivable		68,000

(q) Payments to Creditors. Checks issued to creditors in settlement of vouchers payable are recorded in the check register, in which a separate amount column is provided for recording debits to Vouchers Payable. At the end of May, the total of this column is posted to the general ledger as a debit to Vouchers Payable. At the same time, the total of the column headed Purchase Discounts is posted to the general ledger as a credit to Purchase Discounts (Account No. 6110), and the total of the Cash column is posted to the general ledger as a credit to Cash.

The entry, in general journal form, to record these summary data appears as follows:

Vouchers Payable	8,282	
Purchase Discounts		82
Cash		8,200

(r) Vouchering FICA Taxes and Employees' Income Taxes. Periodically, the amounts withheld for employee FICA and income taxes plus the employer's share of FICA tax are paid to a depository (bank). Therefore, after the entries for the employer's and employees' taxes are made, vouchers are prepared to pay the taxes.

During May, vouchers were prepared for the taxes that were recorded for the last week of April and the first three weeks of May. These vouchers were recorded in the voucher register as a debit to FICA Tax Payable, a debit to Employees Income Tax Payable, and a credit to Vouchers Payable. The debits are posted individually to Account Nos. 2230 and 2260, while the amount credited to Account No. 2220 is included in the total of the column headed Vouchers Payable, which is posted at the end of the month.

The entry, in general journal form, to record these summary data appears as follows:

FICA Tax Payable.	7,981	
Employees Income Tax Payable	7,062	
Vouchers Payable.		15,043

(s) Payment of FICA Taxes and Employees' Income Taxes.   The check for $15,043, issued to the depository in payment of the taxes, is recorded in the check register as a debit to Vouchers Payable and as a credit to Cash. At the end of the month, the total of the column headed Vouchers Payable is posted as a debit to Account No. 2220, while the total of the Cash column is posted as a credit to Account No. 1110.

The entry, in general journal form, to record the payment of these taxes appears as follows:

Vouchers Payable.	15,043	
Cash		15,043

(t) General Expenses.   The general expenses incurred during the month include the following:

> Office expense, $1,200
> Miscellaneous general expense, $1,300
> Public relations expense, $1,700

Vouchers are issued for the expense invoices as they are received. The entry, in general journal form, to record these summary data appears as follows:

Office Expense	1,200	
Public Relations Expense	1,700	
Miscellaneous General Expense	1,300	
Vouchers Payable.		4,200

The End of the Month

Following is the general ledger of the Judson Manufacturing Corporation showing the balances of the accounts on May 31 (including adjustments from the work sheet).

General Ledger

Cash					Acct. No. 1110
19--			19--		
May 1 Balance	21,500.00		May 31 Payroll	(d)	40,810.00
31 Deposit	(p) 68,000.00		31 Creditors	(q)	8,200.00
	89,500.00		31 Taxes	(s)	15,043.00
25,447.00					64,053.00

Petty Cash		Acct. No. 1120
19--		
May 1 Balance	100.00	

Marketable Securities		Acct. No. 1200
19--		
May 1 Balance	16,050.00	

Notes Receivable		Acct. No. 1310
19--		
May 1 Balance	10,000.00	

Interest Receivable		Acct. No. 1320
19--		
May 1 Balance	101.66	
31 Adjustment	48.34	
	150.00	

Accounts Receivable				Acct. No. 1330
19--			19--	
May 1 Balance	36,000.00		May 31 Receipts	(p) 68,000.00
31 Sales	(o) 82,376.25			
	118,376.25			
50,376.25				

Allowance for Doubtful Accounts		Acct. No. 1331
	19--	
	May 1 Balance	1,800.00
	31 Adjustment	824.00
		2,624.00

Finished Goods		Acct. No. 1410
19--	19--	
May 1 Inventory 18,000.00	May 31 Cost of goods	
31 Goods completed (n) 52,442.50	sold (o) 54,917.50	
70,442.50		
15,525.00		

Work in Process		Acct. No. 1420
19--	19--	
May 1 Inventory 10,000.00	May 31 Finished goods (n) 52,442.50	
31 Materials (e) 24,700.00		
31 Labor (f) 39,900.00		
31 Overhead (l) 22,511.25		
97,111.25		
44,668.75		

Materials		Acct. No. 1430
19--	19--	
May 1 Inventory 25,000.00	May 31 Requisitions (e) 29,400.00	
31 Purchases (a) 22,200.00		
47,200.00		
17,800.00		

Prepaid Insurance		Acct. No. 1510
19--	19--	
May 1 Balance 2,000.00	May 31 Expired (h) 200.00	
1,800.00		

Land		Acct. No. 1610
19--		
May 1 Balance 25,100.00		

Buildings		Acct. No. 1620
19--		
May 1 Balance 80,000.00		

Accumulated Depreciation—Buildings		Acct. No. 1621
	19--	
	May 1 Balance 12,000.00	
	31 Addition (h) 325.00	
	12,325.00	

Machinery		Acct. No. 1630
19--		
May 1 Balance 120,000.00		

Accumulated Depreciation — Machinery   Acct. No. 1631

	19--		
	May 1 Balance		25,000.00
	31 Addition	(h)	825.00
			25,825.00

Furniture and Fixtures   Acct. No. 1640

19--		
May 1 Balance	14,000.00	

Accumulated Depreciation — Furniture and Fixtures Acct. No. 1641

	19--		
	May 1 Balance		4,480.00
	31 Addition	(h)	116.67
			4,596.67

Small Tools   Acct. No. 1650

19--		
May 1 Balance	14,000.00	

Accumulated Depreciation — Small Tools   Acct. No. 1651

	19--		
	May 1 Balance		8,520.00
	31 Addition	(h)	233.33
			8,753.33

Goodwill   Acct. No. 1710

19--		
May 1 Balance	5,300.00	

Notes Payable   Acct. No. 2210

	19--	
	May 1 Balance	7,000.00

Vouchers Payable   Acct. No. 2220

19--			19--		
May 31 Payroll	(d)	40,810.00	May 1 Balance		15,000.00
31 Creditors	(q)	8,282.00	31 Materials	(a)	22,200.00
31 U.S. Depository	(s)	15,043.00	31 Overhead	(b)	4,664.00
		64,135.00	31 Payroll	(c)	40,810.00
			31 FICA taxes and		
			employees		
			income taxes	(r)	15,043.00
			31 Misc. general		
			expense	(t)	4,200.00
					101,917.00
			37,782.00		

FICA Tax Payable   Acct. No. 2230

19--		19--	
May 31 Vouchered (r) 7,981.00		May 1 Balance	1,800.00
		31 Employees (c)	4,240.00
		31 Employer (g)	4,552.00
			10,592.00
		2,611.00	

Federal Unemployment Tax Payable   Acct. No. 2240

19--	
May 1 Balance	315.00
31 Employer (g)	569.00
	884.00

State Unemployment Tax Payable   Acct. No. 2250

19--	
May 1 Balance	1,215.00
31 Employer (g)	2,276.00
	3,491.00

Employees Income Tax Payable   Acct. No. 2260

19--		19--	
May 31 Vouchered (r) 7,062.00		May 1 Balance	1,500.00
		31 Withheld (c)	7,950.00
			9,450.00
		2,388.00	

Property Tax Payable   Acct. No. 2271

19--	
May 1 Balance	2,000.00
31 Accrued (h)	150.00
	2,150.00

Estimated Income Tax Payable   Acct. No. 2272

19--	
May 1 Balance	16,200.00
31 Adjustment	2,710.50
	18,910.50

Interest Payable   Acct. No. 2273

19--	
May 1 Balance	102.22
31 Adjustment	31.53
	133.75

Accrued Payroll   Acct. No. 2274

19--	
May 31 Accrued (f)	3,900.00

Bonds Payable — Acct. No. 2710

19-- May 1 Balance	25,000.00

Capital Stock — Acct. No. 2910

19-- May 1 Balance	200,000.00

Retained Earnings — Acct. No. 2980

19-- May 1 Balance 31 Net income	75,219.44 6,723.31 81,942.75

Income Summary — Acct. No. 2990

19-- May 31 Closing Retained Earnings	75,783.28 6,723.31 82,506.59	19-- May 31 Closing	82,506.59 82,506.59

Factory Overhead — Acct. No. 3100

19-- May 31 Manufacturing expenses 31 Indirect materials 31 Indirect labor 31 Payroll taxes 31 Fixed expense	(b) 4,664.00 (e) 4,700.00 (f) 7,000.00 (g) 6,097.00 (h) 1,850.00 24,311.00	19-- May 31 Distributed	(i) 24,311.00 24,311.00

Factory Overhead — Department A — Acct. No. 3140

19-- May 31 Distributed 31 Department C 31 Department D	(i) 10,149.00 (j) 2,247.47 (k) 1,683.35 14,079.82	19-- May 31 Applied 31 Trans. to Acct. No. 3180	(l) 13,466.25 (m) 613.57 14,079.82

Factory Overhead — Department B — Acct. No. 3150

19-- May 31 Distributed 31 Department C 31 Department D	(i) 8,336.00 (j) 1,053.50 (k) 841.68 10,231.18	19-- May 31 Applied 31 Trans. to Acct. No. 3180	(l) 9,045.00 (m) 1,186.18 10,231.18

Factory Overhead — Department C   Acct. No. 3160

19--				19--			
May 31	Distributed	(i)	4,214.00	May 31	Distributed	(j)	4,214.00

Factory Overhead — Department D   Acct. No. 3170

19--				19--			
May 31	Distributed	(i)	1,612.00	May 31	Distributed	(k)	2,525.03
31	Department C	(j)	913.03				
			2,525.03				2,525.03

Under- and Overapplied Overhead   Acct. No. 3180

19--				19--		
May 31	Underapplied overhead	(m)	1,799.75	May 31	Cost of goods sold	1,799.75

Sales   Acct. No. 4100

19--			19--			
May 31	Income Summary	82,376.25	May 31	On account	(o)	82,376.25

Cost of Goods Sold   Acct. No. 4600

19--				19--		
May 31	Finished goods	(o)	54,917.50	May 31	Income Summary	56,717.25
31	Under- and over- applied overhead		1,799.75			
			56,717.25			56,717.25

Payroll   Acct. No. 5000

19--				19--			
May 31	Vouchered	(c)	53,000.00	May 31	Distributed	(f)	56,900.00
31	Accrued	(f)	3,900.00				
			56,900.00				56,900.00

Salaries   Acct. No. 5100

19--			19--		
May 31	(f)	10,000.00	May 31	Income Summary	10,000.00

Payroll Tax Expense — Salaries   Acct. No. 5200

19--			19--		
May 31	(g)	1,300.00	May 31	Income Summary	1,300.00

	Office Expense		Acct. No. 5300
19-- May 31	(t) 1,200.00	19-- May 31 Income Summary	1,200.00

	Public Relations Expense		Acct. No. 5500
19-- May 31	(t) 1,700.00	19-- May 31 Income Summary	1,700.00

	Doubtful Accounts Expense		Acct. No. 5800
19-- May 31 Adjustment	824.00	19-- May 31 Income Summary	824.00

	Miscellaneous General Expense		Acct. No. 5900
19-- May 31	(t) 1,300.00	19-- May 31 Income Summary	1,300.00

	Purchase Discounts		Acct. No. 6110
19-- May 31 Income Summary	82.00	19-- May 31	(q) 82.00

	Interest Income		Acct. No. 6120
19-- May 31 Income Summary	48.34	19-- May 31 Adjustment	48.34

	Interest Expense		Acct. No. 6220
19-- May 31 Adjustment	31.53	19-- May 31 Income Summary	31.53

	Provision for Income Tax		Acct. No. 6420
19-- May 31 Adjustment	2,710.50	19-- May 31 Income Summary	2,710.50

Work Sheet

A work sheet, properly designed, is an aid in preparing monthly financial statements. The work sheet for May is presented on pages 250 and 251.

Trial Balance.   The first step in preparing the work sheet is to prepare a trial balance of the general ledger accounts as of May 31. This unadjusted trial balance appears in the first two amount columns.

The balances of the accounts for work in process, accounts receivable, and vouchers payable are verified by preparing schedules of the subsidiary work in process and accounts receivable accounts, and a schedule of the unpaid vouchers. These schedules are reproduced below.

Schedule of Work in Process, May 31, 19--

Job	Name	Amount
311	Patterson Textiles	$19,087.50
312	Plasco Dye and Chemical Corp.	13,668.75
313	International Bleaching	11,912.50
	Total	$44,668.75

Schedule of Accounts Receivable, May 31, 19--

Name	Amount
Chemical Bleachers & Dyers, Newark	$11,175.00
Glen Rock Plumbing Supplies, Glen Rock	5,455.00
Manufacturers Supplies, Dayton	5,860.00
Moline, The City of, Moline	9,400.00
Pinehurst Dairies, Inc., Marysville	9,610.00
Plasco Dye & Chemical Corp., New Milford	8,876.25
Total	$50,376.25

Schedule of Vouchers Payable, May 31, 19--   *vouche reg. unpaid voucher*

Voucher No.	To Whom Issued	Amount
17	Rockford Pipe Co., Inc.	$ 2,365
32	Acme Steel Corp.	1,735
35	Synthetic Resins, Inc.	3,850
53	Baker Roller Mills Co.	1,870
58	Acme Steel Corp.	3,700
60	Buckeye Steel Co.	7,350
61	Arco Plastics	2,570
62	Synthetic Resins, Inc.	1,950
64	Automation, Inc.	2,730
66	The Globe Valve Co.	6,250
67	Rockford Pipe Co., Inc.	3,412
	Total	$37,782

Adjustments.   It is usually necessary to adjust certain accounts before financial statements can be prepared. The adjustments required on May 31 are as follows:

(a)   Increase in accrued interest receivable, $48.34

(b)   Increase in accrued interest payable, $31.53

Account	Acct. No.	Trial Balance	
		Debit	Credit
Cash	1110	25,447.00	
Petty Cash	1120	100.00	
Marketable Securities	1200	16,050.00	
Notes Receivable	1310	10,000.00	
Interest Receivable	1320	101.66	
Accounts Receivable	1330	50,376.25	
Allowance for Doubtful Accounts	1331		1,800.00
Finished Goods	1410	15,525.00	
Work in Process	1420	44,668.75	
Materials	1430	17,800.00	
Prepaid Insurance	1510	1,800.00	
Land	1610	25,100.00	
Buildings	1620	80,000.00	
Accumulated Depreciation — Buildings	1621		12,325.00
Machinery	1630	120,000.00	
Accumulated Depreciation — Machinery	1631		25,825.00
Furniture and Fixtures	1640	14,000.00	
Accumulated Depreciation — Furniture and Fixtures	1641		4,596.67
Small Tools	1650	14,000.00	
Accumulated Depreciation — Small Tools	1651		8,753.33
Goodwill	1710	5,300.00	
Notes Payable	2210		7,000.00
Vouchers Payable	2220		37,782.00
FICA Tax Payable	2230		2,611.00
Federal Unemployment Tax Payable	2240		884.00
State Unemployment Tax Payable	2250		3,491.00
Employees Income Tax Payable	2260		2,388.00
Property Tax Payable	2271		2,150.00
Estimated Income Tax Payable	2272		16,200.00
Interest Payable	2273		102.22
Accrued Payroll	2274		3,900.00
Bonds Payable	2710		25,000.00
Capital Stock	2910		200,000.00
Retained Earnings	2980		75,219.44
Under- and Overapplied Overhead	3180	1,799.75	
Sales	4100		82,376.25
Cost of Goods Sold	4600	54,917.50	
Salaries	5100	10,000.00	
Payroll Tax Expense — Salaries	5200	1,300.00	
Office Expense	5300	1,200.00	
Public Relations Expense	5500	1,700.00	
Doubtful Accounts Expense	5800		
Miscellaneous General Expense	5900	1,300.00	
Purchase Discounts	6110		82.00
Interest Income	6120		
Interest Expense	6220		
		512,485.91	512,485.91
Provision for Income Tax	6420		
Net Income (to Retained Earnings)			

Manufacturing Corporation
Sheet
Ended May 31, 19--

	Adjustments		Income Statement		Balance Sheet	
	Debit	Credit	Debit	Credit	Debit	Credit
					25,447.00	
					100.00	
					16,050.00	
					10,000.00	
	(a) 48.34				150.00	
		(c) 824.00			50,376.25	2,624.00
					15,525.00	
					44,668.75	
					17,800.00	
					1,800.00	
					25,100.00	
					80,000.00	12,325.00
					120,000.00	
						25,825.00
					14,000.00	
						4,596.67
					14,000.00	
						8,753.33
					5,300.00	
						7,000.00
						37,782.00
						2,611.00
						884.00
						3,491.00
						2,388.00
						2,150.00
	(d) 2,710.50					18,910.50
	(b) 31.53					133.75
						3,900.00
						25,000.00
						200,000.00
			1,799.75			75,219.44
			54,917.50	82,376.25		
			10,000.00			
			1,300.00			
			1,200.00			
	(c) 824.00		1,700.00			
			824.00			
			1,300.00			
		(a) 48.34		82.00		
				48.34		
	(b) 31.53		31.53			
			73,072.78	82,506.59	440,317.00	433,593.69
	(d) 2,710.50		2,710.50			
			6,723.31			6,723.31
	3,614.37	3,614.37	82,506.59	82,506.59	440,317.00	440,317.00

(c)   Increase in allowance for doubtful accounts, 1% of the account sales for May, $824

(d)   Provision for estimated income tax, $2,710.50

The proper adjustments are entered in the third and fourth amount columns on the work sheet.

Income Statement.   The adjusted balances of the temporary or nominal accounts are extended to the fifth and sixth amount columns on the work sheet, after which these columns provide the information for preparing the income statement for May.

Balance Sheet.   The adjusted balances of the assets, liabilities, and capital, or real accounts, are extended to the seventh and eighth amount columns on the work sheet; these columns provide the information for preparing the balance sheet as of May 31.

Financial Statements

It is generally desirable to prepare monthly financial statements for the use of the principal executives of the company. These statements can be prepared only if inventories are taken monthly or if a system of cost accounting is made a part of the accounting procedure of the company. Ordinarily, it is impractical to take monthly physical inventories of materials, work in process, and finished goods. A properly developed cost accounting system, however, makes a monthly physical inventory unnecessary, inasmuch as it provides for recording the cost of work in process and finished goods and the maintenance of book inventories of materials, work in process, and finished goods.

The Judson Manufacturing Corporation follows the practice of preparing a monthly manufacturing statement, income statement, and balance sheet. The statements prepared at the end of May are reproduced on pages 253 to 255.

Statement of Cost of Goods Manufactured.   In preparing the manufacturing statement for May, the costs of materials, labor, and applied factory overhead are first determined. The work in process account is the source of the information for these costs. Since the application rates are based upon estimates made at the beginning of the fiscal year, it is not unusual that the amount of applied overhead may differ from the actual overhead incurred during any month of the year. It is to be expected that there will be further fluctuations during succeeding months. In preparing the manufacturing statement for any part of the year, the amount of any underapplied overhead should be added in computing the actual cost of the goods manu-factured during the period, while any overapplied overhead should be sub-tracted in computing the actual cost of the goods manufactured.

Income Statement.   The income statement reproduced on page 254 follows the traditional form, with the gross margin on sales shown first, followed by the income from operations and finally the income both before and after deducting income tax. The provision for income tax is based on an estimate, since the actual amount of the tax cannot be computed until the income for the year is determined and the rates applicable to the year are known.

Balance Sheet.   It should be noted that the accounts are listed in the balance sheet in the order of their arrangement in the chart of accounts. Thus, the current assets appear first in the assets section of the balance sheet, followed by plant assets and goodwill. In the liabilities section, the current liabilities are listed first, followed by the long-term liabilities and capital. In practice, the arrangement of items will depend on the uses for which the balance sheet is intended. If it is to be submitted to a bank with application for a loan, the form of balance sheet to which the particular bank is accustomed would be desirable. If it is prepared at the end of the year for inclusion in the report to stockholders, it should be arranged so as to be most informative to them. If it is prepared monthly for the use of the principal executives, the items may be expressed in more technical language than would be advisable if it were to be submitted to the stockholders.

The Judson Manufacturing Corporation **Statement of Cost of Goods Manufactured** **For the Month Ended May 31, 19--**	
Direct materials used	$24,700.00
Direct labor	39,900.00
Applied factory overhead	22,511.25
Total manufacturing cost	$87,111.25
Add work in process inventory, May 1	10,000.00
Total	$97,111.25
Less work in process inventory, May 31	44,668.75
Cost of goods manufactured during the month at predetermined application rates	$52,442.50
Add underapplied factory overhead	1,799.75
Cost of goods manufactured during the month	$54,242.25

Multiple Step (handwritten)

The Judson Manufacturing Corporation
Income Statement
For the Month Ended May 31, 19--

Net sales		$82,376.25
Less cost of goods sold:		
Finished goods inventory, May 1	$18,000.00	
Add cost of goods manufactured	54,242.25	
Goods available for sale	$72,242.25	
Less finished goods inventory, May 31	15,525.00	
Cost of goods sold		56,717.25
Gross margin on sales		$25,659.00
Operating expenses:		
Salaries	$10,000.00	
Public relations expense	1,700.00	
Office expense	1,200.00	
Doubtful accounts expense	824.00	
Payroll tax expense—salaries	1,300.00	
Miscellaneous general expense	1,300.00	
Total operating expenses		16,324.00
Income from operations		$ 9,335.00
Other revenue:		
Purchase discounts	$ 82.00	
Interest income	48.34	130.34
		$ 9,465.34
Other expense:		
Interest expense		31.53
Income before provision for income tax		$ 9,433.81
Less income tax (estimated)		2,710.50
Net income		$ 6,723.31

✗ Retained - Earnings (handwritten)

The Judson Manufacturing Corporation
Balance Sheet
May 31, 19--

Current assets:		
Cash		$ 25,447.00
Petty cash		100.00
Marketable securities		16,050.00
Notes receivable		10,000.00
Interest receivable		150.00
Accounts receivable	$ 50,376.25	
Less allowance for doubtful accounts	2,624.00	47,752.25

Finished goods.............................	15,525.00	
Work in process	44,668.75	
Materials..................................	17,800.00	
Prepaid insurance	1,800.00	
Total current assets		$179,293.00

Property, plant, and equipment:

Land		$ 25,100.00	
Buildings....................	$ 80,000.00		
Less accumulated depreciation................	12,325.00	67,675.00	
Machinery....................	$120,000.00		
Less accumulated depreciation................	25,825.00	94,175.00	
Furniture and fixtures..........	$ 14,000.00		
Less accumulated depreciation................	4,596.67	9,403.33	
Small tools..................	$ 14,000.00		
Less accumulated depreciation................	8,753.33	5,246.67	
Total property, plant, and equipment			201,600.00

Intangibles:

Goodwill		5,300.00
Total assets		$386,193.00

Liabilities

Current liabilities:

Notes payable.............................	$ 7,000.00	
Vouchers payable..........................	37,782.00	
FICA tax payable	2,611.00	
Federal unemployment tax payable	884.00	
State unemployment tax payable	3,491.00	
Employees income tax payable..............	2,388.00	
Property tax payable	2,150.00	
Estimated income tax payable..............	18,910.50	
Interest payable	133.75	
Accrued payroll...........................	3,900.00	
Total current liabilities		$ 79,250.25

Long-term liability:

Bonds payable		25,000.00
Total liabilities		$104,250.25

Stockholders' Equity

Capital stock		$200,000.00	
Retained earnings, May 1........	$ 75,219.44		
Net income for month	6,723.31		
Retained earnings, May 31....................		81,942.75	
Total stockholders' equity			281,942.75
Total liabilities and stockholders' equity.........			$386,193.00

Adjusting Entries

After the financial statements have been prepared, the adjustments entered on the work sheet are journalized as shown below and posted to the accounts to bring them into agreement with the statements.

Adjusting Entries, May 31

Interest Receivable..............................	48.34	
Interest Income...............................		48.34
Increase in accrued interest receivable.		
Interest Expense................................	31.53	
Interest Payable		31.53
Increase in accrued interest payable.		
Doubtful Accounts Expense......................	824.00	
Allowance for Doubtful Accounts		824.00
Increase in allowance for doubtful accounts.		
Provision for Income Tax........................	2,710.50	
Estimated Income Tax Payable..................		2,710.50
Provision for estimated income tax applicable		
to the income for May.		

Closing Entries

The Judson Manufacturing Corporation prepares monthly financial statements but does not close the temporary accounts until the end of the fiscal year. However, to illustrate the procedure in closing the accounts of a manufacturing company, the closing entries that would be required if the accounts were to be closed at the end of May are journalized below and on page 257 and are posted to the accounts on pages 242 to 248.

Closing Entries, May 31

Cost of Goods Sold	1,799.75	
Under- and Overapplied Overhead		1,799.75
Underapplied overhead transferred to Cost of		
Goods Sold.		
Sales...	82,376.25	
Purchase Discounts.............................	82.00	
Interest Income................................	48.34	
Income Summary		82,506.59
Closing the income accounts to Income		
Summary.		

Income Summary	75,783.28	
Cost of Goods Sold		56,717.25
Salaries....................................		10,000.00
Payroll Tax Expense — Salaries.................		1,300.00
Office Expense		1,200.00
Public Relations Expense		1,700.00
Doubtful Accounts Expense....................		824.00
Miscellaneous General Expense.................		1,300.00
Interest Expense.............................		31.53
Provision for Income Tax......................		2,710.50

Closing the cost of goods sold and expense
accounts to Income Summary.

Income Summary	6,325.01	
Retained Earnings		6,325.01

Balance of the income summary account
transferred to Retained Earnings.

Post Closing Trial Balance.

QUESTIONS

This chapter reviews subjects discussed in previous chapters. These chapters should be referred to for answers to some of the following questions, exercises, and problems.

1. Explain the difference between direct costs and indirect costs.
2. A manufacturer of an electronic component ran short of a part needed to complete an assembly. The reason for the shortage was that the purchasing department inaccurately estimated the materials requirements. The required parts were shipped by air freight at a cost of $4,000. When these materials are shipped by regular transportation methods, these items cost $3,600. How would you recommend recording the amount paid for these rush-order materials?
3. Due to an improperly adjusted machine, 50 of the 200 units produced during the day on a job order are damaged beyond repair. How should these units be accounted for?
4. A company that is using departmental predetermined rates is considering changing to a blanket predetermined rate for all departments. The controller believes the change will substantially reduce accounting costs, because only one rate will have to be developed and applied to all production. Do you believe the "saving" is justifiable?
5. The Judson Manufacturing Corporation is organized on a departmental basis. Name the departments and indicate which are service departments and which are production departments.
6. What subsidiary ledgers are maintained for the Judson Manufacturing Corporation and what are the numbers and titles of their control accounts in the general ledger?

7. Name the books of original entry used by the Judson Manufacturing Corporation.
8. Are the deductions for FICA tax and employees' income tax entered in the voucher register at the time of recording the voucher, or in the check register at the time of recording the payroll check?
9. List and describe the purpose of each form used in accounting for materials.
10. Name the control accounts affected and explain how they are affected by the general journal entry required at the end of each month to record materials requisitioned during the month.
11. List and describe the purpose of each form used in accounting for labor.
12. Explain how the control account for factory overhead is closed at the end of each month.
13. Assume that the direct labor hour method is used to apply factory overhead and that the following estimates were made for each department:

	Total Direct Labor Hours for the Year	Total Factory Overhead for the Year
Department A	170,400	$86,904
Department B	117,600	85,848
Department C	40,800	11,016

What amount should be charged to the work in process account for the month of June if the departments used the following number of direct labor hours?

Department A — 15,100 hours
Department B — 11,000 hours
Department C — 3,750 hours

14. Refer to the ledger of the Judson Manufacturing Corporation and ascertain the amounts of the inventories of finished goods, work in process, and materials at the end of May.
15. Refer to the ledger of the Judson Manufacturing Corporation and ascertain the amount of the under- and overapplied overhead for each production department at the end of May.
16. Refer to the financial statements of the Judson Manufacturing Corporation prepared at the end of May and ascertain the following:
    (a) Cost of goods manufactured during May.
    (b) Cost of goods sold during May.
    (c) Net income for May.
    (d) Retained earnings as of the end of May.

EXERCISES

Exercise 5-1   Journal entries and cost of goods manufactured statement.

Certain selected accounts from the general ledger of the Koufax Manu-facturing Co. are shown below.

Work in Process		Materials	
14,700.00	34,300.00	1/1 2,850.00	16,250.00
14,250.00		. . . . *	
9,120.00		1/31 Bal. 6,525.00	

Payroll		Factory Overhead	
15,600.00	15,600.00	1,550.00	. . . . *
		1,350.00	
		2,137.20	
		175.00	
		. . . . *	

Under- and Overapplied Overhead	
	175.00

*To be calculated.

From an analysis of these accounts, complete the following requirements:
(a)   Prepare all entries, in general journal form, that were made during the month to the various manufacturing accounts. (For recording payroll taxes, use the arbitrary rates of: FICA, 8%; federal income tax, 10%; federal unemployment tax, 1%; and state unemployment tax, 4%.)
(b)   Prepare a statement of cost of goods manufactured.
(c)   If the ending work in process balance has the same proportion of mate-rials, labor, and factory overhead as the goods processed during the month, how much of each cost is included in the ending balance?
(d)   If the average cost of direct labor per hour was $7.50, what is the over-head application rate based on direct labor hours?

Exercise 5-2   Journal entry for factory overhead.

The Treble Machine Tool Company uses the job order cost system of ac-counting. Following is a summary of the factory overhead incurred during the month of January. The information needed to prepare this summary was ob-tained from the accounts in the subsidiary factory overhead ledger. Prepare an entry in general journal form to distribute the factory overhead expenses to the proper departments.

Summary of Factory Overhead for January

Acct. No.		Dept. A Machine Shop	Dept. B Assembly	Dept. C Mainte- nance	Dept. D Engi- neering	Total
51	Depreciation	$1,400.00	$1,250.00	$ 700.00	$ 250.00	$ 3,600.00
52	Property tax.............	75.00	50.00	25.00	12.00	162.00
53	Insurance...............	100.00	75.00	20.00	10.00	205.00
54	Power	100.00	50.00	35.00	10.00	195.00
55	Indirect materials	2,000.00	1,600.00	590.00	440.00	4,630.00
56	Indirect labor............	900.00	500.00	600.00	300.00	2,300.00
57	Heat, light, and power....	200.00	150.00	85.00	25.00	460.00
58	Payroll taxes	245.00	110.00	95.00	70.00	520.00
	Total.................	$5,020.00	$3,785.00	$2,150.00	$1,117.00	$12,072.00

Exercise 5-3   Worksheet and journal entries for distributing service department costs.

Departments C and D of the Treble Machine Tool Company are service departments, while departments A and B are production departments. Department C expenses are distributed to departments A, B, and D on the basis of the number of square feet occupied by each department, as follows:

Department	Area (Square Feet)
A...	15,000
B...	10,000
D...	8,000

Department D expenses are distributed to the production departments on a basis of 75% to A and 25% to B.

Prepare a work sheet showing the proper distribution of the service department expenses and draft the required entries in general journal form to record the distribution of the service department expenses to the production departments.

Exercise 5-4   Job cost, variances, journal entry.

The Salsa Company, using a job order cost system, has compiled the following data on work started during the week:

Job	Direct Materials	Direct Labor Hours
101	$ 2,750	180
102	3,100	210
103	2,500	170
104	1,500	100
105	1,850	120
106	2,100	160
107	800	40
108	1,000	50
109	600	30
	$16,200	1,060

The direct labor rate is $10 an hour. The overhead rate is $8 per direct labor hour at standard volume of 1,000 hours (fixed — $5,000; variable — $3 an hour). The actual factory overhead costs for the week were $9,015. Jobs 101, 102, 103, and 106 were completed.
(a) Determine the total cost of each job for the week.
(b) Compute the under- or overapplied factory overhead for the week.
(c) Determine the volume and budget variances.
(d) Calculate the work in process at the end of the week.
(e) Prepare a general journal entry to transfer the completed jobs to finished goods.

PROBLEMS

Problem 5-1   Scrap material.

The Gotham Company manufactures a product that is started in department A and is finished in department B. All materials required for the product are issued in department A. When the materials are introduced in department A, about 10% are usually spoiled and have to be sold as scrap. The receipts from the sale of scrap are credited to the department. *Cost of goods manufactured.*
The following costs were incurred for one month's production: *scrap 10%*

	Department A	Department B
Materials	$ 35,800	–0–
Direct labor.	62,400	$21,300
Factory overhead	78,000	21,450
	$176,200	$42,750

Receipts from the sale of scrap during the month amounted to $1,200. Production data for the month were as follows:

	Department A	Department B
Units started or received from preceding department	11,000	10,000
Units spoiled (material only)	1,000	
Units completed and transferred . .	10,000	10,000

Required:

1. Prepare a schedule that shows the unit cost of production in department A, department B, and in total.
2. Suppose that department B, at the point of final inspection before the goods are transferred to finished goods, discards 500 units as spoiled with no salvage value. How much will the total cost per unit increase if this spoilage is not charged to factory overhead?

Problem 5-2   Effect of change in capacity on unit costs.

The Ruxpin Company has just negotiated a new labor contract that increases direct labor costs by 10%. The company is already experiencing a serious decline in sales and profit. As a consequence, the president has requested production and sales statistics which include the following:

(a) The maximum capacity the plant can achieve is 200,000 units per year. At this capacity, the production costs will be:

Materials		$ 500,000
Direct labor.		1,000,000
Factory overhead:		
Fixed cost.	$1,000,000	
Variable cost	1,000,000	2,000,000
Total		$3,500,000

(b) Sales are not expected to exceed 180,000 units per year, nor can the units be sold for more than $25 per unit because of market competition.
(c) To maintain its position in the industry, a 40% gross margin on sales should be realized on a volume of 160,000 units per year.
(d) A cost study shows that at 160,000 units per year, fixed costs can be reduced by 60%, and there is some possibility of reducing the variable factory overhead costs.

Required:

1. What are the unit costs for materials, labor, and overhead at the 200,000 unit level? What is the gross margin per unit?

2. If direct labor costs increase by 10% but only 160,000 units are produced and sold, what is the gross margin per unit?
3. What unit cost will result if at the 200,000 unit capacity, the fixed costs are reduced by 60%, labor cost increases 10%, and 160,000 units are produced and sold?
4. At the 160,000 unit level for production and sales, with a 60% fixed cost reduction and 10% labor cost increase, how much per unit must variable factory overhead be reduced to achieve a 40% gross margin?

Problem 5-3   Calculation of budget and volume variances.

The Fong Company has accumulated the following data pertaining to factory overhead costs for the year. Each department is budgeted for $15,000 of fixed costs for the year. The company uses the direct labor hour method of applying factory overhead to the jobs.

	Department A	Department B	Department C
Total budgeted factory overhead...........	$51,000	$75,000	$105,000
Budgeted direct labor hours	12,000	15,000	20,000
Total actual factory overhead...........	$55,000	$70,000	$105,000
Actual direct labor hours	10,000	18,000	20,000

Required:
1. Compute the under- or overapplied factory overhead for each department.
2. Compute the budget variances due to cost factors and indicate whether they are favorable or unfavorable.
3. Compute the volume variances and indicate whether they are favorable or unfavorable.

Problem 5-4   Comprehensive review of job order procedures.

The Faust Chrome Products Co. manufactures special chromed parts made to the order and specifications of the customer. It has two production departments, Stamping and Plating, and two service departments, Power and Maintenance. In any production department, the job in process is wholly completed before the next job is started.

The company operates on a fiscal year which ends March 31. Following is the post-closing trial balance as of March 31:

Faust Chrome Products Co.
Post-Closing Trial Balance
March 31, 19--

Cash	19,000	
Accounts Receivable	24,200	
Finished Goods	8,400	
Work in Process	2,400	
Materials	10,000	
Prepaid Insurance	2,700	
Factory Building	60,000	
Accumulated Depreciation — Factory Building		20,000
Machinery and Equipment	30,000	
Accumulated Depreciation — Machinery and Equipment		15,000
Office Equipment	16,000	
Accumulated Depreciation — Office Equipment		8,000
Vouchers Payable		3,700
FICA Tax Payable		3,120
Federal Unemployment Tax Payable		364
State Unemployment Tax Payable		1,404
Employees Income Tax Payable		5,200
Capital Stock		100,000
Retained Earnings		15,912
	172,700	172,700

Additional information:

1. The balance of the materials account represents the following:

Materials	Units	Unit Cost	Total
A	100	$24	$ 2,400
B	300	12	3,600
C	150	20	3,000
Factory Supplies			1,000
			$10,000

The company uses the fifo method of accounting for all inventories. Material A is used in the stamping department and materials B and C in the plating department.

2. The balance of the work in process account represents the following costs that are applicable to Job 312. (The customer's order is for 1,000 units of the finished product.)

Direct materials	$1,000
Direct labor	800
Factory overhead	600
	$2,400

(3.) The finished goods account reflects the cost of Job 311, which was finished at the end of the preceding month and is awaiting delivery orders from the customer.

(4.) At the beginning of the year, factory overhead application rates were based on the following data:

	Stamping Dept.	Plating Dept.
Estimated factory overhead for the year	$135,000	$94,500
Estimated direct labor hours for the year	25,000	7,000

In April, the following transactions were recorded:

(a) Purchased the following materials and supplies on account:

Material A	1,500 units @ $26
Material B	1,400 units @ $14
Material C	1,200 units @ $20
Factory Supplies	$2,800

(b) The following materials were issued to the factory:

	Job 312	Job 313	Job 314
Material A		600 units	400 units
Material B		400 units	200 units
Material C	200 units	400 units	
Factory Supplies — $2,600			

Customers' orders covered by Jobs 313 and 314 are for 1,000 and 500 units of finished product, respectively.

(c) Factory wages and office, sales, and administrative salaries are paid at the end of each month.

The following data, provided from an analysis of labor time tickets and salary schedules, will be sufficient for the preparation of the entries to voucher the payroll (assume FICA and federal income tax rates of 8% and 10%, respectively); record the company's liability for state and federal unemployment taxes (assume rates of 4% and 1% respectively); and record the payroll distribution for the month of April.

	Stamping Dept.	Plating Dept.
Job 312	100 hrs. @ $8	300 hrs. @ $10
Job 313	1,200 hrs. @ $8	300 hrs. @ $10
Job 314	800 hrs. @ $8	

Wages of the supervisors, custodial personnel, etc., totaled $9,200; and administrative salaries were $19,200.

(d) Miscellaneous factory overhead incurred during the month totaled $2,965. Miscellaneous selling and administrative expenses were $1,700. Vouchers were prepared for these items as well as for the FICA tax and federal income tax withheld for March. (See account balances on the post-closing trial balance for March 31.)

(e)   Annual depreciation on plant assets is calculated using the following rates:

Factory buildings — 5%
Machinery and equipment — 20%
Office equipment — 20%

(f)   The balance of the prepaid insurance account represents a three-year premium for a fire insurance policy covering the factory building and machinery. It was paid on the last day of the preceding month and became effective on April 1.

(g)   The summary of factory overhead prepared from the factory overhead ledger is reproduced below:

Summary of Factory Overhead for April

Trans- action	Account	Stamping	Plating	Power	Mainte- nance	Total
(b)	Factory supplies........	$1,040.00	$ 780.00	$ 260.00	$ 520.00	$ 2,600.00
(c)	Indirect labor..........	3,680.00	2,760.00	920.00	1,840.00	9,200.00
(c)	Payroll taxes	1,646.36	1,247.81	415.60	850.23	4,160.00
(d)	Miscellaneous	1,286.00	1,089.50	393.00	196.50	2,965.00
(e)	Depreciation	300.00	225.00	75.00	150.00	750.00
(f)	Insurance.............	30.00	25.00	10.00	10.00	75.00
	Total...............	$7,982.36	$6,127.31	$2,073.60	$3,566.73	$19,750.00

(h)   The total expenses of the maintenance department are distributed on the basis of floor space occupied by the power department (8,820 sq. ft.), stamping department (19,500 sq. ft.), and plating department (7,875 sq. ft.). The power department expenses are then allocated equally to the stamping and plating departments.

(i)   After the actual factory expenses have been distributed to the departmental accounts and the applied factory overhead has been recorded and posted, any balances in the departmental accounts are transferred to Under- and Overapplied Overhead.

(j)   Jobs 312 and 313 were finished during the month. Job 314 is still in process at the end of the month.

(k)   During the month, Jobs 311 and 312 were sold at a markup of 150% on cost.

(l)   Received $51,500 from customers in payment of their accounts.
(m)   Checks were issued during the month in the amount of $53,500 for payment of vouchers.
(n)   The estimated provision for federal income tax applicable to the earnings for April was $2,000.00

Required:

1.   Set up the beginning trial balance in T-accounts.
2.   Prepare materials inventory ledger cards and enter April 1 balances.
3.   Set up job cost sheets as needed.
4.   Record all transactions and related entries in general journal entry form for the month of April and post to T-accounts.
5.   Prepare a service department expense distribution work sheet for April.
6.   At the end of the month:
     (a)   Analyze the balance in the materials account, the work in process account, and the finished goods account.
     (b)   Prepare the statement of cost of goods manufactured, income statement, and balance sheet for April 30.

Retained earnings

Problem 5-5   Review of job order cost procedures.

The Terkel Manufacturing Company uses a job order cost system. The balances in the inventory accounts on September 1 were:

Finished Goods $210,000
Work in Process   94,100
Materials   100,000

The job cost sheets on September 1 contained the following data:

Job	Materials	Labor	Overhead	Total
1234	$ 1,200	$ 2,000	$ 2,500	$ 5,700
1235	3,000	3,300	3,900	10,200
1238	4,100	5,100	6,100	15,300
1244	2,500	3,000	3,200	8,700
1250	12,000	15,000	17,000	44,000
1251	2,800	3,400	4,000	10,200
Total	$25,600	$31,800	$36,700	$94,100

The transactions for September were:
(a)   Materials purchased, $74,000.
(b)   Materials requisitioned by the factory were as follows:

Job 1234	$ 2,200
Job 1235	1,200
Job 1244	1,500
Job 1252	5,300
Job 1253	3,700
Job 1254	4,800
Job 1255	12,000
Indirect Materials — Dept. A.	4,700
Indirect Materials — Dept. B.	3,000
Indirect Materials — Dept. C	2,500
Total	$40,900

(c)   Actual labor costs incurred were as follows:

Job	Dept. A	Dept. B	Dept. C	Total
1234		$ 700	$ 500	$ 1,200
1235	$ 100	300	700	1,100
1238	800	1,100	2,800	4,700
1244	900	800	400	2,100
1250	1,000	2,200	1,800	5,000
1251	1,100	800	1,300	3,200
1252	2,300	1,800	800	4,900
1253	1,700	1,300	1,000	4,000
1254	2,700	1,600	700	5,000
1255	7,000	6,000	300	13,300
Indirect	5,000	2,700	4,200	11,900
Total	$22,600	$19,300	$14,500	$56,400

(d)   Other factory overhead costs were:

	Dept. A	Dept. B	Dept. C	Total
Supervision	$ 1,600	$ 1,200	$ 800	$ 3,600
Heat, light, and water	1,500	1,400	1,900	4,800
Maintenance	700	600	900	2,200
Payroll taxes, vacation				
pay, etc.	8,600	8,100	6,200	22,900
Depreciation	4,400	2,600	3,600	10,600
Miscellaneous.	600	400	500	1,500
Total	$17,400	$14,300	$13,900	$45,600

(e)   The direct labor cost method is used to apply factory overhead to the jobs. The rates for the departments are:

Dept. A — 150%
Dept. B — 130%
Dept. C — 180%

(f)   The jobs completed and transferred to finished goods were: Jobs 1234, 1235, 1238, 1250, and 1251.

(g)   Finished goods sold totaled $235,000.

Required:

1.   Set up individual job cost sheets and record the September costs for each job.
2.   Record the beginning balances in the inventory accounts and record the September transactions in inventory, overhead, and cost of goods sold accounts. Each department has a factory overhead account.
3.   Compute the under- or overapplied overhead for each department.
4.   Prepare a statement of cost of goods manufactured.

Problem 5-6   Service department allocations and determining overhead rates.

The Manning Manufacturing Company has two production departments (fabrication and assembly) and three service departments (general factory administration, factory maintenance, and factory cafeteria). A summary of overhead costs and other data for each department prior to allocation of service department costs is as follows:

	General Factory Admin.	Factory Mainte- nance	Factory Cafeteria	Fabrication	Assembly	Total
Indirect labor	$90,000	$82,100	$87,000	$1,950,000	$2,050,000	$4,259,100
Indirect material	—	65,000	91,000	3,130,000	950,000	4,236,000
Other factory overhead.....	70,000	56,100	62,000	1,650,000	1,850,000	3,688,100
Direct labor hours				562,500	437,500	1,000,000
Number of employees	12	8	20	280	200	520
Square footage occupied ..	1,750	2,000	4,800	88,000	72,000	168,550

The costs of the general factory administration department, factory maintenance department, and factory cafeteria are allocated on the basis of direct labor hours, square footage occupied, and number of employees, respectively.

Required:

1.   Allocate the service departments' costs directly to production without inter-service department cost allocation and calculate an overhead rate for each production department based on direct labor hours.
2.   Allocate the service departments' costs sequentially, starting with the service department with the greatest total costs, to other service departments as well as to the production departments. Calculate an overhead rate for each production department based on direct labor hours.

(AICPA adapted)

Problem 5-7   Determining overhead variances.

The Zulu Company is a manufacturer of heavy machinery. It applies factory overhead to production on the basis of an average percentage of direct labor cost. At the time the rate was established, it was based on the following information as to expected operations:

Direct labor hours.		136,000
Direct labor cost.		$578,000.00
Average rate per hour		$4.25
Fixed overhead.	$208,080.00	
Variable overhead	462,400.00	
Total overhead		$670,480.00

At December 31, the end of the first accounting period, the records disclosed the following information:

Direct labor hours.		130,000
Direct labor cost.		$574,990.00
Average rate per hour		$4.423
Fixed overhead.	$225,400.00	
Variable overhead	475,100.00	$700,500.00
Underapplied overhead		$ 33,511.60

Management is concerned that the year's operations failed to absorb overhead of $33,511.60.

Required:
1. Calculate the application rates for fixed cost, variable cost, and total overhead.
2. Show the computation of the underapplied overhead as determined by the company.
3. Compute the budget variances due to cost factors.
4. Compute the volume variances.
5. Analyze the volume variance in additional detail by giving consideration to the effect of the increase in labor rate and the decrease in the number of labor hours used on the factory overhead.
6. Compute the budget and volume variances if the company had used the direct labor hour method.
7. Show a reconciliation between the direct labor cost and direct labor hour variances calculated.

(AICPA adapted)

Problem 5-8   Analysis of under- and overapplied factory overhead.

The Angelo Company, engaged in production of heavy equipment, has applied factory overhead to its product on the basis of an average rate of 115%

of direct labor cost. This rate, at the time it was established, was based on the following information as to expected operations:

Direct labor hours		13,600
Direct labor cost		$163,200
Average rate per hour		$12
Fixed overhead	$ 57,936	
Variable overhead	129,744	
Total overhead		$187,680

At December 31, the end of the first accounting period, the records disclosed the following information:

Direct labor hours		13,000
Direct labor cost		$183,040
Average rate per hour		$14.08
Fixed overhead	$ 75,400	
Variable overhead	145,600	
Total overhead (actual expense)		$221,000
Underapplied overhead		$10,504

The management is concerned with the fact that it failed to apply overhead of $10,504 in the year's operations.

Required:

1. Evaluate the system currently being used to apply overhead.
2. Prepare an explanation for management showing why the $10,504 under-application existed. Compute and show the effect of variation in direct labor rates and direct labor hours on the application of both fixed and variable overhead. Support your conclusions with computations and explanatory comments setting forth the significance of each item in the analysis. (Computations should be rounded to the nearest dollar.)

(AICPA adapted)

PROCESS COST ACCOUNTING—

GENERAL PROCEDURES

LEARNING OBJECTIVES

In studying this chapter, you will learn about the:

- Similarities and differences between job order and process cost accounting
- Average cost method of assigning costs to inventories
- Concept of equivalent production
- Preparation of a cost of production summary
- Computation of unit costs with and without beginning inventories when there is one department
- Computation of unit costs with and without beginning inventories when there are two or more departments

The basic purpose of cost accounting is the accumulation of data designed to provide management with accurate information on the cost of manufacturing a product. The appropriate cost accounting system for a particular entity depends on the nature of manufacturing operations. The preceding chapter focused on the job order cost system. This chapter and Chapter 7 focus on procedures applicable in a process cost system.

As mentioned in Chapter 1, standard cost accounting procedures may be used with a process cost accounting system. Standard costs are discussed in Chapters 8 and 9.

COMPARISON OF BASIC COST SYSTEMS

As explained in Chapter 1, a job cost system is appropriate when products are manufactured on a special order basis. Process costing is appropriate when goods of a similar or homogeneous nature are manufactured in a continuous or mass production operation.

The focal point of job order costing is the "job," even though the factory may be departmentalized. The costs of materials, direct labor, and factory overhead are gathered for each job and divided by the number of units produced to determine the unit cost for that particular job. The primary objective is to ascertain the costs of producing each job completed during the accounting period as well as the cost incurred on each job in process at the end of the period. Management uses this information not only for inventory valuation but also for planning, control, and measurement of performance.

The focus of process costing is the cost center, which, as discussed in Chapter 1, is a unit of activity within the factory to which costs may be practically and equitably assigned. It is usually a department, but could be a process or an operation. Costs are accumulated for a particular cost center or function and are divided by the number of units produced to determine the average cost per unit in that cost center for the period. The primary objective, like that of the job order system, is to ascertain the unit cost of the products manufactured during the period and of those in process at the end of the period and to promote efficiency within the factory.

Many of the procedures studied for job order cost accounting are also applicable to process cost accounting. The main difference in the two methods is the manner in which costs are accumulated.

Materials and Labor Costs

Under the job order cost system, the costs of materials and labor, as determined from the summaries of materials requisitions and time tickets, are charged to specific jobs or to factory overhead. Under the process cost system, the costs of materials and labor are charged to the departments in which they are incurred. However, the indirect materials and indirect labor costs that cannot be directly associated with a particular department are charged to Factory Overhead. Examples of such costs would include custodial supplies for the factory and the salary of a supervisor who is responsible for several departments.

Less clerical effort is required in a process system than in a job order system because some of the direct and indirect materials and labor are not separated, and also because costs are charged to a few departments rather than to many jobs. For example, in accounting for labor costs, detailed time tickets might be eliminated completely in a process cost system. While a typical factory employee under the job order cost system might work on several jobs, requiring allocation of labor to each job, the employee in a process cost system usually works only in one department so that only a simple time record is required.

Other than the differences discussed above, the procedures for acquiring, controlling, accounting for, and paying for materials and labor are similar in both systems. At the end of each month, the materials requisitions summary provides the data for the journal entry debiting Work in Process and Factory Overhead and crediting Materials. Similarly, the labor cost summary provides the data for the journal entry debiting Work in Process and Factory Overhead and crediting Payroll.

Factory Overhead Costs

In a process cost system, overhead costs are accumulated from the various journals in the same manner as in a job order cost accounting system. The actual costs for the period are gathered in a control account in the general ledger to which postings are made from the general journal (for certain indirect materials, indirect labor, and fixed costs), from the voucher register, and from other appropriate journals. This control account is supported by a subsidiary ledger which consists of factory overhead analysis sheets showing the detailed allocation of costs to the departments. At the end of the month, based on the data reflected in the analysis sheets, the total actual factory overhead is distributed to the departmentalized overhead accounts.

Service Departments.   As with job order cost accounting, the applicable factory overhead is charged to the service departments. These service department expenses are distributed to the production departments. A distribution work sheet is prepared showing the allocation of each service department's expenses to other service departments and to the production departments. A journal entry also records the distribution of the service departments' expenses to the production departments and thus closes the service departments' accounts for factory overhead. Service department costs will not be considered in the following discussion because the fundamentals were developed in Chapter 4.

Application of Factory Overhead.   In the job order cost system, overhead is applied to the jobs through the use of predetermined rates. The use of predetermined rates is also quite common in a process cost system but overhead is applied on the basis of departments rather than jobs. As in the job order cost system, the amount of overhead applied is determined by multiplying the predetermined rate by the appropriate base. This base might be direct labor cost, direct labor hours, machine hours, or any other method that will equitably distribute overhead to the departments in reasonable proportion to the benefit received by each department. Under- or overapplied overhead is treated in the same manner as discussed in Chapter 4.

PRODUCT COST IN A PROCESS COST SYSTEM

The basic principle established in this comparison of the two cost accounting systems is that all costs of manufacturing must eventually be charged to production departments, either directly or indirectly, in a process cost system. The unit cost in each department is the total cost charged to that department for the period divided by the number of units produced in the department during the same period. The total cost of each item produced is the combined unit costs from each department.

Nondepartmentalized Factory

When the factory is operated as a single department producing a single product in a continuous output, the process cost system is particularly appropriate and simple. The costs of operating the factory are summarized at the end of each accounting period. Then the total of these costs is divided by the quantity of units produced to determine the cost of each unit manufactured during the period.

The following cost of production summary illustrates this procedure:

Materials.	$ 50,000
Labor.	75,000
Factory overhead	35,000
Total cost of production.	$160,000
Unit output for period.	40,000 units

Unit cost for period: $160,000 ÷ 40,000 units = $4

Departmentalized Factory

In other than the simplest type of manufacturing operation, a company has several production and service departments. Products accumulate costs as they pass through each successive production department. Costs are recorded by departments according to the following procedure: (1) the costs of the service departments are allocated to the production departments; (2) the costs added in prior departments are carried over to successive departments; and (3) the costs of materials and labor directly identifiable with a department, as well as applied overhead, are charged to that department. The unit cost within a department is determined by dividing the sum of these costs by the number of units produced during the period.

WORK IN PROCESS INVENTORIES

If there is no work in process at the end of an accounting period, ascertaining the unit cost under the process cost system is relatively simple; divide total cost by number of units produced. Usually, however, each department will have work in process at the end of each accounting period. The valuation of work in process inventories presents one of the most important and difficult problems in process cost accounting. Normally, a factory will have (1) units started and finished during the current period; (2) units started in a prior period and completed during the current period; and (3) units started during the current period but not finished at the end of the period. Since materials, labor, and overhead may have been applied to each of the unfinished items, such charges cannot be ignored in computing the cost of the units finished during the accounting period. Therefore, consideration must be given to not only the number of items finished during the period but also the units in process at the beginning and at the end of the period. The primary problem is the allocation of total cost between (1) units finished during the period and (2) units still in process at the end of the period.

Two procedures are commonly used for assigning costs to the ending inventories: the **average cost** method and the **first-in, first-out (fifo)** method. The average cost method is discussed and illustrated in the remainder of this chapter. The first-in, first-out method is discussed in Chapter 7.

Average Cost Method

Under the **average cost method,** the cost of the work in process at the beginning of the period is added to the production costs for the current period. Average unit cost for the period is then determined by dividing the total of these costs by the total equivalent production. Equivalent production represents the number of units that could have been completed during a period using the production costs incurred during the period. The calculation of equivalent production requires the restatement, in terms of completed units, of goods in process at the end of the period. To illustrate, assume that the production costs of a department during a certain period are as follows:

Materials	$12,000
Labor	18,000
Factory overhead	6,000
Total cost of production	$36,000

If 18,000 units were produced during the period and there was no work in process at the beginning or at the end of the period, the unit cost of production is easily calculated to be $2, and $36,000 would be transferred to the finished goods account in the general ledger.

Assume, instead, that the production report for the period shows that there was no beginning work in process, that 17,000 units were finished during the period, and that there are 2,000 units in process at the end of the period. The problem that now arises is allocating the production cost for the period, $36,000, between the goods that were finished and the goods that are still in process. What portion of the total production cost was incurred during the month by the remaining 2,000 units in process?

If the 2,000 units are almost finished, clearly more cost has been incurred to bring them to that stage of completion than would have been incurred if they had just been started in process. In order to make a rational measurement, the stage of completion of the units still in process must be taken into consideration. Stage of completion represents the fraction or percentage of materials, labor, and overhead costs of a completed unit that have been applied during the period to goods that have not been completed. An estimate of the stage of completion is made by the department head. This estimate is obviously subject to the inaccuracies that may result with the use of any method of averaging. The possibility of error is minimized because the department head usually has the skills and the familiarity with the work to make reliable estimates.

At the end of the accounting period, the department head submits a production report showing: (1) the number of units in process at the beginning of the period, (2) the number of units completed during the period, and (3) the number of units in process at the end of the period and their estimated stage of completion.

Continuing the example, assume that the 2,000 units in process are half finished. If materials, labor, and overhead are applied evenly throughout the process, one half of the total cost for completing 2,000 units can be applied to these units. Expressed in another way, the cost to bring these 2,000 units to the halfway point of completion is equivalent to the cost of fully completing 1,000 units. Therefore, in terms of equivalent production, 2000 units one-half completed are equal to 1,000 units fully completed. Unit cost is calculated as follows:

Units finished during the period	17,000
Equivalent units of work in process at the end of the period (2,000 units one-half completed)	1,000
Equivalent production for the period	18,000 units

$36,000 ÷ 18,000 = $2 unit cost for the month.

The inventory cost can now be calculated as follows:

Transferred fo finished goods (17,000 units at $2)	$34,000
Work in process (2,000 units × ½ × $2)	2,000
Total production costs accounted for	$36,000

Determining equivalent units of work in process at the end of the period is frequently more complex than suggested above. When it is not reasonable to assume that all production costs are incurred evenly throughout the production process, for example, when all materials are added at the beginning of a process, the amount of materials, labor, and overhead applicable to the work in process would have to be evaluated separately in estimating the stage of completion. In addition, the work in process at the end of the period may consist of a large number of units in widely varying stages of completion, thus requiring a more detailed analysis to determine equivalent units. These situations are discussed in Chapter 7.

Cost of Production Summary.   In a process cost system, the reporting of production and related costs in each department involves:

1.   Accumulating costs for which the department is accountable.
2.   Calculating equivalent production for the period.
3.   Computing the unit cost for the period.
4.   Summarizing the disposition of the production costs.

These data are reported on a cost of production summary which presents the necessary information for inventory valuation and can also serve as the source for summary journal entries. The procedures previously discussed are further developed through the four illustrative problems that follow.

Illustrative Problem No. 1 — Computing the unit cost when there is no beginning inventory and only one department.

The Pyramid Toy Corp. manufactures a plastic toy. The small factory is operated as a single department and the finished goods are placed in stock to be withdrawn as orders are received. At the end of January, the first month of operation for the company, the factory supervisor submits the following production report. The estimate of the stage of completion indicates that the units in process at the end of the month were examined and found to be, on the average, about one-half completed.

PRODUCTION REPORT
For Month Ending   January 31, 19--

In process, beginning of month _____ none

Finished during the month _____ 4,900 units

In process, end of month _____ 200 units

Estimated stage of completion of work in process, end of month ___ 1/2

Remarks

_R. L. B._

Supervisor

After receiving the production report, the cost accountant begins the preparation of the cost of production summary by collecting the period's production costs from summaries of materials requisitions, payroll, and factory overhead analysis sheets. The units in process are then converted to equivalent units. In this case, the supervisor's estimate that the 200 units in process are one-half completed implies that approximately one-half the total cost of the materials, labor, and factory overhead needed to produce 200 units has been incurred. On the basis of this reasoning, the equivalent of 200 units in process, one-half completed, is 100 units. In other words, the costs incurred in partially completing 200 units is considered to be the equivalent of the entire cost of producing 100 units. The cost of producing 4,900 fully completed units and 200 units one-half completed during the month is therefore the equivalent of the cost of producing 5,000 fully completed units.

Pyramid Toy Corp.
Cost of Production Summary
For the Month Ended January 31, 19--

Cost of production for month: ~W/P acct~		
Materials....................................		$ 5,000
Labor.......................................		3,000
Factory overhead		2,000
Total costs to be accounted for		$10,000
Unit output for month:		
Finished during month......................		4,900
Equivalent units of work in process, end of month (200 units, one-half completed)......................		100
Total equivalent production		5,000
Unit cost for month:		
Materials ($5,000 ÷ 5,000 units)......................		$1.00
Labor ($3,000 ÷ 5,000 units)......................		.60
Factory overhead ($2,000 ÷ 5,000 units)		.40
Total......................................		$2.00
Inventory costs:		
Cost of goods finished during month (4,900 × $2)		$ 9,800
Cost of work in process, end of month:		
Materials (200 × ½ × $1)	$100	
Labor (200 × ½ × $.60)......................	60	
Factory overhead (200 × ½ × $.40)	40	200
Total production costs accounted for		$10,000

Since the work in process is estimated to be one-half completed, its value for inventory purposes is one-half the unit cost of finished goods.

At the end of the month, the following journal entries record the factory operations for January:

Jan. 31	Work in Process	5,000	
	Materials		5,000
	Work in Process	3,000	
	Payroll		3,000
Jan. 31	Factory Overhead	2,000	
	Various accounts		
	(Accumulated Depreciation, Prepaid Insurance,		
	Accrued Taxes, Accounts Payable)		2,000
	Work in Process	2,000	
	Factory Overhead		2,000

After preparing the cost of production summary, the accountant can make the following entry:

Jan. 31	Finished Goods	9,800	
	Work in Process		9,800

After posting these entries, the work in process account, as shown below, has a debit balance of $200, representing the valuation of the work in process on January 31.

Work in Process			
Jan. 31	5,000	Jan. 31	9,800
	3,000		
	2,000		
	10,000		
200			

The cost accountant can now prepare the January statement of the cost of goods manufactured, shown below.

Pyramid Toy Corp. Statement of Cost of Goods Manufactured For the Month Ended January 31, 19--	
Materials	$ 5,000
Labor	3,000
Factory overhead	2,000
Total	$10,000
Less work in process inventory, January 31	200
Cost of goods manufactured during the month	$ 9,800

Illustrative Problem No. 2 — Computing the unit cost when there is a beginning inventory and only one department.

At the end of February, the second month of operations for the Pyramid Toy Corp., the factory supervisor submits the following production report.

PRODUCTION REPORT

For Month Ending <u>February 28, 19--</u>

In process, beginning of month ___ ~~200 units~~

Finished during the month ___ 6,900 units

In process, end of month ___ 600 units $\times \frac{1}{3} + 6,900$

Estimated stage of completion of work in process, end of month ___ 1/3

ignore beginning units

The cost accountant prepares the following cost of production summary for February.

Pyramid Toy Corp.
Cost of Production Summary
For the Month Ended February 28,19--

Cost of work in process, beginning of month:		
Materials....................................	$ 100	
Labor.......................................	60	
Factory overhead	40	$ 200
Cost of production for month:		
Materials....................................	$7,000	
Labor.......................................	4,200	
Factory overhead	2,800	14,000
Total costs to be accounted for		$14,200
Unit output for month:		
Finished during month........................		6,900
Equivalent units of work in process, end of month		
(600 units, one-third completed)....................		200
Total equivalent production		7,100
Unit cost for month:		
Materials ($7,100 ÷ 7,100).........................		$1.00
Labor ($4,260 ÷ 7,100)...........................		.60
Factory overhead ($2,840 ÷ 7,100)		.40
Total.......................................		$2.00

Inventory costs:
  Cost of goods finished during month (6,900 × $2)...... $13,800
  Cost of work in process, end of month:
    Materials (600 × ⅓ × $1) .... $ 200
    Labor (600 × ⅓ × $.60)............................   120
    Factory overhead (600 × ⅓ × $.40)   80   400
  Total production costs accounted for .... $14,200 ✗

Note that the cost of the ending work in process in January is added to the total costs incurred in February because all costs must be accounted for. The calculation of unit output for the month takes into consideration the units finished during the month, including those that had been started in process during the prior month, as well as the stage of completion of the units in process at the end of the current month. The fact that one half of the work had been completed on 200 units in the prior month does not have to be considered in this calculation, because the cost of doing that work is included with the current month's costs for the purpose of calculating unit costs. In determining the unit cost of materials, labor, and factory overhead, the accountant considers not only the current month's cost of each element, but also the cost carried over from the prior month. This procedure is the identifying characteristic of the average costing method.

Since the ending work in process is estimated to be one-third completed, its value for inventory purposes is one-third of the $2 unit cost of finished goods, or $.66667. If a company does not carry out its unit costs to several decimal places, a common practice is to use a rounding procedure as shown below:

Item	Unit Cost	Rounded to Nearest Ten
Materials..............	$1.00 ÷ 3 = $.33 × 600 = $198	$200
Labor.................	.60 ÷ 3 = .20 × 600 = 120	120
Factory overhead	.40 ÷ 3 = .13 × 600 = 78	80
Total................		$400

From the data developed on the cost of production summary on page 282, the accountant can now make this entry:

Feb. 28 Finished Goods...............................   13,800
            Work in Process   13,800

After posting this entry and the entries for the month's production costs, the work in process account has a debit balance of $400, as shown on page 284.

Work in Process		
Jan. 31	5,000	Jan. 31	9,800
	3,000		
	2,000		
	10,000		
200			
Feb. 28	7,000	Feb. 28	13,800
	4,200		23,600
	2,800		
	24,000		
400			

The following statement of the cost of goods manufactured can now be prepared:

Pyramid Toy Corp.
Statement of Cost of Goods Manufactured
For the Month Ended February 28,19--

Materials.	$ 7,000
Labor.	4,200
Factory overhead	2,800
Total.	$14,000
Add work in process inventory, February 1	200
Total.	$14,200
Less work in process inventory, February 28.	400
Cost of goods manufactured during the month.	$13,800

Illustrative Problem No. 3 — Computing the unit cost when there are no beginning inventories and two or more departments.

The business of the Pyramid Toy Corp. continued to grow until management decided to departmentalize the factory and reorganize the cost records. Accordingly, on January 1 of the following year the factory was divided into three departments as follows:

> Department A — Cutting
> Department B — Forming
> Department C — Painting

Separate control accounts are maintained in the general ledger for recording the costs of operating each department. Departmental expense analysis sheets are used in recording the manufacturing expenses incurred. The departmental production reports for January are reproduced on pages 285 and 288. Note that there were no beginning inventories of work in process in any department.

```
┌────────────────────────────────────────────────────────────────────┐
│                        PRODUCTION REPORT                           │
│                                                                    │
│              For Month Ending    January 31, 19--                  │
│                       Dept.   A--Cutting                           │
│                                                                    │
├────────────────────────────────────────────────────────────────────┤
│                                              none                  │
│  In process, beginning of period _____  │
│                                                                    │
│  Stage of completion _____  │
│                                            3,300  units            │
│  Placed in process during period _____  │
│                                                                    │
│  Received from dept. _____ during period _____   │
│                              B                  2,700  units       │
│  Transferred to dept. _____ during period _____   │
│                                              none                  │
│  Transferred to stockroom during period _____    │
│                                         600  units                 │
│  In process, end of period _____  │
│                                            1/2                     │
│  Stage of completion _____  │
└────────────────────────────────────────────────────────────────────┘
```

After receiving the production reports from the department heads, the cost accountant prepares a cost of production summary for each department and prepares the journal entries to record the operations of each department and the transfer of costs.

Note that the costs accumulated in the department are transferred to the next department for those units completed during the period and sent on for further processing. Thus, costs follow the flow of goods through the manufacturing process.

Pyramid Toy Corp.
Cost of Production Summary—Department A
For the Month Ended, January 31, 19--

Cost of production for month:	
Materials...	$15,000
Labor...	8,000
Factory overhead	7,000
Total costs to be accounted for	$30,000
Unit output for month:	
Finished and transferred to dept. B during month	2,700
Equivalent units of work in process, end of month	
(600 units, one-half completed).......................	300
Total equivalent production	3,000

Unit cost for month:
  Materials ($15,000 ÷ 3,000 units)................... $ 5.000
  Labor ($8,000 ÷ 3,000 units).......................   2.667
  Factory overhead ($7,000 ÷ 3,000 units) 2.333
    Total...................................... $10.000

Inventory costs:
  Cost of goods finished and transferred to dept. B during
  month (2,700 × $10.00) $27,000
  Cost of work in process, end of month:
    Materials (600 × ½ × $5.00)..................... $1,500
    Labor (600 × ½ × $2.667) 800*
    Factory overhead (600 × ½ × $2.333).............   700*   3,000
Total production costs accounted for $30,000

*Rounded

After posting the usual end-of-month entries, the work in process account for department A, as shown below, has a debit balance of $3,000, representing the cost of the partially completed ending inventory.

Work in Process — Dept. A			
Jan. 31	15,000	Jan. 31	27,000
	8,000		
	7,000		
	30,000		
3,000			

The only difference in procedure between this problem and Illustrative Problem No. 1 is that the goods finished in department A are transferred to department B for further processing rather than being transferred to the stockroom as finished goods.

Although still in process, the transferred units and their related costs are treated as completed products in department A and as raw materials added at the beginning of the process in department B. The cost of the units includes the costs of materials, labor, and factory overhead incurred in department A. However, the individual cost elements are combined and transferred in total to department B.

In reviewing the cost of production summary for department B on the next page, note that the calculation of unit cost for the month in department B takes into consideration only those costs incurred during the month in that department and the equivalent units produced in the department. The transferred-in costs and units from the prior department are not included in the computation.

However, in determining the cost transferred to department C and the cost of the work in process, the prior department costs must be considered. Also, in the calculation of the ending work in process valuation, the full cost of $10 per unit from department A is attached to the 500 units still in process in department B, while only a fraction of cost from department B, based on the stage of completion, is considered.

Pyramid Toy Corp.
Cost of Production Summary — Department B
For the Month Ended January 31, 19--

Cost of goods received from dept. A during month			
(2,700 units × $10.00)			$27,000
Cost of production for month:			
Materials.		$ 1,000	
Labor.		3,000	
Factory overhead		2,000	$ 6,000
Total costs to be accounted for			$33,000
Unit output for month:			
Finished and transferred to dept. C during month			2,200
Equivalent units of work in process, end of month			
(500 units, two-fifths completed)			200
Total equivalent production			2,400
Unit cost for month:			
Materials ($1,000 ÷ 2,400 units)			$ .417
Labor ($3,000 ÷ 2,400 units)			1.250
Factory overhead ($2,000 ÷ 2,400 units)			.833
Total.			$ 2.500
Inventory costs:			
Cost of goods finished and transferred to dept. C			
during month:			
Cost in dept. A (2,200 × $10.00)		$22,000	
Cost in dept. B (2,200 × 2.50)		5,500	$27,500
$12.50			
Cost of work in process, end of month:			
Cost in dept. A (500 × $10.00)		$ 5,000	
Cost in dept. B:			
Materials (500 × ⅖ × $.417)	$ 83		
Labor (500 × ⅖ × $1.25)	250		
Factory overhead (500 × ⅖ × $.833)	167	500	5,500
Total production costs accounted for			$33,000

```
┌─────────────────────────────────────────────────────────────┐
│                    PRODUCTION REPORT                          │
│                                                               │
│          For Month Ending   January 31, 19--                  │
│                     Dept.   B-Forming                         │
├─────────────────────────────────────────────────────────────┤
│                                                               │
│  In process, beginning of period _____     none           │
│                                                               │
│  Stage of completion _____                │
│                                                               │
│  Placed in process during period _____     none           │
│                                                               │
│  Received from dept. ___A___ during period _2,700 units_     │
│                                                               │
│  Transferred to dept. ___C___ during period _2,200 units_    │
│                                                               │
│  Transferred to stockroom during period ____  none           │
│                                                               │
│  In process, end of period _____   500 units            │
│                                                               │
│  Stage of completion _____      2/5               │
└─────────────────────────────────────────────────────────────┘
```

After posting the end-of-month entries, the work in process account for department B, as shown below, has a debit balance of $5,500.

Work in Process — Dept. B

Jan. 31		1,000	Jan. 31	27,500
		3,000		
		2,000		
		27,000		
		33,000		
5,500				

```
┌─────────────────────────────────────────────────────────────┐
│                    PRODUCTION REPORT                          │
│                                                               │
│          For Month Ending   January 31, 19--                  │
│                     Dept.   C-Painting                        │
├─────────────────────────────────────────────────────────────┤
│                                                               │
│  In process, beginning of period _____     none           │
│                                                               │
│  Stage of completion _____                │
│                                                               │
│  Placed in process during period _____     none           │
│                                                               │
│  Received from dept. ___B___ during period _2,200 units_     │
│                                                               │
│  Transferred to dept. _____ during period _____        │
│                                                               │
│  Transferred to stockroom during period   2,000 units        │
│                                                               │
│  In process, end of period _____   200 units            │
│                                                               │
│  Stage of completion _____      1/2               │
└─────────────────────────────────────────────────────────────┘
```

The cost of production summary illustrated below for department C is prepared in a manner similar to the department B summary, as explained previously.

Pyramid Toy Corp.
Cost of Production Summary—Department C
For the Month Ended January 31, 19--

Cost of goods received from dept. B during month (2,200 units × $12.50)...........................		$27,500
Cost of production for month:		
Materials.......................................	$ 3,000	
Labor..	2,400	
Factory overhead	3,000	8,400
Total costs to be accounted for		$35,900
Unit output for month:		
Finished and transferred to finished goods during month		2,000
Equivalent units of work in process, end of month (200 units, one-half completed)......................		100
Total equivalent production		2,100
Unit cost for month:		
Materials ($3,000 ÷ 2,100 units).....................		$ 1.429
Labor ($2,400 ÷ 2,100 units)........................		1.142
Factory overhead ($3,000 ÷ 2,100 units)		1.429
Total..		$ 4.000
Inventory costs:		
Cost of goods finished and transferred to finished goods during month:		
Cost in dept. A (2,000 × $10.00)	$20,000	
Cost in dept. B (2,000 × 2.50)	5,000	
Cost in dept. C (2,000 × 4.00)	8,000	$33,000
$16.50		
Cost of work in process, end of month:		
Cost in dept. A (200 × $10.00).....................	$ 2,000	
Cost in dept. B (200 × $ 2.50).....................	500	
Cost in dept. C:		

Materials (200 × ½ × $1.429)	$143		
Labor (200 × ½ × $1.142)	114		
Factory overhead (200 × ½ × $1.429)....	143	400	2,900
Total production costs accounted for			$35,900

After posting the end-of-month entries, the work in process account for department C, as shown on page 290, has a debit balance of $2,900.

Work in Process—Dept. C

Jan. 31		3,000	Jan. 31		33,000
		2,400			
		3,000			
		27,500			
		35,900			
	2,900				

As a means of classifying and summarizing the factory operations for January, the cost accountant prepares the work sheet reproduced on page 291. This work sheet provides the information for the following statement of cost of goods manufactured.

Pyramid Toy Corp.
Statement of Cost of Goods Manufactured
For the Month Ended January 31, 19--

Materials..	$19,000
Labor...	13,400
Factory overhead	12,000
Total...	$44,400
Less work in process inventories, January 31	11,400
Cost of goods manufactured during the month...................	$33,000

At the end of the month, the following general journal entries are made:

Jan. 31	Work in Process—Dept. A	15,000	
	Work in Process—Dept. B	1,000	
	Work in Process—Dept. C	3,000	
	Factory Overhead	1,000	
	Materials		20,000

The amount charged to Factory Overhead for indirect materials is an arbitrary amount chosen to illustrate how the costs are gathered and distributed. This amount represents the cost of various expenses and supplies that were issued but could not be charged directly to a department.

Jan. 31	Work in Process—Dept. A	8,000	
	Work in Process—Dept. B	3,000	
	Work in Process—Dept. C	2,400	
	Factory Overhead	1,500	
	Payroll		14,900

Analysis	Cost per unit transferred	Units received in department	Units transferred or on hand	Amount charged to department	Amount credited to department
Dept. A—Cutting:					
Started in process		3,300			
Costs for month:					
Materials				15,000 00	
Labor				8,000 00	
Factory overhead				7,000 00	
Finished and transferred to dept. B .	10 00		2,700		27,000 00
Closing work in process			600		3,000 00
Total	10 00	3,300	3,300	30,000 00	30,000 00
Dept. B—Forming:					
Received during month from Dept. A		2,700		27,000 00	
Costs added during month:					
Materials				1,000 00	
Labor				3,000 00	
Factory overhead				2,000 00	
Finished and transferred to dept. C .	2 50		2,200		27,500 00
Closing work in process			500		5,500 00
Total	12 50	2,700	2,700	33,000 00	33,000 00
Dept. C—Painting:					
Received during month from dept. B		2,200		27,500 00	
Costs added during month:					
Materials				3,000 00	
Labor				2,400 00	
Factory overhead				3,000 00	
Finished and transferred to stock . . .	4 00		2,000		33,000 00
Closing work in process			200		2,900 00
Total	16 50	2,200	2,200	35,900 00	35,900 00

				Amount	Total
Summary:					
Materials:					
Dept. A				15,000 00	
Dept. B				1,000 00	
Dept. C				3,000 00	19,000 00
Labor:					
Dept. A				8,000 00	
Dept. B				3,000 00	
Dept. C				2,400 00	13,400 00
Factory overhead:					
Dept. A				7,000 00	
Dept. B				2,000 00	
Dept. C				3,000 00	12,000 00
Total production costs for January					44,400 00
Deduct work in process inventory, end of month:					
Dept. A				3,000 00	
Dept. B				5,500 00	
Dept. C				2,900 00	11,400 00
Cost of production, goods fully manufactured during January					33,000 00

Again, the amount charged to Factory Overhead is an arbitrary amount chosen for purposes of illustration and represents payroll costs that could not be charged directly to any given department.

```
Jan. 31   Factory Overhead...........................    9,000
               Various accounts (Accumulated
               Depreciation, Prepaid Insurance,
               Payroll Taxes)...........................              9,000
```

This entry is a summary of several entries that are made in the general journal and possibly other journals to reflect the current month's provision for depreciation, insurance, payroll taxes, and other expenses.

```
Jan. 31   Factory Overhead — Dept. A .................    6,600
          Factory Overhead — Dept. B .................    2,100
          Factory Overhead — Dept. C .................    2,800
               Factory Overhead...........................            11,500
```

This entry distributes the actual overhead for the period to the departments. The basis for this entry would be the factory overhead analysis sheets, which show in detail the allocation or apportionment of the actual expenses to the various departments. Note that these actual amounts do not appear on the cost of production summaries, which contain the estimated amounts of factory overhead that were applied to production.

```
Jan. 31   Work in Process — Dept. A ...................    7,000
          Work in Process — Dept. B ...................    2,000
          Work in Process — Dept. C ...................    3,000
               Factory Overhead — Dept. A .............              7,000
               Factory Overhead — Dept. B .............              2,000
               Factory Overhead — Dept. C .............              3,000
```

This entry charges the applied factory overhead appearing on the cost of production summaries to the work in process control accounts. The amounts are calculated by multiplying a predetermined overhead application rate by the base used for applying overhead to each department, such as labor hours or machine hours. A different base might be used for different departments, so that overhead would be equitably applied according to the benefit each department has received.

The cost of production summary is used to develop the entries to record the transfer of costs from one department to another and to Finished Goods, as shown on page 293.

Jan. 31	Work in Process — Dept. B.....................		27,000	
	Work in Process — Dept. A...................			27,000
31	Work in Process — Dept. C....................		27,500	
	Work in Process — Dept. B..................			27,500
31	Finished Goods..............................		33,000	
	Work in Process — Dept. C..................			33,000

These journal entries are reflected in the T-accounts below. The balances remaining in the work in process accounts are reflected in total on the statement of cost of goods manufactured. The balances in the departmental factory overhead accounts represent under- or overapplied overhead and would usually be carried forward to future months; however, these balances can be transferred to an under- and overapplied factory overhead account. As discussed in previous chapters, these amounts of under- and overapplied overhead would be analyzed to determine if they are expected normal or seasonal variances, or if they represent inefficiencies that must be corrected.

Work in Process — Dept. A				Work in Process — Dept. B			
Jan. 31	15,000	Jan. 31	27,000	Jan. 31	1,000	Jan. 31	27,500
	8,000				3,000		
	7,000				2,000		
	30,000				27,000		
3,000					*33,000*		
				5,500			

Work in Process — Dept. C				Materials		
Jan. 31	3,000	Jan. 31	33,000		Jan. 31	20,000
	2,400					
	3,000			**Payroll**		
	27,500				Jan. 31	14,900
	35,900					
2,900						

Finished Goods			Factory Overhead — Dept. A			
Jan. 31	33,000		Jan. 31	6,600	Jan. 31	7,000
					400	

Factory Overhead				Factory Overhead — Dept. C			
Jan. 31	1,000	Jan. 31	11,500	Jan. 31	2,800	Jan. 31	3,000
	1,500					*200*	
	9,000						
	11,500						
–0–							

Factory Overhead — Dept. B			
Jan. 31	2,100	Jan. 31	2,000
	100		

Illustrative Problem No. 4—Computing the unit cost when there are beginning inventories and two or more departments.

The February production reports submitted by the department heads for the Pyramid Toy Corp. are reproduced below and on pages 296 and 298. These reports differ from the January production reports in that they show inventories for work in process in each department at the beginning of the month. Note that the number of units in process at the beginning of the

```
┌─────────────────────────────────────────────────────────┐
│                   PRODUCTION REPORT                        │
│                                                            │
│          For Month Ending  February 28, 19--               │
│                     Dept.  A-Cutting                       │
├─────────────────────────────────────────────────────────┤
│                                                            │
│  In process, beginning of period        600  units        │
│                                                            │
│  Stage of completion                        1/2           │
│                                                            │
│  Placed in process during period       3,800  units       │
│                                                            │
│  Received from dept. _____ during period    none         │
│                                                            │
│  Transferred to dept. __B__ during period  3,900  units   │
│                                                            │
│  Transferred to stockroom during period      none         │
│                                                            │
│  In process, end of period              500  units        │
│                                                            │
│  Stage of completion                        4/5           │
└─────────────────────────────────────────────────────────┘
```

period plus the units placed in process or received from another department during the period are equal to the number of units transferred to another department or to the stockroom during the period plus the units in process at the end of the period. After receiving the production reports for February, the cost accountant prepares a cost of production summary for each department and drafts the entries to record the operations of each department in the general ledger accounts.

It should be noted in the following cost of production summary that in determining unit cost, as with an earlier example, the cost of beginning work in process from the prior month is added to the total costs incurred during the current month. The calculation of unit output for the month takes into consideration all units finished during the month, including those that had been in process at the beginning as well as those in process at the end of the period. Although the total unit cost is the same as in January, the unit cost of labor has increased and the unit cost of factory overhead has decreased. Management would likely investigate the causes for these changes and take whatever action might be necessary.

Pyramid Toy Corp.
Cost of Production Summary—Department A
For the Month Ended February 28, 19--

Cost of work in process, beginning of month:		
Materials...	$ 1,500	
Labor..	800	
Factory overhead	700	$ 3,000
Cost of production for month:		
Materials...	$20,000	
Labor..	10,810	
Factory overhead	9,190	40,000
Total costs to be accounted for		$43,000
Unit output for month:		
Finished and transferred to dept. B during month		3,900
Equivalent units of work in process, end of month		
(500 units, four-fifths completed)...................		400
Total equivalent production		4,300
Unit cost for month:		
Materials ($21,500 ÷ 4,300).......................		$5.00
Labor ($11,610 ÷ 4,300)		2.70
Factory overhead ($9,890 ÷ 4,300).................		2.30
Total......................................		$ 10.00
Inventory costs:		
Cost of goods finished and transferred to dept. B		
during month: (3,900 × $10.00)		$39,000
Cost of work in process end of month:		
Materials (500 × ⅘ × $5.00).....................	$ 2,000	
Labor (500 × ⅘ × $2.70)	1,080	
Factory overhead (500 × ⅘ × $2.30)..............	920	4,000
Total production costs accounted for		$43,000

At this time the following general journal entry can be made:

Feb. 28	Work in Process—Dept. B.....................	39,000	
	Work in Process—Dept. A..................		39,000

The work in process account for this department now appears as follows:

Work in Process — Dept. A

Jan. 31		15,000	Jan. 31	27,000
		8,000		
		7,000		
		30,000		
	3,000			
Feb. 28		20,000	Feb. 28	39,000
		10,810		*66,000*
		9,190		
		70,000		
	4,000			

PRODUCTION REPORT

For Month Ending ___February 28,___ 19--
Dept. ___B-Forming___

In process, beginning of period _____ 500 units

Stage of completion _____ 2/5

Placed in process during period _____ none

Received from dept. ___A___ during period ___3,900 units___

Transferred to dept. ___C___ during period ___4,100 units___

Transferred to stockroom during period _____ none

In process, end of period _____ 300 units

Stage of completion _____ 1/3

In determining the unit cost in department B at the end of February, the amounts considered are the production costs incurred by the department during the month added to the departmental cost of work in process at the beginning of the month. The cost from department A that is included in the beginning work in process valuation ($5,000) is not used in this calculation.

Pyramid Toy Corp.
Cost of Production Summary—Department B
For the Month Ended February 28, 19--

Cost of work in process, beginning of month:			
Cost in dept. A.................................		$ 5,000	
Cost in dept. B:			
Materials................................	$ 83		
Labor....................................	250		
Factory overhead	167	500	$ 5,500
Cost of goods received from dept. A during month......			39,000
Cost of production for month:			
Materials...	$ 1,681		
Labor...	5,000		
Factory overhead	3,319	10,000	
Total costs to be accounted for			$54,500
Unit output for month:			
Finished and transferred to dept. C during month			4,100
Equivalent units of work in process, end of month			
(300 units, one-third completed).....................			100
Total equivalent production			4,200
Unit cost for month:			
Materials ($1,764 ÷ 4,200)...........................			$ .42
Labor ($5,250 ÷ 4,200)..............................			1.25
Factory overhead ($3,486 ÷ 4,200)			.83
Total...			$ 2.50
Inventory costs:			
Costs of goods finished and transferred to dept. C			
during month:			
Cost in dept. A (4,100 × $10.00)..................	$41,000		
Cost in dept. B (4,100 × ___2.50)	10,250	$51,250	
$12.50			
Cost of work in process, end of month:			
Cost in dept. A (300 × $10.00).....................	$ 3,000		
Cost in dept. B:			
Materials (300 × ⅓ × $.42)................	$ 42		
Labor (300 × ⅓ × $1.25)	125		
Factory overhead (300 × ⅓ × $.83)	83	250	3,250
Total production costs accounted for			$54,500

The following journal entry can now be made:

Feb. 28	Work in Process — Dept. C....................	51,250	
	Work in Process — Dept. B..................		51,250

The general ledger account for work in process in department B appears as follows:

Work in Process — Dept. B

Jan. 31		1,000	Jan. 31	27,500
		3,000		
		2,000		
		27,000		
		33,000		
	5,500			
Feb. 28		1,681	Feb. 28	51,250
		5,000		78,750
		3,319		
		39,000		
		82,000		
	3,250			

PRODUCTION REPORT

For Month Ending ___February 28, 19--___
Dept. ___C-Painting___

In process, beginning of period _____ 200 units

Stage of completion _____ 1/2

Placed in process during period _____ none

Received from dept. ___B___ during period ___4,100 units___

Transferred to dept. _____ during period _____

Transferred to stockroom during period _____ 3,900 units

In process, end of period _____ 400 units

Stage of completion _____ 1/2

Pyramid Toy Corp.
Cost of Production Summary — Department C
For the Month Ended February 28, 19--

Cost of work in process, beginning of month:
Cost in dept. A		$ 2,000*	
Cost in dept. B		500*	
Cost in dept. C:			
Materials.................................	$143		
Labor....................................	114		
Factory overhead	143	400	$ 2,900
Cost of goods received from dept. B during month			51,250
Cost of production for month:			
Materials..	$ 5,720		
Labor..	4,560		
Factory overhead	5,720	16,000	
Total costs to be accounted for			**$70,150**

Unit output for month:
Finished and transferred to finished goods during
month 3,900
Equivalent units of work in process, end of month
(400 units, one-half completed)...................... 200

Total equivalent production 4,100

Unit cost for month:
Materials ($5,863 ÷ 4,100)............................	$1.43
Labor ($4,674 ÷ 4,100)...............................	1.14
Factory overhead ($5,863 ÷ 4,100)	1.43
Total...	$4.00

Inventory costs:
Cost of goods finished and transferred to finished
goods during month:
Cost in dept. A (3,900 × $10.00)	$39,000	
Cost in dept. B (3,900 × 2.50)	9,750	
Cost in dept. C (3,900 × 4.00)	15,600	$64,350

$16.50

Cost of work in process, end of month:
Cost in dept. A (400 × $10.00)......................		$ 4,000	
Cost in dept. B (400 × $ 2.50)......................		1,000	
Cost in dept. C:			
Materials (400 × ½ × $1.43)..............	$286		
Labor (400 × ½ × $1.14)	228		
Factory overhead (400 × ½ × $1.43).......	286	800	5,800
Total production costs accounted for			**$70,150**

*Not to be considered in calculating February unit cost in department C.

The following journal entry can now be made:

Feb. 28   Finished Goods............................   64,350
                Work in Process — Dept. C..................   64,350

The general ledger account for work in process in department C appears as shown below.

Work in Process — Dept. C

Jan. 31	3,000	Jan. 31	33,000
	2,400		
	3,000		
	27,500		
	35,900		
2,900			
Feb. 28	5,720	Feb. 28	64,350
	4,560		97,350
	5,720		
	51,250		
	103,150		
5,800			

The cost accountant can now prepare the work sheet, reproduced below and on page 301, which summarizes the factory operations for February and provides the data needed for preparing the statement of cost of goods manufactured.

Pyramid Toy Corp.
Departmental Cost Work Sheet
For the Month Ended February 28, 19--

Analysis	Cost per unit transferred		Units received in department	Units transferred or on hand	Amount charged to department		Amount credited to department	
Dept. A — Cutting:								
Opening inventory in process......			600		3,000	00		
Started in process................			3,800					
Costs for month:								
Materials.....................					20,000	00		
Labor........................					10,810	00		
Factory overhead..............					9,190	00		
Finished and transferred to Dept. B.	10	00		3,900			39,000	00
Closing work in process..........				500			4,000	00
Total........................	10	00	4,400	4,400	43,000	00	43,000	00

Analysis	Cost per unit transferred		Units received in department	Units transferred or on hand	Amount charged to department		Amount credited to department	
Dept. B—Forming:								
Opening inventory in process			500		5,500	00		
Received during month from Dept. A			3,900		39,000	00		
Costs added during month:								
Materials					1,681	00		
Labor					5,000	00		
Factory overhead					3,319	00		
Finished and transferred to Dept. C	2	50		4,100			51,250	00
Closing work in process				300			3,250	00
Total	12	50	4,400	4,400	54,500	00	54,500	00
Dept. C—Painting:								
Opening inventory in process			200		2,900	00		
Received during month from Dept. B			4,100		51,250	00		
Costs added during month:								
Materials					5,720	00		
Labor					4,560	00		
Factory overhead					5,720	00		
Finished and transferred to stock . . .	4	00		3,900			64,350	00
Closing work in process				400			5,800	00
Total	16	50	4,300	4,300	70,150	00	70,150	00

		Amount		Total	
Summary:					
Materials:					
Dept. A		20,000	00		
Dept. B		1,681	00		
Dept. C		5,720	00	27,401	00
Labor:					
Dept. A		10,810	00		
Dept. B		5,000	00		
Dept. C		4,560	00	20,370	00
Factory overhead:					
Dept. A		9,190	00		
Dept. B		3,319	00		
Dept. C		5,720	00	18,229	00
Total production costs for February . . .				66,000	00
Add work in process, beginning of month:					
Dept. A		3,000	00		
Dept. B		5,500	00		
Dept. C		2,900	00	11,400	00
Total				77,400	00
Deduct work in process, end of month:					
Dept. A		4,000	00		
Dept. B		3,250	00		
Dept. C		5,800	00	13,050	00
Cost of production, goods fully manufactured during February				64,350	00

Pyramid Toy Corp.
Statement of Cost of Goods Manufactured
For the Month Ended February 28, 19--

Materials..	$27,401
Labor...	20,370
Factory overhead	18,229
Total...	$66,000
Add work in process inventories, February 1..................	11,400
	$77,400
Less work in process inventories, February 28	13,050
Cost of goods manufactured during the month..................	$64,350

Occasionally finished goods in a department at the end of the month may not be transferred to the next department until the following month. Because these units are still on hand in the first department at the end of the first month, they cannot be accounted for as being transferred even though they have been finished. They are accounted for as "goods completed and on hand" and priced out at the full unit price. However, it is important to remember that these goods are considered to be work in process for financial statement purposes. Although the goods are finished in the department, they are still in process as far as the factory is concerned.

Change in Unit Costs

In the preceding illustrative problem, it was assumed that the cost from prior departments was the same in the current month as it had been in the previous month. Often, however, the cost from prior departments will change from one month to the next, so that these costs must be averaged for purposes of assigning the total costs. The method is similar to that used for the cost of materials, labor, and factory overhead in the department.

To illustrate, assume that 2,000 units are in process in department 2 at the beginning of the month with an accumulated cost of $15,000. During the month, 10,000 units with a cost of $50,000 are received from department 1; 11,000 units are finished and transferred to department 3; and 1,000 units are in process in department 2 at the end of the month, one-half completed. The following is a schedule of costs for department 2 in such a situation.

	Units	Unit Cost	Cost from Dept. 1	Costs in Dept. 2 Materials	Labor	Overhead	Total Cost
In process, beginning of month	2,000	$5.30	$10,600	$ 2,000	$ 1,400	$ 1,000	$ 15,000
Received from dept. 1 during month	10,000	$5.00	50,000				50,000
Cost incurred this month.....				21,000	14,700	10,500	46,200
Total units and costs to be accounted for..............	12,000		$60,600	$23,000	$16,100	$11,500	$111,200
Average cost of units from dept. 1 ($60,600 ÷ 12,000)..		$5.05					$5.05
Unit cost for month in dept. B with equivalent production of 11,500 units...............				$2.00	$1.40	$1.00	4.40
Unit cost for finished goods..							$9.45
Assignment of costs: Transferred to dept. 3	11,000	$5.05	$55,550	$22,000	$15,400	$11,000	$103,950
In process end of month (½ complete)..............	1,000	$5.05	5,050	1,000	700	500	7,250
Total units and costs accounted for	12,000	$5.05	$60,600	$23,000	$16,100	$11,500	$111,200

KEY TERMS

Average cost method (276)
Cost center (273)
Cost of production summary (279)
Equivalent production (277)
Production report (277)
Stage of completion (277)
Transferred-in costs (286)

QUESTIONS

1. What are the two basic systems of cost accounting and under what conditions may each be used advantageously?

2. Following is a list of manufactured products. For each product, indicate whether a job order or a process cost system would be used to account for the costs of production.

(a) Lumber   (e) Cereal
(b) Buildings   (f) Textbooks
(c) Airplanes   (g) Paint
(d) Gasoline   (h) Women's hats

3. Is there any situation in which a manufacturing company might use both the job order cost system and the process cost system?

4. What is the primary difference between the two cost accounting systems regarding the accumulation of costs and the calculation of unit costs?

5. What is the difference between the term "unit cost" as commonly used in the process cost system and the term "job cost" as commonly used in the job order system of cost accounting?

6. How do the two cost accounting systems differ in accounting for:
(a) materials
(b) labor
(c) factory overhead

7. What is the primary objective in accumulating costs by departments?

8. What is meant by the term "equivalent production" as used in the process cost system?

9. Explain why it is necessary to estimate the stage or degree of completion of work in process at the end of the accounting period under the process cost system.

10. What would be the effect on the unit cost of finished goods if an inaccurate estimate of the stage of completion of work in process is made?

11. What information is reflected on a production report?

12. What are the four divisions of a cost of production summary?

EXERCISES

Exercise 6-1   Identifying cost flows in process cost system.

List in columnar form the transactions and the accounts debited and credited to reflect the flow of costs through a process cost accounting system.

Exercise 6-2   Computing equivalent production.

Compute the equivalent production (unit output) for the month for each of the following situations:

	Units Completed During Month	Units in Process End of Month	Stage of Completion	
(a)	8,000	2,000	1/2	
(b)	21,000	4,000	3/4	
(c)	6,000	1,000	3/4	
		500	2/5	
(d)	18,000	5,000	1/2	
		5,000	3/4	
(e)	32,000	1,500	1/5	
		4,000	3/4	

[Handwritten annotations: "Eq. Prod.", 29,000, 24,000, 750, 200, 2500, and various marginal figures.]

Exercise 6-3   Computing units in process, units completed, and equivalent production.

Using the data presented below, compute the figures that should be inserted in the blank spaces.

	Beginning Units in Process	Units Started in Production	Units Transferred to Finished Goods	Ending Units in Process	Equivalent Units
(a)	600	8,000	8,600	—	—
(b)	900	6,500	—	400 — ½ completed	—
(c)	1,500	—	12,900	1,200 — ¼ completed	—
(d)	—	7,250	7,200	150 — ⅓ completed	—
(e)	—	8,400	8,200	200 — ½ completed	—
(f)	400	6,200	6,200	—	6,300

Exercise 6-4   Determining unit cost.

During the month, a company with no departmentalization incurred costs of $45,000 for materials, $30,000 for labor, and $20,625 for factory overhead. There were no units in process at the beginning or at the end of the month, and 7,500 units were completed. Determine the unit cost for the month for materials, labor, and factory overhead.

Exercise 6-5   Determining unit cost.

The Crux Manufacturing Co. recorded costs for the month of $15,750 for materials, $40,950 for labor, and $25,200 for factory overhead. There was no beginning work in process; 9,000 units were finished, and 2,000 units were in process at the end of the period, three-fourths completed. Compute the month's unit cost for each element of manufacturing cost.

Exercise 6-6   Determining unit cost.

The records of Leba, Inc., reflect the following data:

Work in process, beginning of month—2,000 units one-half completed at a cost of $1,250 for materials, $675 for labor, and $950 for overhead.

Production costs for the month—materials, $99,150; labor, $54,925; factory overhead, $75,050.

Units completed and transferred to stock—38,500.

Work in process, end of month—3,000 units one-half completed.

Calculate the unit cost for the month for materials, labor, and factory overhead.

Exercise 6-7   Determining unit cost for department and for completed units.

Read Products Company has two production departments. The nature of the process is such that there are no units left in process in department 2 at the end of the period. During the period, 8,000 units with a cost of $27,200 were transferred from department 1 to department 2. Department 2 incurred costs of $9,600 for materials, $6,400 for labor, and $8,000 for factory overhead, and finished 8,000 units during the month. Determine:

(a)   the unit cost for the month in department 2.

(b)   the unit cost of the products transferred to finished goods.

Exercise 6-8   Determining unit cost.

The Mayfair Manufacturing Co. had 500 units, three-fifths completed, in process at the beginning of the month. During the month 2,000 units were started in process and finished. There was no work in process at the end of the month. Unit cost of production for the month was $1.20. Costs for materials, labor, and factory overhead incurred in the current month totaled $2,655. Calculate the unit cost for the prior month.

PROBLEMS

Problem 6-1   Cost of production summary, one department; beginning and ending work in process.

The Ottowa Products Co. produces a household cleansing liquid and uses the process cost system. The following information was obtained from the accounts of the company at the end of February:

Production Costs

Work in process, beginning of period:

Materials	$ 5,000	
Labor	3,750	
Factory overhead	3,750	$12,500
Costs incurred during month:		
Materials	$30,000	
Labor	22,500	
Factory overhead	22,500	75,000
Total		$87,500

Production Report	Units
Finished and transferred to stockroom during month	34,000
Work in process, end of period, one-fourth completed.	4,000

Required:

Prepare a cost of production summary for February.

Problem 6-2   Cost of production summary, one department; beginning and ending work in process.

The Hammer Company uses the process cost system. The following data taken from the books of the organization reflect the results of manufacturing operations during the month of October:

Production Costs

Work in process, beginning of period:

Materials	$ 2,600	
Labor	2,300	
Factory overhead	1,000	$ 5,900
Costs incurred during month:		
Materials	$10,000	
Labor	7,500	
Factory overhead	6,000	23,500
Total		$29,400

Production Report	Units
Finished and transferred to stockroom during month	13,000
Work in process, end of period, one-half completed	2,000

Required:

Prepare a cost of production summary for October.

Problem 6-3 Cost of production summary, two departments.

Zano Inc., which manufactures products on a continuous basis, had 800 units in process in department 1, one-half completed at the beginning of May. The costs in April for processing these units were: materials, $1,200; labor, $900; and factory overhead, $1,000. During May, department 1 finished and trans- ferred 10,000 units to department 2 and had 400 units in process at the end of May, one-half completed.

Department 2 had 200 units in process at the beginning of the month, one-half completed. April costs for these units were: cost transferred from department 1, $1,550; materials, $200; labor, $175; factory overhead, $225. During May, department 2 completed 9,000 units and had 1,200 units in pro- cess at the end of the period, two-thirds completed.

Production costs incurred by the two departments during May were as follows:

	Department 1	Department 2
Materials	$29,400	$19,400
Labor	22,050	16,975
Factory overhead	24,500	21,825

Required:

Prepare a cost of production summary for each department.

Problem 6-4   Change in unit cost from prior department and valuation of inventory.

The Royal Products Co. has two departments — mixing and cooking. At the beginning of the month, the cooking department had 2,000 units in process with costs of $8,600 from the mixing department and its own departmental costs of $500 for materials, $1,000 for labor, and $2,500 for factory overhead. During the month, 8,000 units were received from the mixing department with a cost of $36,400. The cooking department incurred costs of $4,250 for materials, $8,500 for labor, and $21,250 for factory overhead, and finished 9,000 units. At the end of the month there were 1,000 units in process, one-half completed.

Required:
1. Determine the unit cost for the month in the cooking department.
2. Determine the new average unit cost for all units received from the mixing department.
3. Determine the unit cost of goods finished.
4. Determine the accumulated cost of the goods finished and of the ending work in process. *Note: A schedule similar to the illustration on page 303 will be helpful.*

Problem 6-5   Cost of production summary, three departments; change in unit cost from prior department; departmental cost work sheet; journal entries; manufacturing statement.

The Lake Manufacturing Co. uses the process cost system. The following information for the month of December was obtained from the books of the company and from the production reports submitted by the department heads:

B or C cost change

Production Report	Dept. A	Dept. B	Dept. C
Units in process, beginning of period ..	2,500	1,500	3,000
Started in process during month.......	12,500	—	—
Received from prior department	—	13,000	10,000
Finished and transferred.............	13,000	10,000	11,000
Finished and on hand	—	500	—
Units in process, end of period........	2,000	4,000	2,000
Stage of completion.................	1/4	4/5	1/2

Production Costs	Dept. A	Dept. B	Dept. C
Work in process, beginning of period:			
Cost in dept. A		$ 3,075	$ 6,150
Materials........................	$ 1,470		
Labor...........................	650		
Factory overhead	565		
Cost in dept. B			3,660
Materials........................		240	
Labor...........................		905	
Factory overhead		750	
Cost in dept. C			
Materials........................			900 (own)
Labor...........................			3,100
Factory overhead			3,080
Costs incurred during month:			
Materials........................	15,000	2,500	1,500 (own)
Labor...........................	4,750	8,000	6,500
Factory overhead	5,240	6,100	7,000
Total.........................	$27,675	$21,570	$31,890

Required:
1. Prepare cost of production summaries for Departments A, B, and C.
2. Prepare a departmental cost work sheet.
3. Draft the journal entries required to record the month's operations.
4. Prepare a statement of cost of goods manufactured for December.

Problem 6-6   Departmental cost work sheet analysis; cost of production summary, three departments; journal entries; manufacturing statement.

The West Manufacturing Co. uses the process cost system of accounting. A portion of the departmental cost work sheet prepared by the cost accountant at the end of July is reproduced below.

Departmental Cost Work Sheet
For the Month Ended July 31, 19--

Analysis	Cost per unit transferred		Units received in department	Units transferred or on hand	Amount charged to department		Amount credited to department	
Dept. A:								
Started in process			6,600					
Costs for month:								
Materials.......................					30,000	00		
Labor..........................					16,000	00		
Factory overhead					14,000	00		
Completed and transferred to dept. B	10	00		5,400			54,000	00
Closing inventory in process				1,200			6,000	00
Total........................	10	00	6,600	6,600	60,000	00	60,000	00
Dept. B:								
Received during month from dept. A			5,400		54,000	00		
Costs added during month:								
Materials.......................					1,200	00		
Labor..........................					6,000	00		
Factory overhead					4,800	00		
Completed and transferred to dept. C	2	50		4,400			55,000	00
Closing inventory in process				1,000			11,000	00
Total........................	12	50	5,400	5,400	66,000	00	66,000	00
Dept. C:								
Received during month from dept. B			4,400		55,000	00		
Costs added during month:								
Materials.......................					6,300	00		
Labor..........................					4,200	00		
Factory overhead					6,300	00		
Completed and transferred to stock.	4	00		4,000			66,000	00
Closing inventory in process				400			5,800	00
Total........................	16	50	4,400	4,400	71,800	00	71,800	00

Required:

1. Prepare a cost of production summary for each department. The stage of completion of ending units in process must be computed.
2. Draft the necessary entries in general journal form to record the manufacturing costs incurred during the month of July.
3. Prepare a statement of cost of goods manufactured for the month ended July 31.

Problem 6-7   Ledger account analysis; cost of production summary.

Analyze the information presented in the general ledger account of the Lexington Manufacturing Co. shown below.

Departmentalized

Work in Process — Dept. B

Mar. 1 b/s	10,250	Mar. 31	50,000 *outflow*
31 Materials	4,000		
31 Labor	8,000		
31 Factory overhead	6,000		
31 Dept. A	36,000		

apt from

Additional facts:

$5.125 (a)   2,000 units were in process at the beginning of the month, one-half com- *1000 units*
pleted.

$4.00 (b)   9,000 units were received from department A during the month.
6.25 (c)   8,000 units were transferred to department C during the month.

(d)   The unit costs in departments A and B were the same for March as for the prior month.

(e)   The ratio of materials, labor, and factory overhead costs for department B in the beginning and ending balances of Work in Process was in the same ratio as the costs incurred in department B during the current month.

Required:

Prepare a cost of production summary for March.

18,000

4/9 - material

4/9 labor

3/9 factory overhead

PROCESS COST ACCOUNTING—

ADDITIONAL PROCEDURES

LEARNING OBJECTIVES

In studying this chapter you will learn about the:

■ Computation of unit cost when materials are not added uniformly throughout the process
■ Accounting for units lost in the production process
■ Accounting for units gained in the production process
■ First-in, first-out method of assigning costs to inventories
■ Nature of joint costs and the methods used to apportion these costs to joint products
■ Differences between joint products and by-products and the accounting for by-products

The illustrative problems presented in Chapter 6 are based on the assumption that materials, labor, and factory overhead are uniformly applied during the period of processing. If the work in process at the end of the accounting period was considered to be one-half completed, it was assumed that one half of the materials cost, one half of the labor cost, and one half of the factory overhead cost had been incurred.

EQUIVALENT PRODUCTION — MATERIALS NOT UNIFORMLY APPLIED

In many industries where the process cost system is used, the materials may be put into production in irregular quantities and at varying points in the processing cycle.

For example, before any manufacturing process can begin, materials must be introduced into the first production department. This might be a sheet of metal that will be cut or trimmed to size, shaped, and formed through the application of labor and the use of machines. In this case, all of the materials are added at the start of the process, and then labor and factory overhead are incurred to begin converting this material into the finished product. No matter what stage of completion the work is in at the end of the month in this department, it will have had all the materials costs added. If the work is unfinished in the department, it will have had only a portion of the labor and overhead costs applied to it.

In the second production department, this same material may be processed further through the application of other labor operations such as buffing and polishing, and then, at the end of the process in this department, have several coats of enamel applied to it. In this case, the units that are uncompleted in the department at the end of the month would have a part of the departmental labor and overhead costs applied to them but have had no materials cost added in this department.

In the next department, other materials such as a knob, a handle, or pads may be added to the unit immediately, then a final polishing involving labor and equipment would be applied. After this process, in the same department, the unit may be placed in a plastic container which is additional material, and the package would be sealed, incurring more labor and overhead cost.

In this third department, the units not completed may have the first items of material and some labor and overhead applied, or they may have the first material, some labor and overhead, and the additional materials added; in any event, the stage of completion must be carefully determined to measure accurately how much of each element of cost to apply to these unfinished units.

Compared with the principles and procedures developed in the preceding chapter, the only new procedure presented here is that equivalent production must be computed for each element of production cost, rather than one equivalent production figure being determined for materials, labor, and overhead. In addition, the allocation of cost for each element must be carefully considered when valuing the ending work in process.

As an aid in explaining the problems involved in ascertaining unit costs under these conditions, three illustrative problems are presented. In these examples, materials are added at different stages in the process. Labor and factory overhead are assumed to be applied evenly throughout the process. This situation is typical in that the incurrence and application of overhead is usually so closely related to labor costs or hours that overhead is generally thought of as being incurred or applied in the same ratio as labor expense.

Illustrative Problem No. 1

Computing the unit cost in department A where all the materials are added at the beginning of processing. The production report for the month, submitted by the department head, is shown below. It is similar to those studied in the previous chapter.

PRODUCTION REPORT

For Month Ending __April 30, 19--__
Dept. ____A____

In process, beginning of period	500 units
Stage of completion	2/5
Placed in process during period	2,500 units
Received from dept. _____ during period	
Transferred to dept. __B__ during period	2,600 units
Transferred to stockroom during period	
In process, end of period	400 units
Stage of completion	3/4

The cost of production summary is illustrated on page 315. Note that it too is similar to the ones previously discussed, with the additional step of determining equivalent production for materials separately from that of labor and factory overhead.

```
                    Modern Manufacturing Corp.
              Cost of Production Summary—Department A
                  For the Month Ended April 30, 19--

Cost of work in process, beginning of month:
    Materials.......................................    $1,500
    Labor...........................................       250
    Factory overhead................................       150      $ 1,900
Cost of production for month:
    Materials.......................................    $7,500
    Labor...........................................     3,375
    Factory overhead................................     2,025       12,900
Total costs to be accounted for.....................                $14,800

Unit output for month:
  Materials:
    Finished and transferred to dept. B during month ....             2,600
    Equivalent units of work in process, end of month
    (400 units, three-fourths completed, all materials).....            400
        Total equivalent production .....................            3,000

  Labor and factory overhead:
    Finished and transferred to dept. B during month ....             2,600
    Equivalent units of work in process, end of month
    (400 units, three-fourths completed)................               300
        Total equivalent production .....................            2,900

Unit cost for month:
    Materials ($9,000 ÷ 3,000)...........................            $3.00
    Labor ($3,625 ÷ 2,900)...............................             1.25
    Factory overhead ($2,175 ÷ 2,900)...................               .75
        Total........................................              $5.00

Inventory costs:
    Cost of goods finished and transferred to dept. B
    during month (2,600 × $5)...........................           $13,000
    Cost of work in process, end of month:
        Materials (400 × $3)............................    $1,200
        Labor (400 × ¾ × $1.25) ........................       375
        Factory overhead (400 × ¾ × $.75)...............       225        1,800
Total production costs accounted for ...................                $14,800
```

In this department, because all materials are added at the start of processing, it is simple to determine the equivalent units for materials. The production report from the factory indicates that 500 units were in process at the beginning of the month with all materials added, and that 2,500 units were started in process; therefore, the equivalent production for materials is 3,000 units. Another way of calculating the figure by the method used in this chapter is: the 2,600 units finished during the month and the 400 units in process at the end of the month have all of the materials added. The total of these two figures is 3,000 units, which is the equivalent production for materials for the month.

The unit output for labor and factory overhead is calculated as shown in the preceding chapter: 2,600 completed units, plus the equivalent of 300 completed units (400 units three-fourths completed), gives a total of 2,900 for the unit output for the month for labor and overhead.

With the equivalent production figures determined for materials, labor, and overhead, the cost accountant can now calculate the unit cost for the month as illustrated in previous discussions. The cost of each element in the beginning work in process is added to the cost of production for that element incurred in the current month; this total cost is then divided by the appropriate equivalent production figure to determine the unit cost of the month for each element of cost. In this example, the unit cost of materials is $3.00, of labor $1.25, and of overhead $.75, giving a total unit cost of $5.00.

The 2,600 units transferred to department B are costed at $5.00 each, or a total of $13,000. In costing the ending work in process, the accountant must consider the stage of completion and the point at which materials are added. In this instance, because materials are put into production at the beginning of the manufacturing cycle, the 400 units in process at the end of the month have all of the materials added and are, therefore, costed at the full unit cost of $3.00 for materials. Because the goods are three-fourths completed, and labor and factory overhead are added evenly throughout the process, the 400 units are costed at three-fourths of the month's unit cost for labor and overhead.

Illustrative Problem No. 2

Computing the unit cost in department B where all the materials are added at the close of processing. In department B, because the materials are added at the end of the manufacturing process, only those units finished will have materials cost applied; therefore, the equivalent production for the month for materials in this department is 2,500 units. The calculation for labor and factory overhead adds the 2,500 finished units to the equivalent production for the ending work in process, 350 units two-fifths completed, or 140, giving a total of 2,640 units as the output for the month. The production report for department B is shown below. The cost of production summary is presented on page 318.

```
┌──────────────────────────────────────────────────────────────┐
│                    PRODUCTION REPORT                         │
│                                                              │
│            For Month Ending   April 30, 19--                 │
│                       Dept. _____B_____                    │
│                                                              │
│  In process, beginning of period _____    250 units        │
│                                                              │
│  Stage of completion _____                 1/2             │
│                                                              │
│  Placed in process during period _____                     │
│                                                              │
│  Received from dept. ___A___ during period  2,600 units      │
│                                                              │
│  Transferred to dept. ___C___ during period 2,500 units      │
│                                                              │
│  Transferred to stockroom during period _____             │
│                                                              │
│  In process, end of period _____          350 units        │
│                                                              │
│  Stage of completion _____                 2/5             │
└──────────────────────────────────────────────────────────────┘
```

As in department A, the unit cost for each element of manufacturing cost is determined by adding the cost included in the beginning work in process to the cost for that element incurred during the month, and dividing this total by the unit output for the month. For department B these unit costs for materials, labor, and factory overhead are $4, $3, and $3, respectively.

The units finished and transferred to department C are valued at the full unit cost of $5, carried over from department A, plus the unit cost of $10 added in department B, giving a total cost transferred of $37,500.

The cost of the units in process at the end of the period includes the full cost of $5 from department A. There is no materials cost for department B to be considered because no materials have been added. If materials had been added, the units would have been finished. Because the units are two-fifths completed, two-fifths of the current unit costs for labor and factory overhead is used in costing the units. The combination of these items results in a cost of $2,590 for the ending work in process.

Modern Manufacturing Corp.
Cost of Production Summary—Department B
For the Month Ended April 30,19--

Cost of work in process, beginning of month:			
Cost in dept. A		$ 1,250	
Cost in dept. B:			
Materials..............................	−0−		
Labor..................................	$375		
Factory overhead	375	750	$ 2,000
Cost of goods received from dept. A during month			13,000
Cost of production for month:			
Materials....................................	$10,000		
Labor...	7,545		
Factory overhead	7,545	25,090	
Total costs to be accounted for			$40,090

Unit output for month:	
Materials:	
Finished and transferred to dept. C during month ...	2,500
Equivalent units of work in process, end of month ...	−0−
Total equivalent production	2,500
Labor and factory overhead:	
Finished and transferred to dept. C during month ...	2,500
Equivalent units of work in process, end of month	
(350 units, two-fifths completed)...................	140
Total equivalent production	2,640

Unit cost for month:	
Materials ($10,000 ÷ 2,500).......................	$ 4.00
Labor ($7,920 ÷ 2,640)...........................	3.00
Factory overhead ($7,920 ÷ 2,640)	3.00
Total.......................................	$10.00

Inventory costs:			
Cost of goods finished and transferred to dept. C			
during month:			
Cost in dept. A (2,500 × $5)......................	$12,500		
Cost in dept. B (2,500 × $10).....................	25,000	$37,500	
Cost of work in process, end of month:			
Cost in dept. A (350 × $5).......................	$ 1,750		
Cost in dept. B:			
Materials..............................	−0−		
Labor (350 × ⅖ × $3)	$420		
Factory overhead (350 × ⅖ × $3)........	420	840	2,590
Total production costs accounted for			$40,090

Illustrative Problem No. 3

Computing the unit cost in department C where 60 percent of the materials cost is added to production at the beginning of processing and 40 percent when the processing is one-half completed. In department C, the calculation of equivalent production is more complex because materials are added at different stages throughout the process. The stage of completion of units in process cannot be averaged but must be reported in groups of units at varying points in the manufacturing process as shown in the following production report. In calculating the unit of output for the month, the stage of completion of each group must be carefully computed.

PRODUCTION REPORT

For Month Ending ___April 30, 19--___
Dept. ___C___

In process, beginning of period ___500 units___

Stage of completion ___200 units 3/4 completed-300 units 1/3 completed___

Placed in process during period _____

Received from dept. ___B___ during period ___2,500 units___

Transferred to dept. _____ during period _____

Transferred to stockroom during period ___2,400 units___

In process, end of period ___600 units___

Stage of completion ___200 units 1/4 completed-400 units 3/4 completed___

The equivalent production for the month for materials is determined as follows: 2,400 units were finished and therefore include all the materials. Two hundred units are one-fourth completed at the end of the period; since they are not yet at the halfway point of the process, they have had only 60 percent of the materials added, or the equivalent of 120 units. The 400 units that are three-fourths completed are past the halfway stage, and therefore have all of the materials added, or a total of 400 units. Combining these figures — 2,400, 120, and 400 — results in the unit output for materials of 2,920 units.

A simpler calculation is made for labor and factory overhead: 2,400 completed units, plus the equivalent of 50 completed units (200 units one-fourth completed), plus the equivalent of 300 completed units (400 units three-fourths completed) equals total equivalent production for the month for labor and overhead of 2,750 units.

The unit costs for the month are calculated as previously illustrated and are determined to be $1.75, $1.20, and $.60 for materials, labor, and factory overhead respectively, for a total unit cost in department C of $3.55. The cost of the units finished and transferred to the stockroom includes the unit costs from department A of $5, from department B of $10, and from department C of $3.55.

In calculating the cost to be assigned to the ending work in process, the stage of completion must be considered. The 200 units that are one-fourth completed will have all the costs from departments A and B assigned to them. The costs in department C are determined as follows: 60 percent of the materials cost has been added, and therefore the units will be costed at 60 percent of the unit cost for materials, or 200 units × 60% × $1.75 = $210; the costs allocated for labor and overhead are one-fourth of the month's unit cost for each, or 200 units × 25% × $1.20 = $60 for labor and 200 units × 25% × $.60 = $30 for overhead.

Modern Manufacturing Corp.
Cost of Production Summary — Department C
For the Month Ended April 30, 19--

Cost of work in process, beginning of month:			
Cost in dept. A		$ 2,500	
Cost in dept. B		5,000	
Cost in dept. C:			
Materials	$665		
Labor	300		
Factory overhead	150	1,115	$ 8,615
Cost of goods received from dept. B during month			37,500
Cost of production for month:			
Materials		$ 4,445	
Labor		3,000	
Factory overhead		1,500	8,945
Total costs to be accounted for			$55,060

Unit output for month:
  Materials:
    Finished and transferred to finished goods during
    month 2,400
    Equivalent units of work in process, end of month:
      200 units, one-fourth completed (60% of materials) . 120
      400 units, three-fourths completed (all materials) .. 400

        Total equivalent production 2,920

  Labor and overhead:
    Finished and transferred to finished goods during
    month 2,400
    Equivalent units of work in process, end of month:
      200 units, one-fourth completed 50
      400 units, three-fourths completed 300

        Total equivalent production 2,750

Unit cost for month:
  Materials ($5,110 ÷ 2,920).......................... $1.75
  Labor ($3,300 ÷ 2,750).............................. 1.20
  Factory overhead ($1,650 ÷ 2,750).................. .60

      Total... $3.55

Inventory costs:
  Cost of goods finished and transferred to finished goods
  during month:
    Cost in dept. A (2,400 × $5)..................... $12,000
    Cost in dept. B (2,400 × $10).................... 24,000
    Cost in dept. C (2,400 × $3.55) 8,520 $44,520

  Cost of work in process, end of month:
    200 units, one-fourth completed:
      Cost in dept. A (200 × $5)..................... $ 1,000
      Cost in dept. B (200 × $10).................... 2,000
      Cost in dept. C:
        Materials (200 × 60% × $1.75) $210
        Labor (200 × 25% × $1.20) 60
        Factory overhead (200 × 25% × $.60).. 30   300

    400 units, three-fourths completed:
      Cost in dept. A (400 × $5)..................... 2,000
      Cost in dept. B (400 × $10).................... 4,000
      Cost in dept. C:
        Materials (400 × $1.75) $700
        Labor (400 × 75% × $1.20) 360
        Factory overhead (400 × 75% × $.60).. 180   1,240   10,540

Total production costs accounted for $55,060

The 400 units that are three-fourths completed are assigned all of the unit costs from departments A and B. Although these units are still in process, they have all of the materials added, and therefore are charged for the full unit cost of materials in department C—400 units × $1.75 = $700. Three-fourths of the unit costs for labor and factory overhead would be included in the cost of these units: 400 units × 75% × $1.20 = $360 for labor; 400 units × 75% × $.60 = $180 for overhead.

After the cost of production summaries have been prepared for each department, the journal entries, as illustrated in the previous chapter, can be made. Entries would be made to transfer costs from one department to another and finally to Finished Goods. The actual costs incurred during the month for materials, labor, and factory overhead would be recorded in the journals and ledgers. After all entries have been made, the work in process accounts in the general ledger should have balances that equal the cost assigned to work in process on the cost of production summaries. If desired, a departmental cost work sheet can be prepared as illustrated in Chapter 6.

UNITS LOST IN PRODUCTION

In many industries that have a process manufacturing operation, the process is of such a nature that there will always be some loss of units during the process due to evaporation, shrinkage, spillage, or other factors. The effect of such losses is that the number of units completed during a given period of time plus the number of units still in process at the end of the period will be less than the number of units in process at the beginning of the period plus the number of units placed in process during the period.

Normal losses are inherent to the manufacturing process and cannot be avoided; they represent a necessary cost of producing the marketable units. The usual procedure is to treat normal losses as product costs, that is, to include the cost of the lost units in the cost of all units finished or still in process. The effect is that the unit cost of the remaining units is greater than if there had been no losses, since there are a smaller number of units over which to spread the production costs for the period. The following examples illustrate the procedures involved.

Illustrative Problem No. 1

Units lost in the first department. Assume that materials, labor, and factory overhead are applied evenly throughout the process and that the monthly production report for department A reports the following data:

Units started in process		10,000
Units finished and transferred to the next department	9,000	
Units still in process, one-half completed	800	9,800
Units lost in production		200

This report is significant to factory management, who review these figures to determine whether they represent normal unavoidable losses or abnormal losses that require action. With the production figures above and the costs of production for the month, the cost accountant can prepare the cost of production summary below.

Notice that on the cost of production summary the lost units have not been considered; they have been completely ignored in the calculation of equivalent production and in the determination of inventory costs. If the

Chemical Refining Corporation
Cost of Production Summary — Department A
For the Month Ended July 31, 19--

Cost of production for month:		
Materials		$18,800
Labor		9,400
Factory overhead		4,700
Total costs to be accounted for		$32,900
Unit output for month:		
Finished and transferred to dept. B during month		9,000
Equivalent units of work in process, end of month (800		
units, one-half completed)		400
Total equivalent production		9,400
Unit cost for month:		
Materials ($18,800 ÷ 9,400)		$2.00
Labor ($9,400 ÷ 9,400)		1.00
Factory overhead ($4,700 ÷ 9,400)		.50
Total		$3.50
Inventory costs:		
Cost of goods finished and transferred to dept. B during		
month (9,000 × $3.50)		$31,500
Cost of work in process, end of month:		
Materials (800 × ½ × $2)	$800	
Labor (800 × ½ × $1)	400	
Factory overhead (800 × ½ × $.50)	200	1,400
Total production costs accounted for		$32,900

units had not been lost but had been finished, equivalent production would have been 9,600 units, and the unit costs for materials, labor, and factory overhead would have been lower. The cost of the lost units is absorbed by the production for the month.

Illustrative Problem No. 2

Units lost in subsequent department. The July production report for department B reflects the following data:

Units received from department A		9,000
Units finished and transferred to finished goods.............	8,000	
Units still in process, two-thirds completed	750	8,750
Units lost in production....................................		250

On the cost of production summary, the procedures are identical to those for department A through the calculation of unit costs for the month. The 250 units lost in the department during the period are ignored in the computations, so that the higher unit costs for the month reflect the absorption of the costs relating to the lost units.

Before determining the cost of the goods finished and in process at the end of the month, however, a new computation must be made. The 250 units that were lost in department B were ignored in determining unit costs for department B, but these units carried a cost of $3.50 each from department A that must now be taken into consideration.

Chemical Refining Corporation
Cost of Production Summary—Department B
For the Month Ended July 31, 19--

Cost of production for month:		
Materials.....................................	$15,300	
Labor..	10,200	
Factory overhead	6,375	
Total......................................		$31,875
Cost of goods received from dept. A during month......		31,500
Total costs to be accounted for		$63,375

Unit output for month:
Finished and transferred to finished goods during
month   8,000
Equivalent units of work in process, end of month
(750 units, two-thirds completed)   500
    Total equivalent production   8,500

Unit cost for month:
Materials ($15,300 ÷ 8,500).......................... $1.80
Labor ($10,200 ÷ 8,500) 1.20
Factory overhead (6,375 ÷ 8,500) 75
    Total... $3.75

Inventory costs:
Cost of goods finished and transferred to finished
goods:
  Cost in dept. A (8,000 × $3.60, adjusted unit cost).. $28,800
  Cost in dept. B (8,000 × $3.75) 30,000 $58,800

Cost of work in process, end of month:
  Cost in dept. A (750 × $3.60, adjusted unit cost).... $ 2,700
  Cost in dept. B:
    Materials (750 × ⅔ × $1.80)............ $900
    Labor (750 × ⅔ × $1.20)   600
    Factory overhead (750 × ⅔ × $.75)   375   1,875   4,575
Total production costs accounted for **$63,375**

During the month, 250 of the 9,000 units transferred from department A were lost in department B. Therefore, the cost transferred, $31,500, must now be spread over the remaining 8,750 units, producing a new unit cost of $3.60. This new cost is called the adjusted unit cost in the cost of production summary. The adjustment of unit cost does not affect department A's cost of production summary, since the units were lost in department B.

Another way of making this calculation is as follows:

Units from dept. A lost in dept. B.................................   250
Multiplied by the unit cost from dept. A.......................... $3.50
Cost applicable to the units lost $875.00

Number of units transferred from dept. A.........................   9,000
Number of units lost...   250
Number of units remaining.......................................   8,750

The cost applicable to lost units must be spread over the remaining units:

$$\frac{\$875}{8,750} = \$.10 \text{ adjustment in unit cost.}$$

Original unit cost...	$3.50
Add adjustment in unit cost...................................	.10
Adjusted unit cost..	$3.60

Illustrative Problem No. 3

Units lost at the end of the process. In the previous illustrations, the units lost were treated as though they had never been put into production. Both finished goods and units still in process absorbed the cost of the lost units. However, if the units are lost at the end of the process or are rejected at the final inspection, the cost of the lost units may be absorbed by the completed units only. In this case, no part of the loss is charged to the units remaining in process. The lost units are included in the number of units used to determine equivalent production and unit costs are then calculated in the usual way, thus producing a lower unit cost than if the lost units had been ignored. This unit cost is applied to goods finished and transferred, to those still in process, and to those units that were lost. The cost assigned to lost units is then added to the cost of the goods completed, and this total cost is transferred to the next department or to Finished Goods. The unit cost of the goods transferred will, of course, be higher than the monthly unit cost of production. These calculations are shown in the cost of production summary on page 327, using the same data as that used on page 323.

The preceding discussion has considered only normal losses, with the cost of lost units being treated as a product cost, that is, charged to the remaining units. But abnormal losses may also occur. Such losses are not inherent to the manufacturing process and are not expected under normal, efficient operating conditions. Units lost under these circumstances would be included in the calculation of equivalent production and unit costs as shown in the preceding example of units lost at the end of the process. However, abnormal losses are not included as part of the cost of transferred or finished goods, but are treated as a period cost, that is, charged to a separate expense account and shown as a separate item of expense on the current income statement. If the number of units lost in the previous example was considered to be abnormal, the cost transferred to the next department would be $30,843; $686 would be charged to Abnormal Loss of Units, and the cost of work in process would remain unchanged at $1,371.

Chemical Refining Corporation
Cost of Production Summary — Department A
For the Month Ended July 31, 19--

Cost of production for month:		
Materials...		$18,800
Labor...		9,400
Factory overhead		4,700
Total costs to be accounted for		**$32,900**
Unit output for month:		
Finished and transferred to dept. B during month		9,000
Equivalent units of work in process, end of month		
(800 units, one-half completed).....................		400
Lost at end of process		200
Total equivalent production		9,600
Unit cost for month:		
Materials ($18,800 ÷ 9,600)........................		$1.958
Labor ($9,400 ÷ 9,600)............................		.979
Factory overhead ($4,700 ÷ 9,600)		.490
Total..		$3.427
Inventory costs:		
Cost of goods finished and transferred to dept. B		
during month (9,000 × $3.427).....................	$30,843	
Add cost of units lost (200 × $3.427)	686	
Total cost of good units finished and transferred to		
department B during month (9,000 × $3.503*)......		$31,529
Cost of work in process, end of month:		
Materials (800 × ½ × $1.958)	$ 783	
Labor (800 × ½ × $.979)	392	
Factory overhead (800 × ½ × $.49)	196	1,371
Total production costs accounted for		**$32,900**

*200 units lost × $3.427 = $686 cost of lost units.
$686 ÷ 9,000 units completed = $.076 unit cost adjustment for lost units.
$3.427 + $.076 = $3.503 adjusted unit cost of units completed.

Illustrative Problem No. 4

Abnormal loss of units at the beginning of the process. If an abnormal loss occurs at the beginning of processing in a department, only materials and/or transferred-in costs are affected. Since these units are lost early in the process, no labor or overhead should be added for these lost units. Using the department A data, the abnormal loss is calculated and accounted for as follows:

Chemical Refining Corporation
Cost of Production Summary—Department A
For the Month Ended July 31, 19--

Cost of production for month:		
Materials..		$18,800
Labor...		9,400
Factory overhead		4,700
Total costs to be accounted for		$32,900
Unit output for month:		
Materials:		
Finished and transferred to dept. B during month		9,000
Equivalent units of work in process, end of month (800 units, one-half completed)		400
Lost in process................................		200
Total equivalent production		9,600
Labor and factory overhead:		
Finished and transferred to dept. B during month		9,000
Equivalent units of work in process, end of month (800 units, one-half completed)		400
Total equivalent production		9,400
Unit cost for month:		
Materials ($18,800 ÷ 9,600)......................		$1.9583
Labor ($9,400 ÷ 9,400)...........................		1.0000
Factory overhead ($4,700 ÷ 9,400)		.5000
Total.......................................		$3.4583
Inventory costs and abnormal loss:		
Cost of goods finished and transferred to dept. B (9,000 × $3.4583).....................................		$31,125
Cost of work in process, end of month:		
Materials (800 × ½ × $1.9583)	$783	
Labor (800 × ½ × $1.00)	400	
Factory overhead (800 × ½ × $.50)	200	1,383
Cost of abnormal loss (200 × $1.9583).............		392
Total production costs accounted for		$32,900

The journal entry to transfer costs would be as follows:

Work in Process — Department B	31,125	
Abnormal Loss of Units	392	
Work in Process — Department A		31,517

UNITS GAINED IN PRODUCTION

With some manufactured products, the addition of materials in a subsequent department increases the number of units being processed. For example, assume a liquid product is being produced. In the first department, 1,000 gallons of various materials are put into production. In the next department an additional 500 gallons of another material is added, increasing the number of units being manufactured to 1,500. This increase in units has the opposite effect of lost units and requires an adjustment to the unit cost in the second or subsequent departments. The calculation of this adjusted unit cost is similar to that made when units are lost, except that the total cost for the original units must be spread over a greater number of units in the subsequent department, thereby reducing the unit cost.

To illustrate, assume that a concentrated detergent, Super-Glo, is manufactured. During the month 10,000 gallons of the partially processed product have been transferred to department B at a cost of $15,000, or a unit cost of $1.50. In department B, 5,000 gallons of additional materials are added to these units in process. As these materials are added, the mixing and refining of the liquid involves the equal application of materials, labor, and overhead. A production report shows that 13,000 gallons were completed and transferred to finished goods, leaving 2,000 gallons in process, one-half completed. The cost of production summary is on page 330. The cost transferred from department A for 10,000 gallons was $15,000, or a unit cost of $1.50. The addition of 5,000 gallons in department B increases the liquid in process to 15,000 units. The cost from department A of $15,000 must now be spread over these 15,000 units, resulting in an adjusted unit cost of $1.00.

It is possible that in addition to gaining a number of units, some units will also be lost during processing in department B. This factor presents no additional problem, since the equivalent production and unit costs are calculated as though the lost units had not existed, and the type of computation shown in the preceding example would be the same. As mentioned previously in this chapter, if management wishes to have a dollar accounting

Super-Glo Manufacturing Company
Cost of Production Summary—Department B
For the Month Ended May 31, 19--

Cost of goods received from dept. A during month (10,000 gallons × $1.50)		$15,000
Cost of production for month:		
Materials..	$15,400	
Labor..	3,500	
Factory overhead	2,800	21,700
Total costs to be accounted for		$36,700
Unit output for month:		
Finished and transferred to finished goods		13,000
Equivalent units of work in process, end of month (2,000 gallons, one-half completed).................		1,000
Total equivalent production		14,000
Unit cost for month:		
Materials ($15,400 ÷ 14,000)		$1.10
Labor ($3,500 ÷ 14,000)		.25
Factory overhead ($2,800 ÷ 14,000)...............		.20
Total.......................................		$1.55
Inventory costs:		
Cost of goods finished and transferred to finished goods:		
Cost in dept. A (13,000 × $1.00*, adjusted unit cost)	$13,000	
Cost in dept. B (13,000 × $1.55)	20,150	$33,150
Cost of work in process, end of month:		
Cost in dept. A (2,000 × $1.00, adjusted unit cost)..	$ 2,000	

Cost in dept. B:			
Materials (2,000 × ½ × $1.10).........	$1,100		
Labor (2,000 × ½ × $.25).............	250		
Factory overhead (2,000 × ½ × $.20) ..	200	1,550	3,550
Total production costs accounted for			$36,700

*$15,000 ÷ 15,000 gal. = $1 per gal.

for lost units, then the number lost would be included in equivalent production as though no loss had occurred. The unit cost would be computed and a dollar cost assigned to lost units by multiplying the unit cost by the number of units lost.

EQUIVALENT PRODUCTION — FIRST-IN, FIRST-OUT METHOD

The previous discussion and illustrations have used the average method of costing. As mentioned in Chapter 6, another method of costing commonly used is the first-in, first-out (fifo) method. This approach assumes that the costs of the current period are first applied to complete the beginning units in process; secondly, to start and finish a number of units; and finally, to start other units in process.

The two problems that follow illustrate this method of costing compared with average costing. When studying these examples, note that fifo costing differs from average costing only if there are units in process at the start of the period; if there is no beginning work in process, both methods will produce the same results.

Also note that under the fifo method, if units are lost, there must be a decision made as to whether these units are from the beginning inventory in process or from the units started during the period. Assuming that unit costs differ from one period to the next, this decision is necessary in order to determine which unit cost should be adjusted.

Whether the fifo or the average cost method is used, the first step in preparing the cost of production summary is to list the costs that must be accounted for, that is, the beginning balance of work in process, the current period's costs of production, and the cost of units transferred from a prior department, if any. With the fifo method, there is no necessity to break down the cost of the beginning work in process into its cost elements as is required with the average cost method.

The second step under the fifo method, as with the average cost procedure, is to determine the unit output for the month. If there were units in process at the start of the period, the total equivalent production figures for the fifo method will differ from those for the average cost method because the unit output required to complete the beginning work in process must also be calculated.

Illustrative Problem No. 1

Fifo cost method compared with average cost method — materials added at start of process. Assume that in department 1, materials are added at the start of processing, and labor and factory overhead are applied evenly throughout the process. The production report for March reflects the following data:

Units in process, beginning of month, two-thirds completed	3,000
Units started in process	9,000
Units finished and transferred to department 2	8,000
Units in process, end of month, one-half completed	4,000

Cost data are as follows:

Beginning work in process, prior month's cost:

Materials.	$ 9,600
Labor.	3,600
Factory overhead	2,800
Total.	$16,000

Current month's production costs:

Materials.	$27,000
Labor.	16,000
Factory overhead	8,000
Total.	$51,000

Using the fifo method, a cost of production summary is prepared as shown on the following page. For comparative purposes, a cost of production summary under the average cost method is shown on page 334.

There were 3,000 units in process at the beginning of the month; these units were complete as to materials and two-thirds complete as to labor and factory overhead.

In the current month, no materials had to be added to these units; however, the equivalent of 1,000 units (3,000 × ⅓) of labor and overhead had to be applied to these units to finish them in Department 1.

Of the 8,000 units finished and transferred to department 2 during the month, 3,000 were from the beginning units in process; therefore, 5,000 units must have been fully manufactured during the month. Under the fifo cost method, the beginning units in process are not merged with the units started and finished during the month.

The calculation of equivalent production for the ending work in process is the same under fifo as under the average cost method. There are 4,000 units in process with all materials and with one half of the labor and overhead. Thus, the equivalent production for materials is 4,000 units and for labor and overhead, 2,000 units.

The calculation of unit costs with the fifo method takes into consideration only the current period data. The total cost of each element — materials, labor, and factory overhead — is divided by the equivalent

FIFO METHOD

Gage Manufacturing Company
Cost of Production Summary — Department 1
For the Month Ended March 31, 19--

Cost of work in process, beginning of month............		$16,000
Cost of production for month:		
Materials...	$27,000	
Labor...	16,000	
Factory overhead	8,000	51,000
Total costs to be accounted for		**$67,000**

Unit output for month:

	Materials	Labor and Factory Overhead
To complete beginning units in process	–0–	1,000
Units started and finished during month	5,000	5,000
Ending units in process...............................	4,000	2,000
Total equivalent production	9,000	8,000

Unit cost for month:		
Materials ($27,000 ÷ 9,000)........................		$3.00
Labor ($16,000 ÷ 8,000)		2.00
Factory overhead ($8,000 ÷ 8,000).................		1.00
Total..		$6.00

Inventory costs:		
Cost of goods finished and transferred to department 2 during month:		
Beginning units in process:		
Prior month's cost.............................	$16,000	
Current cost to complete:		
Materials....................................	–0–	
Labor (3,000 × ⅓ × $2).....................	2,000	
Factory overhead (3,000 × ⅓ × $1)...........	1,000	$19,000
Units started and finished during month (5,000 × $6.00)		30,000
Total cost transferred (8,000 × $6.125*)........		$49,000
Cost of work in process, end of month:		
Materials (4,000 × $3)............................	$12,000	
Labor (4,000 × ½ × $2)...........................	4,000	
Factory overhead (4,000 × ½ × $1)................	2,000	18,000
Total production costs accounted for		**$67,000**

*$49,000 ÷ 8,000 = $6.125

production for the month to determine the unit cost for each element. The cost of the beginning work in process is not merged with current costs under the fifo method as it is under the average cost method.

When assigning costs to the units finished and transferred, the average cost approach simply charges the 8,000 units transferred with the total unit cost of $6.09, as computed on page 335. Under the fifo method, however, two calculations are necessary to determine the cost assigned to units transferred. First, the 3,000 units in process at the beginning of the month were complete as to materials, so no cost for materials is added. However, the units had been two-thirds completed during the previous month as to labor and overhead and therefore must have been completed as to the other one-third during the current month. Thus, one-third of the current period's unit cost for labor and overhead is assigned to each of the 3,000 units and then added to the $16,000 cost carried over from the prior period.

Second, the 5,000 units fully manufactured during the month are priced at the unit cost of $6 for the period. The total accumulated cost of the 3,000 units in process at the beginning of the month and the cost of the 5,000 units started and finished during the month is then transferred to department 2. Note that when making this transfer of cost, the costs related to the starting units in process lose their identity and are merged with the costs of those units started and finished during the current period. Thus, the $49,000 of the total cost transferred to department 2 is divided by the 8,000 units transferred to department 2 to arrive at a single unit cost of $6.125. The costs assigned to the ending work in process inventory are determined in the same manner under the fifo method as under the average cost approach. The 4,000 units are complete as to materials and are charged with the full unit cost; they are one-half complete as to labor and overhead and are allocated one half of the unit cost. Although the method of calculation is the same, the total costs charged to the ending units in process differ between the fifo and average cost methods because of the difference in unit costs that result under each procedure.

Illustrative Problem No. 2

Fifo cost method compared with average cost method — materials added at end of process and units lost during process. Assume that in department 2 materials are added at the end of the process and labor and factory overhead are applied

AVERAGE COST METHOD

Gage Manufacturing Company
Cost of Production Summary — Department 1
For the Month Ended March 31, 19--

Cost of work in process, beginning of month:

Materials..	$ 9,600	
Labor...	3,600	
Factory overhead	2,800	$16,000

Cost of production for month:

Materials...	$27,000	
Labor...	16,000	
Factory overhead	8,000	51,000
Total costs to be accounted for		$67,000

Unit output for month:
Materials:

Finished and transferred to dept. 2 during month....	8,000
Work in process, end of month	4,000
Total equivalent production	12,000

Labor and factory overhead:

Finished and transferred to dept. 2 during month....	8,000
Work in process, end of month	2,000
Total equivalent production	10,000

Unit cost for month:

Materials ($36,600 ÷ 12,000)	$3.05
Labor ($19,600 ÷ 10,000)	1.96
Factory overhead ($10,800 ÷ 10,000)...............	1.08
Total...	$6.09

Inventory costs:

Cost of goods finished and transferred to dept. 2 during month (8,000 × $6.09)......................		$48,720
Cost of work in process, end of month:		
Materials (4,000 × $3.05)........................	$12,200	
Labor (4,000 × ½ × $1.96)......................	3,920	
Factory overhead (4,000 × ½ × $1.08)	2,160	18,280
Total production costs accounted for		$67,000

evenly throughout the process. The production for March reflects the following information:

Units in process, beginning of month, three-fourths completed......	2,000
Units received from department 1	8,000
Units finished...	8,000
Units in process, end of month, one-half completed	1,000
Units lost...	1,000
Cost data are as follows:	
Beginning work in process, prior month's cost:	
Prior department cost	$12,000
Materials...	–0–
Labor...	4,160
Factory overhead	3,000
Total...	$19,160
Cost of units received from department 1......................	$49,000
Current month's production costs:	
Materials...	$16,000
Labor...	21,000
Factory overhead	14,000
Total...	$51,000

The cost of production summary for department 2 is shown below and on the following page, using the fifo method, and on pages 338–339, using the average cost method. In the cost of production summary using the fifo method, the costs to be accounted for are listed and then the unit output for the period is determined. In this department, materials are added at the end of the process; therefore, in order to finish the 2,000 units in process at the beginning of the period, all of the materials had to be added — a total of 2,000. Three-fourths of the labor and factory overhead had been applied

---

FIFO METHOD

Gage Manufacturing Company
Cost of Production Summary — Department 2
For the Month Ended March 31, 19--

Cost of work in process, beginning of month...........		$ 19,160
Cost of goods received from dept. 1 during month		49,000
Cost of production for month:		
Materials..	$16,000	
Labor..	21,000	
Factory overhead	14,000	51,000
Total costs to be accounted for		$119,160

Unit output for month:

	Materials	Labor and Factory Overhead
To complete beginning units in process	2,000	500
Units started and finished during month	6,000	6,000
Ending units in process........................	–0–	500
Total equivalent production	8,000	7,000

Unit cost for month:

Materials ($16,000 ÷ 8,000)......................	$2.00
Labor ($21,000 ÷ 7,000)	3.00
Factory overhead ($14,000 ÷ 7,000)...............	2.00
Total..	$7.00

Inventory costs:
Cost of goods finished:
  Beginning units in process:

Prior month's cost............................	$19,160	
Current cost to complete:		
Materials (2,000 × $2)......................	4,000	
Labor (2,000 × ¼ × $3).....................	1,500	
Factory overhead (2,000 × ¼ × $2)	1,000	$ 25,660
Units started and finished during month:		
Cost in Dept. 1 (6,000 × $7*)	$42,000	
Cost in Dept. 2 (6,000 × $7)	42,000	84,000
Total (8,000 × $13.7075)		$109,660
Cost of work in process, end of month:		
Cost in dept. 1 (1,000 × $7*)	$ 7,000	
Cost in dept. 2:		
Materials...................................	–0–	
Labor (1,000 × ½ × $3).....................	1,500	
Factory overhead (1,000 × ½ × $2)	1,000	9,500
Total production costs accounted for		**$119,160**

The adjusted unit cost is calculated as follows:

Units received from dept. 1 during the current month	*8,000*
Units lost in dept. 2.........................	*1,000*
Units remaining..............................	*7,000*

Cost transferred from dept. 1—$49,000 ÷ 7,000 units = $7 adjusted unit cost.

to these units in process during the prior period, so one-fourth of these cost elements would be applied in the current month to finish the 2,000 units—an equivalent of 500 units.

Of the 8,000 units completed during the period, 2,000 were in process at the start of the month; therefore, 6,000 have been fully manufactured during the current month. The 1,000 units in process at the end of the month have had no materials added but are one-half complete as to labor and overhead — an equivalent of 500 units.

Notice that with both the fifo and average cost methods, the units lost in processing are ignored for purposes of calculating the unit output. This procedure is based on the assumption that the losses are normal and occur during the process. If the losses were incurred at the end of the process, or were abnormal, the lost units would be included in the determination of equivalent production under either method, and a separate dollar accounting would be made for these units.

As in department 1, unit cost under the fifo method is determined by dividing the current period's cost of each element by the unit output for the period. Under the average cost method, unit cost is calculated by dividing the merged costs of the current period and those carried over as work in process by the unit output, which is determined by merging current production and the units in process at the beginning of the period.

In determining the total costs to be charged to the beginning work in process, the balance from the prior month is added to the costs incurred to complete these units in the current period. The 2,000 units are charged for

---

AVERAGE COST METHOD

Gage Manufacturing Company
Cost of Production Summary — Department 2
For the Month Ended March 31, 19--

Cost of work process, beginning of month:			
Cost in dept. 1		$12,000	
Cost in dept. 2:			
Materials	–0–		
Labor	$4,160		
Factory overhead	3,000	7,160	$ 19,160
Cost of goods received from dept. 1 during month			48,720
Cost of production for month:			
Materials		$16,000	
Labor		21,000	
Factory overhead		14,000	51,000
Total costs to be accounted for			$118,880

Unit output for month:
Materials finished during month 8,000

Labor and overhead:
Finished during month....................... 8,000
Work in process, end of month 500   8,500

Unit cost for month:
Materials ($16,000 ÷ 8,000)...................... $2.00
Labor ($25,160 ÷ 8,500) 2.96
Factory overhead ($17,000 ÷ 8,500).............. 2.00
Total...................................... $6.96

Inventory costs:
Cost of goods finished:
Cost in dept. 1 (8,000 × $6.74667*) $53,973
Cost in dept. 2 (8,000 × $6.96) 55,680 $109,653

Cost of work in process, end of month:
Cost in dept. 1 (1,000 × $6.74667*) .... $ 6,747
Cost in dept. 2:
Materials...................................... –0–
Labor (1,000 × ½ × $2.96)..................... 1,480
Factory overhead (1,000 × ½ × $2.00) 1,000   9,227
Total production costs accounted for $118,880

*The adjusted unit cost is calculated as follows:
Total units processed during the month that had
been received from dept. 1.................... 10,000
Units lost 1,000
Units remaining.............................. 9,000

Total cost from dept. 1 — $60,720 ÷ 9,000 = $6.74667 adjusted unit cost.

the full unit cost of materials and with one-fourth of the current unit costs for labor and overhead. This computation is not made under the average cost method.

Under the fifo method, when calculating the cost to be allocated to those units fully manufactured during the month, the lost units must be taken into consideration, and the unit cost from the prior department must be adjusted. As mentioned previously, a determination must be made as to whether the lost units are from those in process at the beginning of the period or from those received during the period. In this case, the assumption is made that the units lost are from those received from department 1 during the month.

Eight thousand units had been received but 1,000 units were lost in processing, leaving 7,000 units in department 2 that had been received during the month from department 1. The cost transferred from department 1 during the period, $49,000, is divided by the 7,000 units remaining, to result in an adjusted unit cost from department 1 of $7. The 6,000 units started and finished during the month are charged with the $7 adjusted unit cost from the prior department as well as the $7 current unit cost in department 2.

Under the average cost method, all of the units that had come from department 1, whether this month or last month, must be considered in determining the adjusted unit cost. The 2,000 units in process at the beginning of the period, as well as the 8,000 units received during the month, are included in the calculation, and the prior department cost of $12,000, carried over from the prior month, is added to the current month's cost transferred from department 1. The total prior department cost of $60,720 is divided by the 9,000 remaining units to produce an adjusted unit cost of $6.74667. The 8,000 units completed during the period are charged with this unit cost as well as with the current unit cost in department 2 of $6.96.

The calculation of the costs to be charged to the units in process at the end of the month is similar under either the fifo or the average cost method. The resulting figures differ as a result of the differences between prior department and current month unit costs under the two methods.

In comparing the fifo and the average cost methods, the argument for fifo is that units started within the current period are valued at the current period's costs and are not distorted by the merging of these costs with costs from the preceding period. The units and costs in the beginning inventory maintain their separate identity while they are in the department. This aids in controlling costs by having separate per unit costs each month for comparison purposes. Use of the fifo method, however, means that the units in the beginning inventory are valued, when completed, at a cost that represents neither the prior cost nor the current period's cost, but a combination of the two. Also, the identity of the beginning units in process is typically not maintained when these units are transferred to the next department, so the cost of these units is usually combined with the cost of units fully manufactured during the month.

The average cost method has the advantage that all units completed during the period have the same unit cost assigned to them; therefore, this method is easier to use than the fifo cost method. In the final analysis, however, a manufacturing concern should choose the method that most accurately depicts to management the unit cost of producing in that firm's particular industrial and economic environment.

JOINT PRODUCTS AND BY-PRODUCTS

In many industries, the manufacturing process is such that from one or more materials started in process, two or more distinct products are derived. Examples of these industries are petroleum refineries, lumber mills, and meat packing plants. Petroleum yields gasoline, heating oils, and lubricants. Lumber mills produce various grades of lumber and salable sawdust. Meat packing processes result in a variety of different cuts of meat and other products. The several items obtained from a common process are divided into two categories; those that are the primary objectives of the process are called joint products, while secondary products with relatively little value are designated as by-products.

Accounting for Joint Products

The costs of materials, labor, and overhead incurred during the process are called joint costs. When the separate products become identifiable, that is, at the split-off point, the manufacturing costs up to that point cannot usually be specifically identified with any one of the individual products. Therefore, some method must be adopted to equitably allocate the joint costs to each of the products. If further processing of any of the products is required, these additional costs are applied directly to the specific products as discussed in this and previous chapters.

Typical bases for apportionment of joint costs to joint products are as follows:

1. A physical unit of measure such as volume, weight, size, or grade.
2. Relative sales value of each product (or adjusted sales value).
3. Chemical, engineering, or other types of analyses.

The allocation of joint costs according to physical unit of measure is a simple method of apportionment in which each product is assumed to have received similar benefits from the process and therefore is charged with a proportionate share of the total processing costs.

To illustrate, assume that the Chemi-Pro Co. produces two liquid products from one process. In the manufacturing process, various materials are mixed in a huge vat and allowed to settle, so that a light liquid rises to the top and a heavier liquid settles to the bottom of the vat. The products, A and B, are drawn off separately and piped directly into tank cars for shipment. The costs of materials, labor, and overhead total $120,000 to produce 20,000 gallons of A and 10,000 gallons of B. The allocation of costs would be:

Product	Units (Gals.)	Percent of Total Quantity	Assignment of Joint Costs
A	20,000	66⅔%	$ 80,000
B	10,000	33⅓%	40,000
Total	30,000	100 %	$120,000

This method is satisfactory if all of the units manufactured are quite similar in their revenue-producing ability. It would not be satisfactory if it created large variances in gross margins of the products. It could also conceivably allocate to a product costs that would be greater than the sales value of that product.

Because the allocation of costs based on physical measure can be misleading, the assignment of costs in proportion to the relative sales value of each product is more commonly used. This method assumes a direct relationship between selling price and joint costs and follows the logic that the greatest share of joint cost should be assigned to the product that has the highest value.

Assume the same facts as given for Chemi-Pro Co. and assume that product A sells for $5.00 a gallon and product B for $8.50 a gallon. Using the relative sales value method, the joint costs of $120,000 would be allocated as follows:

Product	Units Produced (Gals.)		Unit Selling Price (per Gal.)		Total Sales Value	Percent of Sales Value (Rounded)	Assignment of Joint Costs
A	20,000	×	$5.00	=	$100,000	54%	$ 64,800
B	10,000	×	8.50	=	85,000	46	55,200
Total	30,000				$185,000	100%	$120,000

Some companies make a further refinement of this method by subtracting the estimated selling expenses for each product from its sales value to determine the net realizable value of the product. If a product is to be processed further after the point of separation, costs should not be assigned on the basis of ultimate sales value because the additional processing adds value to the product. In this case, an adjusted sales value is used that takes into consideration the cost of the processing after split-off.

Assume that Chemi-Pro Co. market researchers determine that product B would have a better market if the product is sold in powder form in individual packages. After studying this proposition, the company decides to pipe product B into ovens to dehydrate it. The resulting powder is packaged in one-pound packages that will sell for $21 each.

During the month of October, when the new process began, the costs of materials, labor, and factory overhead in the mixing and settling department were $99,000, $6,000, and $15,000 respectively, and 20,000 gallons of product A were transferred to tank cars. In the Baking Department, costs totaled $5,000 for baking and packaging the 10,000 gallons of product B received from mixing and settling and 5,000 one-pound packages were produced.

The assignment of costs of $120,000 in the mixing and settling department, using the adjusted sales value method, is as follows:

Product	Units Produced	Unit Selling Price	Ultimate Sales Value	Less Cost After Split-Off	Sales Value at Split-Off	Percent of Sales Value	Assignment of Joint Costs
A	20,000 gals. ×	$ 5.00 =	$100,000	–0–	$100,000	50%	$ 60,000
B	5,000 lbs.* ×	21.00 =	105,000	$5,000	100,000	50	60,000
Total			$205,000	$5,000	$200,000	100%	$120,000

*10,000 gallons of liquid is further processed into 5,000 lbs. of powder.

The allocated cost of product A is transferred to a finished goods inventory account. The assigned cost of product B is transferred to a work in process account to which the additional costs of processing are also charged. The total cost of product B is then transferred to a finished goods inventory account.

Occasionally the makeup of the joint products is such that chemical or engineering analyses, or some other type of examination of component parts, can be employed to determine the amount of raw materials present in each completed product. This procedure is complex and must be carried out by highly qualified experts, but the accountant's allocation of costs, based on these analyses, follows the procedures previously discussed.

If the Chemi-Pro Co. found, upon analysis, that 40% of the raw materials introduced into the process were present in the finished product A and 60% in product B and that labor and overhead were added evenly, the following allocation of costs could be made.

		Allocated to Products	
October Processing Costs (A/B)		A	B
Materials..................	$ 99,000 (40/60)	$39,600	$59,400
Labor.....................	6,000 (50/50)	3,000	3,000
Factory overhead	15,000 (50/50)	7,500	7,500
Total...................	$120,000	$50,100	$69,900

Accounting for By-Products

In accounting for by-products, the common practice is to make no allocation of the processing costs up to the split-off point. Costs incurred up to that point are chargeable to the main products. If no further processing is required to make the by-products marketable, they may be accounted for by debiting an inventory account, By-Products, and crediting Work in Process for the estimated sales value of the by-products recovered. Under this procedure, the estimated sales value of the by-products is treated as a reduction in cost of the main products and is so reflected in the inventory costs section of the cost of production summary. If the by-products are sold for more or less than the estimated sales value, the difference may be credited or debited to Gain and Loss on Sales of By-Products.

Assume that the production management of the Chemi-Pro Co. finds that nonusable residue at the bottom of the vat can be sold for $2,000 without further processing. Also assume that other data for the month of November are the same as for October. The cost of production summary shown on page 345 reflects the assignment of joint costs under the adjusted sales value method, as illustrated on page 343, and uses the by-product value as a reduction in the cost of the joint products and as the cost assigned to the by-product.

Chemi-Pro Co.
Cost of Production Summary — Mixing and Settling Department
For the Month Ended November 30, 19--

Cost of production for month:	
Materials..	$ 99,000
Labor..	6,000
Factory overhead	15,000
Total costs to be accounted for	**$120,000**
Unit output for month:	
Finished and transferred to finished goods (product A)	20,000
Finished and transferred to baking department (product B)......	10,000
Total...	30,000
Unit cost for month:	
Materials ($99,000 ÷ 30,000)	$3.30
Labor ($6,000 ÷ 30,000)	.20
Factory overhead ($15,000 ÷ 30,000)...........................	.50
Total...	$4.00
Total costs to split-off point....................................	$120,000
Less market value of by-product...............................	2,000
Total cost to be assigned to joint products finished and transferred	**$118,000**
Inventory costs:	
Cost of goods finished (product A) and transferred to finished goods*	$ 59,000
Cost of goods finished (product B) and transferred to baking department*..	59,000
Cost of by-product finished and transferred to by-product inventory...	2,000
Total production costs accounted for	**$120,000**

*50% × $118,000

In many instances, the sales value of the by-product will be so insignificant or so uncertain, due to an unstable market, that the cost of the main products will not be reduced. In this case, no entry for the by-product is made at the point of separation. When the by-product is sold, the transaction is recorded by debiting Cash or Accounts Receivable and crediting By-Product Sales or Miscellaneous Income. The revenue account will usually be treated as "other income" on the income statement, although some companies, if the amount is significant, will show this revenue as sales income, as a deduction from the cost of the main products sold, or as a reduction in the total cost of the main products manufactured.

If further processing is required to make the by-product salable, an account entitled By-Products in Process may be opened, and all subsequent processing costs incurred are charged to that account. As with other products, when the processing is completed, an entry is made to transfer the costs from the in-process account to an inventory account.

KEY TERMS

Abnormal losses (326)
Adjusted sales value (343)
Adjusted unit cost (325)
By-products (341)
First-in, first-out (331)
Joint costs (341)
Joint products (341)

Normal losses (322)
Period cost (326)
Physical unit of measure (341)
Product cost (322)
Relative sales value (342)
Split-off point (341)

QUESTIONS

1. Under what conditions may the unit costs of materials, labor, and overhead be computed by using only one equivalent production figure?
2. When is it necessary to use separate equivalent production figures in computing the unit costs of materials, labor, and overhead?
3. If materials are not put into process uniformly, what must be considered when determining the cost of the ending work in process?
4. In what way does the cost of production summary on page 315 differ from the cost of production summaries presented in Chapter 6? What is the reason for this difference in treatment?
5. Explain why the total number of units completed during a month plus the number of units in process at the end of a month, may be less than the total number of units in process at the beginning of the month plus the number of units placed in process during the month.
6. What is the usual method of handling the cost of normal processing losses?

7. If some units are normally lost during the manufacturing process and all units absorb the cost, what effect does this have on the unit cost of goods finished during the period and work in process at the end of the period?

8. In what way is the cost of units normally lost in manufacturing absorbed by the unit cost for the period?

9. What computations must be made if units are lost in a department other than the originating one?

10. What is the method for handling the cost of units lost or rejected at the end of a process?

11. Describe the method of treatment for the cost of abnormal processing losses.

12. What computations must be made if materials added in a department increase the number of units being processed?

13. If materials added in a department increase the number of units being processed and units are also lost through evaporation in that same department, what calculations must be made, assuming the company follows the practice of letting all units absorb the cost of lost units?

14. Differentiate between the average cost method and the first-in, first-out cost method.

15. Define:
    (a) Joint products
    (b) By-products
    (c) Joint costs
    (d) Split-off point

16. (a) Name three methods of allocating joint costs.
    (b) Under what conditions might each of the three methods be used?

17. Describe two ways of accounting for by-products for which no further processing is required.

EXERCISES

Note: The average cost method is to be used with Exercises 1 through 6.

Exercise 7-1   Equivalent units of production for materials, labor, and overhead.

Using the data given for Cases 1–3, compute the separate equivalent units of production, one for materials and one for labor and overhead, under each of the following assumptions (labor and factory overhead are applied evenly during the process in each assumption):

(a) All materials go into production at the beginning of the process.

(b) All materials go into production at the end of the process.

(c) 75% of the materials go into production at the beginning of the process and 25% when the process is one-half completed.

Case 1 — Started in process 5,000 units; finished 4,000 units; work in process, end of period 1,000 units, three-fourths completed.

Case 2 — Opening inventory 10,000 units, three-fifths completed; started in process 40,000 units; finished 44,000 units; work in process, end of period 6,000 units, one-fourth completed.

Case 3 — Opening inventory 2,000 units, one-half completed, and 6,000 units, one-fourth completed; started in process 27,000 units; finished 29,000 units; closing inventory goods in process 3,000 units, one-third completed, and 3,000 units, one-half completed.

Exercise 7-2   Unit costs; cost of units finished; cost of units in process.

The following data appeared in the accounting records of The Allied Manufacturing Company:

Started in process. . . . .   12,000 units
Finished and transferred . . . .   10,500 units
Work in process, end of month . . . .   1,500 units ($\frac{2}{5}$ completed)
Materials. $36,000
Labor. $44,400
Factory overhead $22,200

Case 1 — All materials are added at the beginning of the process and labor and factory overhead are added evenly throughout the process.

Case 2 — One half of the materials are added at the start of the manufacturing process and the balance of the materials are added when the units are one-half completed. Labor and factory overhead are applied evenly during the process.

Using the above information, calculate for each case:

(a) the unit cost of materials, labor, and factory overhead for the month

(b) the cost of the units finished during the month

(c) the cost of the units in process at the end of the month

Exercise 7-3   Computing costs and units.

Assuming that all materials are added at the beginning of the process and the labor and factory overhead are applied evenly during the process, compute the figures to be inserted in the blank spaces of the following data.

	Case 1	Case 2	Case 3
Units in process, beginning of period .	300	None	—
Materials cost in process, beginning of period	$ 915	None	$˙ 568
Labor cost in process, beginning of period	$ 351	None	$ 200
Overhead cost in process, beginning of period	$ 300	None	$ 188
Units started in process.............	—	—	19,200
Units transferred	1,300	8,000	—
Units in process, end of period	200	—	1,400
Stage of completion	1/4	—	1/5
Equivalent units — materials	—	—	—
Equivalent units — labor and factory overhead...........................	—	—	18,440
Materials cost current month	$ 3,660	$13,120	$ —
Labor and factory overhead current month..............................	$ 5,100	$16,200	$ —
Materials unit cost for period	$ —	$ 1.60	$ .30
Labor and factory overhead unit cost for period	$ —	$ 2.00	$ .20

Exercise 7-4   Equivalent units for materials and labor.

The Master Manufacturing Company uses a process cost system to account for the costs of its only product, product D. Production begins in the fabrication department where units of raw materials are molded into various connecting parts. After fabrication is complete, the units are transferred to the assembly department. There are no materials added in the assembly department. After assembly is complete, the units are transferred to the packaging department where packing materials are placed around the units. After the units are ready for shipping, they are sent to a shipping area.

At year end, June 30, the following inventory of product D is on hand:
(1)   no unused raw materials or packing materials
(2)   fabrication departments — 900 units, ⅓ complete as to raw material and ½ complete as to direct labor
(3)   assembly department — 3,000 units, ⅖ complete as to direct labor
(4)   packaging department — 300 units, ¾ complete as to packing materials and ¼ complete as to direct labor
(5)   shipping area — 1,200 units

Determine:
(a)   the number of equivalent units of raw materials in all inventories at June 30.

(b)   the number of equivalent units of fabrication department direct labor in all inventories at June 30.

(c)   the number of equivalent units of packing materials in all inventories at June 30.

(AICPA adapted)

Exercise 7-5   Unit costs; cost of units transferred and in process.

The Mayfield Products Company manufactures a liquid product. Due to the nature of the product and the process, units are regularly lost during production. Goods finished in the mixing department are transferred to the refining department. Material and conversion costs are added evenly throughout the process. The following summaries were prepared for the month of January.

	Units	
	Mixing	Refining
Production Summary	Dept.	Dept.
Started in process or received from prior department	10,000	8,000
Finished and transferred to the next department or the stockroom	8,000	7,000
In process, end of the month	1,000	500
Stage of completion	1/4	1/2
Lost in process	1,000	500
Cost Summary		
Materials	$99,000	$14,500
Labor	14,850	7,250
Factory overhead	9,900	14,500

Calculate the unit cost for materials, labor, and factory overhead for January and show the costs of units transferred and in process for:

(a)   the mixing department
(b)   the refining department

Exercise 7-6   Unit costs; costs of units transferred and in process.

A company manufactures a liquid product called Easy-Go. The basic ingredients are put into process in department 1. In department 2, other materials are added that increase the number of units being processed by 50%. There are only two departments in the factory.

	Units	
Production Summary	Dept. 1	Dept. 2
Started in process............................	18,000	– 0
Received from prior department		14,000
Added to units in process......................		7,000
Finished and transferred......................	14,000	15,000
In process, end of month	4,000	6,000
Stage of completion	1/4	1/2
Cost Summary		
Materials..................................	$90,000	$36,000
Labor.....................................	30,000	13,500
Factory overhead	15,000	4,500

On the basis of the information given above, calculate the following for each department:

(a) unit cost for the month for materials, labor, and factory overhead
(b) the cost of the units transferred
(c) the cost of the work in process.

Exercise 7-7   Equivalent units, fifo method.

Using the data given below for Cases 1–3 and the fifo cost method, compute the separate equivalent units of production, one for materials and one for labor and overhead, under each of the following assumptions (labor and factory overhead are applied evenly during the process in each assumption):

(a) All materials go into production at the beginning of the process.
(b) All materials go into production at the end of the process.
(c) 75% of the materials go into production at the beginning of the process and 25% when the process is one-half completed.

Case 1 — Started in process 5,000 units; finished 4,000 units; work in process, end of period 1,000 units, three-fourths completed.

Case 2 — Opening inventory 10,000 units, three-fifths completed; started in process 40,000 units; finished 44,000 units; work in process, end of period 6,000 units, one-fourth completed.

Case 3 — Opening inventory 2,000 units, one-half completed, and 6,000 units, one-fourth completed; started in process 27,000 units; finished 29,000 units; closing inventory work in process 3,000 units, one-third completed, and 3,000 units, one-half completed.

Compare your answers with those of Exercise 1 on the average cost basis.

Exercise 7-8   Equivalent units, fifo and average cost methods.

Assume each of the following conditions concerning the data given below:
1. All materials are added at the beginning of the process.

2. All materials are added at the end of the process.
3. One half of the materials are added at the beginning of the process and the balance of the materials are added when the units are three-fourths completed.

In all cases, labor and factory overhead are added evenly throughout the process.

Production Summary

	Units		
	Dept. 1	Dept. 2	Dept. 3
Work in process, beginning of month......	3,000	1,500	1,200
Stage of completion...................	1/2	3/5	4/5
Started in process......................	18,000	16,000	21,000
Finished and transferred...............	19,000	15,500	21,000
Work in process, end of month...........	2,000	2,000	1,200
Stage of completion...................	1/4	4/5	1/5

Compute separate equivalent units of production, one for materials and one for labor and factory overhead for each of the conditions listed, using:
(a) the average cost method
(b) the fifo cost method

Exercise 7-9   Journal entry—joint products.

The River City Lumber Co. processes rough timber to obtain three grades of finished lumber, A, B, and C. The company allocates costs to the joint products on the basis of market value. During the month of May, total production costs of $52,000 were incurred in producing the following:

Grade	Thousand Board Feet	Selling Price per 1,000 Board Feet
A...................................	100	$200
B...................................	300	100
C...................................	500	160

Draft the journal entry to transfer the finished lumber to separate inventory accounts.

Exercise 7-10   Joint costs—relative sales value and physical units.

The LaBreck Company's joint cost of producing 1,000 units of product A, 500 units of product B, and 500 units of product C is $100,000. The unit sales values of the three products at the split-off point are product A—$20; product B—$200; product C—$160. Ending inventories include 100 units of product A, 300 units of product B, and 200 units of product C.

Compute the amount of joint cost that would be included in the ending inventory valuation of the three products on:
(a)   the basis of their relative sales value
(b)   the basis of physical units

(AICPA adapted)

Exercise 7-11   Journal entry — by-product.

The Kingston Chemical Co. manufactures product X. During the process, a by-product, AX, is obtained and placed in stock. The estimated sales value of AX produced during the month of April is $1,020. Assume that the value of the by-product is treated as a reduction of production cost.
Prepare the journal entry for April to record:
(a)   the placing of AX in stock
(b)   the sale of three-fourths of the AX for $800

Exercise 7-12   Journal entries — by-product.

The Broadbeck Manufacturing Co. makes one main product, X, and a by-product, Z, which splits off from the main product when the work is three-fourths completed. Product Z is sold without further processing and without being placed in stock. During June, $800 is realized from the sale of the by-product.
Journalize the entries to record the recovery and sale of the by-product on the assumption that the recovery is treated as:
(a)   a reduction in the cost of the main product
(b)   other income

PROBLEMS

Note: The average cost method is to be used with Problems 1 through 7.

Problem 7-1   Cost of production summaries, one department, two months; journal entries.

Manufacturing data for the months of January and February in department A of the Fox Manufacturing Co. are shown on page 354.

	January	February
Materials used.....	$16,000	$13,790
Labor.....	$11,400	$ 9,600
Factory overhead	$ 7,600	$ 6,400
Finished and transferred to dept. B	3,600	3,200
Work in process, end of month	400	600
Stage of completion	1/2	1/3

All materials are added at the start of the process. Labor and factory overhead are added evenly throughout the process. There were no units in process at the beginning of January. Goods finished in department A are transferred to department B for further processing.

Required:
1. From an analysis of this information, prepare a cost of production summary for each month.
2. Journalize the entries necessary to record each month's transactions.

Problem 7-2   Cost of production summaries, three departments; departmental cost work sheet; journal entries; statement of cost of goods manufactured.

The Atlas Manufacturing Company is engaged in the manufacture of a cement sealing compound called Patchtite. The process requires that the product pass through three departments:
Dept. 1—Sorting and Cleaning
Dept. 2—Mixing
Dept. 3—Clarifying and Packaging
In department 1, all materials are put into production at the beginning of the process; in department 2, materials are put into production evenly throughout the process; and in department 3, all materials are put into production at the end of the process. In each department it is assumed that the labor and factory overhead are applied evenly throughout the process.
At the end of January, the production reports for the month show the following:

	Dept. 1	Dept. 2	Dept. 3
Started in process.....	50,000	—	—
Received from prior department	—	40,000	30,000
Finished and transferred	40,000	30,000	28,000
Finished and on hand	—	5,000	—
Work in process, end of month	10,000	5,000	2,000
Stage of completion	1/2	1/4	3/4

The cost summary for January shows the following:

	Dept. 1	Dept. 2	Dept. 3
Materials	$22,500	$23,200	$19,600
Labor	7,200	14,500	11,800
Factory overhead	10,800	14,500	8,850
	$40,500	$52,200	$40,250

Required:

1. Prepare a cost of production summary for each department for January.
2. Prepare a departmental cost work sheet for January.
3. Prepare the required general journal entries to record the January operations.
4. Prepare a statement of cost of goods manufactured for the month ended January 31.

Problem 7-3   Equivalent production; unit costs; cost of work in process.

The Walsch Company manufactures a single product, a mechanical device known as "Klebo." The company maintains a process cost type of accounting system. The manufacturing operation is as follows:

Material K, a metal, is stamped to form a part that is assembled with one of the purchased parts "X". The unit is then machined and cleaned, after which it is assembled with two units of part "Y" to form the finished device known as a "Klebo." Spray priming and enameling is the final operation.

Time and motion studies indicate that of the total time required for the manufacture of a unit, the first operation required 25% of the labor cost, the first assembly an additional 25%, machining and cleaning 12.5%, the second assembly 25%, and painting 12.5%. Factory overhead is considered to follow the same pattern by operations as does labor.

The following data were collected on October 31, the end of the first month of operation:

Material K purchased — 100,000 lbs.	$25,000
Part X purchased — 80,000 units.	16,000
Part Y purchased — 150,000 units.	15,000
Primer and enamel used	1,072
Direct labor cost	45,415
Factory overhead	24,905

	Units
Units finished and sent to finished goods warehouse.	67,000
Units assembled but not painted.	5,000
Units ready for the second assembly.	3,000

Inventories at the end of the month:

Finished units.	7,500
Material K (lbs.).	5,800
Part X (units of part X)	5,000
Part Y (units of part Y)	6,000
Klebos in process (units).	8,000

Required:
1. Prepare a schedule of equivalent units of production for labor.
2. Prepare a schedule of total and unit costs incurred in production for:
   (a) Each kind of material
   (b) Labor cost
   (c) Factory overhead
   (d) Total cost of production
3. Prepare a schedule of detailed materials, labor, and factory overhead costs assigned to the units left in process.

(AICPA adapted)

Problem 7-4   Lost units; cost of production summaries.

The Monroe Products Co. uses the process cost system. Following is a record of the factory operations for the month of October:

Production Summary

	Units
Started in process.	12,500
Finished and transferred to stockroom.	9,500
In process, end of month, one-half completed.	1,000

Cost Summary

Materials.	$15,000
Labor.	6,000
Factory overhead	9,000

Required:
Prepare a cost of production summary for each of the following conditions.
1. The cost of lost units is absorbed by all units.
2. The cost of lost units is charged only to units completed.
3. The cost of lost units is charged to an expense account.

Problem 7-5   Lost units; cost of production summaries.

The Mantis Manufacturing Company manufactures a single product that passes through two departments: extruding and finishing-packing. The product is shipped at the end of the day in which it is packed. The production in the extruding and finishing-packing departments does not increase the number of units started.

The cost and production data for January are as follows:

Cost Data	Extruding Department	Finishing-Packing Department
Work in process, January 1:		
Cost from preceding department	—	$60,200
Materials	$ 5,900	—
Labor	1,900	1,500
Factory overhead	1,400	2,000
Costs added during January:		
Materials	20,100	4,400
Labor	10,700	7,720
Factory overhead	8,680	11,830
Percentage of completion of work in process:		
January 1:		
Materials	70%	0%
Labor	50	30
Factory overhead	50	30
January 31:		
Materials	50	0
Labor	40	35
Factory overhead	40	35
Production Data		
Units in process, January 1	10,000	29,000
Units in process, January 31	8,000	6,000
Units started or received from preceding department...........................	20,000	22,000
Units completed and transferred or shipped.................................	22,000	44,000

In the extruding department, materials are added at various phases of the process. All lost units occur at the end of the process when the inspection operation takes place.

In the finishing-packing department, the materials added consist only of packing supplies. These materials are added at the midpoint of the process when the packing operation begins. Cost studies have disclosed that one-half of the labor and overhead costs apply to the finishing operation and one-half to the packing operation. All lost units occur during the finishing operation. All of the work in process in this department at January 1 and January 31 was in the finishing operation phase of the manufacturing process.

Required:
1. Compute the units lost, if any, for each department during January.
2. Prepare a cost of production summary for each department for January. The report should disclose the equivalent units of production for the calcu-

lation of unit costs for each department for January, the departmental total cost, and cost per unit (for materials, labor, and overhead) of the units transferred to the finishing-packing department and for units shipped. Assume that January production and costs were normal. (Submit all supporting computations in good form.)

(AICPA adapted)

Problem 7-6 Units gained and lost; cost of production summaries.

The South Manufacturing Co. uses the process cost system. There are three departments, A, B, and C. In department A, all of the materials are put into production at the beginning of the process; in department B, no materials are added to the process; in department C, all of the materials are put into production at the beginning of the process. The materials added in department C increase the number of units being processed by 25%. Labor and factory overhead are incurred uniformly throughout the process in all departments. Losses of units in any department are considered unavoidable due to the nature of the manufacturing process and can occur at any time during the process.

Following is a record of the factory operations for May:

Cost Summary	Dept. A	Dept. B	Dept. C
Materials	$25,000		$ 7,500
Labor	10,800	$ 6,910	10,150
Factory overhead	8,100	6,910	7,250

Production Summary	Units		
	Dept. A	Dept. B	Dept. C
Started in process.	11,000		
Received from prior department		8,500	6,000
Added to units in process.			1,500
Finished and transferred	8,500	6,000	7,000
Units in process, end of month	1,500	1,820	500
Stage of completion	1/3	1/2	1/2

Required:

Prepare a cost of production summary for each department for the month of May.

Problem 7-7 Fifo cost method; cost of production summary.

The McKay Products Co. uses the fifo cost method. Following is a record of the factory operations for the month of October:

Production Summary	Units	
Work in process, beginning of month, <u>one-fourth completed</u>	5,000	1250
Started in process.....................................	13,000	
Finished and transferred to stockroom...................	11,000	
Work in process, end of month, <u>three-fourths completed</u>....	7,000	5250
Cost Summary		
Work in process, beginning of month....................	$ 3,750	
Materials..	36,000	
Labor...	24,000	
Factory overhead	12,000	

Required:

Prepare a cost of production summary for the month.

Problem 7-8   Fifo cost method, lost units; cost of production summary.

The Cascade Company manufactures gewgaws in three steps or departments. The finishing department is the third and last step before the product is transferred to finished goods inventory.

All materials needed to complete the gewgaws are added at the beginning of the process in the finishing department, and lost units, if any, occur only at this point. The company uses the fifo cost method in its accounting system and has accumulated the following data for July for the finishing department:

Production of gewgaws:	Units
In process, July 1 (labor and factory overhead three-fourths complete)	10,000
Transferred from preceding department during July.......	40,000
Finished and transferred to finished goods inventory during July...	35,000
In process, July 31 (labor and factory overhead one-half complete)	10,000
Cost of work in process inventory, July 1:	
Cost from preceding departments	$ 38,000
Cost added in finishing department prior to July 1:	
Materials..	21,500
Labor...	39,000
Factory overhead	42,000
Total......................................	$140,500

Gewgaws transferred to the finishing department during July had costs of $280,000 assigned from preceding departments.

During July, the finishing department incurred the following production costs:

Materials	$ 70,000
Labor	162,500
Factory overhead	130,000
Total	$362,500

Required:
1. Calculate the number of gewgaws lost in production during July.
2. Prepare a cost of production summary for July.

(AICPA adapted)

Problem 7-9   Fifo cost method; equivalent production; units gained and lost.

Poole, Inc., produces a chemical compound by a unique chemical process which Poole has divided into two departments, A and B, for accounting purposes. The process functions as follows:
(a) The formula for the chemical compound requires one pound of chemical X and one pound of chemical Y. In the simplest sense, one pound of chemical X is processed in department A and transferred to department B for further processing where one pound of chemical Y is added when the process is 50% complete. When the processing is complete in department B, the finished chemical compound is transferred to finished goods. The process is continuous, operating twenty-four hours a day.
(b) Normal processing losses occur in department A. Five percent of chemical X is lost in the first few seconds of processing.
(c) No processing losses occur in department B.
(d) In department A, conversion costs are incurred uniformly throughout the process and are allocated to good pounds produced because processing losses are normal.
(e) In department B, conversion costs are allocated equally to each equivalent pound of output.
(f) Poole's unit of measure for work in process and finished goods inventories is pounds.
(g) The following data are available for the month of October:

	Department A	Department B
Work in process, October 1..	8,000 pounds	10,000 pounds
Stage of completion of beginning inventory (one batch per department)	3/4	3/10
Started or transferred in	50,000 pounds	?
Transferred out	46,500 good pounds	?
Work in process, October 31	?	?

	Department A	Department B
Stage of completion of ending inventory (one batch per department).............	1/3	1/5
Total equivalent pounds of material added in department B	—	44,500 pounds

Required:
1. Determine the amounts indicated by the question marks.
2. Prepare schedules computing equivalent "good" pounds of production (materials and conversion costs) for department A and for department B for the month of October, using the first-in, first-out method for inventory cost.

(AICPA adapted)

Problem 7-10   Allocation of joint costs.

Center Manufacturing Company buys zeon for $.80 a gallon. At the end of processing in department 1, zeon splits off into products A, B, and C. Product A is sold at the split-off point with no further processing. Products B and C require further processing before they can be sold; product B is processed in department 2 and product C is processed in department 3. Following is a summary of costs and other related data for the year ended December 31.

	Dept. 1	Dept. 2	Dept. 3
Cost of zeon....................	$ 76,000	—	—
Direct labor....................	14,000	$45,000	$ 65,000
Factory overhead	10,000	21,000	49,000
Total.........................	$100,000	$66,000	$114,000

	Product A	Product B	Product C
Gallons sold....................	20,000	30,000	45,000
Gallons on hand at December 31 ...	10,000	—	15,000
Sales in dollars	$ 30,000	$96,000	$141,750

There were no inventories on hand at the beginning of the year, and there was no zeon on hand at the end of the year. All gallons on hand at the end of the year were complete as to processing. Center uses the relative sales value method of allocating joint costs.

Required:
1. Calculate the allocation of joint costs.
2. Calculate the cost of product B sold.

(AICPA adapted)

Problem 7-11   Allocation of joint costs.

The Harrison Corporation produces three products—Alpha, Beta, and Gamma. Alpha and Gamma are joint products, while Beta is a by-product of Alpha. No joint cost is to be allocated to the by-product. The production processes for a given year are as follows:

(a)   In department 1, 110,000 pounds of raw material, Rho, are processed at a total cost of $120,000. After processing in department 1, 60% of the units are transferred to department 2 and 40% of the units (now Gamma) are transferred to department 3.

(b)   In department 2, the material is further processed at a total additional cost of $38,000. Seventy percent of the units (now Alpha) are transferred to department 4 and 30% emerge as Beta, the by-product, to be sold at $1.20 per pound. Selling expenses related to disposing of Beta are $8,100.

(c)   In department 4, Alpha is processed at a total additional cost of $23,660. After this processing, Alpha is ready for sales at $5 per pound.

(d)   In department 3, Gamma is processed at a total additional cost of $165,000. In this department, a normal loss of units of Gamma occurs that equals 10% of the marketable output of Gamma. The remaining marketable output of Gamma is then sold for $12 per pound.

Required:

1.   Prepare a schedule showing the allocation of the $120,000 joint cost between Alpha and Gamma using the relative sales value approach. The net realizable value of Beta should be treated as an addition to the sales value of Alpha.

2.   What is the cost of Alpha transferred to finished goods, assuming that the net realizable value of Beta available for sale is to be deducted from the cost of producing Alpha?

(AICPA adapted)

8

STANDARD COST ACCOUNTING—
MATERIALS AND LABOR

LEARNING OBJECTIVES

In studying this chapter, you will learn about the:

- Purpose of standard cost accounting
- Types of standards that may be used in determining standard costs
- Procedures for recording standard costs for materials and labor
- Meaning of variances and how they are analyzed and disposed of
- Specific features of a standard cost system

In previous chapters cost control has been emphasized. The primary means of control discussed was the comparison of current costs with historical costs — costs of yesterday, last week, last month, or last year. When a current cost differed unfavorably from an earlier cost, it was shown that management should immediately investigate the cause of this variation and try to eliminate it before the results became too costly. It was also indicated that management has the responsibility not only to watch for these fluctuations and attempt to correct them but also to consider all possible ways of controlling costs.

While this method of cost control is useful, there is the danger that management will tend to become complacent if the costs of manufacturing do not differ significantly from period to period. There may be a feeling that the manufacturing operation is efficient because unit and overall costs are stabilized at a certain level. But stability of costs does not necessarily indicate efficiency when the earlier costs with which current costs are compared may reflect inefficiency. There is always the possibility that costs can be utilized more effectively.

The purpose of standard cost accounting is to control costs and promote efficiency. This system is not a third cost accounting method, but is used with either job order or process manufacturing operations. It is based on a predetermination of what it should cost to manufacture a product and the subsequent comparison of the actual costs with the established standard. Any deviation from the standard can be quickly detected and responsibility pinpointed so that appropriate action can be taken to eliminate inefficiencies or to take advantage of efficiencies.

Standard costs are usually determined for a period of one year and are revised annually. However, if cost analyses during the year indicate that a standard is incorrect, or if a significant change has occurred in costs or other related factors, management should not hesitate to adjust the standard accordingly.

TYPES OF STANDARDS

A standard is a norm against which performance can be measured. The objective of setting standards is to measure efficiency and to monitor costs by assigning responsibility for deviations from the standards. Also, a standard can motivate employees by providing a goal for achievement. But a question that often arises is "What is the proper standard to use?" A company can estimate materials, labor, and factory overhead usage and costs, but what about the unforeseen costs, such as spoilage, lost time, and equipment breakdowns? Should these items be considered in determining the standard cost to manufacture a product?

Some companies set their standards at the maximum degree of efficiency. Using an ideal standard, costs are determined by considering estimated materials, labor, and overhead costs, the condition of the factory and machinery, and time for rest periods, holidays, and vacations; but no allowances are made for inefficient conditions such as lost time, waste, or spoilage. This ideal standard can be achieved only under the most efficient operating conditions, and therefore it is practically unattainable, giving rise to unfavorable variances. Companies using this type of utopian standard feel that it provides a maximum objective for which to strive in the attempt to improve efficiency. There is, however, a psychological disadvantage — the factory personnel may become discouraged and lose their incentive to meet standards that are almost impossible to attain except under perfect operating conditions.

Recognizing this potential problem, most companies set **attainable standards** that include such factors as lost time, spoilage, or waste. These companies realize that some inefficiencies cannot be completely eliminated, and so they design a standard that can be met or even bettered in efficient production situations. The primary concern of the manufacturer should be to set a standard that is high enough to provide motivation and promote efficiency, yet not so high that it is unreasonable and thus unattainable.

STANDARD COST PROCEDURES

Standard cost accounting is based on the following procedures:

1. Standard costs are determined for the three elements of cost — direct materials, direct labor, and factory overhead.
2. The standard costs, the actual costs, and the variances, or differences between the two costs, are recorded in appropriate accounts.
3. All variances are analyzed and investigated and appropriate action taken.

Determination of Standard Costs for Materials and Labor

The first step, the determination of standard costs for manufacturing a product, is a complex task that requires considerable experience and familiarity with manufacturing operations as well as cooperation between employees in various departments of the factory. The cost accountant may be consulted to help determine historical costs, to point out prevalent trends, and to otherwise assist in accomplishing the job. A **materials cost standard** is based on estimates of the quantity of materials required for a unit of product and the cost of the materials. In setting a materials cost standard, the production engineering department may be consulted to determine the amounts and types of materials that are needed, and the purchasing agent must supply knowledge of suppliers' prices to calculate the cost of these materials.

A **labor cost standard** is based on estimates of the labor hours required to produce a unit of product and the hourly wage rates. In establishing a labor cost standard, the heads of various departments might be asked to contribute their knowledge of the operations that are necessary to process a product. The services of time-study engineers may be utilized to establish the time necessary to perform each operation, and the personnel manager may be consulted regarding prevailing wage rates for the various types of labor needed.

Historical costs and processes should be studied to gain familiarity with these items, but the persons who set the standards should also consider that prevailing trends may cause changes in the future. In setting standards for materials and labor, factors to be considered might include:

1. The trend of prices for raw materials.
2. The use of different types of materials due to new processing or market developments.
3. The effect of negotiations with labor unions on labor rates.
4. The possible saving of labor time due to the use of more modern machinery and equipment.

The following illustrates a simple standard cost summary:

Race Products, Inc.
Standard Cost Summary
Product X

Materials—1 lb. @ $4 per lb.	$ 4.00
Labor—½ hr. @ $10 per hr.	5.00
Factory overhead	2.00
Standard cost per unit	$11.00

The development of factory overhead standards will be discussed in the following chapter.

Recording Standard Costs for Materials and Labor

Once the standard cost for manufacturing a product has been determined, the second phase of the system can be put into effect: the standard costs, the actual costs, and the variances are recorded in the various journals and transferred to the general ledger. Usually this process takes place at the end of the month.

Determination of Variances.   A variance represents the difference, during an accounting period, between the actual and the standard costs of materials, labor, and overhead. The variances measure efficiencies or inefficiencies in usage (quantity of materials used or number of labor hours worked) and price (cost of materials and hourly wage rates).

Assume that the production report of Race Products, Inc., whose standard cost summary is shown above, indicates that equivalent production for the month, calculated as discussed in previous chapters, was 10,000 units. The standard cost of this production is determined as follows:

Materials cost—10,000 units × $4.00	$ 40,000
Labor cost—10,000 units × $5.00	50,000
Factory overhead cost—10,000 units × $2.00..................	20,000
Total standard cost of manufacturing 10,000 units...............	$110,000

Assume that the materials requisitions, the time tickets or payroll records, and the factory overhead records indicate the following actual costs of manufacturing these units:

Cost of direct materials used (11,000 lbs. @ $3.80)..............	$ 41,800
Cost of direct labor (4,500 hrs. @ $11.00)	49,500
Factory overhead applied	20,000
Total actual cost of manufacturing 10,000 units..................	$111,300

The cost accountant can now compare the standard with the actual costs to determine whether any variances exist. This analysis is done as follows:

	Standard Cost	Actual Cost	Net Variances— Favorable or (Unfavorable)
Materials........................	$ 40,000	$ 41,800	$(1,800)
Labor...........................	50,000	49,500	500
Factory Overhead................	20,000	20,000	—
Total...........................	$110,000	$111,300	$(1,300)

The information presented by these comparative figures is significant to the extent that it shows that the total actual manufacturing costs have exceeded the standards previously established. The variances indicate that the cost of materials was $1,800 higher than it should have been, and that the cost of labor was $500 less than the established standards, resulting in an overall unfavorable variance of $1,300. For these figures to be of value, however, a further breakdown of the variances must be made.

The accounts used to indicate the materials and labor variances are as follows:

Materials Quantity (Usage) Variance — represents the actual quantity of direct materials used above or below the standard quantity for the actual level of production at standard price.

Materials Price Variance — reflects the actual unit cost of materials above or below the standard unit cost, multiplied by the actual quantity of materials used.

Labor Efficiency (Usage) Variance — indicates the number of actual direct labor hours worked above or below the standard for the actual level of production at standard price.

Labor Rate (Price) Variance — represents the average of the actual hourly rates paid above or below the standard hourly rate, multiplied by the actual number of hours worked.

A debit balance in any of these accounts indicates an unfavorable variance; that is, actual costs have exceeded the established standard cost. A credit balance reflects a favorable variance meaning that actual costs were less than the standard cost.

Formulas that are commonly used to calculate the materials and labor variances are on page 369, using the figures previously presented for materials and labor.

This type of analysis points out the effects of the deviations from the standard. The manufacturing effort exceeded the established materials standard for 10,000 units which, at a standard price of $4.00 per pound, created an unfavorable materials quantity variance of $4,000 (1,000 pounds used in excess of standard × $4.00). This variance was partially offset by the fact that the 11,000 pounds of materials used were obtained at a cost below standard of $3.80 per pound thereby creating a favorable price variance of $2,200 (11,000 pounds used at a saving of $.20 per pound).

The calculation of labor variances indicates a favorable labor efficiency variance of $5,000, because the number of hours worked was 500 hours below the standard for the production of 10,000 units (500 hours times the standard rate of $10.00). However, during the period, a labor rate ($11.00 per hour) higher than standard was paid, creating an unfavorable rate variance of $4,500 (4,500 hours paid at a rate $1.00 over standard).

Formula for Calculating Materials Variances

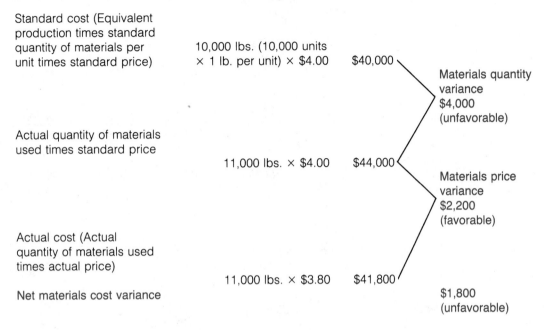

Standard cost (Equivalent production times standard quantity of materials per unit times standard price)

10,000 lbs. (10,000 units × 1 lb. per unit) × $4.00 $40,000

Materials quantity variance $4,000 (unfavorable)

Actual quantity of materials used times standard price

11,000 lbs. × $4.00 $44,000

Materials price variance $2,200 (favorable)

Actual cost (Actual quantity of materials used times actual price)

11,000 lbs. × $3.80 $41,800

Net materials cost variance

$1,800 (unfavorable)

Formula for Calculating Labor Variances

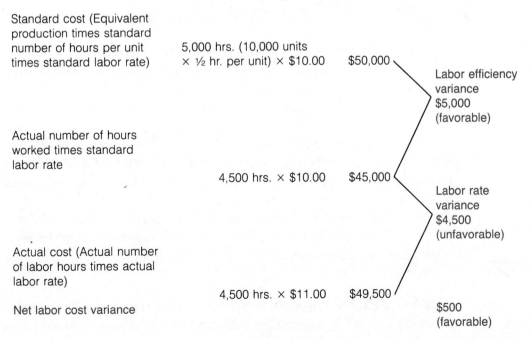

Standard cost (Equivalent production times standard number of hours per unit times standard labor rate)

5,000 hrs. (10,000 units × ½ hr. per unit) × $10.00 $50,000

Labor efficiency variance $5,000 (favorable)

Actual number of hours worked times standard labor rate

4,500 hrs. × $10.00 $45,000

Labor rate variance $4,500 (unfavorable)

Actual cost (Actual number of labor hours times actual labor rate)

4,500 hrs. × $11.00 $49,500

Net labor cost variance

$500 (favorable)

Another method of calculating the variances, which displays the specific deviations from standard, is as follows:

	Standard Quantity or Hours	Actual Quantity or Hours	Difference	Standard Cost	Variance
Materials Quantity Variance	10,000 lbs.	11,000 lbs.	1,000 lbs. (unf.)	$4.00 lb.	$4,000 (unf.)
Labor Efficiency Variance	5,000 hrs.	4,500 hrs.	500 hrs. (fav.)	$10.00 hr.	$5,000 (fav.)

	Standard Cost	Actual Cost	Difference	Actual Quantity or Hours	Variance
Materials Price Variance	$4.00 lb.	$3.80 lb.	$.20 (fav.)	11,000 lbs.	$2,200 (fav.)
Labor Rate Variance	$10.00 hr.	$11.00 hr.	$1.00 (unf.)	4,500 hrs.	$4,500 (unf.)

It is important to understand that the terms *favorable* and *unfavorable* indicate only a deviation of the actual cost below or above standard. Further analysis and investigation may indicate that the unfavorable variance is not necessarily reflecting an inefficiency, nor is the favorable variance always indicating a desirable situation. An apparently unfavorable condition may be offset completely by a favorable situation. For example, a favorable materials price variance that results from buying less expensive materials than are called for in the standards may more than offset an unfavorable materials quantity variance that results from additional spoilage due to the use of cheaper materials. In any event, all variances, favorable or unfavorable, must be analyzed to determine the cause for and the effect of the deviations. Appropriate action should then be taken to improve the problem areas.

Accounting Procedure.   The work in process account is always debited with the standard cost of equivalent production for the period. The materials inventory account is credited for the actual cost of materials issued to the factory as indicated by materials requisitions and inventory ledger cards. The payroll account is credited with the actual cost of labor incurred for the period. The differences between the debits (at standard costs) and the credits (at actual costs) are debited (unfavorable variances) or credited (favorable variances) to the variance accounts. The standard cost of units finished is transferred from Work in Process to Finished Goods.

To illustrate, use the figures previously presented for materials and labor costs.

1. To record the entry for direct materials cost:

Work in Process	40,000	
Materials Quantity Variance	4,000	
Materials Price Variance		2,200
Materials		41,800

2. To record the entry for direct labor cost:

Work in Process	50,000	
Labor Rate Variance	4,500	
Labor Efficiency Variance		5,000
Payroll		49,500

3. To record the entry applying factory overhead to work in process (assuming no variances):

Work in Process	20,000	
Factory Overhead		20,000

4. To record the entry for finished goods at standard cost (assuming no beginning or ending inventory of work in process, 10,000 units @ $11.00):

Finished Goods	110,000	
Work in Process		110,000

Under a standard cost system, the balance sheet of Race Products, Inc., would reflect inventories for work in process and finished goods at standard cost, while the materials inventory account would be shown at actual cost. This procedure will be followed in this text. The materials inventory account, however, may also be shown at standard cost, as explained below.

Alternative Method of Recording Materials Cost.   Some companies recognize materials price variances at the time materials are purchased by recording a purchase price variance, which represents the deviation of the purchase cost above or below the standard cost. The rationale for recording this variance at the time of purchase is that the difference between actual and standard cost is known at this time, so there is no reason for delaying the recognition of this variance until the materials are used.

Using the above price figures and assuming that 12,000 pounds are purchased, the purchase entry under this method is as follows:

```
Materials (12,000 lbs. @ $4.00 standard price)..........   48,000
   Materials Purchase Price Variance...................           2,400
   Accounts Payable (12,000 lbs. @ $3.80 actual price)..         45,600
```

Under these conditions, the materials inventory account on the balance sheet would reflect standard cost. At the time of materials usage, there would be no price variance to record, and the quantity variance would be recorded as follows:

```
Work in Process (10,000 lbs. @ $4.00 standard price) ...    40,000
Materials Quantity Variance ...........................      4,000
   Materials (11,000 lbs. @ $4.00).....................           44,000
```

Another benefit of using this method is that the individual materials inventory accounts are maintained at standard cost. This saves recordkeeping expense because it is necessary to keep track only of the quantities purchased, issued, and on hand. It is not necessary to post individual materials costs nor to continuously calculate dollar amounts on the inventory ledger cards. Because the materials inventory account is kept at standard cost, the balance, in dollars, can be determined at any time by multiplying the standard price times the quantity on hand.

Disposition of Standard Cost Variances.   At the end of the accounting period, the variances of actual cost from standard must be reflected in some appropriate manner on the financial statements. There are different approaches for handling these items:

1.   Some companies prorate these variances to cost of goods sold, work in process, and finished goods. The net effect of this method is the adjustment of these expense and inventory accounts to actual or historical cost. The rationale is that standard costs are important for management's evaluation of operations but are not proper for external financial reports; therefore, the variances, being a part of actual manufacturing cost, should be included in inventory costs. When this method is followed, the allocation of materials, labor, and overhead variances will

be in proportion to the standard materials, labor, and overhead costs included in cost of goods sold, work in process, and finished goods.

2. A more common approach, however, is to show the unfavorable net variance as an addition to the cost of goods sold for the period and the favorable net variance as a deduction. This is shown in the partial income statement below.

The basis for this approach is that these variances are the result of favorable or unfavorable conditions or inefficiencies during the period, and so they should be charged or credited to the period. These items should not be charged to future periods by including them in inventory costs.

Sales....................................			$100,000
Cost of goods sold at standard		$80,000	
Add unfavorable variance:			
Materials quantity variance		800	
		$80,800	
Less favorable variances:			
Materials price variance...................	$410		
Labor efficiency variance.................	100		
Labor rate variance......................	105	615	
Cost of goods sold (actual cost)..............			80,185
Gross margin on sales (actual cost)			$ 19,815

3. If the variances are significant or have been caused by the use of an incorrect standard, then the variances should be allocated to inventory and to cost of goods sold, and the standard cost adjusted accordingly.

4. If production is seasonal, with extreme peaks and valleys during the year, variances should be shown as deferred charges or credits on interim balance sheets, using the logic that they would be mostly offset in future periods. At the end of the year, however, some disposition of these variances, as described above, must be made, and the variance accounts closed.

5. If the variances are due to abnormal or unusual circumstances, such as strikes, fires, storms, or floods, there is justification for charging off these items as extraordinary losses on the income statement.

The material in this text will, unless otherwise indicated, use the more common approach of reflecting the materials and labor variances as adjustments to the standard cost of goods sold, as illustrated in Item 2. Variances of factory overhead costs, to be discussed in the next chapter, would also be reflected in the statements in a similar manner. Illustration 8-1 will aid the student in understanding the cost flow through a standard cost system.

Analyses of Variances

In analyzing materials and labor variances, two factors are considered — usage and price. The cost accountant considers the quantity of materials used, the cost per unit of each type of material, the number of direct labor hours worked, and the cost of each labor hour. If management can discover in what respect the usage and/or price differ from standard, the reason for this variance can be determined, and action can be taken to correct any deficiency before the loss becomes significant.

In analyzing the materials cost variance, the usage of materials might be above, below, or at standard, or the cost per unit of the materials used might be above, below, or at standard. This relevant information is required by management in order to make intelligent decisions. Consider the following three possibilities in the manufacture of 10,000 units:

Example 1:
Standard cost, 10,000 lbs. of materials @ $4.00................ $40,000
Actual cost, 10,000 lbs. of materials @ $4.18 41,800
Unfavorable materials price variance.......................... $(1,800)

This analysis shows that the factory usage of materials is at standard, but the price of the materials is not. The variance is caused by the fact that the company used materials costing $.18 more than the standard price. With 10,000 pounds used, this $.18 per unit variance causes a total variance of $1,800.

Management now has the data with which to investigate why the materials cost per unit is higher than the standard of $4.00 per pound. There are several possibilities, some of which are:

1. Inefficient purchasing methods.
2. Use of a slightly different material as an experiment.
3. Increase in market price.

Inefficient purchasing can be corrected by better planning and by careful selection of suppliers. If the different material (2) is adopted by the company for use in its manufacturing operations, the standard cost per unit of materials will have to be increased. The standard cost would also have to be

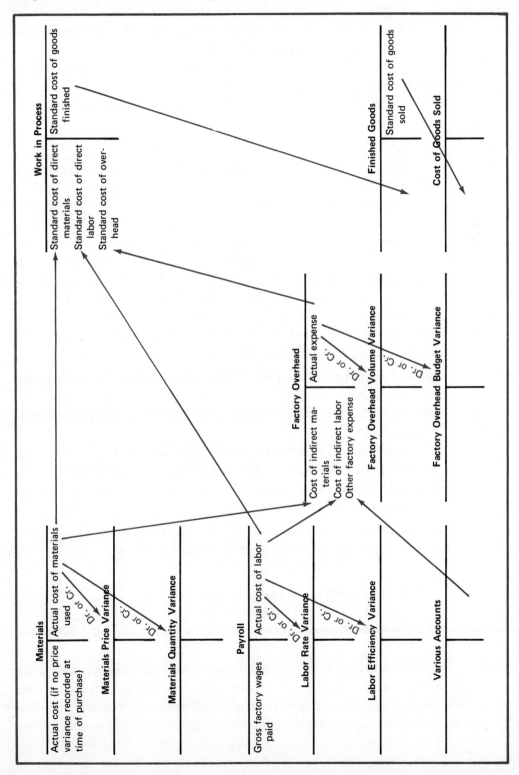

Illustration 8-1   Cost Flow Through a Standard Cost System

increased if the situation mentioned in (3) is found to be the cause of the variance and is considered to be a permanent condition.

This example illustrates the principle that any variance, favorable or unfavorable, must be carefully investigated so that corrective action can be taken. This action may involve elimination of inefficiencies or a change in the standard cost of the product.

Example 2:

Standard cost, 10,000 lbs. of materials @ $4.00.................	$40,000
Actual cost, 10,450 lbs. of materials @ $4.00	41,800
Unfavorable materials quantity variance	$(1,800)

In this case, the cost of the materials is at standard but the materials usage is not. The manufacturing operation used 450 pounds of materials more than it should have, as indicated by the standard. This additional 450 pounds at a cost of $4.00 created the variance of $1,800 over standard cost.

As with the previous example, management must now determine why the extra materials were used. Again, there are various circumstances that might have created this situation. Some are:

1. Materials were spoiled or wasted. This loss could have been due to the fact that a different type of material was used, that workers were careless, or that supervisory personnel were lax. If possible, this condition must be eliminated.
2. More materials were deliberately used per manufactured unit as an experiment to determine if the quality of the product could be increased. If management decides to continue this usage, the standard cost per unit must be changed.

An analysis of the cause of this variance might also result in the elimination of inefficiencies or in a change in the standard cost.

Example 3:

Standard cost, 10,000 lbs. of materials @ $4.00.................	$40,000
Actual cost, 11,000 lbs. of materials @ $3.80	41,800
Unfavorable net materials variance	$(1,800)

In this example, a combination of usage and price variances causes the overall unfavorable variance. The factory has used 1,000 pounds of materials over standard but has purchased these materials at a cost which is $.20 below standard. Once again management should investigate the reason for the usage of additional materials and take appropriate action. It is important to recognize that the price variance of $.20 will also be investigated. The fact that this variance is favorable, below standard cost, is no reason for production personnel to be complacent and to ignore it. This "better" price may have been created by more efficient buying techniques, a bargain purchase, or a general price reduction. On the other hand, materials of a lesser quality may have been purchased, thereby reducing the quality of the product and possibly causing an unfavorable effect on the marketing of the product.

It is also possible that the greater usage of materials may be related to the lower price. Waste and spoilage might be created by (1) use of cheaper materials, or by (2) unfamiliarity in the use of a different material by the production workers. Of course, an investigation may reveal that the standard was not properly determined and should be revised.

The important points that have been illustrated by the three examples with identical net variances are these:

1. The total variance between standard and actual cost must be broken down by usage and price.
2. The variances in usage and price, whether unfavorable or favorable, must be analyzed as to cause and effect. Variances may be stated in dollar amounts, or in terms of units such as pounds or hours. The method chosen should be that which is of greatest benefit in aiding analysis.
3. Appropriate action must be taken. This action might include a change in methods of manufacturing, supervision, or purchasing, or a change in the standard cost of the product. It might involve taking advantage of efficient operations or functions. If the standard cost is changed, the units in inventory are often revalued at the new figure.

The same principles of analysis apply to the labor cost variances. Three similar examples are presented below.

Example 1:
Standard cost, 5,000 hrs. @ $10.00 per hr.....................	$50,000
Actual cost, 5,000 hrs. @ $9.90 per hr.........................	49,500
Favorable labor rate variance	$ 500

Example 2:
Standard cost, 5,000 hrs. @ $10.00 per hr.....................	$50,000
Actual cost, 4,950 hrs. @ $10.00 per hr.	49,500
Favorable labor efficiency variance	$ 500

Example 3:

Standard cost, 5,000 hrs. @ $10.00 per hr.	....	$50,000
Actual cost, 4,500 hrs. @ $11.00 per hr.	....	49,500
Favorable net labor variance	....	$ 500

In the first instance, it is apparent that the number of actual labor hours was at standard, but the cost per hour was lower than the standard of $10.00. Although this situation appears to be favorable, the reason and the possible effect must still be determined. It may be that the personnel department is doing a more efficient job in hiring qualified employees and should be commended; or it may be that less-than-qualified workers are being hired at a lower rate, possibly reducing the quality of the work on the product. This second condition would not be acceptable.

The second example indicates that the labor rate is at standard, but the time required was 50 hours below standard. Again, the question is, "why?" It is possible that the speed of production has been increased and the employees are working too fast to do top quality work. This possibility could have an adverse effect on sales. Again, of course, there is the possibility that the manufacturing and/or supervisory functions have become more efficient so that more work is done in less time.

In the third example, a saving of 500 hours is indicated, but there has been a payment per hour of $1.00 in excess of standard. These two factors could be related. The hiring of more highly skilled and higher paid personnel quite often results in a reduction in the number of hours worked. But, as with the other examples, management must investigate carefully and determine the cause and the effect of the variances in usage and price. If the labor efficiency variance is unfavorable, it may have been caused by the use of unskilled workers or it may be due to time lost because of machine breakdowns, improper scheduling of production, or an inefficient flow of materials to the production line.

The analyses of materials and labor variances do not stand alone; it is very possible that a difference above or below standard of one is directly tied to a variance of the other. For example, the hiring of more highly skilled personnel at a higher labor rate does not always reduce the number of hours worked, but it may reduce the amount of materials lost through spoilage. Conversely, the use of less skilled workers at a lower rate may cause greater materials loss. In examining any variance, management should look closely at the relationship of that variance to other variances.

Features of Standard Cost Accounting

Some features of standard cost accounting must be emphasized. First, the actual unit cost of manufacturing a product is not determined; only the total actual costs and the total standard costs are gathered.

Second, the fact that standards are based on estimates does not make them unreliable. A close examination and analysis of variances will quickly indicate whether the manufacturing operation is inefficient or whether the standards are reasonable.

Third, standards will change as conditions change. Permanent changes in prices, processes, or methods of operating may indicate the need for adjustment of the standards.

Fourth, the purpose of using a standard cost accounting system is to provide continual incentive for factory personnel to keep costs and performance in line with predetermined management objectives. As mentioned earlier in the chapter, comparisons between actual costs and the predetermined standards are much more effective than comparisons between current actual costs and actual costs of prior periods.

Fifth, a standard cost accounting system, through the recording and analysis of manufacturing cost variances, helps focus management's attention on these questions:

1. Were materials purchased at prices above or below standard?
2. Were materials used in quantities above or below standard?
3. Is labor being paid at rates above or below standard?
4. Is labor being used in amounts above or below standard?

Finally, although the discussion in this text indicates that variances are determined at the end of the month, most manufacturing companies calculate variances on a weekly, or even daily, basis to allow for more timely action in correcting inefficiencies or taking advantage of efficiencies. The variances for the month, however, are still recorded in the accounts at the end of the month.

Illustration of Standard Cost in a Departmentalized Factory

The following example demonstrates standard cost accounting procedures in a factory having two departments.

Standard Cost Summary

	Dept. A	Dept. B	Total
Materials:			
5 lbs. @ $1.00 lb........................	$ 5		
1 lb. @ $2.00 lb.........................		$ 2	$ 7
Labor:			
1 hour @ $8.00.........................	8		
2 hours @ $10.00........................		20	28
Factory overhead:			
Per unit.................................	1	2	3
Standard costs per unit...................	$14	$24	$38

Production Report for the Month

	Dept. A	Dept. B
Beginning units in process...........................	None	None
Units finished and transferred.......................	2,200	1,800
Ending units in process	None	400
Stage of completion.................................		½

Units pass through department A to department B. In both departments, materials, labor, and overhead are added evenly throughout the process. Actual costs for the month, as determined from materials requisitions, payroll records, and factory overhead records are as follows:

	Dept. A		Dept. B		Total
Direct materials:					
12,000 lbs. @ $ .95......		$11,400			
1,900 lbs. @ $2.10......				$ 3,990	$15,390
Direct labor:					
2,000 hrs. @ $8.10.......		16,200			
4,100 hrs. @ $9.90.......				40,590	56,790
Factory overhead:					
Indirect materials.........	$ 400		$1,000		
Indirect labor	600		1,000		
Other items..............	1,200	2,200	2,000	4,000	6,200
		$29,800		$48,580	$78,380

From the data given on the standard cost summary, the cost accountant can determine the standard costs of production. To facilitate the comparison of these figures with actual costs and the determination of variances, the accountant may use a form similar to that shown in Illustration 8-2.

	Dept. A Equivalent Production of 2,200 Units			Dept. B Equivalent Production of 2,000 Units			Total		
	Standard Cost	Actual Cost	Favorable (Unfavorable) Variance	Standard Cost	Actual Cost	Favorable (Unfavorable) Variance	Standard Cost	Actual Cost	Favorable (Unfavorable) Variance
Materials:									
11,000 lbs. @ $1.00	$11,000								
12,000 lbs. @ $ .95		$11,400	$(400)		$ 3,990	$ 10		$15,390	$(390)
2,000 lbs. @ $2.00				$ 4,000			$15,000		
1,900 lbs. @ $2.10									
Labor:									
2,200 hrs. @ $ 8.00	17,600								
2,000 hrs. @ $ 8.10		16,200	1,400		40,590	(590)		56,790	810
4,000 hrs. @ $10.00				40,000			57,600		
4,100 hrs. @ $ 9.90									
Factory overhead:									
Standard cost per unit $1.00	2,200								
Actual cost		2,200	—		4,000	—		6,200	810
Standard cost per unit $2.00				4,000			6,200		
Actual cost									
Total	$30,800	$29,800	$1,000	$48,000	$48,580	$(580)	$78,800	$78,380	$420

Illustration 8-2   Calculation of Variances

Using the data given in Illustration 8-2, the specific variances for materials and labor can be determined as follows:

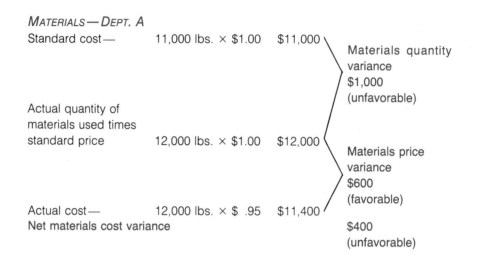

MATERIALS — DEPT. A
Standard cost —   11,000 lbs. × $1.00 $11,000

Materials quantity
variance
$1,000
(unfavorable)

Actual quantity of
materials used times
standard price   12,000 lbs. × $1.00 $12,000

Materials price
variance
$600
(favorable)

Actual cost —   12,000 lbs. × $ .95 $11,400
Net materials cost variance

$400
(unfavorable)

One thousand pounds of materials in excess of standard were used in department A, which, at the standard cost of $1.00, caused an unfavorable variance of $1,000. If prices had not changed, there would have been no other variances. But price did change — 12,000 pounds of materials at a cost of $.05 below standard resulted in a favorable price variance of $600. The combined variances resulted in a net unfavorable materials cost variance of $400 in department A.

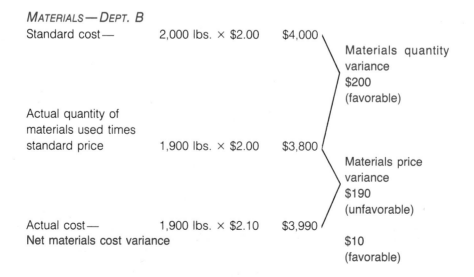

MATERIALS — DEPT. B
Standard cost —   2,000 lbs. × $2.00 $4,000

Materials quantity
variance
$200
(favorable)

Actual quantity of
materials used times
standard price   1,900 lbs. × $2.00 $3,800

Materials price
variance
$190
(unfavorable)

Actual cost —   1,900 lbs. × $2.10 $3,990
Net materials cost variance

$10
(favorable)

In this case, department B used 100 pounds of materials less than standard. At a standard cost of $2.00 per pound, the favorable quantity variance was $200. But this variance was partially offset by the unfavorable price variance created by the increase in the cost per unit of the materials of $.10. With 1,900 pounds being used, the price variance was $190 above standard. The two variances resulted in a net favorable materials cost variance of $10 in department B.

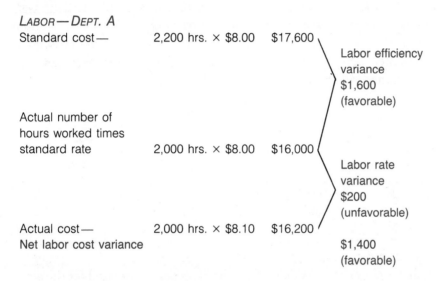

LABOR — DEPT. A

Standard cost —	2,200 hrs. × $8.00	$17,600	
			Labor efficiency variance $1,600 (favorable)
Actual number of hours worked times standard rate	2,000 hrs. × $8.00	$16,000	
			Labor rate variance $200 (unfavorable)
Actual cost —	2,000 hrs. × $8.10	$16,200	
Net labor cost variance			$1,400 (favorable)

During the month, this department saved 200 hours by working fewer hours than the number established as a standard for the number of units

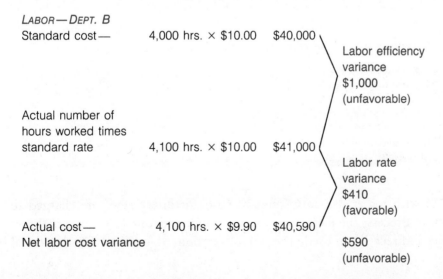

LABOR — DEPT. B

Standard cost —	4,000 hrs. × $10.00	$40,000	
			Labor efficiency variance $1,000 (unfavorable)
Actual number of hours worked times standard rate	4,100 hrs. × $10.00	$41,000	
			Labor rate variance $410 (favorable)
Actual cost —	4,100 hrs. × $9.90	$40,590	
Net labor cost variance			$590 (unfavorable)

produced. At a standard cost of $8.00 per hour, a favorable efficiency variance of $1,600 was realized. The average hourly rate of pay, however, was $.10 above standard so there was also an unfavorable rate variance. The company paid $.10 more per hour than the standard rate for 2,000 hours of work, or a total of $200.

Department B used 100 hours more than the standard and therefore, at the standard rate of $10.00, had an unfavorable efficiency variance of $1,000. Because the actual rate paid was $.10 below standard, there was a favorable rate variance of $410, determined by multiplying the 4,100 hours actually worked by this $.10 rate difference. (For the purposes of discussion in this chapter, no variances have been reflected for factory overhead. This type of variance will be discussed in detail in the next chapter.)

The following journal entries can now be made:

Work in Process — Dept. A	11,000	
Work in Process — Dept. B	4,000	
Materials Quantity Variance — Dept. A	1,000	
Materials Price Variance — Dept. B	190	
Factory Overhead (Indirect Materials)	1,400	
Materials Price Variance — Dept. A		600
Materials Quantity Variance — Dept. B		200
Materials		16,790

Note that the accounts for work in process are charged for the standard cost of direct materials, the factory overhead account is debited for the actual cost of indirect materials used, the materials account is credited at actual cost for all direct and indirect materials used, and the variance accounts are debited if unfavorable and credited if favorable. (If this company followed the practice of recording the materials price variance at time of purchase, no price variances would be recorded at this time.)

Work in Process — Dept. A	17,600	
Work in Process — Dept. B	40,000	
Labor Rate Variance — Dept. A	200	
Labor Efficiency Variance — Dept. B	1,000	
Factory Overhead (Indirect Labor)	1,600	
Labor Efficiency Variance — Dept. A		1,600
Labor Rate Variance — Dept. B		410
Payroll		58,390

As with materials, only standard costs for direct labor are charged to Work in Process; the factory overhead account is debited for the actual cost of the indirect labor used; the payroll account is credited for the actual cost of direct and indirect labor during the month; and the variances are charged or credited to the appropriate accounts.

During the month and at the end of the month, there would be the usual entries in the journals to record the factory overhead other than indirect materials and indirect labor. These entries are summarized as follows:

Factory Overhead....................................	3,200	
Various credits (Accounts Payable, Accumulated		
Depreciation, Prepaid Insurance)......................		3,200

Factory overhead would be applied to work in process by the following entry:

Work in Process — Dept. A (2,200 units × $1).............	2,200	
Work in Process — Dept. B (2,000 units × $2).............	4,000	
Factory Overhead....................................		6,200

The entries are then made to transfer the standard cost of units finished in department A to department B and from department B to finished goods.

Work in Process — Dept. B.............................	30,800	
Work in Process — Dept. A............................		30,800
(2,200 units @ $14)		
Finished Goods......................................	68,400	
Work in Process — Dept. B............................		68,400
(1,800 units @ $38)		

After these entries have been posted, the general ledger accounts would reflect the data as shown below in T-account form.

Materials			Work in Process — Dept. A	
	16,790		11,000	30,800
			17,600	
			2,200	
Work in Process — Dept. B			*30,800*	
4,000	68,400			
40,000			**Finished Goods**	
4,000			68,400	
30,800				
78,800			**Materials Quantity Variance — Dept. B**	
10,400				200
Materials Quantity Variance — Dept. A			**Materials Price Variance — Dept. B**	
1,000			190	

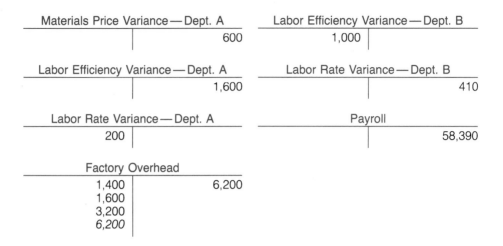

Materials Price Variance — Dept. A		Labor Efficiency Variance — Dept. B	
	600	1,000	

Labor Efficiency Variance — Dept. A		Labor Rate Variance — Dept. B	
	1,600		410

Labor Rate Variance — Dept. A		Payroll	
200			58,390

Factory Overhead	
1,400	6,200
1,600	
3,200	
6,200	

The work in process account for department A has no balance because all work has been completed in this department and transferred to department B. The work in process account for department B has a balance of $10,400 accounted for as follows:

Cost in department A — 400 units @ $14	$ 5,600
Cost in department B — 400 units @ $12 (one-half completed)	4,800
	$10,400

Additional entries, not shown above, would have been made during the month for purchases of materials, vouchering and payment of payrolls, and recording of cost of goods sold.

Mix and Yield Variances

It is quite common for more than one material to be required in a production process. The proportion or ratio of each material to the other is called the mix. Quite often, in industries such as petroleum manufacturing, textiles, chemicals, foundries, rubber goods, and food processing, the mix of materials is deliberately changed from the standard formula. This may be for various reasons, such as (1) achieving economy, (2) an experimental change in the quality of the product, or (3) because a given material is in short supply or is not available. Sometimes a change in mix will affect the yield, which is the number of units produced from a standard amount of materials introduced into the process. For example: If the standard calls for

2 gallons of material X and 1 gallon of material Y to produce 3 gallons of product Z, the mix ratio is ⅔ of X to ⅓ of Y. The yield is three units of Z. If the ratio of ⅔ material X to ⅓ material Y is altered in the production process, there has been a change in mix. If the ratio of 3 gallons of input materials to 3 gallons of output product is different, there has been a change in yield.

As discussed earlier, the materials quantity variance measures the cost of the actual quantity of direct materials used above or below the standard quantity for the actual level of production. If there has been a change in the mix, further analysis must be made to determine the effect of this change. This involves breaking down the materials quantity variance into a mix variance and a yield variance.

A mix variance shows the change in cost that results from changing the proportions of materials added to the production mix. It measures the effect of using a different combination of materials. In the previous example, if materials X and Y were used in equal proportions, the standard mix has changed, and a mix variance would be calculated. This variance is determined by measuring the difference in cost, at standard prices, between the actual mix of quantities used and the standard mix of the total quantity used.

A yield variance measures whether a change in mix affected the yield, and shows the difference in cost that results if the actual yield (output) varies from the standard quantity of yield determined for a given input of materials. In the previous example, if the mix was changed and 3 gallons of direct materials did not produce 3 gallons of product, the yield has also changed and a yield variance should be determined. This variance is calculated by measuring the difference between the actual quantity of materials used, at standard mix and prices, and the standard quantity of materials allowed for the actual amount of production, at standard prices.

To illustrate, assume that the standards for materials are as follows:

Material	Quantity		Price per Pound	Total Cost
A............................	60 lbs.	×	$1	$ 60
B............................	40	×	$3	120
	100 lbs.			$180

Standard yield = 100 lbs. of finished product; mix ratio = 60% A, 40% B.

Also assume that the production records for the month show that 100 pounds of finished product were manufactured at the following cost:

Material	Quantity		Price per Pound	Total Cost
A........................	90 lbs	×	$1	$ 90
B........................	20	×	$3	60
	110 lbs.			$150

The materials quantity variance would be calculated as follows for 100 finished units:

Material	Actual Quantity	Standard Quantity	Quantity Difference	Standard Price	Quantity Variance
A.........	90 lbs.	60 lbs.	(30 lbs.) (U) ×	$1	$(30) (U)
B.........	20	40	20 (F) ×	$3	60 (F)
	110 lbs.	100 lbs.	(10 lbs.) (U)		$ 30 (F)

The mix variance is then calculated:

Material	Actual Quantity	Actual Quantity Converted to Standard Mix	Quantity Difference	Standard Price	Mix Variance
A...........	90 lbs.	66 lbs. (60% × 110 lbs.)	(24) lbs. (U) ×	$1	$(24) (U)
B...........	20	44 (40% × 110 lbs.)	24 (F) ×	$3	72 (F)
	110 lbs.	110 lbs.	–0–		$ 48 (F)

The mix variance is favorable because the actual mix of materials cost less than the standard mix. This was because more of the lower cost material A was used and less of the higher priced material B was used.

The yield variance is determined as follows:

Material	Actual Quantity Converted to Standard Mix	Standard Quantity (100 units)	Quantity Difference	Standard Price	Yield Variance
A...............	66 lbs.	60 lbs.	(6) lbs. (U)	$1	$ (6) (U)
B...............	44	40	(4) (U)	$3	(12) (U)
	110 lbs.	100 lbs.	(10) lbs. (U)		$(18) (U)

This analysis indicates that 110 pounds of input materials were used, rather than the standard 100 pounds, to produce 100 finished units. This creates an unfavorable yield variance which may have been caused by (1) the use of an inferior grade of materials, (2) loss of units due to the different mix, or (3) rejection of units of poorer quality.

Note that the total of the mix and yield variances equals the quantity variance.

Mix variance	$48	(F)
Yield variance	(18)	(U)
Quantity variance	$30	(F)

These variances may be developed for internal use only, in which case only the materials quantity variance would be recorded in a journal entry, as discussed earlier in the chapter. However, if the mix and yield variances are to be recorded in the accounts in lieu of a materials quantity variance, the journal entry is as follows (assuming no price variance):

Work in Process	180	
Materials Yield Variance	18	
Materials Mix Variance		48
Materials		150

This same type of analysis can be applied to determine labor mix and yield variances. A change in labor mix would be created if the relative proportions of skilled (higher paid) and unskilled (lower paid) workers were changed due to (1) cost-cutting, (2) absentee workers, (3) a shortage of one type of labor, or (4) problems in scheduling. In this case, a mix variance would be determined. Because this type of variation from the standard labor mix usually would affect hours worked and unit yield, a yield variance would also be calculated.

Assume that the direct labor standard for manufacturing a unit of product is as follows:

Class 1 labor — 1 hour @ $10	$10	
Class 2 labor — 1 hour @ $5	5	
Total direct labor cost per unit	$15	

Due to a shortage of skilled laborers, it was necessary to hire additional unskilled workers to complete the production process. The production data are as follows:

Number of units manufactured	1,000
Direct labor cost:	
Class 1 labor — 900 hours @ $10	$9,000
Class 2 labor — 1,300 hours @ $5	$6,500

The labor variances would first be calculated in the usual way:

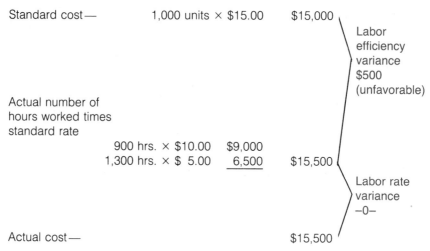

Standard cost—	1,000 units × $15.00	$15,000	Labor efficiency variance $500 (unfavorable)
Actual number of hours worked times standard rate			
	900 hrs. × $10.00	$9,000	
	1,300 hrs. × $ 5.00	6,500	$15,500
			Labor rate variance –0–
Actual cost—		$15,500	

There is no labor rate variance because the two classes of workers were paid standard hourly rates for their classification. The labor efficiency variane is $500 and is unfavorable. This variance seemingly results because the number of hours worked (2,200) exceeded the standard number of hours (2,000) allowed for the production of 1,000 units. However, the breakdown of the efficiency variance into labor mix and yield variances will provide a more definitive analysis. The calculation is as follows:

Labor Class	Actual Hours	Actual Hours Converted to Standard Mix	Quantity Difference	Standard Price	Mix Variance
1	900	1,100 (50%)	200 hrs. (F)	$10	$2,000 (F)
2	1,300	1,100 (50%)	(200) hrs. (U)	5	(1,000) (U)
	2,200	2,200	–0–		$1,000 (F)

The mix variance is favorable because more lower paid workers were used in place of higher paid workers, but when this type of variance arises, management must be concerned as to whether the quality of the product and the yield were affected.

The yield variance is determined next:

Labor Class	Actual Hours Converted to Standard Mix	Standard Hours (1,000 units)	Quantity Difference	Standard Price	Yield Variance
1	1,100 (50%)	1,000	(100) hrs. (U)	$10	$(1,000) (U)
2	1,100 (50%)	1,000	(100) (U)	5	(500) (U)
	2,200	2,000	(200) hrs. (U)		$(1,500) (U)

The yield variance is unfavorable because 2,200 hours of labor produced only 1,000 units, rather than 1,100 units as prescribed by the standards. The total of the mix variance ($1,000 favorable) and the yield variance ($1,500 unfavorable) equals the amount of the efficiency variance ($500 unfavorable). Because a change in materials and/or labor mix can affect yields, costs, and quality of the product, management will carefully study these variances to determine the potential effect of nonstandard mix.

KEY TERMS

Attainable standard (365)
Favorable variance (368)
Ideal standard (364)
Labor cost standard (365)
Labor efficiency (usage)
    variance (368)
Labor rate (price) variance (368)
Materials cost standard (365)
Materials price variance (368)
Materials quantity (usage)
    variance (368)

Mix (386)
Mix variance (387)
Price (367)
Purchase price variance (371)
Standard (364)
Standard cost accounting (364)
Unfavorable variance (368)
Usage (367)
Variance (367)
Yield (386)
Yield variance (387)

QUESTIONS

1. Give a simple explanation of the function and objective of standard cost accounting.
2. Distinguish between standard cost and actual cost of production.
3. What is a "standard"?
4. What are the specific procedures upon which a standard cost accounting system is based?
5. State briefly how standards are determined for materials and labor costs.
6. What is a variance?
7. When are variances usually recorded in the journals?
8. Explain price and quantity variances in relation to materials costs.
9. Explain rate and efficiency variances in relation to labor costs.
10. Is a favorable variance "good" or an unfavorable variance "bad"? Explain.

11. Are actual costs or standard costs charged to Work in Process?
12. Are the inventory accounts—Finished Goods, Work in Process, and Materials—valued at actual cost or standard cost?
13. What two things must the cost accountant consider when breaking down a variance into its components? Explain.
14. What might cause the following variances?
    (a) An unfavorable materials price variance
    (b) A favorable materials price variance
    (c) An unfavorable materials quantity variance
    (d) A favorable materials quantity variance
    (e) An unfavorable labor rate variance
    (f) A favorable labor rate variance
    (g) An unfavorable labor efficiency variance
    (h) A favorable labor efficiency variance
15. Is it possible that a variance of one type might be partially or fully offset by another variance? Explain.
16. If, in a given period, the total actual cost of all materials used is exactly the same as the standard cost so that there is no net variance, is there any reason for further analyzing the data? Explain.
17. Explain a mix variance.
18. Explain a yield variance.

EXERCISES

The following data are to be used for Exercises 1 through 5:

The standard operating capacity of the Modicum Manufacturing Co. is 1,000 units. A detailed study of the manufacturing data relating to the production of one product revealed the following:
1. Two pounds of materials are needed to produce one unit.
2. The standard unit cost of materials is $6 per pound.
3. It takes one hour of labor to produce one unit.
4. The standard labor rate is $10 per hour.
5. Standard overhead for this volume is $3,000.

The following is required for each case in Exercises 1 through 5:
(a) Set up a standard cost summary showing the standard unit cost.
(b) Analyze the variances and prepare journal entries to record the transfer to Work in Process of:
    (1) materials costs
    (2) labor costs

(3)   overhead costs
When making these entries, indicate the types of variances, and state whether each variance is favorable or unfavorable.
(c)   Prepare the entry in general journal form to record the transfer of costs to the finished goods account.

Exercise 8-1   Standard unit cost; variance analysis; journal entries.

1,000 units were started and finished.
Case 1.   All prices and quantities for the cost elements are standard, except for materials cost which is $5.90 per pound.
Case 2.   All prices and quantities for the cost elements are standard, except that 2,100 pounds of materials were used.

Exercise 8-2   Standard unit cost; variance analysis; journal entries.

1,000 units were started and finished.
Case 1.   All prices and quantities are standard, except for the labor rate which is $10.20 per hour.
Case 2.   All prices and quantities are standard with the exception of labor hours which totaled 900.

Exercise 8-3   Standard unit cost; variance analysis; journal entries.

All of the deviations listed in Exercises 1 and 2 took place, and 1,000 units were started and finished.

Exercise 8-4   Standard unit cost; variance analysis; journal entries.

All of the deviations listed in Exercises 1 and 2 took place, and 950 units were started and finished.

Exercise 8-5   Standard unit cost; variance analysis; journal entries.

All of the deviations listed in Exercises 1 and 2 took place, and 1,050 units were started and finished.

Exercise 8-6   Standard cost summary; materials and labor cost variances.

A manufacturing plant produces an average of 10,000 units each month. The factory standards are 20,000 hours of direct labor and 10,000 pounds of materials for this volume. The standard cost of direct labor is $9.00 per hour, and of materials, $4.00 per pound. The standard factory overhead at this level of production is $10,000.

During the current month the production and cost reports reflected the following information:

Beginning units in process..............................	None
Units finished...	9,500
Units in process, end of month	None
Direct labor hours worked..............................	20,000
Pounds of materials used	9,400
Cost of direct labor....................................	$178,000
Cost of materials used.................................	$ 39,480

On the basis of the above information:
(a) Prepare a standard cost summary.
(b) Calculate the materials and labor cost variances and indicate whether they are favorable or unfavorable using formulas as shown on page 369.
(c) Calculate the materials and labor cost variances, using a schedule similar to that shown on page 370.

Exercise 8-7   Standard cost summary; journal entries.

The normal capacity of a manufacturing plant is 30,000 direct labor hours and 20,000 units per month. A finished unit requires 5 pounds of materials at an estimated cost of $2 per pound. The estimated cost of labor is $11.00 per hour. It is estimated that overhead for a month will be $36,000.

During the month of March, 27,200 direct labor hours were worked at an average rate of $10.90 an hour. The number of units produced was 18,000, using 88,000 pounds of materials at a cost of $2.04 per pound.

Prepare:
(a) A standard cost summary showing the standard unit cost.
(b) Journal entries to charge materials and labor to Work in Process. Indicate whether the variances are favorable or unfavorable.

Exercise 8-8   Standard cost summary; journal entries.

Assume that during the month of April the production report of the company in Exercise 7 revealed the following information:

Units produced during the month	21,000
Direct labor hours for the month	31,000
Materials used (in pounds).............................	106,000
Labor rate per hour	$11.04
Materials cost per pound	$1.98

Prepare journal entries to charge materials and labor to Work in Process. Indicate whether variances are favorable or unfavorable.

Exercise 8-9   Determining actual quantities and costs for materials and labor.

From an analysis of the data presented below, determine the actual quantity of materials used and the actual price per pound as well as the actual direct labor hours incurred and the actual cost per hour.

	Standard Quantity or Hours	Standard Price or Rate	Variances Materials Quantity	Materials Price
Materials	(pounds)			
(a)	2,200	$ 2.05	$ 205 Unf.	$115 Fav.
(b)	800	11.00	110 Fav.	79 Fav.
(c)	10,000	3.00	1,200 Unf.	520 Unf.
			Labor Efficiency	Labor Rate
Labor	(hours)			
(d)	5,600	10.00	$ 500 Unf.	$ 565 Fav.
(e)	8,800	9.00	900 Fav.	435 Unf.
(f)	11,500	10.50	1,575 Fav.	1,135 Unf.

Exercise 8-10   Variance analysis and interpretation.

Last year Monitor Corporation adopted a standard cost system. Labor standards were set on the basis of time studies and prevailing wage rates. Materials standards were determined from materials specifications and the prices then in effect.

At June 30, the end of the current fiscal year, a partial trial balance revealed the following:

	Debit	Credit
Materials Price Variance		25,000
Materials Quantity Variance	9,000	
Labor Rate Variance.............................	30,000	
Labor Efficiency Variance	7,500	

Standards were set at the beginning of the year and have remained unchanged. All inventories are priced at standard cost. What conclusions can be drawn from each of the four variances shown in Monitor's trial balance?

(AICPA adapted)

PROBLEMS

Problem 8-1   Materials and labor variance analyses.

The standard cost summary of the Shaft Mfg. Co. is shown below, together with production and cost data for the period.

Standard Cost Summary

Materials:

2 gallons A @ $1.00.............................	$2.00	
2 gallons B @ $2.00.............................	4.00	$ 6.00

Labor:

1 hour @ $10.00...............................	10.00

Factory overhead:

$1.00 per direct labor hour.....................	1.00
Total standard unit cost.........................	$17.00

Production and Cost Summary

Units completed during the month	9,000
Ending units in process (one-fourth completed)	2,000
Gallons of material A used	21,000
Gallons of material B used	20,000
Direct labor hours worked.................................	10,000
Cost of material A used...................................	$20,160
Cost of material B used...................................	$40,000
Cost of direct labor......................................	$97,000

One gallon each of materials A and B are added at the start of processing. The balance of the materials are added when the process is two-thirds complete. Labor and overhead are added evenly throughout the process.

Required:

On the basis of this information:
1. Calculate equivalent production.
2. Calculate materials and labor variances and indicate whether they are favorable or unfavorable, using formulas shown on page 369.
3. Explain all variances by preparing a schedule similar to the one on page 370.
4. Determine the cost of materials and labor in the work in process account at the end of the month.
5. Prove that all materials and labor costs have been accounted for.

Problem 8-2   Variance analysis, journal entries, other analyses.

Cost and production data for the Jetco Products Company are presented below.

Standard Cost Summary

	Dept. I	Dept. II	Total
Materials:			
4 units @ $ .50.................	$ 2		
1 unit @ $ 1.00.................		$ 1	$ 3
Labor:			
1 hour @ $ 8.00...............	8		
1 hour @ $10.00...............		10	18
Factory overhead:			
Per unit	1	2	3
	$11	$13	$24

Production Report

	Dept. I	Dept. II
Beginning units in process...................	None	None
Units finished and transferred	6,000	5,000
Ending units in process.....................	2,000	1,000
Stage of completion	½	½

Cost Data

	Dept. I	Dept. II
Direct materials:		
30,000 units @ $ .52....	$15,600	
5,500 units @ $ .95....		$ 5,225
Direct labor:		
6,800 hours @ $ 8.00....	54,400	
5,600 hours @ $10.20....		57,120
Factory overhead:		
Indirect materials.........	$ 500	$1,000
Indirect labor	2,000	5,000
Other	4,500 7,000	5,000 11,000

Required:
1. Calculate net variances for materials, labor, and factory overhead.
2. Calculate specific materials and labor variances by department.
3. Prepare all journal entries to record production costs in Work in Process and Finished Goods.
4. Prove balances of Work in Process for both departments.
5. Prove that all costs have been accounted for.
   Note: Assume that materials, labor, and overhead are added evenly throughout the process.
6. If 4,000 units were sold @ $40 each,
   (a) what is the gross margin based on standard cost?
   (b) what is the gross margin based on actual cost?

Problem 8-3   Analysis of materials and labor variances.

The Central Products Company manufactures a variety of products made of plastic and aluminum components. During the winter months, substantially all of the production capacity is devoted to the production of lawn sprinklers for the following spring and summer seasons. Other products are manufactured during the remainder of the year.

The company has developed standard costs for its several products. Standard costs for each year are set in the preceding October. The standard cost of a sprinkler for the current year is $3.70, computed as follows:

Direct materials:
Aluminum—0.2 lbs. @ $.40 per lb.	$ .08
Plastic—1.0 lbs. @ $.38 per lb.	.38
Production labor—0.3 hrs. @ $8.00 per hr.	2.40
Factory overhead	.84
Total	$3.70

During February, 8,500 good sprinklers were manufactured. The following costs were incurred and charged to production:

Materials requisitioned for production:
Aluminum—1,900 lbs. @ $.40 per lb.	$ 760
Plastic—Regular grade—6,000 lbs. @ $.38 per lb.	2,280
Low Grade*—3,500 lbs. @ $.38 per lb.	1,330
Production labor—2,700 hrs.	23,220
Factory overhead	7,140
Costs charged to production	$34,730

Materials price variations are not determined by usage, but are charged to a materials price variation account at the time the invoice is entered. All materials are carried in inventory at standard prices. Materials purchases for February were:

Aluminum—1,800 lbs. @ $.48 per lb.	$ 864
Plastic—Regular grade—3,000 lbs. @ $.50 per lb.	1,500
Low grade*—6,000 lbs. @ $.29 per lb.	1,740

*Due to plastic shortages, the company was forced to purchase lower grade plastic than called for in the standards. This increased the number of sprinklers rejected on inspection.

Required:

Calculate price and usage variances for each type of material and for labor.

(CMA adapted)

Problem 8-4   Materials and labor variances analyses.

The Dynamic Company manufactures a fuel additive that has a stable selling price of $44 per drum. The company has been producing and selling 80,000 drums per month.

In connection with your examination of the financial statements of Dynamic Company for the year ended September 30, you have been asked to review some computations made by Dynamic's cost accountant. Your working papers disclose the following about the company's operations:

Standard costs per drum of product manufactured:

Materials:
8 gallons of Miracle Mix @ $2	$16	
1 empty drum	1	$17
Direct labor—1 hour		$ 8
Factory overhead		$ 6

Costs and expenses during September:

Miracle Mix: 500,000 gallons purchased at a cost of $950,000; 650,000 gallons used

Empty drums; 94,000 purchased at a cost of $94,000; 80,000 used

Direct labor: 82,000 hours worked at a cost of $662,560

Factory overhead: $768,000

Required:

Prepare a schedule computing the following variances for September:

1. Materials quantity variance
2. Materials price variance (determined at time of purchase)
3. Labor efficiency variance
4. Labor rate variance

(AICPA adapted)

Problem 8-5   Calculation of materials and labor variances.

The Economy Corporation manufactures and sells a single product. The cost system used by the company is a standard cost system. The standard cost per unit of product is shown below:

Materials—one pound plastic @ $2.00	$ 2.00
Direct labor—1.6 hours @ $8.00	12.80
Factory overhead	4.45
Total	$19.25

The charges to the manufacturing department for November, when 5,000 units were produced, are given below:

Materials—5,300 pounds @ $2.00	$ 10,600
Direct labor—8,200 hours @ $8.20	67,240
Factory overhead	23,815
Total	$101,655

The purchasing department normally buys about the same quantity as is used in production during a month. In November, 5,200 pounds were purchased at a price of $2.10 per pound.

Required:

Calculate the following variances from standard costs for the data given:
1. Materials quantity
2. Materials price (at time of purchase)
3. Labor efficiency
4. Labor rate

(CMA adapted)

Problem 8-6   Allocation of variances.

The Burnett Manufacturing Corporation uses a standard cost system that records raw materials at actual cost, records materials price variances at the time that raw materials are issued to work in process, and prorates all variances at year end. Variances associated with direct materials are prorated based on the direct materials balances in the appropriate accounts, and variances associated with direct labor are prorated based on the direct labor balances in the appropriate accounts. The following information is available for Burnett for the year ended December 31.

Raw materials inventory at December 31	$ 65,000
Finished goods inventory at December 31:	
Direct materials	87,000
Direct labor	130,500
Applied factory overhead	104,400
Cost of goods sold for the year ended December 31:	
Direct materials	348,000
Direct labor	739,500
Applied factory overhead	591,600
Materials quantity variance (favorable)	15,000
Materials price variance (unfavorable)	10,000
Labor efficiency variance (favorable)	5,000
Labor rate variance (unfavorable)	20,000
Factory overhead applied	696,000

There were no beginning inventories and no ending work in process inventory.

Required:

Determine the following:

1. The amount of materials price variance to be prorated to finished goods inventory at December 31.
2. The total amount of direct materials cost in the finished goods inventory at December 31, after all variances have been prorated.
3. The total amount of direct labor cost in the finished goods inventory at December 31, after all variances have been prorated.
4. The total cost of goods sold for the year ended December 31, after all variances have been prorated.

(AICPA adapted)

Problem 8-7   Analysis of materials and labor variances.

Steward Manufacturing Company uses a standard cost system in accounting for the cost of production of its only product, product A. The standards for the production of one unit of product A are as follows:

Direct materials: 10 feet of item 1 at $.75 per foot and 3 feet of item 2 at $1.00 per foot.
Direct labor: 4 hours at $8.00 per hour.
Factory overhead: applied at 150% of standard direct labor costs.

There was no beginning inventory on hand at July 1. Following is a summary of costs and related data for the production of product A during the following year ended June 30.

100,000 feet of item 1 were purchased at $.78 per foot.
30,000 feet of item 2 were purchased at $.90 per foot.
8,000 units of product A were produced that required 78,000 feet of item 1; 26,000 feet of item 2; and 31,000 hours of direct labor at $8.20 per hour.
6,000 units of product A were sold.

At June 30, there are 22,000 feet of item 1; 4,000 feet of item 2; and 2,000 completed units of product A on hand. All purchases and transfers are "charged in" at standard.

Required:

Calculate the following:

1. Materials quantity variance for item 1
2. Materials quantity variance for item 2
3. Materials price variance for item 1 (recorded at purchase)
4. Materials price variance for item 2 (recorded at purchase)
5. Labor efficiency variance
6. Labor rate variance

(AICPA adapted)

Problem 8-8   Materials mix and yield variances.

Using the data presented in Problem 8-3, calculate materials mix and yield variances.

Problem 8-9   Materials mix and yield variances.

Using the data given in Problem 8-7, calculate materials mix and yield variances.

Problem 8-10   Labor efficiency, rate, mix and yield variances.

The direct labor standard for the Reed Company is as follows:

Class A labor — 2 hours @ $12	$24
Class B labor — 3 hours @ $6	18
Standard direct labor cost per unit	$42

During the month 2,000 units were manufactured. Actual labor costs were as follows:

Class A labor — 4,200 hours @ $12.00	$50,400
Class B labor — 6,000 hours @ $5.75	34,500

Required:
1. Calculate the following:
   (a) Labor efficiency variance
   (b) Labor rate variance
   (c) Labor mix variance
   (d) Labor yield variance
2. Explain what might have caused the mix and yield variances.

STANDARD COST ACCOUNTING—

FACTORY OVERHEAD

LEARNING OBJECTIVES

In studying this chapter, you will learn about the:

- Two methods that are commonly used for analyzing overhead variances
- Procedures used to determine standard amounts of factory overhead at different levels of production
- General principles of budgeting
- Various types of budgets prepared by businesses
- Evaluation of budgets by the use of performance reports

The determination of the standard unit cost for factory overhead involves the estimation of factory overhead cost at the standard, or normal, level of production, considering historical data (adjusted for distorting items in the past such as strikes and fire losses) and future changes and trends. This estimated factory overhead cost is divided by the standard number of units to be produced to determine the standard unit cost. For example, assume that the standard amount of production is 1,000 units. At this level of activity, the standard factory overhead is determined to be as follows:

Depreciation on building and machinery.............................	$ 4,000
Taxes and insurance on building and machinery	1,000
Supervisory salaries..	4,000
Maintenance costs...	2,000
Supplies	1,000
Total standard factory overhead	$12,000

Dividing the standard factory overhead cost of $12,000 by the 1,000 units to be produced results in a standard unit cost for overhead of $12. If equivalent production during the period is exactly 1,000 units, Work in Process will be charged with $12,000 of factory overhead (1,000 units × $12 per unit). As illustrated in the following journal entry and T-accounts, if the actual factory overhead was $12,000, all of this cost would be applied to the work in process account, and there would be no over- or underapplied overhead.

```
Work in Process ........................................     12,000
     Factory Overhead......................................             12,000
          To apply factory overhead to work in process.
```

Work in Process		Factory Overhead	
12,000		12,000 (actual costs recorded from various journals)	12,000 (standard cost applied to work in process)

If the actual overhead was greater than $12,000, as illustrated in the following account, Factory Overhead would have a debit balance of $400 after $12,000 of standard cost has been applied to Work in Process. This balance reflects the amount of factory overhead cost that was not charged to or absorbed by the goods produced. This unabsorbed cost represents the amount of overhead incurred over and above the standard for this level of production. The balance in the account would be considered an unfavorable variance.

Factory Overhead	
12,400 (actual costs recorded from various journals) 400	12,000 (standard cost applied to work in process)

TWO-VARIANCE METHOD OF ANALYSIS

Two methods are commonly used for analyzing overhead variances: the two-variance method and the three-variance method. Additional variances can be calculated, but most companies limit their analyses to one of these two methods. The most commonly used approach, the two-variance analysis, is discussed on the following pages; the three-variance method is discussed at the end of the chapter.

Budget Variance

In the previous example, the factory incurred actual overhead cost that exceeded the standard for this level of production; the resulting variance is called an unfavorable budget, or controllable variance. As with any variance, the cause must be immediately determined and action taken to eliminate inefficient conditions.

Conversely, as shown below, if the actual factory overhead had been $11,800, or less than the standard indicated, the factory overhead account would have a credit balance of $200 after $12,000 had been applied to the work in process account. This credit balance indicates a favorable budget variance: the factory did not incur as much overhead as was allowed by the standard at this level of production. However, the variance must still be analyzed and investigated even though it appears to be favorable, because underspending can affect the quality of the product.

Factory Overhead	
11,800 (actual costs recorded from various journals)	12,000 (standard cost applied to work in process)
	200

The underlying principle of budget variance analysis is that a comparison must be made between the actual factory overhead for a given period and the standard amount of overhead allowed by the budget at a given level of production. Differences are classified as favorable or unfavorable budget or controllable variances.

If the actual level of production differs from the standard level, it is reasonable to assume that the standard budgeted amount of factory overhead for the actual level of production would differ from the standard budgeted amount for the standard level of production. This difference is the result of the behavior of the fixed and variable cost items included in the overhead estimate. As discussed in previous chapters, fixed cost items tend to remain the same in total dollars despite normal fluctuations in production, while total variable costs tend to vary more or less proportionately to the changes in production.

In the example given previously, the items of depreciations, taxes, insurance, and supervisory salaries are common items of fixed expense, while maintenance costs and supplies are usually in the category of variable cost.

Assuming that the actual level of production in the previous example on page 403 was 900 units, or 90% of the planned production of 1,000 units, the standard amount of factory overhead allowed in the budget for this level of production might be as follows:

Depreciation on building and machinery (fixed)	$ 4,000
Taxes and insurance on the above (fixed)	1,000
Supervisory salaries (fixed)	4,000
Maintenance costs, 90% × $2,000 (variable)	1,800
Supplies, 90% × $1,000 (variable).	900
Total standard factory overhead	$11,700

The fixed costs remain the same as budgeted at 1,000 units of production, but the variable costs are lower. Production of 900 units is equal to 90 percent of normal production, so the cost of maintenance is budgeted at $1,800 (90 percent of $2,000). The cost of supplies is shown to be $900 (90 percent of $1,000).

Assume that with production of 900 units, the actual factory overhead recorded is $11,700, which is the amount budgeted for this level of production. There will be no budget variance because the actual costs are equal to the costs budgeted for the actual number of units produced. However, another variance, the volume variance, must now be given consideration.

Volume Variance

At the beginning of the period, the standard cost per unit for overhead was determined to be $12; therefore, Work in Process will be charged the standard overhead cost of $12 for each unit produced. In the previous example, the amount of factory overhead applied to production would be $10,800 (900 units × $12). Thus, an unfavorable variance of $900 appears which is caused by the difference between the actual overhead of $11,700 and the standard overhead applied to work in process, $10,800.

Factory Overhead	
11,700 (actual costs recorded from various journals) 900	10,800 (standard cost applied to work in process)

This variance is called a **volume variance** because it is the result of operating at a level of production different from the standard, or normal, level. If the normal level of production had originally been set at 900 units and the budgeted overhead at $11,700, the standard cost would have been

$13 per unit. If 900 units had been produced, the amount charged to Work in Process would have been $11,700 (900 units × $13), and there would have been no variance.

Another way of determining this variance is as follows:

Standard Level of Production — 1,000 units

Fixed costs:		
Depreciation	$ 4,000	
Taxes and insurance	1,000	
Supervisory salaries.	4,000	
Total.	$ 9,000	
Application rate per unit		$ 9
Variable cost:		
Maintenance	$ 2,000	
Supplies	1,000	
Total.	$ 3,000	
Application rate per unit		3
Total standard factory overhead	$12,000	
Total application rate per unit		$12

Actual Level of Production — 900 units

	Budget	Applied	Variance
Fixed cost (applied at $9 per unit)	$ 9,000	$ 8,100	$900
Variable cost (applied at $3 per unit).	2,700	2,700	–0–
Total factory overhead.	$11,700	$10,800	$900

The volume variance can be very significant because it indicates that production was below the established standard. If management feels that 1,000 units should have been produced during the period, it will be concerned that only 900 units were produced and will investigate to determine the cause. This reduced production may be the result of inefficiencies in labor or supervision, machine breakdowns due to faulty maintenance or any number of unfavorable conditions. On the other hand, this level of production might indicate a normal seasonal fluctuation that would be offset by higher than normal production in other periods. It is possible also, if the drop in production is not seasonal, that the factory is not at fault. Production may have been deliberately reduced because sales were not as high as predicted, in which case the marketing department could be held accountable for the situation.

Whatever the circumstances, if the factory is producing below its normal capacity, it has idle and possibly wasted excess capacity. If it is producing above its normal capacity, it may be subject to inefficient operating conditions and excess costs. These types of situations must be constantly scrutinized by management, which has the ultimate responsibility for planning and implementing the most efficient production methods and schedules.

Determination of Variances

Assume the following facts for the accounting period:

Standard overhead cost per unit...................................	$12
Number of units manufactured	900
Actual factory overhead	$11,000
*Standard factory overhead budgeted for the actual level of production	$11,700

*See page 407.

The actual overhead costs incurred during the month are recorded in the various journals by methods previously discussed and posted to the factory overhead account in the general ledger.

At the end of the accounting period, the following journal entry would be made and reflected in the accounts as shown:

Work in Process	10,800	
Factory Overhead.....................................		10,800
To apply factory overhead to production—900 units equivalent production at standard cost of $12 per unit.		

Work in Process		Factory Overhead	
10,800		11,000 (actual costs recorded from various journals) 200	10,800 (standard cost applied to work in process)

As was indicated, the factory overhead account has a debit balance of $200, which represents unabsorbed or underapplied factory overhead. The $200 is the net variance, and the debit balance shows that it is unfavorable. This net unfavorable variance can be analyzed in more detail. Illustrated below is the formula for calculating factory overhead variances using the two-variance method.

Formula for Calculating Factory Overhead Variances
Using Two-Variance Method

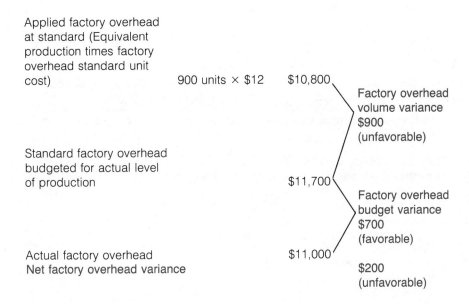

Applied factory overhead
at standard (Equivalent
production times factory
overhead standard unit
cost)   900 units × $12 $10,800

Factory overhead
volume variance
$900
(unfavorable)

Standard factory overhead
budgeted for actual level
of production $11,700

Factory overhead
budget variance
$700
(favorable)

Actual factory overhead $11,000
Net factory overhead variance $200
                                                               (unfavorable)

The amount of overhead applied to production is $900 less than the amount of overhead budgeted for the actual level of production. This variance is unfavorable because fixed overhead was underabsorbed by production. It is a volume variance because it was created when the actual production of 900 units was less than the planned or standard production of 1,000 units. The amount of actual factory overhead was $700 less than the amount budgeted at the actual level of production, creating a seemingly favorable condition and resulting in a favorable budget variance.

After the analysis of the variances, the following journal entry can be made:

```
Factory Overhead Volume Variance......................     900
    Factory Overhead Budget Variance...................            700
    Factory Overhead.....................................           200
```

This entry closes out the account for factory overhead and records the variances in individual accounts.

The entries to apply overhead and to record the variances may be combined in the following manner:

Work in Process	10,800	
Factory Overhead Volume Variance	900	
Factory Overhead Budget Variance		700
Factory Overhead		11,000

Production below the standard number of units will always produce an unfavorable volume variance for the reasons previously explained. Conversely, production greater than the standard number of units will always cause a favorable volume variance. Assume the following facts for the period:

Standard overhead cost per unit	$ 12
Number of units manufactured (120% of normal production)	1,200
Actual factory overhead	$15,000
Standard factory overhead budgeted for the actual level of production:	
Depreciation (fixed)	$ 4,000
Taxes and insurance (fixed)	1,000
Supervisory salaries (fixed)	4,000
Maintenance costs (120% × $2,000)	2,400
Supplies (120% × $1,000)	1,200
Total standard factory overhead	$12,600

Under these circumstances, the work in process account would be charged with $14,400 applied factory overhead (standard cost of $12 per unit × 1,200 units of equivalent production). The factory overhead account, as reflected below, would have a debit balance of $600 which represents a net unfavorable variance. Analysis of this variance is on page 411.

Factory Overhead	
15,000 (actual costs recorded from various journals) 600	14,400 (standard cost applied to work in process)

The breakdown of the net variance shows that there is a favorable volume variance, because factory overhead was overabsorbed in production when the actual volume of production was higher than the established standard. The unfavorable budget variance indicates that the actual overhead exceeded the amount budgeted, or allowed, at the standards for the actual level of production.

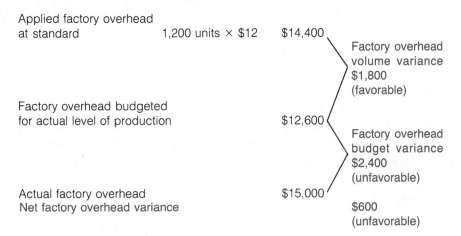

Applied factory overhead
at standard   1,200 units × $12 $14,400

Factory overhead
volume variance
$1,800
(favorable)

Factory overhead budgeted
for actual level of production $12,600

Factory overhead
budget variance
$2,400
(unfavorable)

Actual factory overhead $15,000
Net factory overhead variance $600
(unfavorable)

Both variances should be investigated to determine their cause and effect. The favorable volume variance may be due to a normal seasonal fluctuation that was anticipated, and it may offset all or part of the previous unfavorable volume variances that arose during periods of low production. However, this level of production may have occurred because the company received more orders for goods than it had anticipated. From the standpoint of increased profits, this factor is favorable; however, if the factory worked beyond an established efficient capacity of production, the quality of the product may have suffered.

The unfavorable budget variance should be scrutinized carefully to determine why the costs were higher than they should have been, where the responsibility for this condition lies, and what steps should be taken to keep these costs under control in the future. This variance could be the result of several factors, such as laxity in purchasing, inefficiency in supervision, or weak control of expenditures. However, some portion of the budget variance may result from additional machine maintenance and repair costs, which are attributable to the increased use of facilities at the higher level of production.

On the financial statements, the overhead variances will usually be treated as additions to or deductions from the standard cost of goods sold. If the variances are material, seasonal, or due to unusual circumstances, they will be treated as discussed in Chapter 8.

BUDGETED FACTORY OVERHEAD

In previous pages, there were several references to the standard amount of factory overhead allowed, or budgeted, at different levels of production.

These dollar amounts are predetermined; that is, the expense is estimated at the beginning of the year, before production is started, for varying levels of production. Using these predetermined figures, the cost accountant can determine the factory overhead variances by converting the production report data into standard costs and then comparing these costs with the actual costs that have been posted to the overhead accounts. The purpose of the following section is to discuss the procedures by which the accountant determines in advance what these standard amounts of factory overhead will be at different levels of production.

Budgets

Most successful companies today make use of operating budgets to help them in their constant effort to analyze and control operations, keep costs in line, and reduce expenses. A budget is a planning device that helps a company set goals, and it is a gauge against which actual results can be measured. Many heads of households are familiar with the basic aspects of budgeting whereby they estimate their income for the following year, determine what their living expenses will be, and then, depending on the figures, reduce unnecessary spending, set up a savings plan, or possibly determine additional ways to supplement their income. During the year, they compare their budget with their actual income and expenditures to be sure that expenses do not exceed income, and cause financial difficulties.

Budgeting in business and industry is a formal method of detailed financial planning. It encompasses the coordination and control of every item of significance in the balance sheet and income statement. Its purpose is to help the company reach its objectives, both long-term and short-term. If the principles of budgeting are carried out in a proper manner, the company can be assured that it will efficiently use all of its resources and achieve the most favorable results possible in the long run.

Basically, the primary objective of any company is to maximize its net income or attain the highest volume of sales at the lowest possible cost. Planning and control are absolutely essential in achieving this goal, and the process of budgeting produces the framework within which the organization can reach this objective. The budget then becomes a roadmap that guides management along the way and lets them know when the company is straying from its planned route. It is a chart of the course of operations, and in addition to forecasting costs and profits as a means of controlling costs, it requires those in authority in all areas of the business to analyze carefully all aspects of their responsibility for costs and also to analyze company strengths and weaknesses.

Principles of Budgeting.   The general principles of budgeting are these:

1. Management must clearly define its objectives.
2. Goals must be realistic and possible to attain.
3. Because the budgeting process involves looking to the future, the development of the budget must carefully consider economic developments, the general business climate, and the condition of the industry, as well as changes and trends that may influence sales and costs. Historical data should be used only as a stepping-off point for projections into the future.
4. There must be a plan, which is consistently followed, to constantly analyze the actual results as compared with the budget.
5. The budget must be flexible enough so that it can be modified in the light of changing conditions; it must not be so restrictive that changes cannot be made where more favorable results are foreseeable.
6. Responsibility for forecasting costs must be clearly defined, and accountability for actul results must be enforced. This principle encourages careful analysis and precise evaluation.

Preparing the Budget.   This section is not intended to be an exhaustive survey of budgeting, but is principally concerned with the preparation of the producton plan and the manufacturing expense budget. However, a brief discussion of other budgets is appropriate, so that the cost accountant can see how all budgets are interrelated and how the budget for the factory is influenced by the other budgets.

Forecast of Sales.   In preparing a budget, all the items of income and expense should be considered. The best starting point is a forecast of sales, followed by a determination of inventory policy, a production plan, a budget of manufacturing costs, and a budget for all administrative and selling expenses. The resulting amount is the budgeted net income for the year. A balance sheet forecast should also be prepared, concerned primarily with cash, receivables, and capital additions.

Although all of the aforementioned budgets are important, the forecast of sales is especially significant, because management must use this information as a basis for preparing all other budgets. This forecast is concerned with projecting the volume of sales both in units and dollars. In estimating the sales for the forthcoming year, the sales department must take into consideration present and future economic situations; it must research and carefully analyze market prospects for its products; it must consider the development of new products and the discontinuance of old products. It must make these analyses by territory, by type of product, and possibly by type of customer. Marketing researchers should also carefully survey and evaluate consumer demand. After this detailed examination, the mix of the products to be sold can be determined, as well as the volume and the sales price.

Inventory and Production Planning.   After the sales mix and volume plans have been made, the factory can proceed with the determination of production requirements. In a simple situation, assuming one product, stable production throughout the year, and an ending inventory 2,000 units greater than the beginning inventory, the number of units to be produced can be calculated as follows:

Units to be sold.	100,000
Ending inventory required.	4,500
Total.	104,500
Beginning inventory	2,500
Units to be manufactured	102,000
Units per month (102,000 ÷ 12)	8,500

In actual practice, this computation is more complex. Management must try to achieve a satisfactory balance between production, inventory, and the timely availability of goods to be sold. For example, if the company's sales are seasonal rather than evenly distributed throughout the year, stable production might produce the following situation:

NUMBER OF UNITS

	Produced	Sold	On Hand
Beginning balance			2,500
January.	8,500	1,000	10,000
February	8,500	2,000	16,500
March	8,500	3,000	22,000
April.	8,500	10,000	20,500
May	8,500	15,000	14,000
June.	8,500	15,000	7,500
July	8,500	12,000	4,000
August.	8,500	9,000	3,500
September	8,500	9,000	3,000
October.	8,500	8,000	3,500
November.	8,500	8,000	4,000
December	8,500	8,000	4,500
Total.	102,000	100,000	

The problem created here is that the company must have enough storage facility to handle as many as 22,000 units. However, most of this space would be unused during several months of the year, resulting in a waste of invested capital for inventory and storage facilities and expenditures for upkeep, insurance, and taxes that provide no direct benefit. In this situation, a manufacturing concern might lease some storage facilities during the peak months, thereby requiring a much smaller company-owned facility. However, leasing may present problems of inconvenience, expense, and unavailability of the facilities at the right time and in the right place. In addition, during some months the company would have a considerable amount of capital tied up in finished goods that could be threatened by obsolescence.

Another solution is for management to schedule different levels of production each month in order to maintain a stable inventory and to minimize the number of units stored. The following table shows this approach:

	NUMBER OF UNITS		
	Produced	Sold	On Hand
Beginning balance..................			2,500
January............................	1,500	1,000	3,000
February..........................	2,500	2,000	3,500
March.............................	3,000	3,000	3,500
April..............................	10,000	10,000	3,500
May...............................	15,000	15,000	3,500
June..............................	15,000	15,000	3,500
July...............................	12,000	12,000	3,500
August............................	9,500	9,000	4,000
September.........................	9,500	9,000	4,500
October...........................	8,000	8,000	4,500
November.........................	8,000	8,000	4,500
December.........................	8,000	8,000	4,500
Total.........................	102,000	100,000	

This alternative requires minimum storage space and related expenses, but it creates a new problem; the factory must have enough facilities to handle the peak production of 15,000 units, but these facilities would be from 50 percent to 90 percent idle during some months. A possible solution is to have a smaller facility and to engage two or three shifts of employees during the busier months. Although the facility investment problem is reduced, a bigger problem is created because the working force can vary by 1,000 percent from the slowest period to the most active. This condition would require hiring new employees in the earlier months as production is climbing, with the problem of the high cost of recruiting and training as well as the problem of quality production with new, possibly inexperienced employees. In the later months, as production drops, many workers would be laid off, creating considerable additional expense for unemployment compensation as well as hardship for the employees and a feeling of ill will toward the company.

Management is often faced with the problem of determining which course to follow — whether to maintain stable production, with the necessity of providing for storage capacity, the tie-up of capital funds in inventory, and the possibility of obsolescence; or to maintain a stable inventory, with all of the ensuing expenses of personnel and facilities. Most companies will carefully analyze the alternatives and arrive at a plan that represents a reasonable compromise between the two alternatives.

Budgets for Manufacturing Costs and Administrative and Selling Expenses.   Once the production schedule has been determined, the budget for manufacturing costs can be prepared which involves determining the costs of materials, labor, and factory overhead for each month (or week, or day) of the coming year. After standard costs have been determined, this calculation, whether for one or for several products, is relatively simple for direct materials and direct labor, involving the extension of the number of units to be produced times the standard cost per unit. However, the forecast of the factory overhead is more involved and will be considered in detail later in this section. When the level of activity has been determined for sales and production, the budgets for administrative, selling, and other expenses can be prepared. As with other forecasts, the planners must take into consideration not only the planned volume for the company but also economic conditions, trends for local and national wages and salaries, and other expenses.

Other Budgets.   Completion of these budgets permits the determination of the budgeted income statement for the year. It should be recognized that, although the discussion to this point has centered around units and dollars, the forecasts would also be used for planning the hiring (or laying off) of personnel, scheduling the purchases of materials, arranging for necessary facilities, developing sales promotion, and other appropriate functions.

The balance sheet budgets can now be prepared. The **cash budget** shows the anticipated flow of cash and the timing of receipts and disbursements based upon projected revenues, the production schedule, and expenses. Using this budget, management can plan for necessary financing or for temporary investment of surplus funds. The budget for receivables, based on anticipated sales, credit terms, the economy, and other relevant factors, will influence the cash budget by showing when cash can be expected from the turnover of inventory and receivables. A liabilities budget is also necessary, reflecting how the cash position will be affected by payment of these items.

The company may prepare a capital additions budget, which is a plan for the timing of acquisitions of buildings, equipment, or other significant assets during the year. This plan ties in with the sales and production plans and may influence the cash budget for expenditures to the extent that additional financing may be necessary.

Teamwork and cooperation in preparing the budgets are absolutely necessary. The sales, engineering, manufacturing, and accounting divisions of the company must work together to produce meaningful forecasts, because many of the estimates depend on the plans of other departments. Also, a considerable amount of coordination is required. For example, the sales goal must be compatible with the production that can be attained with the facilities available; at the same time, the amount and scheduling of production relies heavily on the needs of the marketing department. As mentioned before, some budgets can be prepared only after certain others have been completed, and they will be influenced by these other plans.

Another point to be made is that the budgets are not necessarily prepared sequentially. After the sales forecast in units is made, the manufacturing division can begin working on the production schedule and the manufacturing expense budget; the sales department can start preparing its budget for selling expenses; and the administrative expense forecast can begin. The receivables turnover schedule can also be made at this point, and possibly the capital expenditures budget can be prepared. The cash budget and the schedule of liabilities and payments cannot be considered until all of the aforementioned items are completed.

Evaluating Budget Performance. If a budget is to be used successfully as a management tool for control, the actual results must be periodically compared with the budgeted figures, and the differences must be thoroughly analyzed. Without this constant follow-up and analysis, the budget is a useless item. This principle has been discussed previously in connection with standard costs, and the same application may be made to the other planned amounts, both by unit and by dollar volume. If variances are found to exist in the number of units sold or manufactured, or in the dollar amounts of sales or expenses, or in other budgeted items, a careful evaluation of the variances must be made and responsibility determined.

Typically, performance reports are prepared for and distributed to the people who are accountable for the actual results. For example, all supervisors and department heads receive reports for their respective departments. The vice president in charge of production receives information on all elements of manufacturing involving the production and service departments. The president of the company receives reports on all functions of the business — manufacturing, sales, and administrative. These reports should clearly reflect the variances from budget in all areas so that appropriate action can be taken.

Flexible Budgeting.   The comparison of actual results with the budget to see if the planned objectives are being met leads to the use of flexible budgeting. This concept, which was introduced in Chapter 4, will be discussed from the standpoint of the factory overhead budget, but the principles are applicable to any item of expense that involves fixed and variable elements.

Implementation of a flexible budget involves planning what will happen to a company under varying sets of conditions: for example, the sale of 10,000 units per month rather than 9,000; the production of 15,000 units per month rather than 17,000; the effect of the addition or replacement of a machine in a department; or the development of new products or the discontinuance of the old. In other words, the company plans in advance what the effect will be on revenue, expense, and profit if sales or production differ from the budget. To illustrate, if budgeted sales for a month are $100,000 and the budgeted selling expense is $25,000, it is reasonable to assume that if actual sales are $80,000, the actual selling expense would be less than $25,000. If production volume was 10,000 units rather than a budgeted 9,000, the cost of production would logically be greater than the amount budgeted for 9,000 units.

The flexible budget is influenced by the presence of fixed and variable costs as discussed in Chapter 4. Fixed costs have been previously defined as those costs that do not change as production changes over a given range. They are a function of time and generally will be incurred regardless of the level of production. These expenses, such as straight-line depreciation, insurance, taxes, supervisory salaries, and others, will remain the same in dollar total, except in the extreme case of a major change in production that requires more or fewer machines, facilities, and supervisory personnel.

Many costs do vary in total dollar amount in proportion to any change in production. These variable costs, which are a function of activity, include direct labor, direct materials, indirect labor, and maintenance costs. It is because of these variable elements that the total cost differs from amounts originally budgeted when the level of production is different. If the manufacturer has budgeted production of 5,000 units for the month at a cost of $50,000 and the actual production is more or less than 5,000 units, there would be little value in comparing the actual cost of production with the items making up the $50,000 budget. Under such operating conditions, a flexible budget is useful because it shows the planned expenses at various levels of production. Thus, management can quickly determine variances by comparing the actual costs with what the costs of production should have been at the actual level of production.

Preparing the Flexible Budget for Factory Overhead.   Determining the standard overhead cost per unit and preparing the flexible budget for factory overhead follow the basic principles that were suggested for determining standards for materials and labor costs. All costs that might be incurred must be carefully considered. Prior costs, as adjusted, must be studied as well as the effect of new costs, future economic conditions, changes in processes, and trends. As with other standards, the individuals responsible for setting factory overhead standards must have considerable experience in and familiarity with manufacturing operations.

Because costs are affected by the level of production, the first step is to determine what should be the standard volume of production. Standard production is the volume on which the initial calculation of costs is based. There are several approaches used to determine this figure and several related definitions of manufacturing capacity. Some of these types of capacity are as follows:

1. Theoretical capacity represents the maximum number of units that can be produced with the completely efficient use of all available facilities and personnel. Generally this production level is almost impossible to attain. It represents a rigid standard for the factory because it requires maximum production with no allowance for inefficiencies of any kind.

2. Practical capacity is the level of production that provides complete utilization of all facilities and personnel, but allows for some idle capacity due to operating interruptions, such as machinery breakdowns, idle time, and other inescapable inefficiencies.

3. Normal capacity is the level of production that will meet the normal requirements of ordinary sales demand over a period of years. Although

it conceivably can be equal to or greater than practical capacity, normal capacity usually does not involve a plan for maximum usage of manufacturing facilities but allows for some unavoidable idle capacity and some inefficiencies in operations. Most manufacturing firms use this level of capacity for budget development because it represents a logical balance between maximum production capacity and that capacity which is demanded by actual sales volume. Furthermore, over a period of years, all factory overhead expense will normally be absorbed by production. The following discussion will assume the use of normal capacity for planning purposes.

To illustrate the flexible budget, the following figures were determined to be the factory overhead costs at the normal or standard volume of 1,000 units. (To simplify the illustration, only a few overhead classifications are used. In actual practice there would be many types of expenses broken down into fixed and variable categories.)

```
Standard production — 1,000 units
Standard direct labor hours — 2,000
Fixed cost:
    Depreciation of building and equipment..............    $ 4,000
    Property tax and insurance .......................        1,000
    Supervisory salaries...............................        4,000
        Total fixed cost ....................................            $ 9,000
Variable cost:
    Maintenance .....................................    $ 2,000
    Supplies.........................................      1,000
        Total variable cost ............................              3,000
Total factory overhead cost ..........................            $12,000

Standard factory overhead application rate per direct labor hour:
    Fixed cost ($9,000 ÷ 2,000 hours)............................    $ 4.50
    Variable cost ($3,000 ÷ 2,000 hours) .........................      1.50
Total factory overhead rate ($12,000 ÷ 2,000 hours)...............    $ 6.00

Standard overhead cost per unit ($12,000 ÷ 1,000 units)............    $12.00
```

As discussed in Chapter 4, factory overhead can be applied to work in process using different bases, such as direct labor hours, direct labor cost, or machine hours. One of the most commonly used bases is the direct labor hours method, in which overhead is applied in relation to the standard number of direct labor hours allowed for the current actual production.

In the preceding schedule, both standard units and standard hours are given, because production may be expressed in terms of units or the standard number of direct labor hours allowed for the actual production. Whichever base for measuring production is chosen, the results are not affected. Based on the budget above, if 900 units are manufactured, Work in Process would be charged with $10,800 (900 × $12) for factory overhead. If production is expressed in terms of standard direct labor hours, in this case 1,800 (900 units × 2 hours), Work in Process would still be charged with $10,800 (1,800 × $6).

The flexible budget for this illustration is shown below. The individuals responsible for the work have determined what the fixed and variable costs will be at various levels of production. Notice that the factory overhead per direct labor hour decreases as volume increases because the fixed factory overhead is being spread over more production. Further notice that the standard volume of production is expressed as being 100 percent of capacity. This production level is not necessarily the maximum capacity of the manufacturing facility; but it does represent, considering sales demand, the most efficient use of the present facilities under normal operating conditions, with some allowance for operating interruptions. A factory can always produce more than the normal volume by working overtime, adding a shift, or by squeezing in more machinery and workers; but these conditions are not normal. Since it is not uncommon to operate above or below normal, the flexible budget shows expense amounts for production above and below normal capacity of 100 percent.

Factory Overhead Cost Budget

Percent of Normal Capacity	80%	90%	100%	110%	120%
Number of units	800	900	1,000	1,100	1,200
Number of standard direct labor hours.	1,600	1,800	2,000	2,200	2,400
Budgeted factory overhead:					
Fixed cost:					
Depreciation of building and					
equipment	$ 4,000	$ 4,000	$ 4,000	$ 4,000	$ 4,000
Property taxes and insurance	1,000	1,000	1,000	1,000	1,000
Supervisory salaries	4,000	4,000	4,000	4,000	4,000
Total fixed cost	$ 9,000	$ 9,000	$ 9,000	$ 9,000	$ 9,000
Variable cost:					
Maintenance	$ 1,600	$ 1,800	$ 2,000	$ 2,200	$ 2,400
Supplies.	800	900	1,000	1,100	1,200
Total variable cost	$ 2,400	$ 2,700	$ 3,000	$ 3,300	$ 3,600
Total factory overhead cost	$11,400	$11,700	$12,000	$12,300	$12,600
Factory overhead per direct labor hour	$7.125	$6.50	$6.00	$5.59	$5.25

Using the Flexible Budget.   If actual production for a given period is exactly 1,000 units, the accountant can compare total or individual factory overhead costs incurred with these budgeted figures and determine variances as shown below.

Factory Overhead Cost Variances

Normal production . . . . 1,000 units (or 2,000 direct labor hours)
Actual production . . . . 1,000 units (or 2,000 direct labor hours)

	Budget	Actual	Variances Favorable (Unfavorable)
Fixed cost:			
Depreciation of building and equipment	$ 4,000	$ 4,000	
Property taxes and insurance	1,000	1,000	
Supervisory salaries	4,000	4,000	
Total fixed cost	$ 9,000	$ 9,000	
Variable cost:			
Maintenance	$ 2,000	$ 2,500	$(500)
Supplies	1,000	900	100
Total variable cost	$ 3,000	3,400	$(400)
Total factory overhead cost	$12,000	$12,400	$(400)

The net unfavorable variance is considered a budget, or controllable, variance because production was at normal capacity, eliminating the possibility of a volume variance.

Usually, however, factory activity will not be exactly at the normal level. The volume of production invariably fluctuates to a certain extent from the standard level because it is affected by such things as vacations, holidays, absentee employees, work interruptions, and equipment breakdowns. If a seasonal factor is involved, the fluctuation from one month to the next could be significant. Under these circumstances, the flexible budget provides the budgeted figures for the actual levels of production rather than the established normal level.

Upon receiving the report on actual volume for the period, the accountant can determine what the factory overhead costs should have been at that volume and compare these costs with the actual costs to determine variances. If the volume of production falls between two of the amounts shown in the budget, an approximation of budgeted cost can be interpolated as shown on the next page.

Actual production 850 units (85%)		
Budgeted cost at 90%..		$11,700
Budgeted cost at 80%..		11,400
Difference...		$ 300
Range between volume levels................................		10%

Dividing the difference of $300 by 10 determines an additional cost of $30 for each percentage point increase.

Next lower budgeted volume................................		80%
Costs at 80% volume.......................................		$11,400
Plus (5 × $30)..		150
Budgeted costs at 85% volume		$11,550

Semifixed and Semivariable Costs. The preceding method of determining the budgeted amount of factory overhead at a level of production different from that given in the budget is satisfactory if the overhead increases evenly throughout each range of activity, as would be the case if all costs were either fixed or variable. However, if there are significant semifixed or semivariable costs, then this method would not always be accurate enough for a meaningful evaluation.

Semifixed, or step, costs are those that tend to remain the same in dollar amount through a certain range of activity but increase when production exceeds certain limits. For example, the salary of a department head is generally considered a fixed cost, because no other department head will be employed through a given range of activity, and the salary cost will not change as the volume fluctuates. But if the production level exceeds a given number of units, an assistant department head might have to be employed to aid in supervising the greater number of workers that would be necessary. In this case, the fixed expense for supervisory personnel would increase, as illustrated below.

Percent of Normal Capacity	80%	90%	100%	110%	120%	130%
Fixed cost	$20,000	$20,000	$20,000	$20,000	$28,000	$28,000
Variable cost	24,000	27,000	30,000	33,000	36,000	39,000
Total factory overhead	$44,000	$47,000	$50,000	$53,000	$64,000	$67,000

In this case, if the actual volume of production falls into the range between 110% and 120%, the use of interpolation to determine budgeted expense would probably not be satisfactory. A careful analysis of the expenses would need to be made, without the use of interpolation, to determine whether more supervisory personnel would be needed at 119% of capacity or 111% of capacity, for example.

Semivariable costs are those that may change with production but not necessarily in direct proportion. For example, if a company incurs expense to train new employees before they go into the factory, this expense will increase as production increases and new employees are hired. But if the volume of production decreases and no new employees are hired, there will be no training expense.

The existence of semifixed or semivariable costs indicates an even greater need for careful analysis and evaluation of the costs at each level of production. A statistical analysis of semivariable expenses was discussed in Chapter 4. The approach in this chapter, however, assumes that fixed costs remain constant and variable costs vary evenly throughout the ranges of activity given unless stated otherwise.

Service Department Budgets and Variances

The preparation of a budget for a service department follows the same procedure as that for production departments. Expenses at different levels of production are estimated, and a standard rate for application of service department expenses to production departments is determined based on the type of service provided and the estimated usage by the production departments. The production departments will take these expenses into consideration in setting up their budgets.

During the period, the production departments are charged with service department expenses at the standard rate using their actual activity base, such as kilowatt hours or hours of maintenance labor. At the end of the period, the service department's actual expenses are compared with the amount charged to the production departments to determine the variances.

Summary

A summarization of the budgeting process for the factory, the determination of standard costs, and the segregation of the variances is illustrated on page 425.

1 **A Sales Forecast** in units, considering the

2 **Inventory Policy,** minimum-maximum and stable or fluctuating, helps in developing the

3 **Production Plan** in units and by periods.
   This information aids in developing the

4(a)	4(b)	4(c)
Requirements for Direct Materials (quantities and prices)	**Requirements for Direct Labor** (hours and rates)	**Requirements for Indirect Costs, Facilities, and Supplies** (fixed and variable costs)

From this information is developed the

5(a)	5(b)	5(c)
Direct Materials Budget	**Direct Labor Budget**	**Factory Overhead Budget**

From these budgets are developed the

6(a)	6(b)	6(c)
Standard Unit Cost for Direct Materials	**Standard Unit Cost for Direct Labor**	**Standard Unit Cost for Factory Overhead**

(These combined figures determine the **Standard Unit Cost for the Product.**)

7 These unit costs, when multiplied by the equivalent production for the period, determine the amount to be charged to Work in Process for each element of production cost. The costs in *6(a)* and *6(b)* above are

8(a)	8(b)	8(c)
multiplied by the actual quantity of direct materials used.	multiplied by the actual direct labor hours worked.	From the flexible budget is determined the budgeted factory overhead cost, using the standard hours allowed at the actual level of production.

The comparison of *7* and *8* determines the

9(a)	9(b)	9(c)
Materials Quantity Variance	**Labor Efficiency Variance**	**Factory Overhead Volume Variance**

The comparison of *8* above with the actual cost for the period determines the

10(a)	10(b)	10(c)
Materials Price Variance*	**Labor Rate Variance**	**Factory Overhead Budget Variance**

Unless the materials price variance is recognized at the time of purchase.

THREE-VARIANCE METHOD OF ANALYSIS

The three-variance method of factory overhead cost analysis, although not as common as the two-variance method, is used by many manufacturers. This method breaks down the difference between actual and applied overhead into three variances: (1) efficiency, (2) capacity, and (3) budget (spending).

The efficiency variance measures the difference between the overhead applied (standard hours at the standard rate) and the actual hours worked multiplied by the standard rate. It indicates the effect on fixed and variable overhead costs when the actual hours worked are more or less than standard hours allowed for the production volume. Unfavorable variances may be caused by inefficiencies in the use of labor or by other conditions; favorable efficiency variances might indicate an opposite situation.

The capacity variance indicates that the volume of production was more or less than normal. It reflects an under- or overabsorption of fixed costs and is measured by the difference between the actual hours worked, multiplied by the standard overhead rate, and the budget allowance based on actual hours worked. It indicates that the actual hours of work were more or less than the normal hours used in determining the overhead rate. This variance is considered the responsibility of management and can be due to expected seasonal variations, or it can be caused by changes in the volume of production due to poor scheduling of production, improper use of labor, strikes, or other causes.

The budget, or spending, variance reflects the difference between the amount allowed by the budget for the actual hours worked and the actual costs incurred. The saving or overspending is chargeable to a manager or a departmental supervisor who is responsible for the costs.

The budget variances here must not be confused with those used for the two-variance method; the calculations of these variances are slightly different and result in a sharper distinction in variances. The primary difference between the two methods of variance analysis is that the three-variance method determines the budget allowance based on actual hours worked rather than on the standard number of hours for the units produced.

Many accountants feel that the budgeted allowance for overhead is more appropriately based on actual labor hours than on standard labor hours. They believe there is a more definite relationship between actual hours worked and the factory expense involved and feel that the three-variance method provides a more precise analysis of overhead costs.

Formula for Calculating Factory Overhead Variances Using Three-Variance Method

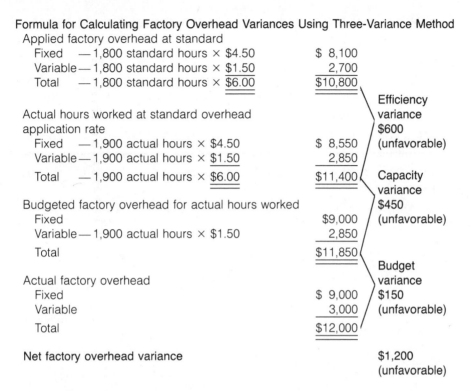

Applied factory overhead at standard
Fixed	— 1,800 standard hours × $4.50	$ 8,100
Variable	— 1,800 standard hours × $1.50	2,700
Total	— 1,800 standard hours × $6.00	$10,800

Efficiency
variance
$600
(unfavorable)

Actual hours worked at standard overhead
application rate
Fixed	— 1,900 actual hours × $4.50	$ 8,550
Variable	— 1,900 actual hours × $1.50	2,850
Total	— 1,900 actual hours × $6.00	$11,400

Capacity
variance
$450
(unfavorable)

Budgeted factory overhead for actual hours worked
Fixed		$9,000
Variable	— 1,900 actual hours × $1.50	2,850
Total		$11,850

Budget
variance
$150
(unfavorable)

Actual factory overhead
Fixed	$ 9,000
Variable	3,000
Total	$12,000

Net factory overhead variance $1,200
                                                 (unfavorable)

The following example illustrates the three-variance method, using the flexible budget presented on page 421. Assume that production was 900 units, direct labor hours worked were 1,900, and actual factory overhead totaled $12,000.

Whichever method is used, two- or three-variance, the overhead applied to production is the same because this figure is based on the standard number of labor hours allowed for the actual production. Similarly, the actual overhead would be the same. Therefore, the net variance in overhead would be the same in either approach.

The efficiency variance illustrated is unfavorable because the number of labor hours worked was more than standard. In this case, the excess of 100 hours times the standard overhead application rate of $6 equals the variance of $600 and reflects the underabsorption of fixed and variable costs.

The budgeted overhead, based on the actual hours worked, is calculated in this manner: the flexible budget is used to determine the amount of fixed overhead allowed, $9,000. Variable cost in the flexible budget is $1.50 per direct labor hour, and is multiplied by the actual number of hours worked to equal $2,850. The capacity variance theoretically reflects the cost of unused plant facilities and involves only fixed costs. At 1,900 actual labor

hours worked, $8,550 (1,900 × $4.50) of fixed cost should have been
absorbed in Work in Process, leaving $450 ($9,000 − $8,550) of fixed cost
unabsorbed. This variance is similar to the volume variance under the
two-variance method but is different in amount because it is based on actual
hours worked rather than the standard hours allowed for 900 units.

The budget variance, which is similar to the budget variance in the two-
variance method, is unfavorable because actual overhead exceeded the budgeted allowance. Again, the amount differs from the two-variance method
because actual rather than standard hours are used to determine the budgeted amount.

For comparison purposes, the two-variance method would produce the
following results:

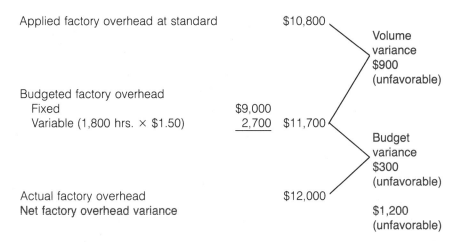

| Applied factory overhead at standard | | $10,800 | Volume variance $900 (unfavorable) |

Budgeted factory overhead			
Fixed	$9,000		
Variable (1,800 hrs. × $1.50)	2,700	$11,700	Budget variance $300 (unfavorable)

| Actual factory overhead | | $12,000 | |
| Net factory overhead variance | | | $1,200 (unfavorable) |

The following is presented as an aid to understanding the three-variance
method:

	Fixed Cost	Variable Cost	Total	
Applied overhead	$8,100	$2,700	$10,800	
Actual hours at standard rate	8,550	2,850	11,400	
Overhead underabsorbed (efficiency variance)	$ 450	$ 150	$ 600	(1)
Actual hours at standard rate	$8,550	$2,850	$11,400	
Budgeted allowance	9,000	2,850	11,850	
Overhead underabsorbed (capacity variance)	$ 450	–0–	$ 450	(2)
Budgeted allowance	$9,000	$2,850	$11,850	
Actual overhead cost	9,000	3,000	12,000	
Overhead underabsorbed (budget variance)	$ –0–	$ 150	$ 150	(3)
Total overhead underabsorbed	$ 900	$ 300	$ 1,200	

1. If the labor hours had been efficiently used, 950 units (1,900 ÷ 2 hours per unit) would have been produced. Factory overhead applied would have been $11,400 (950 units × $12), and there would have been no efficiency variance.

2. Normal capacity is 2,000 direct labor hours. Since only 1,900 hours were worked, the planned capacity was not fully utilized; therefore, all of the fixed overhead was not absorbed by production. Variable cost is not affected. Another way of calculating this variance is: Normal hours (2,000) − actual hours (1,900) = 100 idle hours × the fixed overhead application rate ($4.50) = $450 unfavorable capacity variance.

3. Actual overhead of $12,000 exceeded the budget allowance of $11,850 for 1,900 direct labor hours, therefore the budget variance is unfavorable.

KEY TERMS

Budget (412)
Budget for manufacturing costs (416)
Budget for receivables (417)
Budget variance (405)
Budgeted income statement (416)
Budgets for administrative, selling, and other expenses (416)
Capacity variance (426)
Capital additions budget (417)
Cash budget (416)
Controllable variance (405)
Efficiency variance (426)
Fixed costs (418)
Flexible budgeting (418)

Forecast of sales (413)
Liabilities budget (417)
Normal capacity (419)
Practical capacity (419)
Semifixed costs (423)
Semivariable costs (424)
Spending variance (426)
Standard production (419)
Step costs (423)
Theoretical capacity (419)
Three-variance method (425)
Two-variance method (404)
Variable costs (419)
Volume variance (406)

QUESTIONS

1. How is the standard cost per unit for factory overhead determined?
2. How is factory overhead cost applied to work in process in a standard cost accounting system?

3. What is a budget variance?
4. Why is it important to determine budget variances?
5. Distinguish between fixed and variable costs and give examples of each.
6. What is a volume variance?
7. What is the significance of a volume variance?
8. If production is more or less than the standard volume, is it possible that there would be no budget or volume variances? Explain.
9. What is a budget?
10. What is the advantage of using budgets for business and industry?
11. What are the six principles of good budgeting?
12. Which budget must be prepared before the others? Why?
13. If the sales forecast estimates that 50,000 units of product will be sold during the following year, should the factory plan on manufacturing 50,000 units in the coming year? Explain.
14. Discuss the advantages and disadvantages of
    (a) a stable production policy and
    (b) a stable inventory policy for a company that has greatly fluctuating sales during the year.
15. After budgets have been prepared in units and dollars, what other activities can be planned?
16. What is a flexible budget?
17. Define
    (a) theoretical capacity,
    (b) practical capacity, and
    (c) normal capacity.
18. Is it possible for a factory to operate at more than 100 percent of capacity?
19. If a factory operates at 100 percent of capacity one month, 90 percent of capacity the next month, and at 105 percent of capacity the next, will a different cost per unit be charged to Work in Process each month for factory overhead?
20. At the end of the current fiscal year, the trial balance of Crowley Corporation revealed the following debit balances:

    Budget Variance — $2,000
    Volume Variance — $75,000

    What conclusions can be drawn from these two variances?

(AICPA adapted)

EXERCISES

Exercise 9-1   Factory overhead and various calculations.

The normal capacity of a manufacturing plant is 5,000 units per month. Fixed overhead at this volume is $2,500 and variable overhead is $7,500.

Additional data are as follows:

	Month 1	Month 2
Actual production (units)...................	5,300	4,800
Actual factory overhead......................	$9,900	$9,400

(a)   Determine the amount of factory overhead allowed for the actual levels of production.

(b)   Calculate variances for each month for factory overhead. Indicate whether these variances are favorable or unfavorable.

Exercise 9-2   Factory overhead and various calculations.

The standard capacity of a factory is 8,000 units per month. Cost and production data are as follows:

Standard application rate for fixed overhead	$ .50 per unit
Standard application rate for variable overhead	$1.50 per unit
Production — Month I..............................	7,200 units
Production — Month II	8,400 units
Actual factory overhead — Month I..................	$14,500
Actual factory overhead — Month II.................	$17,600

(a)   Determine the amount of factory overhead allowed for the actual volume of production each month.

(b)   Calculate the variances for factory overhead, indicating whether these variances are favorable or unfavorable.

(c)   Explain the significance of the variances.

The following data and instructions are to be used for Exercises 3 through 5:

The normal operating capacity of the Medley Mfg. Co. is 1,000 units. At this level of production, the standard factory overhead is $3,000 (fixed costs, $1,000; variable costs, $2,000).

For each exercise below, prepare the journal entry to record the application of factory overhead to work in process and to record the variances and state whether each variance is favorable or unfavorable.

Exercise 9-3   Journal entries for factory overhead and variances.

Equivalent production — 1,000 units; actual factory overhead — $3,200.

Exercise 9-4   Journal entries for factory overhead and variances.

Equivalent production — 950 units; actual factory overhead — $3,200.

Exercise 9-5   Journal entries for factory overhead and variances.

Equivalent production — 1,050 units; actual factory overhead — $3,200.

Exercise 9-6   Journal entries for factory overhead and variances; analysis of variances.

The normal capacity of a manufacturing plant is 30,000 direct labor hours or 20,000 units per month. Standard fixed costs are $6,000 and variable costs are $12,000.

Data for two months are as follows:	March	April
Units produced	18,000	21,000
Factory overhead incurred	$16,500	$19,000

For each month, prepare journal entries to charge overhead to Work in Process and to record variances. Indicate the types of variances and state whether each variance is favorable or unfavorable.

Exercise 9-7   Determining amount of factory overhead applied to work in process.

The overhead application rate for a company is $2.50 per unit, made up of $1.00 for fixed overhead and $1.50 for variable overhead. Normal capacity is 10,000 units. In one month there was an unfavorable budget variance of $200. Actual overhead for the month was $27,000. What was the amount of factory overhead applied to work in process?

Exercise 9-8   Preparing production budget and materials budget.

The sales department of your company has forecast sales in March to be 10,000 units. Additional information is as follows:

Finished goods inventory, March 1	1,000 units
Finished goods inventory required, March 31	3,000 units

Materials used in production:

	Inventory March 1	Required Inventory March 31	Standard Cost
A (one gallon per unit)	500 gal.	1,000 gal.	$2 per gal.
B (one pound per unit)	1,000 lbs.	1,000 lbs.	$1 per lb.

Prepare:
(a) a production budget for March (in units).
(b) a materials budget for the month (in units and dollars).

PROBLEMS

Problem 9-1   Overhead application rate; calculation of all variances.

Marley Manufacturing Company uses a job order costing system and standard costs. It manufactures one product whose standard cost is as follows:

Materials, 20 yards @ $.90 per yard	$18
Direct labor, 4 hours @ $9.00 per hour	36
Total factory overhead, (the ratio of variable costs to fixed costs is 3 to 1)	32
Total unit cost.	$86

The standards are set based on normal activity of 2,400 direct labor hours. Actual activity for the month of October was as follows:

Materials purchased, 18,000 yards @ $.92.	$16,560
Materials used 9,500 yards	
Direct labor, 2,100 hours @ $9.15.	19,215
Total factory overhead, 500 units actually produced.	17,760

Required:
1. Compute the variable factory overhead rate per direct labor hour and the total fixed factory overhead based on normal activity.
2. Prepare a schedule computing the following variances for the month of October:
    (a) Materials quantity variance.
    (b) Materials purchase price variance.
    (c) Labor efficiency variance.

    (d)   Labor rate variance.
    (e)   Overhead budget (controllable) variance.
    (f)   Overhead volume variance.
    Indicate whether each variance is favorable or unfavorable.

(AICPA adapted)

Problem 9-2   Journal entries; variance analysis; other analyses.

Cost and production data for the Nature Products Co. are as follows:

Standard Cost Sheet
(Normal capacity — 1,000 units)

	Dept. A	Dept. B	Total
Materials:			
I — 2 lbs. @ $2	$ 4		
II — 2 lbs. @ $1		$ 2	$ 6
Labor:			
2 hours @ $5	10		
1 hour @ $6		6	16
Factory overhead: (per standard labor hour)			
Fixed Variable			
$2 $1	6		
1 3		4	10
Total	$20	$12	$32

Production Report

	Dept. A	Dept. B
Beginning units in process	None	None
Units finished and transferred	1,000	900
Ending units in process	200	100
Stage of completion	½	½

Cost Data

	Dept. A		Dept. B	
Direct materials used:				
I — 2,300 lbs		$ 4,715		
II — 1,850 lbs				$1,813
Direct labor:				
2,150 hours		10,965		
1,000 hours				5,900
Factory overhead:				
Indirect materials	$1,000		$ 500	
Indirect labor	1,300		1,000	
Other	4,400	6,700	2,250	3,750
Total		$22,380		$11,463

During the month 850 units were sold at $50 each.

Note: Materials, labor, and overhead are added evenly throughout the process.

Required:

1. Prepare all entries, in general journal form, to record all transactions and variances. (Use the two-variance method for overhead variance analysis.)
2. Prove balances of Work in Process in both departments.
3. Prove that all costs have been accounted for.
4. Determine the gross margin:
   (a) at standard cost
   (b) at actual cost

Problem 9-3   Flexible budget; overhead variance analysis.

Presented below are the monthly factory overhead cost budget at normal capacity of 5,000 units or 20,000 direct labor hours and the production and cost data for a month.

Factory Overhead Cost Budget

Fixed cost:

Depreciation on building and machinery.........	$1,200	
Taxes on building and machinery...............	500	
Insurance on building and machinery	500	
Superintendent's salary	1,500	
Supervisors' salaries..........................	2,300	
Maintenance wages	1,000	$7,000

Variable cost:

Repairs	$ 400	
Maintenance supplies	300	
Other supplies................................	200	
Payroll taxes.................................	800	
Small tools	300	2,000
Total standard factory overhead		$9,000

Production and Cost Data

Number of units produced	4,000

Factory overhead:

Depreciation on building and machinery...................	$1,200
Supervisors' salaries.....................................	2,300
Insurance on building and machinery	480
Maintenance supplies	200
Maintenance wages.......................................	1,050
Other supplies...	150
Payroll taxes...	650

Repairs	275
Small tools	170
Superintendent's salary	1,500
Taxes on building and machinery	525

Required:

Use the factory overhead cost budget for instructions 1. through 4.:

1. Assuming that variable costs will vary in direct proportion to the change in volume, prepare a flexible budget for production levels of 80 percent, 90 percent, and 110 percent. Also determine the rate for application of factory overhead to work in process at each level of volume.
2. Prepare a flexible budget for production levels of 80 percent, 90 percent, and 110 percent, assuming that variable costs will vary in direct proportion to the change in volume but with the following exceptions:
    (a) At 110 percent of capacity, an assistant department head will be needed at a salary of $10,500 annually.
    (b) At 80 percent of capacity, the repairs expense will drop to one half of the amount at 100 percent capacity.
    (c) Maintenance supplies expense will remain constant at all levels of production.
    (d) At 80 percent of capacity, one part-time maintenance worker, earning $6,000 a year, will be laid off.
    (e) At 110 percent of capacity, a machine not normally in use and on which no depreciation is normally recorded will be used in production. Its cost was $12,000 and it has a ten-year life.
3. Using the flexible budget prepared in (1), determine the budgeted cost at 92 percent of capacity using interpolation.
4. Using the flexible budget prepared in (1), determine the budgeted cost at 104 percent of capacity using a method other than interpolation.
5. Using the production and cost data for a month and the flexible budget prepared in 1.:
    (a) Determine the variances.
    (b) Explain the meaning of the variances.
    (c) Prepare a schedule comparing the actual and budgeted items and showing the variance for each item of factory overhead. Indicate unfavorable variances by putting them in parentheses.

Problem 9-4   Variance analysis.

Nero Shirts, Inc., manufactures men's sport shirts for large stores. Nero produces a single quality shirt in lots of a dozen according to each customer's order and attaches the store's label. The standard costs for a dozen shirts are:

Direct materials	24 yards @ $ .55	$13.20
Direct labor.......................	3 hours @ $7.35	22.05
Factory overhead	3 hours @ $2.00	6.00
Standard cost per dozen..........		$41.25

During October, Nero worked on three orders for shirts. Job cost records for the month disclose the following:

Lot	Units in Lot	Materials Used	Hours Worked
30	1,000 dozen	24,100 yards	2,980
31	1,700 dozen	40,440 yards	5,130
32	1,200 dozen	28,825 yards	2,890

The following information is also available:

(a) Nero purchased 95,000 yards of materials during the month at a cost of $53,200. The materials price variance is recorded when goods are purchased and all inventories are carried at standard cost.

(b) Direct labor incurred amounted to $81,400 during October. According to payroll records, production employees were paid $7.40 per hour.

(c) Overhead is applied on the basis of direct labor hours. Factory overhead totaling $22,800 was incurred during October.

(d) A total of $288,000 was budgeted for overhead for the year based on estimated production at the plant's normal capacity of 48,000 dozen shirts per year. Overhead is 40 percent fixed and 60 percent variable at this level of production.

(e) There was no work in process at October 1. During October, Lots 30 and 31 were completed, and all materials were issued for Lot 32, which was 80 percent completed as to labor.

Required:

1. Prepare a schedule computing the standard cost for October of Lots 30, 31, and 32.

2. Prepare a schedule computing the materials price variance for October and indicate whether the variance is favorable or unfavorable.

3. For each lot produced during October, prepare schedules computing the following (and indicate whether the variances are favorable or unfavorable):
   (a) Materials quantity variance in yards
   (b) Labor efficiency variance in hours
   (c) Labor rate variance in dollars

4. Prepare a schedule computing the total budget and volume overhead variances for October and indicate whether the variances are favorable or unfavorable.

(AICPA adapted)

Problem 9-5   Schedule of production and standard cost; variance analysis; mix and yield variances.

Rossi Pool Product Company processes one compound product known as CLEAN and uses a standard cost accounting system. The process requires preparation and blending of three materials in large batches with a variation from the standard mixture sometimes necessary to maintain quality. Rossi's cost accountant became ill at the end of October and you were engaged to determine standard costs of October production and explain any differences between actual and standard costs for the month. The following information is available for the blending department:

(a)   The standard cost ledger for a 500-pound batch shows the following standard costs:

	Quantity	Price	Total Cost	
Materials:				
Compound #1	250 lbs.	$ .14	$35	
Compound #2	200 lbs	.09	18	
Other ingredients........	50 lbs.	.08	4	
Total per batch........	500 lbs.			$ 57
Labor:				
Preparation and blending .	10 hours	$6.00		60
Factory Overhead:				
Variable	10 hours	$1.00	$10	
Fixed..................	10 hours	.30	3	13
Total standard cost per 500-pound batch				$130

(b)   During October, 410 batches of 500 pounds each of the finished compound were completed and transferred to the packaging department.

(c)   Blending department inventories totaled 6,000 pounds at the beginning of the month and 9,000 pounds at the end of the month (assume both inventories were completely processed but not transferred, and consisted of materials in their standard proportions). Inventories are carried in the accounts at standard cost prices.

(d)   During the month of October, the following materials were purchased and put into production:

	Pounds	Price	Total Cost
Compound #1	114,400	$.17	$19,448
Compound #2	85,800	.11	9,438
Other ingredients................	19,800	.07	1,386
Total	220,000		$30,272

(e)   Wages paid for 4,212 hours of direct labor at $6.25 per hour amounted to $26,325.

(f)   Actual overhead costs for the month totaled $5,519.

(g)   The standards were established for a normal production volume of 200,000 pounds (400 batches) of CLEAN per month. At this level of production, variable factory overhead was budgeted at $4,000 and fixed factory overhead was budgeted at $1,200.

Required:

1. Prepare a schedule for the blending department presenting the computations of the following:
   - (a) October production in both pounds and batches.
   - (b) The standard cost of October production itemized by components of materials, labor, and overhead.
2. Prepare schedules computing the differences between actual and standard costs and analyzing the differences as:
   - (a) Materials variances (for each material) caused by:
     - (1) Quantity difference
     - (2) Price difference
   - (b) Labor variances caused by:
     - (1) Efficiency difference
     - (2) Rate difference
   - (c) Factory overhead variances caused by:
     - (1) Budget factors
     - (2) Volume factors
3. Calculate materials mix and yield variances.

(AICPA adapted)

Problem 9-6   Analyses.

On May 1, Metro Company began the manufacture of a new mechanical device known as "Handy." The company installed a standard cost system in accounting for manufacturing costs. The standard costs for a unit of Handy are as follows:

Raw materials (5 lbs. @ $1 per lb.)	$ 5
Direct labor (1 hour @ $8 per hour)	8
Overhead (50% of direct labor costs)	4
	$17

The following data were obtained from Metro's records for the month of May:

	Units
Actual production	4,000
Units sold	2,500

	Debit	Credit
Sales		$50,000
Purchases (22,000 pounds)	$23,300	
Materials price variance	1,300	
Materials quantity variance....................	1,000	
Direct labor rate variance	770	
Direct labor efficiency variance.................		1,200
Manufacturing overhead total variance	500	

The amount shown above for materials price variance is applicable to raw materials purchased during May.

Required:

Compute each of the following items for Metro for the month of May. Show computations in good form.
1. Standard quantity of raw materials allowed (in pounds)
2. Actual quantity of raw materials used (in pounds)
3. Standard hours allowed
4. Actual hours worked
5. Actual direct labor rate
6. Actual total overhead

(AICPA adapted)

Problem 9-7   Three-variance overhead analysis.

Using the data provided in Problem 9-2, calculate the overhead cost variances under the three-variance method.

Problem 9-8   Variance analysis using the three-variance method for overhead costs.

The Smith Furniture Company uses a standard cost system in accounting for its production costs.

The standard cost of a unit of furniture follows:

Lumber, 100 feet @ $150 per 1,000 feet....................		$15.00
Direct labor, 4 hours @ $10 per hour......................		40.00
Factory overhead: Fixed (15% of direct labor)......	$ 6.00	
Variable (30% of direct labor)....	12.00	18.00
Total unit cost......................................		$73.00

The following flexible monthly overhead budget is in effect:

Direct Labor Hours	Estimated Overhead
5,200	$21,600
4,800	20,400
4,400	19,200
4,000 (normal capacity)..............	18,000
3,600	16,800

The actual unit costs for the month of December were as follows:

Lumber used (110 feet @ $120 per 1,000 feet)..............	$13.20
Direct labor (4¼ hours @ $10.24 per hour)	43.52
Factory overhead ($21,120 ÷ 1,200 units)	17.60
Total actual unit cost	$74.32

Required:

Prepare a schedule that shows an analysis of each element of the total variance from standard cost for the month of December. (Use the three-variance method for overhead costs).

(AICPA adapted)

Problem 9-9   Journal entries; three-variance analysis; income statement.

The P. R. Jones Company uses a standard cost system. The standards are based on a budget for operations at the rate of production anticipated for the current period. The company records in its general ledger variations in materials prices and usage, wage rates, and labor efficiency. The accounts for manufacturing costs reflect variations in activity from the projected rate of operations, variations of actual expense from amounts budgeted, and variations in the efficiency of production.

Current standards are as follows:
  Direct materials:
    Material A . . . . $1.20 per unit
    Material B . . . .   2.60 per unit
    Direct labor. . . . .   6.05 per hour

	Special Widgets	Deluxe Widgets
Finished products (content of each unit):		
Material A	12 units	12 units
Material B	6 units	8 units
Direct labor.	14 hours	20 hours

The general ledger does not include a finished goods inventory account; costs are transferred directly from Work in Process to Cost of Goods Sold at the time finished products are sold.

The budget and operating data for the month of March are summarized as follows:

Budget:
  Projected direct labor hours   9,000
  Fixed factory overhead . . . . $ 4,500
  Variable factory overhead   13,500
  Selling expense.   4,000
  Administrative expense   7,500
Operating data:
  Sales:
    500 special widgets $85,000
    100 deluxe widgets   25,000
  Purchases:
    Material A — 8,500 units . . . . $ 9,725
    Material B — 1,800 units   5,635

Materials requisitions:	Material A	Material B
Issued from stores:		
Standard quantity	8,400 units	3,200 units
Over standard	400 units	150 units
Returned to stores	75 units	none
Direct labor hours:		
Standard.		9,600 hours
Actual		10,000 hours

Wages paid:	Expenses:	
500 hours @ $6.10	Manufacturing.	$20,125
8,000 hours @ 6.00	Selling.	3,250
1,500 hours @ 5.90	Administrative	6,460

Required:

1. Prepare journal entries to record operations for the month of March. Show computations of the amounts used in each journal entry. Materials purchases are recorded at standard.

2. Prepare an income statement for the month supported by an analysis of variations.

(AICPA adapted)

COST ANALYSIS FOR MANAGEMENT DECISION MAKING

LEARNING OBJECTIVES

In studying this chapter, you will learn about the:

■ Differences between the direct costing and absorption costing methods of accounting for manufacturing costs

■ Concept of segment profitability analysis and the necessary distinction between direct and indirect costs

■ Uses and limitations of cost-volume-profit analysis in management decision making

■ Various concepts of "cost", an understanding of which can aid in making choices between alternatives

■ Differential cost studies that highlight the significant cost data of alternatives in decisions such as operation versus shutdown, make or buy, and sell or process further

■ Techniques used to analyze and control the distribution costs incurred in selling and delivering the products

The features that distinguish cost accounting from managerial accounting are not well defined. To a great degree the differences between the two areas are subjective. Most cost accounting textbooks (including this textbook) give considerable attention to the managerial uses of cost data by interweaving the data uses and management needs as part of the discussions involving the cost systems. Most managerial accounting textbooks include at least some discussion of cost systems and the accumulation and processing of cost data. However, the more comprehensive the coverage of cost accounting systems (job order, process, and standard), the more analytical and methodical can be the approach to resolving the special problems that are encountered internally by manufacturing firms.

Most studies that generate special reports for management make use of the regularly accumulated cost data and at times also create additional data. These reports, which are prepared for internal use and are not distributed to external parties, require an understanding of terminology that is not regularly used in operational cost accounting systems. In this chapter, several new terms relating to the special-purpose reports prepared exclusively for internal management decision making are introduced and defined.

DIRECT COSTING AND ABSORPTION COSTING

Under the **direct costing** method, the cost of a manufactured product includes only the costs that vary directly with volume — direct materials, direct labor, and variable factory overhead. This method is also referred to as **variable costing,** since only variable manufacturing costs are assigned to the product, while fixed factory overhead is charged against revenue in the period incurred.

The alternative to direct costing is the **absorption costing** or **full cost method** (the method used in the preceding nine chapters). Under this method, both fixed and variable manufacturing costs are assigned to the product.

Product Costs versus Period Costs

All costs, both manufacturing and nonmanufacturing, can be classified as either product costs or period costs. As discussed in previous chapters, a **product cost** (or inventory cost) is assigned to Work in Process and subsequently to Finished Goods. When inventory is sold, product costs are recognized as expense (cost of goods sold) and matched with the related revenues. In contrast, **period costs** are not assigned to the product but are recognized as expenses in the period incurred. All nonmanufacturing costs are period costs. These include selling expenses and general and administrative expenses.

The only difference between direct costing and absorption costing is the classification of fixed factory overhead. Under the direct costing method, fixed overhead costs are classified as period costs. Under the absorption costing method, they are treated as product costs.

Illustration of Direct and Absorption Costing Methods

To illustrate the differences between direct costing and absorption costing, assume the following conditions for a 3-month period:

Selling price per unit..	$11

Variable cost per unit:	
Direct cost —materials....................................	$ 2
—labor	2
Indirect cost—variable factory overhead......................	1
Variable cost per unit.......................................	$ 5

Fixed cost per unit:	
Fixed factory overhead for the year.........................	$108,000
Normal production for the year in units......................	36,000
Fixed cost per unit—($108,000 ÷ 36,000)....................	$ 3

	Units Produced	Units Sold
January....................................	3,000	1,500
February..................................	500	2,000
March	4,000	2,000

There are no beginning inventories for January.

The comparative production report in Illustration 10-1 shows the costs charged to the product under each costing method. Note that under the absorption costing method, the goods manufactured in January are charged with the standard costs of the direct materials, direct labor, and both fixed and variable factory overhead, totaling $8 per unit. Under the direct costing method, the fixed factory overhead is not charged to the product, resulting in a unit cost of $5.

Illustration 10-2 presents a comparison of the average fixed factory overhead of $9,000 ($108,000 ÷ 12) per month with the amount that is applied to production, using the absorption method. In January, 3,000 units are manufactured, and the manufacturing costs under absorption costing include $9,000 ($3 × 3,000) in fixed factory overhead. February manufacturing costs covering the 500 units produced include fixed factory

Comparative Production Report

	January (3,000 units)		February (500 units)		March (4,000 units)	
	Absorption Costing	Direct Costing	Absorption Costing	Direct Costing	Absorption Costing	Direct Costing
Direct materials	$ 6,000	$ 6,000	$ 1,000	$ 1,000	$ 8,000	$ 8,000
Direct labor.	6,000	6,000	1,000	1,000	8,000	8,000
Variable factory overhead	3,000	3,000	500	500	4,000	4,000
Fixed factory overhead .	9,000	—	1,500	—	12,000	—
Total cost	$24,000	$15,000	$ 4,000	$ 2,500	$32,000	$20,000
Unit cost	$8	$5	$8	$5	$8	$5

Illustration 10-1   **Comparison of Manufacturing Costs for Absorption and Direct Costing Methods**

Fixed Overhead Applied — Absorption Costing

	January	February	March
Monthly fixed factory overhead	$9,000	$9,000	$ 9,000
Fixed factory overhead applied	9,000	1,500	12,000
Under- (over) applied overhead	–0–	$7,500	$ (3,000)

Illustration 10-2   **Schedule of Fixed Overhead Applied under Absorption Costing Method**

overhead of $1,500, and the manufacturing costs for March include $12,000. The result of the overhead charges is that in February $7,500 of fixed expense is not included in manufacturing costs; but in March, the fixed overhead is overapplied by $3,000. These variances of underapplied and overapplied factory overhead are reflected in the income statements for February and March as an addition to and a deduction from cost of goods sold, respectively. Under the direct costing method, no fixed factory overhead expenses are charged to production in any month. These fixed costs appear as an expense on each month's income statement.

Illustration 10-3 shows the comparative effects on income of the direct and absorption methods. Each month, cost of goods sold reflects a cost of $8 per unit under the absorption method and $5 per unit under the direct method. Under the absorption method, the difference between sales revenue and cost of goods sold is termed the gross margin or gross profit. The term commonly used in direct costing to denote the difference between sales and

COMPARATIVE INCOME STATEMENTS
For Three Months Ended March 31, 19--

	January (1,500 units sold)		February (2,000 units sold)		March (2,000 units sold)	
	Absorption Costing	Direct Costing	Absorption Costing	Direct Costing	Absorption Costing	Direct Costing
Sales..................	$ 16,500	$16,500	$ 22,000	$ 22,000	$ 22,000	$ 22,000
Cost of goods sold........	(12,000)	(7,500)	(16,000)	(10,000)	(16,000)	(10,000)
(Under)/overapplied factory overhead	—	—	(7,500)	—	3,000	—
Gross margin (loss)	$ 4,500		$(1,500)		$ 9,000	
Contribution margin		$9,000		$ 12,000		$ 12,000
Less:						
Fixed factory overhead ..		(9,000)		(9,000)		(9,000)
Selling and administrative expenses	(2,000)	(2,000)	(2,000)	(2,000)	(2,000)	(2,000)
Net income (loss)	$ 2,500	$(2,000)	$(3,500)	$ 1,000	$ 7,000	$ 1,000

COMPARATIVE SCHEDULE OF COST OF GOODS SOLD
For Three Months Ended March 31, 19--

Finished goods inventory, January 1................	—	—	$ 12,000	$ 7,500	—	—
Cost of goods manufactured	$ 24,000	$ 15,000	4,000	2,500	$ 32,000	$ 20,000
Goods available for sale...	$ 24,000	$ 15,000	$ 16,000	$ 10,000	$ 32,000	$ 20,000
Less finished goods inventory, March 31	12,000	7,500	—	—	16,000	10,000
Cost of goods sold........	$ 12,000	$ 7,500	$ 16,000	$ 10,000	$ 16,000	$ 10,000

Illustration 10-3 Comparison of Net Income for Absorption and Direct Costing Methods

cost of goods sold is contribution margin. Since cost of goods sold determined under the absorption method includes both fixed and variable overhead, but includes only variable overhead under the direct method, the gross margin under absorption costing is always lower than the contribution margin under direct costing.

Under the absorption method, selling and administrative expenses are deducted from the gross margin to determine net income or loss for the month. In the illustration, these costs are assumed to be $2,000 each month. Under the direct method, the total amount of monthly fixed overhead is deducted from the contribution margin along with selling and administrative expenses. Thus $9,000 of fixed overhead costs are charged against revenue each month regardless of the number of units produced or sold.

An examination of the comparative income statements in Illustration 10-3 reveals the effect that fluctuating production has on reported income under the absorption costing method. Although sales in February are higher than in January, the net income decreased from $2,500 in January to a net loss of $3,500 in February under the absorption method. This decrease is caused in part by adding $7,500 of underapplied overhead at the end of February to the cost of goods sold.

In March the sales are the same as in February, but reported net income increased from a $3,500 net loss in February to a $7,000 net income in March. This increase is due to the increased production which caused considerably more of the fixed factory overhead to be applied to production in March than in February. In fact, overhead is overapplied in March, and this overapplication is shown as a decrease in cost of goods sold on the March statement.

A study of the income statement under the direct costing method shows that as sales increase in February, income also increases. When sales remain the same in March as they were in February, income does not change.

With the absorption costing method, inventories are reported at a higher amount than under the direct costing method, because fixed costs are included in the cost of inventory. This element of fixed cost will not be reported as a deduction from revenue until the goods are sold and the unit cost becomes an expense in the cost of goods sold section of the income statement. Under the direct costing method, no fixed costs are included in inventory; they are charged against revenue in the period in which they are incurred.

Merits and Limitations of Direct Costing

The merits of direct costing may be viewed in terms of the usefulness of the data provided by its application. Some company managers believe that the direct costing method furnishes more understandable data regarding costs, volumes, revenues, and profits to members of management who are not trained in accounting. It presents cost data in a manner that highlights the relationship between sales and variable production costs, which move in the same direction as sales. Furthermore, management planning is aided, because direct costing presents a much clearer picture of the effect of changes in production volume on costs and income. From the direct costing portion of the production report on page 446, management can ascertain that any units produced and sold over and above normal production will cost only $5 each in out-of-pocket expenditures for variable costs, since the fixed manufacturing costs have all been absorbed by normal production, and will therefore produce marginal income of $6 each at a normal selling price of $11. Assume that plant capacity is not fully utilized and that management has the opportunity to fill a special order at a selling price of $7 each. If management incorrectly used the absorption cost of $8 per unit in Illustration 10-1, it would reject the special order. If it correctly compared the selling price of $7 to the additional variable costs of $5 that would be incurred to produce each unit, management would accept the special order and earn additional income of $2 per unit. The point is that the fixed overhead cost of $3 per unit will be incurred whether or not the special order is accepted, and therefore should not be included in the decision analysis.

Although direct costing may provide useful information for internal decision making, it is not a generally accepted method of inventory costing for external reporting purposes. The measurement of income, in traditional accounting theory, is based on the matching of revenues with associated costs. Under absorption costing, product costs include all variable and fixed manufacturing costs. These costs are matched with the sales revenue in the period in which the goods are sold. The direct cost method, however, matches only the variable manufacturing costs with revenue. The absorption method must be applied for income tax purposes as well as for external financial statements. Regulations of the Internal Revenue Service specifically prohibit the direct costing method in computing taxable income.

There are other limitations and criticisms of direct costing. Even when sophisticated statistical techniques are used to separate costs into variable and fixed components, these techniques may lead to erroneous conclusions.

The procedures often use historical data adjusted for future expectations in order to establish the components; but unforeseen occurrences may have a significant effect on such established cost categories. To avoid overlooking significant changes in cost behavior patterns, therefore, a systematic review of the costs and the statistical techniques should be provided in the system. Any unexpected change can then be analyzed for its effect on the categories of costs so that faulty data will not be used in decision making.

Direct costing is also criticized because no fixed factory overhead cost is included in work in process or finished goods inventories. In the opinion of direct costing opponents, both fixed and variable costs are incurred in manufacturing products. Since the inventory figures do not reflect the total cost of production, they do not present a realistic cost valuation.

Adjustments can be made to the inventory figures to reflect absorption cost on published financial reports while retaining the benefits of direct costing internally for income analysis purposes. In the example given, the unit cost was $5 under the direct costing method and $8 under the absorption method. The latter method reflects 60% more cost than the first method; therefore, inventories could be adjusted as follows:

	Ending Inventory Under the Direct Costing Method	Absorption-Direct Cost Ratio ($8 ÷ $5)	Ending Inventory Under the Absorption Costing Method
January...............	$ 7,500	×160%	$12,000
February..............	None		None
March	$10,000	×160%	$16,000

SEGMENT REPORTING FOR PROFITABILITY ANALYSIS

Segment reporting provides data that can be used by management to evaluate the operations and profitability of individual segments within a company. A segment may be a division, a product line, a sales territory, or other identifiable organizational unit.

The results of a segment profitability analysis may be questioned as to validity if it is based on absorption costing data. This is due to the fact that the measure of each company segment's profitability may be distorted by arbitrarily assigning indirect costs to the segments being examined. The contribution margin approach (as used in direct costing), which separates the fixed and variable elements that comprise cost, is often used to overcome these objections.

Segment profitability analysis requires that all costs be classified into one of two categories: direct or indirect. A **direct (traceable) cost** is a cost that can be traced to the segment being analyzed. Direct costs include both variable and fixed costs that are directly identifiable with a specific segment. An **indirect (nontraceable) cost** is a cost that cannot be identified directly with a specific segment. This cost is often referred to in segment analysis as a **common cost**. Under the contribution margin approach, only those costs that are directly traceable to a segment are assigned to the segment. The excess of segment revenue over direct costs assigned to the segment is the **segment margin**. Common costs are excluded from the computation of the segment margin.

Although common costs cannot be directly identified with a specific segment, they are identifiable as common to all segments at a particular level of an organization. Often the differences between direct and common costs are not markedly distinctive; however, the costs that will disappear when the segment is eliminated by the company should be classified as direct costs. Costs that are difficult to classify should not be assigned without a careful evaluation.

The more refinement and sophistication attempted in segment reporting, the larger the amount of costs that will become common costs. For instance, if a company consists of two divisions, each division manager's salary would be a direct cost to each division. However, if each division manufactured two products, each division's product segment report would classify the manager's salary as a common cost. An arbitrary allocation of the manager's salary to a product would distort the profitability shown for each product.

The following is an illustration of two segment reports: (1) by divisions and (2) by products for one of the divisions. The assumed company is divided into two divisions, and each division manufactures two products.

	Segment Report by Divisions			Segment Report by Products — Division One		
	Total Company	Division One	Division Two	Total Division One	Product A	Product B
Sales..............	$1,000,000	$750,000	$250,000	$750,000	$500,000	$250,000
Less variable costs	700,000	600,000	100,000	600,000	400,000	200,000
Contribution margin....	$ 300,000	$150,000	$150,000	$150,000	$100,000	$ 50,000
Less direct fixed costs:						
Production..........	$ 50,000	$ 25,000	$ 25,000	$ 20,000	$ 15,000	$ 5,000
Administration.......	75,000	40,000	35,000	15,000	10,000	5,000
Total direct fixed costs..............	$ 125,000	$ 65,000	$ 60,000	$ 35,000	$ 25,000	$ 10,000
Segment margin.......	$ 175,000	$ 85,000	$ 90,000	$115,000	$ 75,000	$ 40,000
Less common fixed costs:						
Selling.............	$ 30,000					
Production..........				$ 5,000		
Administration.......	20,000			25,000		
Total common fixed costs..........	$ 50,000			$ 30,000		
Segment margin.......				$ 85,000		
Net income	$ 125,000					

An analysis of the segment report by divisions reveals that the division segment margin was $175,000 for the total company. Division One contributed $85,000 to the margin and Division Two, $90,000. The direct fixed costs chargeable to the divisions totaled $125,000, and the non-allocated common fixed costs totaled $50,000.

When Division One is isolated and analyzed to determine how each product contributed to the segment margin of $85,000, the direct fixed costs chargeable to the individual products amount to $35,000. Product A is charged $25,000 and Product B, $10,000. Division One has non-allocated common fixed costs of $30,000, not directly chargeable to either product. For example, the $25,000 for Administration listed under common fixed costs may represent the salary of the manager of Division One who oversees the production of both products.

These reports reveal how costs shift from one category to another depending on the segment under scrutiny. Each segment report prepared for a company isolates those costs, variable and fixed, that can be charged directly to the segment elements. As different segments are analyzed, these costs may be direct costs in one segment and indirect (common) costs in another segment.

The divisions' contribution margins are determined by subtracting the variable costs from the sales. The contribution margin can be used as a guide in making management decisions in regard to shortrun problems such as pricing of special orders.

The direct fixed costs that are chargeable to each segment are subtracted from the contribution margin to determine the segment margin. The segment margin can be used as a guide relating to the segment's long-run profitability. In other words, it measures the ability of the division or product to recover not only the assigned variable costs but also the direct fixed costs that must be recovered in order to keep the company solvent in the long run. In the short run, if a segment margin is positive the segment should be retained even if the company as a whole is operating at a loss. Since the common fixed costs will usually remain at the same level even if a segment is eliminated, deleting a segment with a positive segment margin will only increase the amount of the company's net loss. The remaining revenue, after direct variable and fixed costs have been deducted, is the amount left to be applied toward the unallocated common costs and the net income of the company as a whole. The segment margin analysis is particularly beneficial as an aid to making decisions that relate to a company's long-run requirements and performance, such as changing production capacities, product pricing policies, decisions to retain or eliminate specific segments, analysis of segment managers' performance, and selecting a segment's expected return on investment.

COST-VOLUME-PROFIT ANALYSIS

The net income earned by a business is a measure of management's success in attaining its goals. In planning, management must anticipate how selling prices, costs, expenses, and profits will react to changes in activity with the activity measured in terms of capacity or volume. When the degree of variability in costs is known, the effect of volume changes can be predicted.

Cost-volume-profit (CVP) analysis is an analytical technique that uses the degrees of cost variability for measuring the effect of changes in volume on resulting profits. Such analysis assumes that the plant assets of the firm will remain the same in the short run; therefore, the established level of fixed cost will also remain unchanged during the period being studied.

Break-Even Analysis

The usual starting point in C-V-P analysis is the determination of a firm's break-even point. The break-even point can be defined as the point at which sales revenue is adequate to cover all costs to manufacture and sell the product but no profit is earned. The equation can be stated as follows:

$$\text{Sales revenue (to break even)} = \text{Cost to manufacture} + \text{Cost to sell}$$

Break-even analysis relies on segregating costs according to their degree of variability. The established groupings are usually classed as variable and fixed costs and expenses, and the break-even equation is rewritten as follows:

$$\text{Sales revenue (to break even)} = \text{Fixed costs} + \text{Variable costs}$$

The annual income statement for the Sumo Manufacturing Company in condensed form is shown below.

Sumo Manufacturing Company Income Statement For the Year Ended December 31, 19--		
Net sales (10,000 units at $10)		$100,000
Cost of goods sold:		
Materials	$20,000	
Labor	25,000	
Factory overhead	15,000	60,000
Gross margin on sales		$ 40,000
Operating expenses:		
Selling expense	$15,000	
Administrative expense	10,000	25,000
Net income		$ 15,000

The costs and expenses of the Sumo Manufacturing Company were analyzed and classified as follows:

Items	Total	Variable Costs	Fixed Costs
Materials.............................	$20,000	$20,000	
Labor................................	25,000	25,000	
Factory overhead	15,000	10,000	$ 5,000
Selling expense	15,000	10,000	5,000
Administrative expense................	10,000	5,000	5,000
	$85,000	$70,000	$15,000

The analysis shows that variable costs are 70% of net sales ($70,000 ÷ $100,000).

The break-even equation in mathematical terms is as follows:

$$\frac{\text{Break-even}}{\text{sales volume}} = \frac{\text{Total fixed costs}}{1 - (\text{Total variable costs} \div \text{Total sales volume})}$$

Using this equation, the break-even point for the Sumo Manufacturing Company would be:

$$\text{Break-even sales volume} = \frac{\$15,000}{1 - (\$70,000 \div \$100,000)}$$

$$= \frac{\$15,000}{1 - .70}$$

$$= \frac{\$15,000}{.30}$$

$$= \$50,000$$

The break-even point can also be calculated in terms of units by using the following equation:

$$\frac{\text{Break-even}}{\text{sales volume}} = \frac{\text{Total fixed cost}}{\text{Sales price per unit} - \text{Variable cost per unit}}$$

Using this equation, the break-even point for the Sumo Manufacturing Company would be:

$$\text{Break-even sales volume} = \frac{\$15,000}{\$10 - \$7}$$

$$= \frac{\$15,000}{\$3}$$

$$= 5,000 \text{ units}$$

Note that 5,000 units multiplied by a selling price of $10 per unit equals the $50,000 break-even sales volume computed above.

The break-even point can be rechecked, if desired, as follows:

Sales at break-even point..	$50,000
Less variable costs at break-even point (70% × $50,000)..........	35,000
Margin available for fixed costs..................................	$15,000
Less fixed costs	15,000
Net income (loss)...	–0–

Break-Even Chart.   The break-even point can also be graphically depicted by a break-even chart as in Illustration 10-4. The break-even chart is constructed and interpreted as follows:

1. A horizontal line, the x-axis, is drawn and divided into equal distances to represent the sales volume in dollars.
2. A vertical line, the y-axis, is drawn and spaced into equal parts representing costs and revenues in dollars.
3. A fixed cost line is drawn parallel to the x-axis at the $15,000 point on the y-axis.
4. A total cost line is drawn from the $15,000 fixed cost point on the left side of the y-axis to the $85,000 total cost point on the right side of the y-axis.
5. A sales line is drawn from the intersection of the x-axis and y-axis to the $100,000 total sales point on the right side of the y-axis.
6. The sales line intersects the total cost line at the break-even point, representing $50,000 of sales.
7. The shaded area to the left of the break-even point is the net loss area and the shaded area to the right of the break-even point is the net income area.

Break-Even Analysis for Management Decisions.   Break-even analysis can be used to help management when a decision must be made and several alternatives exist. This analysis is based on the conditions that variable costs will vary in constant proportion to the sales volume and the fixed costs will be fixed over a prescribed or relevant range of activity. If management, therefore, wishes to test new proposals that will change the percentage of variable costs to sales volume, or the total amount of fixed costs, or even a combination of these changes, the basic break-even equation can be used to calculate the results.

For example, assume that the Sumo Manufacturing Company, now that it has established its break-even point in sales volume at $50,000, wishes

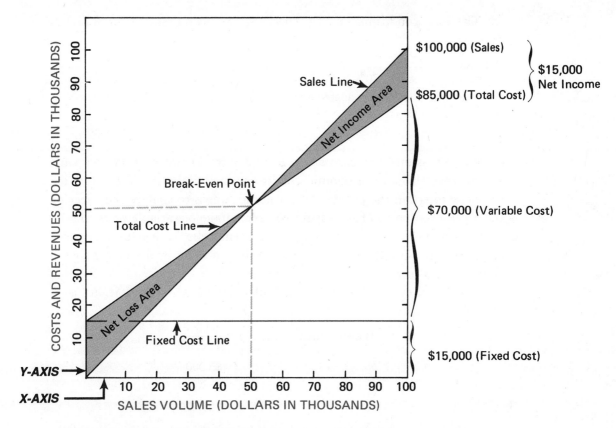

Illustration 10-4   Break-Even Chart

to determine the point at which an $18,000 net income can be expected. The $18,000 net income is viewed as a nonvariable factor, and the sales volume would be calculated as follows, using a modified equation:

$$\text{Sales volume} = \frac{\text{Total fixed costs} + \text{Net income}}{1 - (\text{Total variable costs} \div \text{Total sales volume})}$$

$$= \frac{\$15,000 + \$18,000}{1 - (\$70,000 \div \$100,000)}$$

$$= \frac{\$33,000}{1 - .70}$$

$$= \frac{\$33,000}{.30}$$

$$= \$110,000$$

The new conditions can be checked, in income statement form, as follows:

Sales..	$110,000
Less variable costs (70% × $110,000).........................	77,000
Margin available for nonvariable factors......................	$ 33,000
Less fixed costs	15,000
Net income..	$ 18,000

Further assume that the management of Sumo Manufacturing Company, fearing that changing economic conditions may make it difficult for the company to attain the present sales volume, wants to analyze the effect on the break-even point of increasing the percentage of variable costs to sales and lowering the fixed costs. The management believes that fixed costs can be reduced to $5,000, with a corresponding increase in the percentage of variable costs to 80%.

The break-even sales volume calculated with these conditions is as follows:

$$\text{Break-even sales volume} = \frac{\$5,000}{1 - .80}$$

$$= \frac{\$5,000}{.20}$$

$$= \$25,000$$

If the proposed shift from fixed costs to variable costs is accomplished, the break-even point is reduced from $50,000 to $25,000. The higher the variable costs, the smaller the risk of not attaining the expected break-even point. On the other hand, if the sales volume exceeds expectations, a large portion of the sales revenue will be used to cover the variable costs, and therefore a smaller net income must be anticipated.

To illustrate, assume the Sumo Manufacturing Company achieves a sales volume of $200,000; with a variable cost percentage of 70%, the net income would amount to $45,000. If the fixed costs were reduced to $5,000 and the variable cost percentage increased to 80%, the profit would be only $35,000, a reduction of $10,000 at the same sales volume.

	Variable Cost Rate	
	70%	80%
Sales..	$200,000	$200,000
Variable costs	140,000	160,000
Margin available for nonvariable factors............	$ 60,000	$ 40,000
Fixed costs	15,000	5,000
Net income	$ 45,000	$ 35,000

Contribution Margin Ratio and Margin of Safety

Two terms frequently used in cost-volume-profit relationships are *contribution margin* and *margin of safety*. The contribution margin, introduced in the discussion of direct costing, is the difference between sales revenue and total variable costs and expenses. When an income statement depicts the contribution margin, it can be used by management as a tool for studying the effects of changes in sales volume. The contribution margin ratio, which is also referred to as the marginal income ratio, is the relationship of contribution margin to sales.

The margin of safety indicates the amount that sales can decrease before the company will suffer a loss. The margin of safety ratio is a relationship computed by dividing the difference between the total sales and the break-even point sales by the total sales.

Sales (10,000 units @ $100)	$1,000,000	100%
Variable costs	600,000	60
Contribution margin	$ 400,000	40%
Fixed costs	300,000	30
Net income	$ 100,000	10%

The contribution margin is $400,000. The contribution margin ratio is calculated as follows:

$$\text{Contribution margin ratio} = \frac{\text{Total sales} - \text{Variable costs}}{\text{Total sales}}$$

$$= \frac{\$1,000,000 - \$600,000}{\$1,000,000}$$

$$= \frac{\$400,000}{\$1,000,000}$$

$$= 40\%$$

Using the contribution margin ratio of 40%, the break-even point can be calculated as follows:

$$\text{Break-even sales volume} = \frac{\text{Fixed costs}}{\text{Contribution margin ratio}}$$

$$= \frac{\$300,000}{.40}$$

$$= \$750,000$$

The margin of safety ratio (M/S) is calculated as follows:

$$\text{Margin of safety ratio} = \frac{\text{Total sales} - \text{Break-even sales volume}}{\text{Total sales}}$$

$$= \frac{\$1,000,000 - \$750,000}{\$1,000,000}$$

$$= \frac{\$250,000}{\$1,000,000}$$

$$= 25\%$$

Using the previous data, the margin of safety is 25% of the total sales, or $250,000. If the break-even sales equal $750,000 but the total expected sales are $1,000,000, the M/S ratio shows that the $1,000,000 in sales can decline by 25% before it reaches the firm's break-even level.

Since the margin of safety is directly related to net income, the M/S ratio can be used to calculate net income as a percentage of sales and vice versa.

$$\text{Net income percentage} = \text{Contribution margin ratio} \times \text{Margin of safety ratio}$$

$$= 40\% \times 25\%$$

$$= 10\% \; (\textit{Note} \text{ that this figure agrees with the net income as a percent of sales as shown in the contribution income statement on page 459.}$$

$$\text{Margin of safety ratio} = \frac{\text{Net income percentage}}{\text{Contribution margin ratio}}$$

$$= \frac{.10}{.40}$$

$$= 25\%$$

Cost-Volume-Profit Limitations

Cost-volume-profit analysis assumes that all factors used in the analysis except volume will remain constant for a given period of time. This assumption may be questioned, for it is unrealistic to assume that the established relationship between sales and production will remain as forecast, or even that the sales mix, as established, will remain constant. Some costs and expenses are relatively unpredictable except over very limited ranges of activity. Even price changes that have not been predicted can occur, and the outcome will be substantially affected.

The results from a cost-volume-profit analysis must be interpreted by giving recognition to the basic assumption that the analysis is based on static relationships. Anticipated results depend on the stability of the relationships as they have been established. If a fairly stable set of relationships cannot be established, a series of analyses should be prepared that recognizes the changing sets of circumstances.

COSTS FOR DECISION MAKING

In the previous discussion, it was stated that management, in forecasting, must give recognition to how selling prices, costs and expenses, and profits will react to activity (volume) changes in a firm. However, there are many kinds of problems that are not exclusively associated with activity. In such problems, the analyst is responsible for supplying the quantitative information that will reflect the effect of the alternative choices available in a given situation. These problems may be associated with the expansion or contraction of operations (deleting or adding products), increasing or decreasing the volume of a product or a product line, changing the channel of distribution (selling to wholesalers or selling directly to retailers), selecting between alternative raw materials, selling or further processing a product, and so on. Some of the cost concepts that are related to these problems are discussed in the following section.

Relevant Costs

When comparing alternatives, relevant costs are those costs that are expected to differ from one alternative to another. Other terms are often used for relevant costs, such as marginal costs, differential costs, and incremental costs, but whatever the term used, these costs will change according to the choice of alternatives.

Costs that are not affected by the choice to be made are termed irrelevant costs. For example, assume that the use of a higher quality material is being considered in order to reduce losses from spoiled and defective materials. Such costs as insurance, depreciation, and property tax on the plant would probably not be changed by the decision; therefore, these costs would be disregarded for purposes of comparing alternatives. The relevant and irrelevant costs must be carefully isolated so that management can make the most satisfactory decision.

Escapable and Inescapable Costs

Many costs that are directly chargeable to an operating department would be eliminated if that department's operations were discontinued. These costs are called escapable costs. The costs that would be merely shifted or apportioned to the remaining operational departments are called inescapable costs. Escapable and inescapable classifications of departmental costs are important when management is considering whether or not to discontinue a product, a departmental operation, or a company division or plant.

For example, if a production department in a manufacturing plant is discontinued, the direct materials, direct labor, and factory overhead created by the department's operations would be eliminated. These costs are escapable. However, the apportioned costs, such as depreciation on the building and the department's share of the plant manager's salary, would be assigned to other departments and would thus be classified as inescapable.

Sunk Costs

A sunk cost is the investment that has been made in a tangible productive asset or an intangible right. This investment can be recovered only by using the asset over its service life. Sunk costs are historical costs that have been created by an irrevocable past decision that cannot be changed by any future decision.

For example, assume a replacement is being considered for a machine that originally cost $20,000 and has accumulated depreciation of $10,000. If the machine is scrapped, a loss of $10,000 would result. However, except for the effect on the income tax liability, such a loss should not be included in the consideration for replacement. The undepreciated book value of the existing asset is a sunk cost and is entirely irrelevant to the decision. In this case, the only pertinent information is a comparison of the effect of the two machines on income and the return on the additional investment. Recovery of the book value of the old asset is not possible; therefore, the asset may be considered to be used "free" in manufacturing operations. Although there would be a recorded loss if the asset is scrapped, this loss should be attached to a "wrong" decision of the past, not to the future use of the asset.

Out-of-Pocket Costs

Costs that require additional cash expenditures immediately or in the future are called out-of-pocket costs. This condition is in contrast to sunk costs, in which the expenditure has already been made and will not be affected by the decision under consideration. Out-of-pocket costs are usually relevant costs because they vary with different alternatives.

Suppose a steel manufacturer maintains its own fleet of trucks to bring coke and coal to its mill. The company is considering selling the trucks and contracting with a private trucking firm for delivery of the required fuel. Irrelevant to this decision is the sunk cost of the investment in trucks. The relevant costs are the out-of-pocket costs that will be incurred by the contract, the future costs for maintenance, repairs, insurance, gasoline, tires, and oil that will be eliminated if the company decides to sell the trucks, and the current sales value of the used trucks.

Imputed Costs and Opportunity Costs

In decision making, costs do not always involve cash expenditures. In some cases, additional costs must be assigned or imputed before a fair comparison between alternatives can be made. Imputed costs are hypothetical costs that are not recognized by the traditional accounting system. For example, interest expense is considered a cost only if it is paid or is part of a legal obligation, whereas the interest on capital invested in the firm is not usually recognized as a business cost. However, in the evaluation of a project, failure to give effect to the interest on capital investment may result in an erroneous decision.

Assume that a company is deciding which of two projects it will undertake — Project A, which requires an investment of $100,000, or Project B, requiring $120,000. Both projects are expected to return $30,000 of income, and the risk factors are equal. Using the value of money established by the company, the interest on capital could be directly included as part of the project cost.

Opportunity cost, another type of imputed cost, is the cost associated with a course of action that deprives the company of the opportunity to pursue some other course of action. For example, a company owns a vacant warehouse that is being considered for use as an additional manufacturing facility. The warehouse can be rented to another company for $50,000 per year. In evaluating the expansion proposal, a charge of $50,000 should be included as an opportunity cost.

Replacement Cost

The amount that was actually paid for an asset is its historical cost. The replacement cost is the cost of the same asset at current market prices or current construction costs. In periods of inflation, the use of historical costs results in an overstatement of profits, because part of the reported net income is being plowed back into the business as inventories and fixed assets are replaced at higher costs. For making some decisions, converting to replacement costs may be considered necessary in order to provide a more realistic measurement of profit.

Suppose inventories are purchased for $100,000 and later sold for $125,000. If no other expenses are incurred, a profit of $25,000 would be realized from the transaction. If, however, $110,000 is required to replace the inventory there may be some argument whether the profit on the previous transaction was $25,000 or only $15,000. To further emphasize the importance of this inflationary factor, assume that the company has paid out the $25,000 profit as a dividend to its stockholders. It would then have to borrow $10,000 to replace the inventory.

DIFFERENTIAL COST ANALYSIS

All management requirements cannot be satisfied by one concept or combination of cost data. The designated purpose for which a cost measurement is to be made needs to be studied carefully to determine what items should be included in a specific cost analysis. This study should then provide a series of alternative solutions that compare different sets of relevant cost data. A study that highlights the significant cost data of alternatives is referred to as differential cost analysis.

Assume a company, now operating at 80% capacity, has been asked by a one-time purchaser to sell additional units at less than its established sales price. A study would be made to determine the difference in costs at the two volume levels.

The company produces 30,000 units at 80% of its total capacity. Its fixed factory overhead costs are $20,000, and it sells each unit for $10. A new customer wishes to purchase 7,500 units for $4 per unit. Should the company agree to the terms or reject the offer?

The variable production costs per unit are:

Direct materials.	$2.00
Direct labor	1.00
Variable overhead.	.75
Total variable cost per unit.	$3.75

At the present level of operations, the total production cost per unit is $4.42 ([(30,000 units × $3.75) + $20,000] ÷ 30,000 units). If the additional units are produced, the total cost per unit would be $4.28 ([(37,500 units × $3.75) + $20,000] ÷ 37,500 units). Since the new customer is offering only $4 per unit, the company apparently should not accept such an offer.

However, the total fixed factory overhead cost of $20,000 will not be affected by producing the additional units; only the differential cost, or variable cost, will increase. Thus, each additional unit produced, and sold at $4, will increase the contribution margin by $.25 ($4 selling price − $3.75 variable cost per unit). If the offer is accepted, the total increase in the contribution margin would be $1,875 (7,500 units × $.25); and, since the fixed cost will not change, the gross margin would also increase by $1,875, as shown below:

	Accept Order	Reject Order
Sales:		
30,000 units @ $10	$300,000	$300,000
7,500 units @ $4	30,000	–0–
Total revenues............................	$330,000	$300,000
Variable costs	140,625*	112,500**
Contribution margin	$189,375	$187,500
Fixed overhead costs	20,000	20,000
Gross margin on sales	$169,375	$167,500

* 37,500 units × $3.75 (variable cost)............................. $140,625

** 30,000 units × $3.75 (variable cost)............................. $112,500

The differential cost concept is applicable only when there is excess capacity that can be utilized at little or no increase in fixed cost. Also, in accepting additional orders at selling prices below the usual price levels, care should be exercised so that legislation barring sales to different customers at different prices isn't violated or that regular customers will not expect the same price treatment for their purchases.

Operation Versus Shutdown

Differential cost analysis can also be used to determine whether it is better to shut down a division or to operate at a loss.

Suppose a division is operating at 40% of capacity and producing 80,000 units. The March income statement shows the following:

Sales—80,000 units @ $10......................		$800,000
Less:		
Variable costs—80,000 units @ $8..............	$640,000	
Fixed costs....................................	160,000	800,000
Net income....................................		$ —0—

A new competitor has entered the market, so division management anticipates a decline from the March sales volume for the next few months. However, due to a strong advertising and sales effort new being undertaken, management feels that eventually the sales volume will increase, although there is little hope of increasing revenue in the immediate future. If the division is temporarily shut down, not all fixed costs can be eliminated. Estimates indicate that $60,000 of the $160,000 in fixed costs will be retained. Management states that it would like to continue production as long as the operating loss would be less than the shutdown cost of $60,000.

Pro forma statements at various capacities show the following:

Capacity..............	0%	20%	25%	30%	35%	40%
Number of units	Shutdown	40,000	50,000	60,000	70,000	80,000
Sales ($10 per unit)	—0—	$400,000	$500,000	$600,000	$700,000	$800,000
Variable cost ($8 per unit)	—0—	320,000	400,000	480,000	560,000	640,000
Marginal contribution....	—0—	$ 80,000	$100,000	$120,000	$140,000	$160,000
Fixed costs............	$ 60,000	160,000	160,000	160,000	160,000	160,000
(Loss)	$ (60,000)	$ (80,000)	$ (60,000)	$ (40,000)	$ (20,000)	$ —0—

Not until sales fall below the 50,000 unit level (25% of capacity) will the loss from continuing operation be greater than the cost of shutting down completely. The division should therefore continue operations as long as capacity is above 25%. Since an advertising campaign is being undertaken to improve the prestige of the product, an intangible factor worthy of consideration is keeping the product on the buyers' shelves, although it is presently unprofitable for the division.

Make or Buy Decisions

A company may buy a finished part that could perhaps be more economically manufactured in its own plant. For example, assume that 40,000 parts are purchased each month at a unit price of $1 per part. All the tools and necessary skills required for manufacturing this part are available in Department A.

Department A has a total potential capacity of 30,000 direct labor hours per month. The present capacity is 24,000 direct labor hours, or 80%. Analyses of its factory overhead costs are:

	Budgeted (80%) 24,000 Hours		Normal (100%) 30,000 Hours	
	Total Costs	Per Hour Costs	Total Costs	Per Hour Costs
Fixed costs	$ 72,000	$3.00	$ 72,000	$2.40
Variable costs	48,000	2.00	60,000	2.00
Total....................	$120,000	$5.00	$132,000	$4.40
Differential cost............			$ 12,000	$ .60

The costs to manufacture 40,000 parts are:

Materials...	$ 2,000
Labor, 6,000 Hours @ $4	24,000
Total..	$26,000
Add differential overhead cost of 6,000 labor hours...............	12,000
Total cost to manufacture parts..................................	$38,000
Cost per unit, $38,000 ÷ 40,000................................	$ .95

Since Department A is presently operating at 80% of its total capacity, the company can save $2,000 ($40,000 − $38,000) by making the 40,000 parts rather than buying them. If the 80% capacity level in Department A is temporary, this factor must be considered before the final decision is made. The estimated savings may not be realized if the excess capacity of the department will soon be needed for the company's regularly manufactured products.

Sell or Process Further

There are some instances in which a manufacturing organization may produce goods ready for sale that could be sold for a higher price if given additional processing. In this case, management must make a decision whether to sell these units or process them further. In considering the alternative courses of action, the increase in gross margin generated by further processing must be determined.

Assume that a company manufactures a product (Product A) that it sells in bulk quantities. The manufacturing process also produces a by-product that can be sold for $2,000 without further processing. The main product consists of 20,000 gallons that can be sold either in bulk for $5 a gallon or packaged in 5-gallon cans and sold for $6 a gallon. Joint processing costs incurred up to the split-off point are $61,000. Using the data given, the following analysis can be made. (Recall that the cost to be assigned to the main product is reduced by the estimated market value of the by-product).

Product	Allocated Cost of Product	Cost of Additional Processing	After Additional Processing			Gross Margin Without Further Processing	Increase (Decrease) in Gross Margin
			Cost of Product	Sales Value	Gross Margin		
A	$59,000	$5,000(1)	$64,000	$120,000	$56,000	$41,000(3)	$15,000
By-product	2,000	2,100(2)	4,100	4,000	(100)	–0–	(100)

(1) Cost of additional materials:

20,000 gals. ÷ 5 = 4,000 cans × 50¢ cost per can =	$2,000
Cost of additional labor and overhead..............................	3,000
	$5,000

(2) Cost of additional labor and overhead.............................. $2,100

(3) $100,000 sales value at split-off point − $59,000 share of joint cost = $41,000

Based on this analysis, the company would benefit by further processing Product A but would incur no advantage through additional processing of the by-product. The market value of the by-product at the split-off point is $2,000 and further processing beyond that point adds $2,100 in cost but only $2,000 additional dollars in sales value. Before coming to a final conclusion however, the company must consider other factors, such as the effect on the market, the volume that can be sold, the amount of promotional effort required, the ramifications of setting up an additional process, and the long-run advantages and disadvantages of such a venture.

Equipment Replacement Decisions

An older machine may still have a substantial operating life remaining, but replacement may be considered when a newer, more efficient machine is being marketed. The company already owns the old machine; the decision to purchase it has already been made. The replacement decision, therefore, focuses on retaining the old or buying the new machine.

To illustrate, assume a machine was acquired 4 years ago for $70,000 and has an estimated remaining useful life of 10 years. The machine is depreciated on a straight-line basis and has no salvage value. The present book value of the machine is $50,000 ($70,000 − $20,000). A new machine is now being marketed that can produce the same number of units as the old machine, but at a substantially lower variable cost per unit. The new machine will cost $60,000 and is expected to last for 10 years and have no salvage value. A trade-in allowance of $12,000 will be received for the old machine.

The annual variable and fixed costs expected to be incurred in producing 100,000 units of product on the old and new machines are as follows:

	Old	New
Variable out-of-pocket costs..........................	$70,000	$50,000
Fixed out-of-pocket costs............................	10,000	10,000
Depreciation	5,000	6,000
Total.......................................	$85,000	$66,000
Expected savings....................................		$19,000
Cost per unit	$.85	$.66

The analysis does *not* give consideration to:

1. The trade-in allowance.
2. The fact that the new equipment is not required to maintain present production.
3. The taxes to which part of the additional savings is subject.

Following is a revision of the analysis to include these considerations:

	Old	New
Variable out-of-pocket costs..........................	$70,000	$50,000
Fixed out-of-pocket costs............................	10,000	10,000
Depreciation:		
1/10 of $12,000 (trade-in)*..........................	1,200	
1/10 of $60,000		6,000
Additional costs for new machine:		
Interest on average investment**		4,800
Additional income taxes***		9,500
Total costs	$81,200	$80,300
Cost per unit	$.812	$.803

 * Book value of old equipment, $50,000, is a sunk cost recoverable only through continued use. Cost of old equipment for decision purposes is trade-in value of $12,000 that won't be received if the old machine is kept, depreciated over remaining 10 years.
 ** Additional investment of $48,000 required for the new machine is removed from working capital. Assuming a rate of 10% can be earned on $48,000, the opportunity to earn $4,800 per year is being sacrificed.
 *** Assuming a 50% income tax rate—50% of the expected annual savings ($19,000) would be paid out in taxes—$9,500.

It still appears that the company would save by acquiring the new machine, but the saving is not so large when the sunk cost and the opportunity cost are taken into consideration. If there are any other factors that will change if the new machine is purchased, they should also be included in the cost of the new machine as relevant costs. Such factors may include special electrical wiring, additional power costs, installation costs, and additional space costs.

Operate-the-Department or Lease-the-Space Decisions

A company may consider leasing space in which it has been operating a department. For example, assume that a large manufacturer maintains a hardware and supply department somewhat similar to a retail hardware store. The effort involved to maintain the department causes management to investigate the possibility of leasing this operation to an outside company that specializes in hardware sales. This hardware specialty firm has offered $20,000 annually for the lease. If the offer is accepted, the equipment presently in the department would be scrapped.

The following figures reflect the revenue and expense for the hardware department; in addition to the operating expenses, an average inventory of $50,000 must be maintained.

	Hardware	Other Departments	Total
Gross margin on sales	$50,000	$1,000,000	$1,050,000
Operating expenses	40,000	850,000	890,000
Income before income taxes	$10,000	$ 150,000	$ 160,000

The decision whether or not to lease requires consideration of:

1. The escapable and the inescapable expenses involved in eliminating the department.
2. The sunk costs in equipment in the department.
3. An imputed interest cost on the inventory investment that would be released to earn revenue if operations in the Hardware Department were eliminated.

The following are escapable and inescapable costs:

	Hardware	Other Departments	Total
Gross margin on sales	$50,000	$1,000,000	$1,050,000
Escapable costs:			
Salaries, supplies, bad debts, etc.	$22,000	$ 600,000	$ 622,000
Depreciation	1,000	30,000	31,000
Total escapable costs	$23,000	$ 630,000	$ 653,000
Inescapable costs:			
Building maintenance, utilities, office			
expenses, etc..................	17,000	220,000	237,000
Total costs	$40,000	$ 850,000	$ 890,000
Income before income taxes	$10,000	$ 150,000	$ 160,000

When the Hardware Department is eliminated, the gross margin and the escapable costs of the department will vanish. The inescapable costs will become an added cost to the remaining departments, as shown below:

Gross margin on sales		$1,000,000
Less escapable costs		630,000
Total...		$ 370,000
Less: Other departments—inescapable costs	$220,000	
Hardware department—inescapable costs....	17,000	237,000
Operating income.................................		$ 133,000
Add other revenue:		
Lease rent	$ 20,000	
Interest on investment*	4,000	24,000
Income before income taxes		$ 157,000

*$50,000 (investment in inventory) × 8% (assumed annual interest rate) = $4,000

The depreciation expense charged to the Hardware Department reflects a sunk cost that is irrelevant to the decision; therefore, the $1,000 depreciation expense should be added to the income of the Hardware Department in computing the differential cash flows of the alternatives.

Income—including Hardware Department.......................	$160,000
Add Hardware Department depreciation expense	1,000
Total income—including Hardware Department................	$161,000
Income—leasing Hardware Department's space................	157,000
Income—decrease	$ 4,000

The Hardware Department's contribution to the company's profitability may also be viewed as follows:

	Hardware
Gross margin on sales	$50,000
Less escapable costs—excluding depreciation	22,000
Remainder of gross margin	$28,000
Less: Lease rent $20,000	
Interest on investment 4,000	24,000
Hardware Department's contribution	$ 4,000

It appears that an offer of $20,000 for a department earning only $10,000 should be accepted, according to the financial data gathered by the traditional accounting system. However, when costs of the department are classified as escapable and inescapable, the attractiveness of the lease offer is diminished. Even considering the potential revenue from the lease rental and the interest on investment, the net productivity of the space, as measured by the net income, is not enhanced by leasing. In fact, the company would lose $4,000 from its overall earnings if the department were eliminated.

DISTRIBUTION COSTS

Cost accounting is frequently thought of as a method of accounting only for the costs of manufacturing. However, "cost," as a general term, covers more than merely manufacturing costs; it should include all of the costs of doing business. In other words, efficient control of all costs should cover both the production costs and the distribution costs—costs incurred to sell and deliver the product.

In recent years, state and federal laws prohibiting discriminatory sale prices and the problem of increasing competition, have forced accountants to devote more time to the study of distribution costs. An attempt is being made to determine, by means of close and careful analysis, the answers to such questions as:

1. How much of the selling and administrative expense is allocable to each type of product sold?
2. How much of the selling and administrative expense is allocable to each particular sales office?

3. How much of the selling and administrative expense is allocable to each salesperson?
4. How much of the selling and administrative expense is allocable to each order sold?

Allocating Distribution Costs

To illustrate some of the difficulties to be encountered, assume a company that sells bakery products also operates a fleet of delivery trucks to distribute the finished items. Each driver is a salesperson; therefore each truck is a combination sales and delivery truck. At each stop, the driver takes an order from the store manager for bread, cakes, cookies, and other bakery products carried on the truck and then stocks the shelves. In one store, fifteen minutes may be spent selling four dozen loaves of bread, two dozen breakfast rolls, and a dozen boxes of doughnuts; while in another store it may require forty-five minutes to sell only a dozen loaves of bread. Suppose the daily costs of the operation are: $50 for the salesperson-driver's salary; $30 for truck depreciation; $15 for gasoline and oil; and $5 for miscellaneous operating expenses.

How much of the total truck expense is chargeable to each sale? Should it be allocated on the basis of the number of sales made? Should it be allocated on the basis of the time spent at each stop by the driver? What is the cost of selling a loaf of bread, a dozen doughnuts, or a package of breakfast rolls?

These questions are not academic, and businesses devote a considerable amount of time attempting to arrive at meaningful answers to such questions. The following example will show the usefulness of distribution cost studies.

Assume that a company is making three products, A, B, and C. The manufacturing cost per unit is as follows:

$$
\begin{array}{ll}
\text{A} \ldots\ldots & \$10 \\
\text{B} \ldots\ldots & 15 \\
\text{C} \ldots\ldots & 5
\end{array}
$$

During one month, 1,000 units of each product are sold at $15, $18, and $6 each, respectively. The gross margin for the month would be $9,000 ($39,000 − $30,000). If the selling and administrative expense for the month is $4,000, the net income for the month would be $5,000, a result that management would probably regard as satisfactory.

Now assume that study indicates that the distribution cost per product is as follows:

Expense	A	B	C	Total
Selling expenses:				
Salaries..........................	$ 300	$200	$ 300	$ 800
Commissions.....................			500	500
Advertising.......................	600	200	200	1,000
Telephone and telegraph	40		60	100
Sales manager's salary...........	133	133	134	400
Miscellaneous selling expense	127	17	56	200
Total selling expense...........	$1,200	$550	$1,250	$3,000
Administrative expense..............	300	350	350	1,000
Total........................	$1,500	$900	$1,600	$4,000
Cost per unit	$1.50	$.90	$1.60	

In order to arrive at these figures, it was necessary to make a study of the prevailing conditions and to allocate the various expenses to the products on some reasonable basis. For example, sales salaries might be allocated to the products on the basis of time reports showing the amount of time devoted to selling each product. Advertising might be allocated on the basis of the number of square inches of advertising space purchased for advertising each product. The sales manager's salary might be allocated evenly among the products. Miscellaneous selling expense might be allocated on the basis of the number of orders received for each product or the value of each product sold. There is no standard basis for allocating such expenses, but every effort should be made to use a reasonable basis for allocating each type of expense to the various products.

Using the preceding cost and sales data, it becomes apparent that a profit is actually being made only on Products A and B. Product C is being sold at a loss. The following table, based on the sales for the month, shows the extent of the gain and loss:

Product	Cost to Make	Cost to Sell	Total Cost	Selling Price	Profit (Loss)
A	$10,000	$1,500	$11,500	$15,000	$3,500
B	15,000	900	15,900	18,000	2,100
C	5,000	1,600	6,600	6,000	(600)
Total	$30,000	$4,000	$34,000	$39,000	$5,000

As a result of the analysis of distribution costs, management determines that the company might make more money by selling less. If the sale of

Product C were discontinued, the profit would be greater by the amount of the loss being sustained on C. However, if a more intensive study were undertaken, it may show that Products A and B could not sustain their profit margins if the inescapable costs charged to Product C such as the sales manager's salary had to be charged to A and B. Also, the intangible benefits derived from continuing to carry Product C must be given consideration.

Determining the Optimum Size of the Sales Force

Another distribution cost problem may be the determination of the optimum size of the sales force a company should maintain. This problem requires a study of the marginal income that could result from hiring additional salespeople. The sales saturation point is reached when the marginal revenue from sales generated by one additional salesperson is less than the marginal costs that apply to that person.

Suppose three salespeople are used in a regional area where the following sales have been made during the past three years:

Salesperson	19X1	19X2	19X3
1	$128,000	$132,000	$135,000
2	94,000	98,000	100,000
3	90,000	95,000	95,000
	$312,000	$325,000	$330,000

The sales record of the three salespeople indicates that a dramatic increase in sales should not be expected, although sales have improved a small amount in total each year.

The total costs of the company are analyzed and classified into fixed and variable categories. The costs directly related to selling activities are then summarized to determine whether an increase or decrease in the number of salespeople would be justified. The analysis, which uses only variable factors, is as follows:

		Variable Costs						
Number of Salespeople	Estimated Potential Sales	Variable Factory Costs	Sales Commissions	Other Variable Costs	Total Variable Costs	Marginal Sales	Marginal Costs	Marginal Profit or (Loss)
1	$135*	$ 65	$20.25	$ 25.90	$111.15	$135	$111.15	$23.85
2	235	120	35.25	45.20	200.45	100	89.30	10.70
3	330	170	47.25	73.40	290.65	95	90.20	4.80
4	410	225	57.00	97.60	379.60	80	88.95	(8.95)
5	480	270	66.00	127.30	463.30	70	83.70	(13.70)

*All figures are in thousands of dollars.

Each of the three salespeople employed by the company produces a marginal profit that ranges from $23,850 to $4,800. An additional salesperson should not be added, because that person's marginal contribution would be a loss of $8,950. Although the marginal costs will decline by increasing the volume, the sales dollars generated at the higher production levels are not adequate to improve the company's profitability. The fifth salesperson, for example, would add $70,000 to sales; but the additional costs of using the fifth person would be $83,700.

The preceding illustration shows how the size of a sales force can be determined. Often, however, this problem is resolved incorrectly through intuition rather than by analysis of quantitative data, even though the problem is very significant for most businesses.

KEY TERMS

Absorption costing (444)
Break-even analysis (454)
Break-even point (454)
Common cost (451)
Contribution margin (448)
Contribution margin ratio (459)
Cost-volume-profit (CVP)
  analysis (453)
Differential costs (461)
Differential cost analysis (464)
Direct costing (444)
Direct (traceable) cost (451)
Distribution costs (472)
Escapable costs (461)
Full cost method (444)
Gross margin (447)
Gross profit (447)
Historical costs (463)
Incremental costs (461)

Indirect (nontraceable) costs (451)
Imputed costs (463)
Inescapable costs (462)
Irrelevant costs (461)
Marginal costs (461)
Marginal income ratio (459)
Margin of safety (459)
Margin of safety ratio (459)
Opportunity cost (463)
Out-of-pocket costs (462)
Period costs (444)
Product costs (444)
Relevant costs (461)
Replacement costs (463)
Segment (450)
Segment margin (451)
Sunk cost (462)
Variable costing (444)

QUESTIONS

1. Distinguish between absorption costing and direct costing.

2. What effect will application of the direct costing method have on the income statement and the balance sheet?
3. What are the advantages and disadvantages derived from use of the direct costing method?
4. Why are there objections to using absorption costing when segment reports of profitability are being prepared?
5. What are common costs?
6. How is a contribution margin determined and of what importance is it to management?
7. What are considered direct costs in segment analysis?
8. What is cost-volume-profit analysis?
9. What is the break-even point?
10. List the steps required in the construction of a breakeven chart.
11. Distinguish between contribution margin and the margin of safety ratio.
12. Distinguish between relevant and irrelevant costs.
13. Distinguish between escapable and inescapable costs.
14. Define sunk costs.
15. What are out-of-pocket costs?
16. Do all decision-making costs involve cash expenditures?
17. Distinguish between historical and replacement costs. Why are replacement costs becoming more important to many businesses today?
18. What is differential cost analysis?
19. What is the purpose of an operation versus shutdown study?
20. What is the importance of make or buy studies for a company?
21. What basic decision is involved in determining whether to sell certain products or to process them further?
22. What are some of the important factors to be considered in operate or lease decisions?
23. What are distribution costs?
24. What is the purpose of the analysis of distribution costs?
25. In cost analysis, what governs which costs are to be included in the study?

EXERCISES

Exercise 10-1   Unit cost and cost of inventory—direct and absorption costing.

The Player Products Co. uses a process cost system and applies actual factory overhead to work in process at the end of the month. The following data are taken from the records for the month of March:

Direct materials	$200,000
Direct labor.	$100,000
Variable factory overhead	$ 80,000
Fixed factory overhead	$ 60,000
Selling and administrative expenses.	$ 40,000
Units produced	25,000
Units sold	20,000
Selling price per unit	$ 25

There were no beginning inventories and no work in process at the end of the month.

From the information presented, determine (1) the unit cost of production and (2) the cost of the ending inventory under:
(a)   The absorption costing method
(b)   The direct costing method

Exercise 10-2   Comparative income statements—direct and absorption costing.

Using the information presented in Exercise 1, prepare comparative income statements for March.
(a)   Under absorption costing
(b)   Under direct costing

Exercise 10-3   Income determined by absorption costing.

A company had income of $50,000 using direct costing for a given period. Beginning and ending inventories for the period were 18,000 units and 13,000 units, respectively. If the fixed overhead application rate was $2 per unit, what was the income using absorption costing?

Exercise 10-4   CVP analysis.

The Alpha Company is planning to produce two products, X and Y, and to sell 100,000 units of X at $4 a unit and 200,000 units of Y at $3 a unit. Variable costs are 70% of sales for X and 80% of sales for Y. In order to realize a total profit of $75,000, what must the total fixed costs be?

Exercise 10-5   Break-even analysis.

A company has prepared the following statistics regarding its production and sales at different capacity levels.

Capacity level	60%	80%	100%	120%
Units.	60,000	80,000	100,000	120,000
Sales	$240,000	$320,000	$400,000	$480,000
Total costs:				
Variable	$120,000	$160,000	$200,000	$240,000
Fixed	150,000	150,000	150,000	150,000
Total costs	$270,000	$310,000	$350,000	$390,000
Net profit (loss)	$(30,000)	$ 10,000	$ 50,000	$ 90,000

(a)   At what point is break-even reached in sales? In capacity?
(b)   If the company is operating at 60% capacity, should it accept an offer
from a customer to buy 10,000 units at $3 per unit?

Exercise 10-6   CVP analysis.

A company has sales of $500,000; variable costs of $200,000; and fixed
costs of $150,000. Compute:
(a)   The contribution margin ratio
(b)   The break-even sales volume
(c)   The margin of safety ratio
(d)   Net income as a percentage of sales

Exercise 10-7   Break-even analysis.

A new product is expected to have sales of $100,000, variable costs of 60%
of sales, and fixed costs of $20,000.
(a)   Using graph paper, construct a break-even chart and label the sales line,
total cost line, fixed cost line, break-even point, and net income and net
loss areas.
(b)   From the chart, identify the break-even point and the amount of income
or loss if sales are $100,000.

Exercise 10-8   Operation versus shutdown.

The Pluto Company manufactures a novelty product that sells for $1.95 per
unit. A competitor is now producing a similar product; the demand for the Pluto
product has declined and the selling price has dropped to $1.25. Management
is considering shutting down operations rather than continuing at a loss. A new
product is being developed and will be marketed in the near future.

The 100% capacity level of the plant produces 200,000 units. The production costs are:

Variable costs (materials, labor, and factory overhead) . $.90 per unit
Fixed costs..................................... $125,000

If the plant is completely shut down, it is estimated that $50,000 of the fixed costs will still be incurred. At the new selling price of $1.25, it is estimated that 150,000 units can be sold.
(a)   Should the plant continue to operate at a loss or shut down? Show computations.
(b)   When should shutdown occur?

Exercise 10-9   Differential cost analysis — special customer order.

Dino Company manufactures basketballs. The forecasted income statement for the year before any special orders is as follows:

	Amount	Per Unit
Sales	$4,000,000	$10.00
Manufacturing cost of goods sold..........	3,200,000	8.00
Gross profit............................	$ 800,000	$ 2.00
Selling expenses........................	300,000	.75
Operating income.......................	$ 500,000	$ 1.25

Fixed costs included in the forecasted income statement are $2,000,000 in manufacturing cost of goods sold and $200,000 in selling expenses.
A special order offering to buy 50,000 basketballs for $5.00 each was made to Dino. There will be no additional selling expenses if the special order is accepted. Assuming Dino has sufficient capacity to manufacture 50,000 more basketballs, by what amount would operating income be increased or decreased as a result of accepting the special order?

(AICPA adapted)

Exercise 10-10   Make or buy decision.

Lindsey Company needs 20,000 units of a certain part to use in its production cycle. The following information is available:

Cost to Lindsey to make the part:	
Direct materials	$ 4
Direct labor...	16
Variable factory overhead	12
Fixed factory overhead applied	6
Total...	$38
Cost to buy the part from the COE Company..................	$36

If Lindsey buys the part from COE instead of making it, Lindsey could *not* use the released facilities in another manufacturing activity. Sixty percent of the fixed factory overhead applied will continue regardless of what decision is made.

(a)   In deciding whether to make or buy the part, what are the total relevant costs to make the part?
(b)   What decision should be made?

(AICPA adapted)

Exercise 10-11   Equipment replacement decision.

Equipment that a company is considering replacing was purchased 3 years ago for $39,000. Its remaining useful life is estimated to be 10 years with no salvage value. The new equipment will operate more efficiently at a higher rate of speed, thereby reducing the variable operating costs. The new equipment will cost $50,000, have a useful life of 10 years and no salvage value. A trade-in allowance of $20,000 will be given for the old equipment. No additional costs for removal of the old equipment and installation of the new equipment are anticipated. The company pays income tax at the 50% rate and estimates that it should earn 10% interest on its investments. The following are estimated costs of the old and new equipment at the normal 100,000 unit level:

	Old	New
Variable costs—out-of-pocket...............	$50,000	$43,000
Fixed costs—out-of-pocket...................	8,000	10,000
Depreciation................................	3,000	5,000
	$61,000	$58,000
Expected savings............................		$ 3,000
Cost per unit	$.61	$.58

Should the company replace the old equipment? Show computations.

Exercise 10-12   Operate or lease decision.

A manufacturer has been offered a lease of $20,000 for space now being used by a small division of the company. The leasing company will supply its own equipment and furnishings. The manufacturer estimates interest on investment at the rate of 10%. An analysis shows the following escapable and inescapable costs (the division to be leased carries an average inventory of $40,000):

	Division to be Leased	Other Divisions	Total
Gross margin on sales..........	$50,000	$700,000	$750,000
Escapable costs:			
Other than depreciation........	$30,000	$400,000	$430,000
Depreciation.................	3,000	40,000	43,000
	$33,000	$440,000	$473,000
Inescapable costs..............	10,000	140,000	150,000
Total costs	$43,000	$580,000	$623,000
Income before income tax	$ 7,000	$120,000	$127,000

Should the division be leased? Show computations.

Exercise 10-13   Comparative net income analysis.

The Bass Manufacturing Co. wishes to determine the profitability of its products and asks the cost accountant to make a comparative analysis of sales, cost of sales, and distribution costs of each product for the year. The accountant gathers the following information which will be useful in preparing the analysis:

	Product X	Product Y	Product Z
Number of units sold	30,000	20,000	20,000
Number of orders received.......	5,000	2,500	1,000
Selling price per unit	$50	$75	$100
Cost per unit	$30	$50	$ 75

Advertising expenses total $600,000 for the year, an equal amount being expended to advertise each product. The sales representative's commission is based on the selling price of each unit and is 8% for Product X, 12% for Product Y, and 16% for Product Z. The sales manager's salary of $75,000 per year is allocated evenly to each product. Other miscellaneous selling and administrative expenses are estimated to be $15 per order received.

Prepare an analysis for the Bass Manufacturing Co. that will show in comparative form the net income derived from the sale of each product for the year.

PROBLEMS

Problem 10-1   Absorption and direct costing income statements.

The Zoe & Zoe Manufacturing Co. has determined the cost of manufacturing a unit of product to be as follows, based on normal production of 100,000 units per year:

Direct materials	$ 5
Direct labor	4
Variable factory overhead	3
Fixed factory overhead	3
	$15

Operating statistics for the months of March and April are:

	March	April
Units produced	12,000	6,000
Units sold	6,000	10,000
Selling and administrative expenses	$12,000	$12,000

The selling price is $18 per unit. There were no inventories on March 1, and there is no work in process at April 30.

Required:

Prepare comparative income statements for each month under:
1. The absorption costing method
2. The direct costing method

Problem 10-2   Segmented income statement.

The Greek Manufacturing Company manufactures two products, Alpha and Beta, which are sold in two territories designated by the company as East Territory and West Territory. The income statement prepared for the company shows the product-line segments.

Greek Manufacturing Company
Income Statement

	Total Sales	Alpha		Beta	
Sales	$1,000,000	$600,000	100%	$400,000	100%
Less variable expenses	600,000	420,000	70	180,000	45
Contribution margin	$ 400,000	$180,000	30%	$220,000	55%
Less direct fixed costs	200,000	50,000		150,000	
Segment margin	$ 200,000	$130,000		$ 70,000	
Less common fixed costs	120,000				
Net income	$ 80,000				

The territorial product sales are:

	East	West
Alpha.....................................	$400,000	$200,000
Beta.......................................	200,000	200,000
Total.....................................	$600,000	$400,000

The common fixed costs are partially identifiable with East Territory, West Territory, and the general administration as follows:

East Territory	$ 54,000
West Territory.....................................	36,000
General administration............................	30,000
Total common fixed costs	$120,000

Required:

1. Prepare a segmented income statement by territories. The direct fixed costs of the product lines should be treated as common fixed costs on the segmented statement being prepared.
2. What is the significance of this analysis?

Problem 10-3   Break-even analysis.

The production of a new product required the Hughes Manufacturing Company to lease additional plant facilities. Based on studies, the following data have been made available:

Estimated annual sales — 24,000 units

Estimated costs:	Amount	Per Unit
Materials.....................................	$ 96,000	$4.00
Direct labor....................................	14,400	.60
Factory overhead	24,000	1.00
Administrative expense	28,800	1.20
Total.....................................	$163,200	$6.80

Selling expenses are expected to be 20% of sales and net income is to amount to $1.20 per unit.

Required:

1. The selling price per unit.
2. An income statement for the year.
3. A break-even point expressed in dollars and in units assuming that administrative expense and overhead are fixed but other costs are fully variable.

(AICPA adapted)

Problem 10-4   Break-even point: absorption and direct cost analysis.

The Wilz Company has a maximum productive capacity of 210,000 units per year. Normal capacity is 180,000 units per year. Standard variable manufacturing costs are $10 per unit. Fixed factory overhead is $360,000 per year. Variable selling expense is $5 per unit and fixed selling expense is $252,000 per year. The unit sales price is $20.

The operating results for the year are: sales, 150,000 units; production, 160,000 units; beginning inventory, 10,000 units; and the net unfavorable variance for standard variable manufacturing costs, $40,000. All variances are written off as additions to (or deductions from) the standard cost of sales.

Required:
1. What is the break-even point expressed in dollar sales?
2. How many units must be sold to earn a net income of $100,000 per year?
3. How many units must be sold to earn a net income of 15% on sales?
4. Prepare a formal income statement for the year under:
   (a) Absorption costing (Hint: Don't forget to compute the volume variance.)
   (b) Direct costing
5. Explain briefly the difference in net income between the two income statements.

(AICPA adapted)

Problem 10-5   Contribution margin and break-even analysis.

Hernandez, Inc., produces and sells a product with a price of $100 per unit. The following cost data have been prepared for its estimated upper and lower limits of activity:

	Lower Limit	Upper Limit
Production (units)	4,000	6,000
Production costs:		
Direct materials	$ 60,000	$ 90,000
Direct labor.	80,000	120,000
Overhead:		
Indirect materials.	25,000	37,500
Indirect labor	40,000	50,000
Depreciation.	20,000	20,000
Selling and administrative expenses:		
Sales salaries.	50,000	65,000
Office salaries	30,000	30,000
Advertising	45,000	45,000
Other	15,000	20,000
Total	$365,000	$477,500

Required:
1. Classify each cost element as either variable, fixed, or semivariable.
2. Calculate the break-even point in units and dollars.
3. Prepare a break-even chart.
4. Prepare a contribution income statement, similar in format to the statement appearing at the top of page 458, assuming sales of 5,000 units.
5. Recompute the break-even point in units and dollars, assuming that variable costs increase by 20% and fixed costs are reduced by $50,000.

Problem 10-6   Expanding a market with a special order.

Laser Manufacturing, Inc., is presently operating at 50% of practical capacity, producing annually about 50,000 units of a patented surgical component. Laser recently received an offer from a company in Yokohama, Japan, to purchase 30,000 components at $6 per unit, FOB Laser's plant. Laser has not previously sold components in Japan. Budgeted production costs for 50,000 and 80,000 units of output follow:

Units.	50,000	80,000
Costs:		
Direct materials	$ 75,000	$120,000
Direct labor.	75,000	120,000
Factory overhead	200,000	260,000
Total cost	$350,000	$500,000
Cost per unit	$7.00	$6.25

The sales manager thinks the order should be accepted, even if it results in a loss of $1 per unit, because the sales may build up future markets. The production manager does not wish to have the order accepted primarily because the order would show a loss of $.25 per unit when computed on the new average unit cost. The treasurer has made a quick computation indicating that accepting the order will actually increase gross margin.

Required:
1. Explain what apparently caused the drop in cost from $7 per unit to $6.25 per unit when budgeted production increased from 50,000 to 80,000 units. Show supporting computations.
2. Explain:
   (a) Whether (either or both) the production manager or the treasurer is correct.
   (b) Why the conclusions of the production manager and treasurer differ. Assuming that this order is a one time occurrence, whose conclusion would you support?

3. Explain why each of the following may affect the decision to accept or reject the special order:
    (a) The likelihood of repeat special sales and/or all sales to be made at $6 per unit.
    (b) Whether the sales are made to customers operating in two separate, isolated markets or whether the sales are made to customers competing in the same market.

Problem 10-7   Analysis of an unprofitable product.

The Perez Company manufactures and sells three different products—A, B, and C. Projected income statements by product line for the year ended December 31, are presented below:

	A	B	C	Total
Units sold	10,000	500,000	125,000	635,000
Sales	$925,000	$1,000,000	$575,000	$2,500,000
Variable cost of units sold	$285,000	$ 350,000	$150,000	$ 785,000
Fixed cost of units sold	304,200	289,000	166,800	760,000
Gross margin.......	$335,800	$ 361,000	$258,200	$ 955,000
Variable general and administrative expenses	$270,000	$ 200,000	$ 80,000	$ 550,000
Fixed general and administrative expenses	125,800	136,000	78,200	340,000
Income (loss) before income tax	$ (60,000)	$ 25,000	$100,000	$ 65,000

Production costs are similar for all three products. The fixed general and administrative expenses are allocated to products in proportion to revenues. The fixed cost of units sold is allocated to products by various bases, such as square feet for depreciation, property taxes, and insurance on the factory building; machine hours for repairs, etc.

The management is concerned about the loss for Product A and is considering two alternative courses of corrective action.

Alternative A — The company would purchase some new machinery for the production of Product A. This new machinery would involve an immediate cash outlay of $650,000. Management expects that the new machinery would reduce variable production costs so that total variable costs (cost of units sold and general and administrative expenses) for Product A would be 55% of Product A revenues. The new machinery would increase total fixed costs allocated to Product A to $460,000 per year. No additional fixed costs would be allocated to Products B or C.

Alternative B — The company would discontinue the manufacture of Product A. Selling prices of Products B and C would remain constant. Management expects that Product C production and revenues would increase by 50%. Some of the present machinery devoted to Product A could be sold at scrap value which equals its removal costs. The removal of this machinery would reduce fixed costs allocated to Product A by $50,000 per year. The remaining fixed costs allocated to Product A include $155,000 of depreciation, property taxes, and insurance on the factory building per year. The space previously used for Product A can be rented to an outside organization for $175,000 per year.

Required:

Prepare a schedule analyzing the effects of Alternative A and Alternative B on projected total company income before income taxes.

(AICPA adapted)

Problem 10-8   Allocation of joint costs; sell or process further.

From a particular joint process, Glenn Company produces three products, X, Y, and Z. Each product may be sold at the point of split-off or processed further. Additional processing requires no special facilities, and production costs of further processing are entirely variable and traceable to the products involved. During one year, all three products were processed beyond split-off. Joint production costs for the year were $60,000. Sales values and costs needed to evaluate Glenn's production policy are as follows:

| | | | Additional Costs and Sales Values If Processed Further | |
| | Units | Sales Values | Sales | Added |
Product	Produced	at Split-Off	Values	Costs
X	6,000	$25,000	$42,000	$9,000
Y	4,000	41,000	45,000	7,000
Z	2,000	24,000	32,000	8,000

Joint costs are allocated to the products in proportion to the relative physical volume of output.

Required:

Prepare an analysis to show which products Glenn should subject to additional processing in order to maximize profits.

(AICPA adapted)

Problem 10-9   Analysis of discontinuing an operation.

The S-W Publishing Company is in the business of publishing and printing guide books and directories. The board of directors has engaged you to make a cost study to determine whether the company is economically justified in continuing to print, as well as publish, its books and directories. You obtain the following information from the company's cost accounting records for the preceding fiscal year:

| | DEPARTMENTS | | | |
	Publishing	Printing	Shipping	Total
Salaries and wages	$375,000	$200,000	$20,000	$ 595,000
Telephone and telegraph	22,000	6,000	1,000	29,000
Materials and supplies...	100,000	400,000	20,000	520,000
Occupancy costs	100,000	110,000	12,000	222,000
General and administrative expenses...........	80,000	70,000	8,000	158,000
Depreciation...........	10,000	80,000	10,000	100,000
	$687,000	$866,000	$71,000	$1,624,000

Additional data:

(a)   A review of personnel requirements indicates that if printing is discontinued, the publishing department will need one additional clerk at $10,000 per year to handle correspondence with the printer. Two layout planners and a proofreader will be required at an aggregate annual cost of $35,000; other personnel in the printing department can be released. One mailing clerk will be retained at $9,000; others in the shipping department can be released. Employees whose employment would be terminated would immediately receive, on the average, three months' termination pay. The termination pay would be amortized over a five-year period.

(b)   Long distance telephone and telegraph charges are identified and distributed to the responsible department. The remainder of the telephone bill, representing basic service at a cost of $6,000, was allocated in the ratio of 10 to publishing, 5 to printing, and 1 to shipping. The discontinuance of printing is not expected to have a material effect on the basic service cost.

(c)   Shipping supplies consist of cartons, envelopes, and stamps. It is estimated that the cost of envelopes and stamps for mailing material to an outside printer would be $7,500 per year.

(d)   If printing is discontinued, the company would retain its present building, but would sublet the space previously occupied by printing at an annual rental of $100,000. Taxes, insurance, heat, light and other occupancy costs would not be significantly affected.

(e)   One cost clerk would not be required ($12,000) if printing is discontinued. Other general and administrative personnel would be retained.
(f)   Included in administrative expenses is interest expense on a mortgage loan of $500,000.
(g)   Printing and shipping room machinery and equipment having a net book value of $300,000 can be sold without gain or loss. Those funds in excess of termination pay would be invested in marketable securities earning 8%.
(h)   The company has received a proposal for a five-year contract from an outside printer, under which the volume of work done last year would be printed at a cost of $750,000 per year.
(i)   Assume continued volume and prices at last year's level.

Required:
   Prepare a statement in comparative form showing the costs of operation of the printing and shipping departments under the present arrangement and under an arrangement in which inside printing is discontinued. Summarize the net saving or extra cost in case printing is discontinued.

(AICPA adapted)

Problem 10-10   Distribution cost analysis.

   Katz Corporation's actual and standard distribution cost data for the month of January follow.

	Budget at Standard Cost	Actual Operations
Sales	$750,000	$750,000
Direct distribution costs:		
Selling	$ 12,000	$ 15,000
Shipping salaries.....................	7,000	9,450
Indirect distribution costs:		
Order-filling........................	17,250	21,500
Other	2,100	2,500
Total costs	$ 38,350	$ 48,450

Additional data:
(a)   Katz Corporation sells a single product for $10 per unit.
(b)   Shipping salaries and indirect distribution costs — other are allocated on the basis of shipping hours.
(c)   Data on January shipping hours follow:

	Shipping Hours
Budgeted..	3,500
Standard operating level	4,400
Actual...	4,500

(d)   Order-filling costs are allocated on the basis of sales and are comprised of freight, packing, and warehousing costs. An analysis of the amount of these standard costs by unit order-size follows:

Unit-Volume Classifications	Order-Filling Standard Costs Classified by Unit Order-Size			
	1–15	16–50	Over 50	Total
Freight	$1,200	$1,440	$2,250	$ 4,890
Packing	2,400	3,240	4,500	10,140
Warehousing	600	720	900	2,220
Total	$4,200	$5,400	$7,650	$17,250
Units sold.	12,000	18,000	45,000	75,000

Required:
1.   Compute rate and efficiency variances from standard cost for the following. (The analyses should compare actual costs and standard costs at the standard operating level.)
     (a)   Shipping salaries
     (b)   Indirect distribution costs-other
2.   Management realizes that the distribution cost per unit decreases with an increase in the size of the order and, hence, wants to revise its unit sales prices upward or downward on the basis of the quantity ordered to reflect the allocated freight, packing, and warehousing standard costs. Management assumes that the revised unit prices will require no changes in standards for sales volume, the number of units sold in each order-size classification and the profit per unit sold.
     (a)   For each unit-volume classification, prepare a schedule computing the standard cost per unit for each order-filling cost: freight, packing, and warehousing. Use the format shown in (d) above.
     (b)   Prepare a schedule computing the revised unit sales prices for each unit-volume classification that would enable total sales revenue to remain at $750,000. (Hint: let x = the unit sales price of 1–15 units.)

                                                                        (AICPA adapted)

Problem 10-11   Optimum size of sales force.

     A new company has completed a study showing that if 5 salespeople are hired, the sales to be made by each salesperson would be as follows:

Salesperson	Sales
1	$200,000
2	180,000
3	160,000
4	140,000
5	120,000
	$800,000

An analysis of the total costs of the company shows that variable costs associated with the different levels of sales are:

Sales	Variable Costs
$200,000	$105,000
380,000	217,500
540,000	337,500
680,000	465,000
800,000	592,500

Additionally, each salesperson will be paid a commission of 10% on total sales.

Required:

Determine the number of salespeople the company should hire. Show computations.

GLOSSARY

A

Abnormal losses. Units lost in production due to circumstances that are not inherent in the manufacturing process. Such losses are not expected under normal, efficient operating conditions and are accounted for as period costs.

Absorption costing. A method of accounting for manufacturing costs that charges both fixed and variable costs to the product; also referred to as the "full cost" method.

Adjusted sales value. A basis for allocating joint costs which takes into consideration the cost of processing after split-off.

Adjusted unit cost. The unit cost of a product after adjustment for units lost in the manufacturing process.

Algebraic distribution method. A method for allocating service department costs to production departments using algebraic techniques. While this method may provide the most accurate distribution of costs, it is more complicated than the other methods and the results obtained may not justify the additional effort involved.

Applied Factory Overhead. The account that is credited when applying estimated overhead to production; the debit is to Work in Process. Use of a separate "applied" account avoids confusion with actual overhead costs, which are charged to Factory Overhead, the control account in the general ledger.

Attainable standard. A performance criterion that recognizes inefficiencies that are likely to result from such factors as lost time, spoilage, or waste.

Average cost method. A commonly used procedure for assigning costs to the ending inventories under a process cost accounting system. Under this method, ending inventories are valued using an average unit cost, which is calculated as follows: (cost of beginning work in process + current period production costs) ÷ total equivalent production for the period.

B

Bonus pay. An amount paid to employees in addition to regular earnings for outstanding performance, as a result of higher-than-usual company profits, or for a variety of other reasons.

Break-even analysis. An analytical technique based on the determination of a break-even point expressed in terms of sales revenue or sales volume.

Break-even point. The point at which sales revenue is adequate to cover all costs to manufacture and sell the product but no profit is earned.

Budget. Management's operating plan expressed in quantitative terms, such as units of production and related costs.

Budgeted income statement. A summary of anticipated revenues and expenses for the coming year based on budgets for sales, manufacturing costs, and nonmanufacturing expenses (selling, administrative, and other).

Budget for manufacturing costs. Budget of the costs of materials, labor, and factory overhead for each month (or shorter period) of the coming year.

Budget for receivables. Shows when cash can be expected from the turnover of inventory and receivables.

Budgets for administrative, selling, and other expenses. Individual budgets showing anticipated expenses for administrative, selling, and other nonmanufacturing activities; prepared after the level of activity for sales and production have been determined.

Budget (or spending) variance. The difference between budgeted factory overhead at the capacity attained and the actual factory overhead incurred.

By-products. Secondary products with relatively little value that are obtained in the process of manufacturing the primary product.

C

Capacity variance. The difference between the actual hours worked multiplied by the standard overhead rate and the budget allowance based on actual hours worked; indicates that the actual hours worked were more or less than the normal hours used in determining the overhead rate.

Capital additions budget. A plan for the timing of acquisitions of buildings, equipment, and other operating assets during the year.

Carrying costs. The costs incurred as a result of maintaining (carrying) inventories. These costs generally include: materials storage and handling costs; interest, insurance, and taxes; losses from theft, deterioration, or obsolescence; and recordkeeping and supplies.

Cash budget. Budget showing the anticipated flow of cash and the timing of receipts and disbursements based on projected sales, manufacturing costs, and other expenses.

Clock card. A preprinted card used to record the total amount of time spent in the factory by an employee.

Common cost. The term used in segment analysis to describe a cost that cannot be traced to, or specifically identified with, a particular business segment.

Contribution margin. The difference between sales revenue and variable manufacturing costs.

Contribution margin ratio. The relationship of contribution margin to sales.

Control. The process of monitoring the company's operations and determining whether the objectives identified in the planning process are being accomplished.

Controllable variance. *See* Budget variance.

Conversion cost. The combined cost of direct labor and factory overhead, which are necessary to convert the direct materials into finished goods.

Cost accounting. The branch of accounting that focuses on providing the detailed cost data that management needs in controlling current operations and planning for the future.

Cost accounting system. A set of methods and procedures used by a manufacturing organization to accumulate detailed cost data relating to the manufacturing process.

Cost and production report. A summary of cost and production data for a particular cost center.

Cost center. A unit of activity, such as a department, within the factory to which costs may be practically and equitably assigned.

Cost of production summary. A report that summarizes production costs for a period for each department and provides the information necessary for inventory valuation.

Cost-volume-profit analysis. An analytical technique that uses the degrees of cost variability for measuring the effect of changes in volume on resulting profits.

D

Debit-credit memorandum. A document used to notify the vendor that materials received do not correspond with materials ordered.

Defective units. Units of product with imperfections that are considered correctible because the market value of the corrected unit will be greater than the total cost incurred for the unit.

Department-type analysis sheet. One form of factory overhead analysis sheet; a separate analysis sheet is maintained for each department, with individual amount columns for each type of overhead expense.

Differential cost analysis. A study that highlights the significant cost data of alternatives.

Differential costs. *See* Relevant costs.

Direct (traceable) cost. The term used in segment analysis to describe a cost that can be traced to a specific business segment.

Direct costing. A method of accounting for manufacturing costs that charges the product with only the costs that vary directly with volume — direct materials, direct labor, and variable factory overhead. This method is also referred to as "variable costing."

Direct distribution method. A method for allocating service department costs to production departments. No attempt is made to determine the extent to which service departments provide services to each other; instead, all service department costs are distributed directly to the production departments.

Direct labor. The cost of labor for employees who work directly on the product being manufactured.

Direct labor cost method. A method of applying factory overhead to production based on the amount of direct labor cost incurred for a job or process.

Direct labor hour method. A method of applying factory overhead to production based on the number of direct labor hours worked on a job or process.

Direct materials. Materials which become part of the product being manufactured and which can be readily identified with a certain product.

Distribution costs. Costs incurred to sell and deliver a product.

E

Economic order quantity. The optimal (most economical) quantity of materials that should be ordered at one time; represents the order size which minimizes total order and carrying costs.

Efficiency variance. The difference between overhead applied (standard hours at the standard rate) and the actual hours worked multiplied by the standard rate; indicates the effect on fixed and variable overhead costs when actual hours worked are more or less than standard hours allowed for the production volume.

Employee earnings record. A form prepared for each employee showing the employee's earnings each pay period and cumulative earnings for each quarter and for the year.

Equivalent production. The number of units that could have been completed during a period using the total production costs for the period.

Escapable costs. Costs that are directly chargeable to an operating department and would be eliminated if that department's operations were discontinued.

Expense-type analysis sheet. One form of factory overhead analysis sheet; a separate analysis sheet is used for each type of overhead expense with individual amount columns for each department.

F

Factory ledger. A separate ledger containing all the accounts relating to manufacturing, including the inventory accounts; it is maintained at the factory and tied to the general ledger through a special account.

Factory overhead. All costs related to the manufacturing of a product except direct materials and direct labor; these costs include indirect materials, indirect labor, and other manufacturing expenses such as depreciation, supplies, utilities, maintenance, insurance, and taxes.

Factory overhead analysis sheets. A subsidiary record of factory overhead expenses; replaces a subsidiary factory overhead ledger. Analysis sheets are commonly used by larger enterprises with several departments and many different types of overhead expenses.

Factory overhead ledger. A subsidiary ledger containing the individual factory overhead accounts; the total of the individual account balances in the subsidiary ledger should equal the balance in the control account, Factory Overhead, in the general ledger.

Favorable variance. The difference between actual and standard costs when actual costs are less than standard costs.

Federal Insurance Contributions Act (FICA). Federal legislation requiring both employers and employees to pay social security taxes on wages and salaries.

Federal Unemployment Tax Act (FUTA). Federal legislation requiring employers to pay an established rate of tax on wages and salaries to provide for compensation to employees if they are laid off from their regular employment.

Financial accounting. The branch of accounting that focuses on the gathering of information to be used in the preparation of external financial statements; i.e., balance sheet, income statement, and statement of cash flows.

Finished Goods. The inventory account that represents the total cost incurred in manufacturing goods that are complete but still on hand at the end of the accounting period.

First-in, first-out. An inventory costing method based on the assumption that materials issued are taken from the oldest materials in stock. Thus, materials issued are costed at the earliest prices paid for materials in stock and ending inventories are costed at the most recent purchase prices.

Fixed costs. Manufacturing costs that remain constant when production levels increase or decrease; examples include straight-line depreciation, periodic rent payments, insurance, and salaries paid to production executives.

Flexible budget. A budget that shows expected costs at different production levels.

Forecast of sales. A budget of projected sales expressed in both units and dollars; serves as a basis for preparation of all other budgets.

Full cost method. *See* Absorption costing.

G

General factory overhead expenses. Overhead expenses that cannot be identified with a specific department and must be charged to departments by a process of allocation.

Gross margin. The difference between sales revenue and cost of goods sold; also referred to as "gross profit."

Gross profit. *See* Gross margin.

Gross profit percentage (or mark-on percentage). A percentage of manufacturing cost per unit; the percentage is applied to manufacturing cost to determine the gross profit which, in turn, is added to manufacturing cost to determine selling price.

Guaranteed annual wage (GAW). An amount to be paid to employees over a specified period of time in the event of a layoff or plant shutdown.

H

High-low method. A method used to isolate the fixed and variable elements of a semivariable cost; involves comparison of a high volume and its related cost with a low volume and its related cost to determine the variable amount per unit and the fixed element.

Historical cost. The amount actually paid to acquire an asset.

Holiday pay. An amount paid to employees for designated holidays on which the employee is not required to work.

Hourly-rate plan. A wage plan under which an employee is paid an established rate per hour for each hour worked.

I

Ideal standard. A performance criterion that reflects maximum efficiency, with no allowance for lost time, waste, or spoilage.

Imputed costs. Hypothetical costs that are not recognized by the traditional accounting system but are considered in comparing alternatives.

Incentive wage. A feature included in some modified wage plans to increase worker productivity by paying a bonus rate per hour when an employee meets or exceeds established production quotas.

Incremental costs. *See* Relevant costs.

Indirect (nontraceable) cost. *See* Common cost.

Indirect labor. The wages and salaries of employees who are required for the manufacturing process but who do not work directly on the units being produced; examples include department heads, inspectors, materials handlers, and maintenance personnel.

Indirect materials. Materials and supplies that are necessary for the manufacturing process but cannot be readily identified with any particular product manufactured or whose relative cost is too insignificant to measure.

Individual production report. A daily report prepared for each employee when labor costs are calculated on a piece-rate basis. The report shows the employee's work assignment and the number of units completed.

Inescapable costs. Costs that would not be eliminated if a particular department's operations were discontinued but would merely be shifted or apportioned to the remaining operating departments.

Information system. A set of procedures designed to provide the financial information needed within a business organization.

Inventory report. A form prepared when making a physical count of inventory on hand and used to reconcile differences between recorded inventory and the inventory quantities determined by physical count.

Irrelevant costs. Costs that are not expected to differ from one alternative to another and therefore are not considered when comparing alternatives.

J

Job cost sheet. A form used to accumulate costs applicable to each job under a job order cost accounting system.

Job order cost system. A method or system of cost accounting that is appropriate for manufacturing operations that produce custom-made or special-order goods. Manufacturing costs are accumulated separately for each job and recorded on a job cost sheet.

Joint costs. The costs of materials, labor, and overhead incurred during the production of joint products.

Joint products. Two or more products that are obtained from the same manufacturing process and are the primary objectives of the process.

L

Labor cost standard. A predetermined estimate of the direct labor cost required for a unit of product.

Labor cost summary. A form showing the allocation of total payroll to Work in Process and Factory Overhead.

Labor efficiency (usage) variance. The difference between the actual number of direct labor hours worked and the standard hours for the actual level of production at the standard price.

Labor rate (price) variance. The difference between the average hourly direct labor rate actually paid and the standard hourly rate, multiplied by the number of hours worked.

Last-in, first-out. An inventory costing method based on the assumption that materials issued are the most recently purchased materials. Thus, materials issued are costed at the most recent purchase prices and ending inventories are costed at the prices paid for the earliest purchases.

Lead time. The estimated time interval between the placement of an order and the receipt of materials.

Least-squares method. A method used to isolate the fixed and variable elements of a semivariable cost. Using this method, a straight line is fitted to the observed production and cost data using a mathematical procedure that minimizes the sum of the squared deviations between the observed data and the fitted line.

Liabilities budget. Shows how the cash position will be affected by payment of liabilities.

M

Machine hour method. A method of applying factory overhead to production based on the number of machine hours used for a job or process.

Make-up guarantee. An amount paid to employees under a modified wage plan when established production quotas are not met during a work period. The make-up guarantee is charged to the factory overhead account.

Manufacturing costs (or production costs). All costs incurred in the manufacturing process; the costs are classified into three basic elements: direct materials, direct labor, and factory overhead.

Manufacturing process. The activities involved in converting raw materials into finished goods through the application of labor and incurrence of various factory expenses.

Marginal costs. *See* Relevant costs.

Marginal income ratio. *See* Contribution margin ratio.

Margin of safety. The amount that sales can decrease before the company will suffer a loss.

Margin of safety ratio. A relationship computed by dividing the difference between the total sales and the break-even point sales by total sales.

Materials. The inventory account that represents the cost of all materials purchased and on hand to be used in the manufacturing process, including raw materials, prefabricated parts, and other factory materials and supplies.

Materials control. Procedures incorporated in the system of internal control that are designed to physically protect or safeguard materials (physical control) and to maintain the proper balance of materials on hand (control of the investment in materials).

Materials cost standard. A predetermined estimate of the cost of the direct materials required for a unit of product.

Materials ledger. *See* Stores ledger.

Materials price variance. The difference between the actual unit cost of direct materials and the standard unit cost, multiplied by the actual quantity of materials used.

Materials quantity (usage) variance. The difference between the actual quantity of direct materials used and the standard quantity for the actual level of production at standard price.

Materials (or stores) requisition. A form, prepared by authorized factory personnel and usually approved by the production department supervisor, to request materials from the storeroom; represents authorization for the storeroom keeper to issue materials for use in production.

Mix. The proportion or ratio of each material to the other materials required in the production process.

Mix variance. The change in cost that results from changing the proportions of materials added to the production mix; measures the effect of using a different combination of materials.

Modified wage plan. A wage plan that combines certain features of the hourly-rate and piece-rate plans.

Moving average. An inventory costing method based on the assumption that materials issued at any time are withdrawn from a mixed group of like materials, and no attempt is made to identify materials as being from the earliest or most recent purchases. Under this method, an average unit price is computed each time a new lot of materials is received and the new unit price is used to cost all issues of materials until another lot is received and a new unit price is computed.

N

Normal capacity. The level of production that will meet the normal requirements of ordinary sales demand over a period of time; frequently used for budget development because it represents a logical balance between maximum capacity and the capacity demanded by actual sales volume.

Normal losses. Units lost due to the nature of the manufacturing process. Such losses are unavoidable and represent a necessary cost of producing goods.

O

Observation method. A technique used to classify a semivariable cost as either fixed or variable; involves examination and analysis of past relationships between the expense and production volume. Based on the observed pattern of cost behavior, a decision is made to classify the expense as either a fixed or variable cost, depending on which it more closely resembles.

Opportunity cost. The cost associated with a course of action that deprives the company of the opportunity to pursue some other course of action.

Order costs. The costs incurred as a result of ordering materials; includes salaries and wages of employees involved in purchasing, receiving, and inspecting materials; communications costs such as telephone, postage, and forms; and recordkeeping costs.

Order point. The point at which an item of inventory should be ordered; occurs when a predetermined minimum level of inventory on hand is reached. Determining an order point requires consideration of usage, lead time, and safety stock.

Out-of-pocket costs. Additional cash expenditures that must be considered in choosing among alternative courses of action.

Overapplied (or overabsorbed) factory overhead. The amount by which applied factory overhead exceeds actual factory overhead expenses incurred; represented by a remaining credit balance in Factory Overhead.

Overtime pay. The amount earned by employees at the regular hourly rate for hours worked in excess of the regularly scheduled time.

Overtime premium. An additional pay rate that is added to the employee's regular rate for hours worked in excess of the regularly scheduled time.

P

Payroll department. The department responsible for maintaining payroll records and determining each employee's gross and net earnings.

Payroll record. A form prepared each pay period showing the earnings of each employee for the period.

Payroll summary. A schedule summarizing employee earnings for each payroll period. The schedule serves as the basis for recording the payroll in the voucher register.

Pension costs. The costs incurred by an employer to provide retirement benefits to employees.

Performance report. A periodic summary of cost and production data that are controllable by the manager of a particular cost center.

Period costs. All costs that are not assigned to the product, but are recognized as expense and charged against revenue in the period incurred.

Periodic inventory system. A method of accounting for inventory that requires estimating inventory during the year for interim statements and shutting down operations to count all inventory items at the end of the year.

Perpetual inventory system. A method of accounting for inventory which provides a continuous record of purchases, issues, and balances of all goods in stock.

Physical unit of measure. A basis for allocating joint costs. Each product is assumed to have received similar benefits from the production process and therefore is charged with a proportionate share of the total processing costs.

Piece-rate plan. A wage plan under which an employee is paid a specified rate for each unit or "piece" completed.

Planning. The process of establishing objectives or goals for the organization and determining the means by which the objectives will be attained.

Practical capacity. The level of production that provides complete utilization of all facilities and personnel, but allows for some idle capacity due to operating interruptions such as machinery breakdowns, idle time, and other inefficiencies.

Predetermined factory overhead rate. A percentage or amount determined by dividing budgeted factory overhead cost by budgeted production; budgeted production may be expressed in terms of machine hours, direct labor hours, direct labor cost, or units. The predetermined rate is an estimate used in applying factory overhead to production.

Price. In the context of variance analysis, refers to the cost of materials or the hourly wage rate for direct labor.

Prime cost. The combined costs of direct materials and direct labor incurred in manufacturing a product.

Product costs. Costs that are included as part of inventory costs and expensed when goods are sold.

Production department. A department in which actual manufacturing operations are performed, and the units being produced are physically changed.

Production department supervisor. The employee who is responsible for supervising the operational functions of a production department.

Production report. A report, used in a process cost accounting system and prepared by the department head, showing: beginning units in process; number of units completed during the period; ending units in process and their estimated stage of completion.

Purchase order. A form, prepared by the purchasing agent and addressed to the chosen vendor, that describes the materials ordered, credit terms and prices, and the date and method of delivery; represents the vendor's authorization to ship goods.

Purchase price variance. The difference between the actual cost of materials and the standard cost.

Purchase requisition. A form, usually prepared by the storeroom keeper or employee with similar responsibility, that is used to notify the purchasing agent that additional materials are needed; represents the agent's authority to purchase materials.

Purchasing agent. The employee who is responsible for purchasing the materials needed for production.

R

Receiving report. A form prepared by the receiving clerk for each incoming shipment of materials. The clerk identifies the materials, determines the quantity received, and records this information on the receiving report as well as the name of the shipper, date of receipt, and the number of the purchase order identifying the shipment.

Receiving clerk. The employee who is responsible for supervising incoming shipments of materials and making sure that all incoming materials are checked as to quantity and quality.

Relative sales value. A basis for allocating joint costs proportionally based on the respective selling prices of the separate products.

Relevant costs. Costs that are considered when comparing alternative courses of action; includes only those costs that are expected to differ from one alternative to another.

Replacement cost. The cost to duplicate or replace an existing asset at current market prices or current construction costs.

Responsibility accounting. The assignment of accountability for costs or production results to those individuals who have the authority to influence costs or production.

Returned materials report. A form prepared to accompany materials being returned to the storeroom that had been previously requisitioned but were not used in production.

Return shipping order. A form prepared by the purchasing agent when goods are to be returned to the vendor.

S

Safety stock. The estimated minimum level of inventory needed to protect against stockouts.

Schedule of fixed costs. A listing of fixed overhead costs, such as depreciation, insurance, and property taxes; provides the source from which fixed costs can be allocated to the various departments. Since fixed costs are assumed not to vary in amount from month to month, a schedule can be prepared in advance for several periods; at the end of a period, a journal entry can be prepared to record total fixed costs from the information provided in the schedule.

Scrap materials. By-products that are generated in the manufacturing process; usually, such materials have some value and their costs and revenues are accounted for separately.

Segment. A division, a product line, a sales territory, or other organizational unit that can be separately identified for reporting purposes and profitability analysis.

Segment margin. The term used in segment analysis for the excess of segment revenue over direct costs assigned to the segment; common costs are excluded in computing segment margin.

Semifixed costs. Costs that tend to remain the same in dollar amount over a certain range of activity but increase when production exceeds certain limits.

Semivariable costs. Manufacturing costs that are somewhat responsive to changes in production, but do not change proportionally with increases or decreases in volume; examples include indirect materials, indirect labor, repairs and maintenance, and power.

Sequential distribution method. A method for allocating service department costs to production departments, recognizing the interrelationship of the service departments. Costs are first allocated, sequentially, to other service departments and then to production departments. The sequence may begin by distributing the costs of the service department that renders the greatest amount of service to all other departments. Alternatively, the costs of the service department with the largest total overhead can be distributed first.

Service department. A department within the factory that does not work directly on the product but provides needed services to other departments; examples include a department that generates power for the factory; a maintenance department that maintains and repairs buildings and equipment; and a cost accounting department that maintains factory accounting records.

Shift premium. An additional rate of pay added to an employee's regular rate as compensation for working an evening or night shift.

Spending variance. *See* Budget variance.

Split-off point. The point where joint products become separately identifiable; may occur during, or at the end of, the manufacturing process.

Spoiled units. Units of product with imperfections that cannot be economically corrected; they are sold as items of inferior quality or "seconds."

Stage of completion. The fraction or percentage of materials, labor, and overhead costs of a completed unit that have been applied during the period to goods that have not been completed.

Standard. A norm or criterion against which performance can be measured.

Standard cost accounting. *See* Standard cost accounting system.

Standard cost accounting system. A method of accounting for manufacturing costs that can be used in conjunction with either a job order system or process cost system. Standard costing makes it possible to determine what a product should have cost as well as what the product actually cost.

Standard costs. The costs that would be incurred under efficient operating conditions and are forecast before the manufacturing process begins. The predetermined standard costs are compared with actual manufacturing costs incurred and used by management as a basis for evaluating operating efficiency and taking corrective action when necessary.

Standard production. The volume on which the initial calculation of standard costs is based.

Step costs. *See* Semifixed costs.

Stockout. Running out of an item of inventory; may occur due to inaccurate estimates of usage or lead time or other unforeseen events, such as the receipt of damaged or inferior materials from a supplier.

Storeroom keeper. The employee who is responsible for the storing and maintaining of materials inventories.

Stores (or materials) ledger. A subsidiary ledger supporting the Materials control account in the general ledger. The individual accounts in the stores ledger are used to record receipts and issues of materials and show the quantity and cost of materials on hand.

Summary of factory overhead. A schedule of all factory overhead expenses incurred during a period; prepared from the factory overhead analysis sheets, the schedule shows each item of overhead expense by department and in total.

Summary of materials issued and returned. A form used to record all issuances of materials to the factory, returns of materials previously requisitioned, and returns of materials to the vendors from which they were purchased. The summary, when completed at the end of a period, provides the information needed to record the cost of materials for the period.

Sunk cost. A cost that has been incurred as a result of an irrevocable past decision and that cannot be changed or recovered by any future decision.

T

Theoretical capacity. The maximum number of units that can be produced with the completely efficient use of all available facilities and personnel.

Three-variance method. The analysis of factory overhead costs based on the computation of efficiency, capacity, and budget (spending) variances.

Timekeeping department. The department responsible for determining the number of hours that employees should be paid for and the type of work performed by employees.

Time ticket. A document used to record the time spent by an employee on specific assignments. The time ticket is the basis for allocating the cost of factory labor to jobs or departments.

Transferred-in costs. The portion of a department's total costs that were incurred by and transferred from a prior production department.

Two-variance method. The analysis of factory overhead costs based on the computation of the volume variance and the budget variance.

U

Under- and Overapplied Factory Overhead. An account used to accumulate differences from period to period between actual and applied factory overhead. At the end of the year, the balance in this account may be closed to Cost of Goods Sold (if the amount is relatively small) or allocated on a prorata basis to Work in Process, Finished Goods, and Cost of Goods Sold (if the amount is material).

Underapplied (or underabsorbed) factory overhead. The amount by which actual factory overhead exceeds applied factory overhead; represented by a remaining debit balance in Factory Overhead.

Unfavorable variance. The difference between actual and standard costs when actual costs exceed standard costs.

Unit cost. The cost of manufacturing one unit of product.

Usage. The quantity of materials used or the number of direct labor hours worked.

V

Vacation pay. An amount paid to employees during their vacation periods as part of the employees' compensation for services to the employer.

Variable costing. *See* Direct costing.

Variable costs. Manufacturing costs which vary in proportion to changes in production volume; includes direct labor, direct materials, and some types of factory overhead.

Variance. The difference, during an accounting period, between the actual and standard or budgeted costs of materials, labor, and overhead.

Vendor's invoice. A form, usually received from the vendor before goods are delivered, confirming a purchase of materials and representing a "bill" for the ordered goods. The purchasing agent should compare the invoice with the related purchase order to verify the description of materials, price, terms of payment, method of shipment, and delivery date.

Volume variance. The difference between budgeted fixed overhead and the fixed overhead applied to work in process; the result of operating at a level of production different from the standard, or normal, level.

Voucher system. A system for recording purchases in a voucher register that is widely used by manufacturing enterprises because it is more efficient than the alternative approach of using a purchases journal.

W

Weighted (or month-end) average. An inventory costing method used with a periodic inventory system where a physical count is required to determine the quantity of inventory on hand at the end of a designated period. The unit cost of inventory is computed by dividing total inventory cost incurred for the period by the total units available during the period.

Work in Process. The inventory account that includes all the manufacturing costs incurred to date for goods that are in various stages of production but are not yet completed.

Work shift. A regularly scheduled work period for a designated number of hours.

Y

Yield. The number of units produced from a standard amount of materials introduced in the production process.

Yield variance. Measures whether a change in materials mix affected the yield (output) and shows the difference in cost that results if the actual yield varies from the standard yield determined for a given input of materials.

INDEX

A

AAA, 37
Abnormal losses, *def.*, 326
Absorption costing, *def.*, 444
  and direct costing, 444
  comparison of manufacturing costs for, and
    direct costing methods, *illus.*, 446
  comparison of net income for, and direct
    costing methods, *illus.*, 447
  schedule of fixed overhead applied under,
    method, *illus.*, 446
Accounting, illustration of, for
    manufacturing costs, 13
Adjusted sales value, *def.*, 343
Adjusted unit cost, *def.*, 325
AICPA, 37
Algebraic distribution method, 177
American Accounting Association (AAA), 37
American Institute of Certified Public
    Accountants (AICPA), 37
Applied factory overhead, 189
  closing, to departmental factory overhead
    accounts, *illus.*, 197
  departmental, *illus.*, 197
  summary of actual and, *illus.*, 193
Attainable standards, *def.*, 365
Average cost, 276
Average cost method, 276

B

Bonus pay, 136
Break-even analysis, 454
Break-even chart, *illus.*, 457
Break-even point, *def.*, 454
Budget(s), 405
def., 7, 165, 412
  capital additions, 417
  cash, 416

for administrative expenses, 416
for manufacturing costs, 416
for other expenses, 416
for receivables, 417
for selling expenses, 416
liabilities, 417
variance, 426
Budgeted factory overhead, 411
Budgeted income statement, 416
Budgeting, flexible, 418
Budget variance, 199
  def., 195, 426
  calculating volume and, 195
By-products, *def.*, 341
  joint products and, 341

C

Capacity variance, *def.*, 426
Capital additions budget, 417
Carrying costs, 55
CASB, 39
Cash budget, *def.*, 416
Certified Public Accountants, American
    Institute of, 37
Check register, and voucher register, *illus.*,
    228
Clock card, *def.*, 112
  employee, *illus.*, 113
Common cost, *def.*, 451
Contribution margin, *def.*, 448, 459
Contribution margin ratio, *def.*, 459
Control, *def.*, 5
Controllable variance, *def.*, 405
Conversion cost, *def.*, 12
Cost(s),
  adjusted unit, *def.*, 325
  analyzing semivariable factory overhead,
    159